AF245520

AFRICAN AMERICAN SERVITUDE AND HISTORICAL IMAGININGS

AFRICAN AMERICAN SERVITUDE AND HISTORICAL IMAGININGS

~ Retrospective Fiction and Representation ~

Margaret I. Jordan

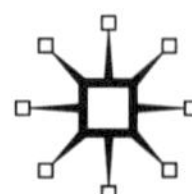

AFRICAN AMERICAN SERVITUDE AND HISTORICAL IMAGININGS

Excerpts from BEING AND RACE: BLACK WRITING SINCE 1970, by Charles Johnson reprinted by permission of Indiana University Press.

First published 2004 by
PALGRAVE MACMILLAN™
175 Fifth Avenue, New York, N.Y. 10010 and
Houndmills, Basingstoke, Hampshire, England RG21 6XS.
Companies and representatives throughout the world.

PALGRAVE MACMILLAN is the global academic imprint of the Palgrave Macmillan division of St. Martin's Press, LLC and of Palgrave Macmillan Ltd. Macmillan® is a registered trademark in the United States, United Kingdom and other countries. Palgrave is a registered trademark in the European Union and other countries.

ISBN 1-4039-6497-1 hardback

Library of Congress Cataloging-in-Publication Data
Jordan, Margaret I.
African American servitude and historical imaginings : retrospective fiction and representation / by Margaret I. Jordan
p. cm.
Includes bibliographical references and index.
ISBN 1-4039-6497-1 (hc : alk. paper)
1. Historical fiction, American—History and criticism. 2. American fiction—20th century—History and criticism. 3. African Americans in literature. 4. Literature and history—United States—History—20th century. 5. Johnson, Charles Richard, 1948– Middle passage. 6. Warren, Robert Penn, 1905– Band of angels. 7. Doctorow, E. L., 1931– Ragtime. 8. Morrison, Toni. Song of Solomon. 9. Domestics in literature. 10. Slavery in literature. 11. Slaves in literature. I. Title.

PS374.N4J67 2004
813'.5409352996073—dc22

2004044579

A catalogue record for this book is available from the British Library.

Design by Letra Libre.

First edition: August 2004
10 9 8 7 6 5 4 3 2 1
Printed in the United States of America

For my parents,

James W. Jordan and V. Ilene Jordan

For Herb Jordan and Maya Jordan

Contents

ACKNOWLEDGEMENTS

A VERY SPECIAL THANKS TO ALL WHO MADE THIS BOOK POSSIBLE. TO paraphrase Lennon and McCartney, I got by with a lot of help from my friends. First, my family. My parents, James Jordan and Ilene Jordan, for all your support and patience. My brother James Jordan, Jr., who gave me support, encouragement and humor. My brother Bruce Jordan, and my sister Marsha Jordan. My daughter, Maya. Your weekly cards and words of encouragement kept me going. Thank you for your constancy. My best friend and brother, Herb Jordan, for helping me to believe in myself and for never losing faith. There is not enough room here or time to list all the ways you have helped. My deepest gratitude.

My heartfelt appreciation goes to Michael Alston, for always coming to the rescue, in so many ways. Katherine DeLoach, thank you so much for your generosity and effort. Many thanks to Phillip Brooks, Jane Mildred, Sneha Misra, Mary McClintock, Ferne Guillebeaux and Lesley Brill. You all know why.

To the staff at Palgrave Macmillan, many thanks for your help and patience. Special thanks to Melissa Nosal, Alan Bradshaw and Farideh Koohi-Kamali.

For all those who have helped sustain me during this endeavor, by word or deed. Family, friends and colleagues, near and far. I could not have done this without your caring, concern and support. Many, many thanks. Words fail.

Preface

WHEN I FIRST BEGAN TO THINK ABOUT AFRICAN AMERICAN SERVANTS and servitude as vehicles or forms of cultural expression as a possible research project, I tried to remember what had first sparked my interest in the subject. I remembered conversations with my paternal grandmother about her experiences and the experiences of others she had known as workers in other people's homes. My grandmother, who was born in the last decade of the nineteenth century in a small town in the Mississippi delta, had tales to tell about what was required on the job. Almost always with a wry humor she recounted strategies for survival and her perceptions and those of her friends about their employers. Her memories of and anecdotes about her employment always centered around how much work she was expected to do for the families, and for so little compensation, and how unself-conscious the families were about their personal habits and business in the presence of their servants. As a child, it was inconceivable to me that in her early life my grandmother performed the same functions for other families that she did for her own. I remembered incidental conversations with other women in my community who worked in domestic service, including African Canadian women who as teenagers worked just after World War II in the homes of wealthy industrialists in Detroit. I was struck by the remarkable similarities of their stories.

I tried to imagine these women I knew as laborers within those other households and was curious about their employers. I had one side of the story, at least a part of it. I knew to some extent how they were treated and could from this infer, to some extent, how they were valued both as employees and as people by their employers.

As a child in the 1950s and early 1960s, because of the stories told by my grandmother and others in service, children's nurses and scullery maids in fairy tales, cooks on pancake and Cream-of-Wheat boxes, and lady's maids and mammies in movies always got my attention. When we watched an "old" movie and an African American made an appearance waiting on or clearing off a table, answering the door and admitting guests into someone else's home, standing quietly at attention in the periphery of a lavishly appointed room, tending to the needs of their employers' children, or stirring the pots and rolling the biscuits in the kitchen, one of us, adults included, would invariably remark that those were the only roles available to black actors in Hollywood "back then," as though there was much discernible difference from the filmic depictions of the 1950s and early 1960s. When a white servant appeared performing the same types of duties, someone invariably remarked that this was an exception. Our perception as African Americans in the 1950s and 1960s was that most servants were black.

As elementary school children on field trips to the Detroit Institute of Arts, we would rush up to paintings with those most noticeable of figures, black servants, marveling at their presence in European works from the seventeenth and eighteenth centuries. We personalized those paintings: Were *we* really there? What were *we* doing? What were *our* lives like? Were *we* only servants? Were *we* only slaves? What's the difference between being a servant and a slave?

We were required to take a class called "Auditorium," in which we watched newsreels and documentaries and listened to music, mostly classical, for our cultural edification. The presence of servants and the concept of servitude were in Negro spirituals in recordings by Marian Anderson and the Robert Shaw Chorale: "Set down servant / I c'aint set down / My soul's so happy that I c'aint set down"; in the liturgy we heard in church that instructed us that "We are God's servants, working together";[1] and in the songs we sang: "My Master, Let me walk with Thee / In lowly paths of service free; / Teach me Thy secret; help me bear / The strain of toil and care."[2]

The "idea" of servitude that resonated in my imagination was inextricably linked to the continuously available presence of servants and the idea of service in my immediate world and in the world I perceived through the images and references to servants in a much larger cultural context. My interest in servants and servitude is informed by personal exposure, and any impulse to a knee-jerk response to the images or presence of African American servants in the products of culture is often mediated and mitigated by a prevailing awareness that on some level, in some significant way, these figures resonate with a certain familiarity. I realize that for a very long time I have been foraging through the products of culture in search of the images and meanings of these people/figures who assist, maintain and support the personal lives of others, in an effort to go beyond the easy predictability of stigmatization to a more comprehensive understanding of these intriguing representations.

I take issue with those who cannot or will not see beyond the presumed lowliness and insignificance of servitude and servants, such as William Henry, who states in *In Defense of Elitism* that "we cannot reinvent the past to pretend that [. . .] studying the quotidian existence of bygone peasants and serving wenches will more than marginally enlighten us about the past's richest legacy, the high-cultural attainments for which these serfs provided, at best, support staff."[3] We need not reinvent. We need not pretend. This study challenges the very notion of the "quotidian existence" of those who serve. The fictive servant, no less quotidian than those in real life, is informed by as well as informs our understanding of American history and cultural values. Through the representation of African American servants and engagement with the idea of African American servitude, writers offer, at the least, myriad ways in which to discover America and Americanness. Furthermore, the ways in which African American servitude is manifested in fiction often provides significant insights into the sensibilities and the philosophies of life and composition of the writers themselves. As Harold Bloom has said, "That the writer somehow is in the work, we need not doubt."[4]

The texts under consideration in this book are works that contemplate the past, retrospective novels, by four twentieth-century writers: *Band of Angels* (1955) by Robert Penn Warren, *Ragtime* (1975) by E. L. Doctorow, *Middle Passage* (1990) by Charles Johnson, and *Song of Solomon* (1977) by Toni Morrison. Why these texts and authors?

What these seemingly disparate texts have in common is that they deal with African Americans as servants in ways that encourage consideration of social and cultural issues, particularly where national and individual identity are concerned. I consider these texts ideal for this project because all four do not simply present African Americans represented as slaves or servants, but actually deal significantly, in both a literary and sociohistorical sense, with the *idea* of African American servitude and what it means or represents to American society and to these individual authors. I regard black servitude in retrospective fiction as the manifestation of deeply ingrained beliefs and attitudes, as an expectation and function of life, and, correspondingly, as identity and status in American society. These texts acknowledge servitude, on some level, as *the* perceived context for African Americans—a context in need of review and revision. Most important, they invoke black servitude in the past to confront the present.

It is how the idea of black servitude, free or otherwise, has driven and continues to drive the social contract that most interests me. A historical approach helps to facilitate this inquiry. Warren deals extensively with both African American slavery and free servitude in mid-nineteenth-century America; Doctorow with servitude, and very particularly with the difficulties whites in the early twentieth century have conceptualizing and dealing with an African

American who is not only *not* a servant, but not servile. In a pre-emancipation context, Johnson deals with slavery, free servitude and the African American who is not a servant; and, Toni Morrison, with slavery and then servitude up to the mid-twentieth century.

Slave and servant are, of course, two very different things, the obvious difference being that one is free and one is not, a distinction I discuss later. But, they do share many common attributes. Long after slavery had ended, African Americans could not escape servitude, having few if any other alternatives for employment. As Gerda Lerner says, "[t]here is always domestic work. The pattern has changed very little since the days of slavery."[5] There are many reasons for this dearth of options, but prominent among them is the assumption of the utilitarian nature of black people based on the conviction of black inferiority, and an accompanying resistance to reconceptualizing the potential for anything else for blacks. This almost immutable belief is what unifies these two categories of service. The consequences of this thinking have troubled the United States for centuries, remain unresolved, and resonate in interesting ways in American retrospective fiction, particularly for Warren, Doctorow, Johnson and Morrison.

Once noticed, they seem to be everywhere, these figures that serve. The Negro washerwomen in William Faulkner's short story "That Evening Sun" walk the dusty streets of a small southern town with their bundles of laundry balanced on their heads. In this powerfully visual scene time seems to stand still, the imagery of an African past superimposed over an American present. Even later, when it is collected in automobiles, it is still "dirty laundry" in a modern world where black women must be washerwomen.[6]

It may be the precarious friendship between a black *au pair* and her wealthy employers and their family in contemporary New York in Jamaica Kincaid's *Lucy*, or the continual splicing of white women as mistresses/employers, and black women as slaves/servants who facilitate personhood for them in Kate Chopin's *The Awakening*. Whether it is the supporting roles and representations of Negroes compared to Indians in James Fenimore Cooper's pre-Revolutionary tale *Satanstoe, or the Littlepage Manuscripts, A Tale of the Colony*, or the idea of "voluntary" slavery in Octavia Butler's post-apocalyptic *Parable of the Sower*, African American servants and the idea of African American servitude simply abound in American literature, period.

In fact, it must be said that I have not found a single text, retrospective or otherwise, with the presence of African Americans in servitude that does not suggest something meaningful about American history, society, culture or literary representation, or about the author of the text. Indeed, an interesting line of pursuit may be to find texts with black servitude that do *not* provoke consideration of these and other issues. This is, one might say, the point here.

This study is an effort to rehabilitate perceptions of the representations of the African American servant, which I regard as an authoritative figure empowered to influence reading audiences in unexpected and compelling ways. The black fictive servant—the product of authorial wish-fulfillment—elucidates, articulates, demarcates, mirrors and ratifies a discernible system of complex beliefs, both enduring and mutable. Those who serve, even those seemingly innocuous, infrequently visible or silent servants, are vehicles through which history, culture and social values and practices are imagined, cultivated, celebrated, perpetuated and challenged. This occurs not only through the construction of the servants, but also by the social schemata of the past observable in the texts themselves. The resulting didactic potential of the African American servant and servitude in American retrospective fiction is enormous.

CHAPTER 1

INTRODUCTION

IMAGINING THE PAST

The history of the world is none other than the progress of the consciousness of freedom.

—Georg Wilhelm Friedrich Hegel

Faithfulness to the truth of history involves far more than a research, however patient and scrupulous, into special facts. [. . .] The narrator must seek to imbue himself with the life and spirit of the time. [. . .] He must himself be, as it were, a sharer or spectator of the action he describes.

—Francis Parkman

There are more valid facts and details in works of art than there are in history books.

—Charlie Chaplin[1]

STEPPING BACK IN TIME: A PHILOSOPHY OF COMPOSITION

From the first arrival of Europeans in North America, before any notion of nationhood, there was the question of how to get the work done. The acquisition and transformation of land and natural resources for the glory and wealth of European heads of state, and for personal profit, proved too great a challenge for a handful of ambitious explorers, adventurers and settlers. Columbus observed straightaway that the friendly and welcoming Arawaks should be conscripted for this purpose. He wrote in his log: "They were well-built, with good bodies and handsome features. . . . They do not bear arms, and do not know them [. . .]. They would make fine servants. . . . With fifty men we could subjugate them all and make them do whatever we want."[2] But the Indians, clearly assumed to be there, like the land, for the taking, proved an unusable source of free labor in that, as a response to disease and mistreatment by the newcomers, they insisted on perishing in great numbers.

Henry Wiencek writes in *An Imperfect God: George Washington, His Slaves, and the Creation of America*, that "scholars disagree over the origins and fundamental nature of slavery, particularly over the question of which came first, racial prejudice or race-based slavery."[3] One thing is certain, color and slavery/servitude are inextricably linked in American history. As early as 1509 Africans were targeted as a viable, potential source of free labor. Although he later changed his mind, the Roman Catholic Archbishop of Chiapas, Bartolomé de las Casas, recommended that each Spanish settler bring Negro slaves to resolve the labor problem.[4] Race and color as meaningful qualifiers of inferiority and grounds for subjugation and enslavement served the interests of imperialism and colonialism from the beginning.

The idea of blacks as fitting subjects for slavery/servitude continued to be of interest to social critics and other observers in Colonial British America. Cotton Mather wrote in *The Negro Christianized* about the necessity for proper training, particularly by indoctrination into Christianity, for the "Wretched Negroes" so that they might be better servants and not cause trouble for their masters.[5] In *Society in America* Harriet Martineau critiqued the contradictions of a culture that expounds "social virtues" in policy, but "of which injustice is the primary characteristic [. . .] a society which is divided into two classes, the servile and the imperious."[6] Frederick Douglass railed against the hypocrisy of slaveholding culture from his vantage point as a former slave, and takes American Christianity to task in his *Narrative of the Life of Frederick Douglass*. He affirms the humanity of the slave, and the inhumanity of the slave owner "who is the religious advocate of marriage [and] robs whole millions of its sacred influence [. . .]. The warm defender of the sacredness of the family relation is the same that scatters whole families [. . .]. We see the thief preaching against theft, and the adulterer against adultery."[7] Thomas Jefferson's deeply contradictory ideas and equivocation about the nature or absence of black intelligence and talent, and fitness for anything but servitude, are recurring concerns in *Notes on the State of Virginia* and his personal correspondence.[8] Alexis de Tocqueville, in *Democracy in America*, along with many others in early America, was very much interested in how ideas about slavery and servitude were formulated in the American consciousness and identity.[9] George Washington "[i]n his last months [. . .] struggled with the paradox that continues to vex us today: how is it that the nation—conceived in liberty and dedicated to the proposition that all men are created equal—preserved slavery?"[10] The question was and remains, "What to do with the Negroes?" in a nation that defines itself as the land of the free. The works of these authors, and other sociocultural or historical sources, became part of the debate and were often intended as incontrovertible evidence of circumstances and conditions, cause and effect. They disclose the sense some have tried to make of their times and issues surrounding African American slavery and/or servitude. They provide a context for understanding the incipient consciousness of values and social hierarchy in the developing nation, and reveal that this subject has always been socially and politically relevant, has always demanded attention and debate. Correspondingly, the renderings of African American servitude in literature that contextualizes and interprets the past demand attention and debate in the theory and criticism that inform our thinking.

The writers of historical and retrospective fiction share at least one significant characteristic in their work: they choose to step out of the period in which they are writing and reconfigure a past in which characters must grapple with personal dilemmas caused or influenced in some significant way by the political, social and economic pressures of the historical moment. According to the conventions of the historical novel they locate plot, characters, conditions, customs, manners, mentality and setting in ways that engage a particular cultural and social milieu. For this discussion, I use the term "retrospective fiction," not so much to distinguish it as a genre distinct from traditional historical fiction, but to extend the definition to include texts that are dependent upon the past, that look to the past with significant reference to or contemplation of history. Though all historical novels are to some extent retrospective, retrospective novels are not necessarily historical novels as we typically understand them to be. By this definition, it is not necessary for a retrospective novel, such as *Song of Solomon*, to be set in the remote past.

The primary texts considered are twentieth-century novels that deal with historical periods ranging from the early nineteenth century through the 1960s. The enormous political, cultural and social changes during this time period provide a fecund matrix from which to glean examples of the servant as an executor of culture and values and for current authorial concerns. In *Band of Angels* (1955) by Robert Penn Warren, *Ragtime* (1975) by E. L. Doctorow, *Middle Passage* by Charles Johnson (1990) and *Song of Solomon* by Toni Morrison (1977), African American servants and slaves are strategically deployed in ways that encourage a rethinking of our conceptions of the historical past, particularly where American identity and a nation coming of age are concerned.

Robert Penn Warren, as one of the panelists at a conference of historians and novelists entitled "The Uses of History," expressed that he was both "appalled and honored to be invited to a group of historians. It makes you feel that the writing of fiction is more important than you thought it was." But Warren himself, as Thomas Connelly argues,

> is very much a historian, if this means that he employs a philosophy of history and uses past experience as a central theme. History *is* the thematic core of all his writing. It is the great dichotomy—history, the blind force capable of human destruction, but also the salvation of one who seeks self-identity. For Warren, self-understanding comes through the application of the "historical sense."[11]

Warren maintains that although the ground rules are different for novelists and historians, "that the novelist doesn't have to document," the novelist must still be governed by possibility; his or her fiction must always be "historically possible"[12] to be legitimate. It is his commitment to the historically possible that shapes the "thematic patterns" of "Warren's philosophy of history" that recur throughout his work: "The theme [is] self-division within one who searched for his own identity. Often he failed. Fed by idealism or determinism, one compromised with the world, justifying evil in the name of elimination of evil. Salvation—when it came—arose when one came to terms with his own complicity in history."[13]

It may or may not be true that "[b]lack voices produced by white ventriloquism qualify as dubious evidence."[14] Nevertheless, Robert Penn Warren's *Band of Angels* is extraordinary in its efforts to both elucidate and transcend the past, particularly through his choice of the daughter of a slave as the first-person narrator in this tale of race relations in the antebellum planter aristocracy.

For E. L. Doctorow, the novelist is not only in a position to present the most comprehensive picture "as to the truth, reality," but has an obligation to do so

> [b]ecause fiction is the discipline that includes all the others. Its language is indiscriminate, it accepts the diction of science, theology, journalism, poetry, myth, history, everything. That's why Lawrence said fiction is the whole hog. That's basically it. You embrace everything. Dreams, hallucinations, legends, facts, and the mutterings of crazy people in the street—it's all valid, and you use it all. Fiction is, finally, a system of knowledge—that's what I believe it to be. So the writer is not functioning properly if he limits his vision as a journalist might or an ideologue.[15]

Doctorow does not draw a hard distinction between the objectives of writers of fiction and historians. He regards the professional historian as a creative writer who "knows how creative he is." In fact, he somewhat facetiously takes historians to task for the creative liberties that have been taken in the erasure of entire groups of people. He continues: "It turned out that American historians had written, for the most part, as an establishment. They had written out of existence the history of black people and women and Indians and Chinese people in this country. What could be more apparent than the creativity of that?"[16] Doctorow's *Ragtime* is a curative for what he perceives as the erroneous and unreliable historical record that conveniently includes and omits according to an unacknowledged agenda, particularly where white middle-class culture is concerned.[17]

I agree with Barbara Foley, who argues that for Doctorow "the accurate representation of the past is less crucial than revelation of the haunting continuity of the past in the present."[18] Doctorow makes this point clear to people who question his interest in history when he says: "People say to me, why do you write books that take place in the past? Well, I say, we live in it. Any city you walk in is made of the decisions of the dead."[19]

For Charles Johnson it is through the synthesis of all knowledge that we may begin to have a greater understanding of the past. To his way of thinking

> all knowledge, all disclosure, all revelation from the past, from our predecessors, black, white, and otherwise, is our inheritance, and most of the time we just don't know it. [. . .] And in a way, that's how I have to write. I have to know that. We are perpetually indebted to our predecessors for that. It's not something I can ignore or something I can abandon.

Everything, according to Johnson, is "predicated on all that came before," which is the reason his novel *Middle Passage* is so heavily researched, and not just for what he could garner from the historical record. Johnson engages philosophy, theology, mythology and science. Any source that contributes to understanding the human condition he considers, much like Doctorow, fair game. His methods serve his intent. He explains: "It isn't just to do a historical novel. It's not that. It's to understand what others have brought to the rendering and disclosure of the subject. You could call it borrowing, I suppose. My intention is somewhat different, a very synthetic technique."[20] Johnson's phenomenological approach, according to Molly Abel Travis, is a deliberate attempt to augment "[t]he reader's re-seeing and enlightenment. [. . .] This kind of narrative structure makes manifest the constructedness of history, throwing light on the historian's hermeneutics and showing the impossibility of a historical narrative purified of interpretation."[21]

Johnson's protagonist, a former slave and then servant, contemplates "his—representative—position as an African and an American in 1830, on his relationship with and his place in America" within the context of all the "extreme sufferings and perils"[22] of the Middle Passage that correspond to and influence his own personal coming of age. Concomitantly, Johnson invokes long-standing issues about the position, relationship and place of African Americans in America to the present.

Finally, Toni Morrison's *Song of Solomon* is the most straightforward example of how the past shapes the present. It continually meanders through and engages the past to contextualize every life, relationship, circumstance and consequence in the text. In fact, as Susan Willis observes, "No one can read a novel by Toni Morrison [. . .] without confronting history, feeling its influence and experiencing the changes wrought by history."[23] Although Morrison believes it is important "to treat old ideas, old situations,"[24] her mission is to make clear the impact of history and the American system of values on identity. She simultaneously, as Marilyn Sanders Mobley puts it, "suggest[s] that a viable sense of African American identity comes from responding to alternative constructions of self and community other than those received from mainstream American culture."[25]

Each author exemplifies many of the predominating concerns of a historical moment and makes use of some of the most pressing social and political questions. In this interpretive process they modulate the period to accommodate an agenda and a philosophy of composition; sometimes embellishing, massaging, perhaps deliberately exploiting or distorting the established historical record. They do not *read* or *misread* history, they *imagine* history. They operate under a fundamental principle of composition, fairly typical of historical and retrospective novelists, that embraces the uses of history as a meditation on social realities of the past for a variety of reasons, including: to examine, challenge, or promulgate a certain view of culture or history; to offer the possibility of alternate or multiple realities for individuals from a particular period in a way not commonly perceived or represented; to showcase certain sociopolitical or cultural values and ideology; to tell the "truth," that is, to set the historical record straight; or even to simply play fast and loose with historical facts or personages for entertainment value.

African Americans in positions of servitude facilitate the writer's imaginings of a historical moment, clearly one of their primary functions in these texts. I envision fictionalized black servants as telemetrical devices that receive and formulate data from the past and transmit it to future reading audiences through the imagination and subjectivity of the author.[26] In this sense, both novel and servant are powerfully retroactive, and often may validate or emend our understanding of history.

Warren, Doctorow, Johnson and Morrison employ the past, perhaps not so much as attempts to disclose an objective knowledge of history, as if there could be any such thing, but as backward glances that contemplate and interpret social realities. Within those realities, representations of the African American servant as an indicator and executor of specific American values are pervasive. A dreamlike quality presides over the narratives of each text, as is often the case with retrospective fiction. The blend of fact and fiction and the sensibilities of the writers interweave continuously to create an intricate and transmogrified view of the historical moment, much like Toni Morrison's description of the dynamic relationship between writer, text, subject and reader, in terms of the representation of an Africanist presence. Morrison writes:

> As a writer reading, I came to realize the obvious: the subject of the dream is the dreamer. The fabrication of an Africanist persona is reflexive; an extraordinary meditation on the self; a powerful exploration of the fears and desires that reside in the writerly conscious. It is an astonishing revelation of longing, of terror, of perplexity, of shame, of magnanimity. It requires hard work not to see this.[27]

Ultimately, African American servitude, perhaps most illustratively in the retrospective novel, is an imaginative, contrived specimen; a powerful discursive device that is continually engaged in the mercurial business of delivering, mythologizing and rehabilitating cultural history as well as disclosing the "fears and desires that reside in the writerly conscious." Black servitude acts as an indicator of changing social values, but also reveals how certain values or the perception of them remain perhaps paradoxically but resolutely constant. In this regard, these novels are especially useful in that they are not simply a forum in which to dramatize chronological events of the past, an expectation of historical fiction, but are narratives that are, by definition, retrospective. Within their historicized narratives the writers are engrossed with causality, agency, disclosure. The fictive constructions of the slaves and servants and the historiocultural matrix in which they reside, or from which they arise, are based wholly on remote observations and perceptions of the past—observations and perceptions colored by the imaginings of the author.

To Excavate the Past

Fact or fiction? These are the war words in the debate about privileging history over fiction in the effort to disclose the "truth" about the past. The assumption here is that fiction, particularly historical fiction, is *not true* by definition, but is a product of the imagination, which may or may not use actual events and historical personages for creative or other purposes. Fiction, therefore, can lay no claim to disclosing the reality of the past. History, on the other hand, has often enjoyed a special status as documented fact, largely provable, and, therefore, objective truth delivered for posterity. These assumptions have often been challenged not only by the writers of historical fiction, but by those who question the integrity of and unexamined reverence often paid to the so-called historical record. This latter group includes many contemporary historians who investigate and provide new contexts for interpreting and understanding the past. The utility of the synthesis of fact and art in the construction of both narrative and meaning in the world around us is a driving principle in Doctorow's work. He writes in his seminal essay "False Documents" that

> [m]oral values are inescapably esthetic. In the modern world it is the moral regime of factual reality that impinges on the provinces of art. News magazines present the events of the world as an ongoing weekly serial. Weather reports are constructed on television with exact attention to conflict (high pressure areas clashing with lows), suspense (the climax of tomorrow's weather prediction coming after the commercial), and other basic elements of narrative. The creating, advertising, packaging, and marketing of factual products is unquestionably a fictional enterprise. The novelist looking around him has inevitably to wonder why he is isolated by a profession when everywhere the factualists have appropriated his techniques and even brought a kind of exhaustion to the dramatic modes by the incessant exploitation of them.[28]

I agree with Mark Carnes, who argues in *Novel History: Historians and Novelists Confront America's Past (and Each Other)* that the usages and modification of historical facts by novelists may be somewhat of a moral obligation, which "they justified, after Aristotle, on the grounds that their art cast light on the human condition rather than on any particular historical episode."[29]

As moderator of a panel entitled "The Uses of History in Fiction," historian C. Vann Woodward makes no apologies for the validity or authority of historical novels, and even celebrates historical fiction in his opening address to the conference in which he makes clear where and why the battle lines have been drawn in this debate. He says that

> [h]istorians have too long cultivated a rather priggish, Nineteenth-Century cult of fact, a creed that borrowed its tenets and prestige from the sciences and the heyday of their ascendency [sic]. Like scientists, we said, historians stuck to the facts, preferably to hard facts. This conception, this prestige of hard facts, derives especially from the English. It was Oscar Wilde who said that the English are always degrading Truth into Fact, and he went on to say that when a Truth becomes a Fact, it loses all its intellectual value.

Woodward argues that it is historians' "eager[ness] to claim kinship with scientists" that creates an over-reliance on fact, which actually serves to obscure the truth. Historians' "kinship is actually much closer to novelists. We are, in fact, siblings, historical siblings," which has led to "sibling rivalry."[30] Warren Susman writes in *Culture as History* that "[t]he task is never to gather facts or develop intellectual structures alone. For history, like the culture of which it is a part, is something lived, something used." He adds that the usage of history in fiction serves a very important function, a function recognized by "major literary figures [. . . who] believed that somehow it was [their] special function [. . .] to make history [their] own, to offer in [their] art a vision of that history that would be more meaningful for culture."[31] Some critics, such as James Thompson, advance the argument that "[t]he decline of historical positivism and the accompanying deterioration of faith in an objective history (i.e., an ascertainable empirical reality), as well as some historians' insistence on an imaginative as opposed to analytical synthesis—both no doubt reflect the influence of modern relativism on historiography."[32]

The distinctions between the two disciplines are often very slippery if one acknowledges that written history is in significant ways shaped and even driven by the writer's point of view. As Peter Freese puts it: "the difference between historiography and the novel, be it historical or not, is for us no longer one of principle but of accentuation. [. . .] [T]he historical novel is no longer a freakish interloper between two disparate ontological realms, but just one of several possibilities to 're-invent' the past by means of language."[33] Perhaps Doctorow repudiates the distinctions most decisively when he states that "there is no fiction or nonfiction as we commonly understand the distinction: there is only narrative,"[34] and that "history belongs more to the novelists and the poets than it does to the social scientists. *At least we admit that we lie.*"[35] A popular conception, the middle ground in the debate, suggests that "neither history nor fiction is itself a stable, universally agreed upon, concept"[36] and neither are truth or reality. Ultimately, "history shares with fiction a mode of mediating the world for the purpose of introducing meaning, and it is the cultural authority from which they both derive that illuminates those facts so that they can be perceived."[37]

Retrospective novels, such as those considered here, are clearly more than simple romance or costume dramas, fanciful vehicles through which we may glorify the past. It is through the interpretation of the past, rather than any claims of objective knowledge of the past, that these novels offer insights and useful ways in which to explicate history through social and cultural context and the imagined lives of individuals who lived during a particular time. As Susman argues, "[t]raditional historical narrative does not lend itself to the expression of the logic of culture, and the writing of cultural history has always meant a search for a new form, a new language, a new perspective: theme and variation, a fugue-like principle of over-all organization, perhaps repeating but also discovering new notes to describe and probe."[38]

Consider, for example, that the slave or servant in the retrospective novel, as an abandoned, lost or orphaned child, may offer ways in which to think about social displacement and dissociation and may also bring into sharp focus the consequences of abandonment of responsibility in a larger social context. Doctorow argues that "redressing grievance could include a metaphysical disturbance of some sort of longing apart from one's own personal psychic construction, and certainly to be orphaned or the state of orphanage is just a useful metaphor for all sorts of injustice."[39]

Amantha Starr in *Band of Angels* is abandoned by her white father, who dies without making provisions for her in his will. She is sold into slavery as part of a property settlement. In *Ragtime* the washerwoman Sarah feels hopeless and abandoned by her lover in her pregnancy, isolated and without prospects in a strange place. She buries her newborn baby in a garden—the most extreme form of abandonment. In *Middle Passage* Rutherford Calhoun and his brother Jackson have been abandoned by their father, or so they think, and these orphans are left to the care and discretion of their slave master. Pilate and Macon Dead in *Song of Solomon* are orphaned when a white family murders their father and confiscates his property. The consequences of these abandonments and orphanings, which are literal and metaphorical, are catastrophic for the individuals directly affected and for the societies in which they live. The abandonment of responsibility, orphanage complicated or caused by social forces and the resulting consequences and accountability are unifying themes for these texts. The abandoned or orphaned child raises interesting questions about social triage, as well as the perceived necessity for and abuses of it in a society in which the guiding principles are hierarchy and power based on race, state of freeness, socioeconomic status, class, ethnicity and gender, and in which vulnerability spells oppression.

Some critics, including Henry James and Georg Lukács, argue that all novels, particularly realistic novels, contain some aspects of the "historical," and that the same problems, principles, structures, characterizations, expectations and conventions that apply to realistic fiction apply to historical fiction as well. James even claims that "[i]t is impossible to imagine what a novelist takes himself to be unless he regards himself as an historian and his narrative as history."[40] It may be true that "[i]n a sense, all novels are historical novels. They all seek to understand, to describe, to recapture the past, however remote, however recent."[41] As Joseph Turner points out in "The Kinds of Historical Fiction: An Essay in Definition and Methodology":

> a theory of aesthetic response obviates the need to define in advance what history is or how a novel should relate to it; instead, it allows us to follow the way the implied reader adjusts his conception of history to the one the novelist is creating. Its focus on the actions involved in responding to a literary text is thus ideally suited to the process of expectation and revision that is engaged when novelists write about the past.

Arguably, "[t]he best historical fiction [. . .] is ultimately about itself, about the meaning and making of history, about man's fate to live in history and his attempt to live in awareness of it."[42]

This is certainly the case for *Band of Angels*, *Ragtime*, *Middle Passage* and *Song of Solomon*, which are strategically positioned in past historical moments for very specific reasons. Could the same story be told in the same way and to the same ends by making it contemporary to when it was written? For these texts, absolutely not. Questions of artistic and perhaps political motives for creating historical/retrospective fiction are unavoidable. The authors in this project require the past to draw attention to certain events, persons or circumstances that are available only during a particular period in the past.

Social Issues, Then and Now

The texts in this discussion share a range of unifying issues and concerns. For example, power relations, dominance hierarchies, class and caste distinctions, are crucial. Servants are utilized as literary devices that articulate an observable social taxonomy in American society—a society both obsessed with and repulsed by the idea of social divisions governed by differences in economic status, inherited rank or privilege, and occupation; social divisions sanctioned by tradition or custom. The United States has been grappling with this issue, which is not supposed to be an issue, from its infancy.

Consider Thomas Jefferson, who acquired his place in posterity as the sacred icon of American freedom and egalitarianism during the nation's nativity; his commitment to the promulgation of a democratic society based on natural rights is well known. He favors a society that affirms equal rights before the law and respect for all people, but that also acknowledges and rewards "virtue and talents," a "natural aristocracy." In this meritocratic system, personal effort and character are the basis for acquiring status and the accompanying rewards of achievement.[43]

"Natural" and "artificial" are the operative words here. Jefferson privileges "natural" as more egalitarian than "artificial" and draws a moral distinction between the two systems. Despite the organizing principles that differ from English primogeniture and the laws of entail, Jefferson's natural aristocracy is still a class-dependent social configuration in that it is necessarily categorical and strata-bound. A belief in social, moral and cultural equality for all governs a true egalitarian society, if any such state really exists. Jefferson's idealized society is still hierarchical—ever striving toward a typological superordination and social taxonomy that is inherently incompatible with the concept of egalitarianism. By definition there can be no aristocracy, "[a] group or class considered superior to others," without a group or groups that are inferior by comparison. There is no upper echelon without the lower echelons comprised of those with, perhaps, inferior and/or lesser abilities, achievements and virtues by comparison.

A complex man in matters of race, Jefferson appears to grapple with some of his conflicted and contradictory ideas about class through his notions about black servitude. In his view, Negroes could not, even after emancipation, become part of a meritocratic system because of, among other reasons, an innate inability to compete in society as a result of the "degraded condition of their existence, both in Africa and America." Apparently, these conditions have produced a being "in reason much inferior" to whites. The proof is "that in imagination they are dull, tasteless, and anomalous." Consequently, "[w]hen freed he is to be removed beyond the reach of mixture."[44]

Alexis de Tocqueville postulated that all societies, including democracies, have both the rich and the poor, and as a result masters and servants. Even though Tocqueville acknowledges the existence of class in America, he misapprehends the complexity and rigor of it. His idealized vision of America is of a society in which

> servants are not only equal among themselves, but one can say that in some fashion they are equal to their masters. [. . .] [T]he servant is not a different type of man from the master. [. . .] By nature they are not at all inferior one to the other, and they only become so temporarily by contract. [. . .] [T]his is not just the way in which the servants see their positions. The masters see domestic service in the same light.[45]

As a foreign observer with limited access, Tocqueville may be forgiven. American society, including the master/servant relationship, is fraught with class distinctions that indeed attach very specific values to individuals and groups. The truth is that "[c]lass distinctions in America are so complicated and subtle that foreign visitors often miss the nuances and sometimes even the existence of a class structure."[46]

Disquisitions on class and caste in the United States are often complicated, self-conscious, defensive. In 1896 John Marshall Harlan wrote in opposition to the ruling in *Plessy v. Ferguson* that "in the eye of the law, there is in this country no superior, dominant, ruling class of citizens. There is no caste here. Our Constitution is color-blind, and neither knows nor tolerates classes among citizens. In respect of civil rights, all citizens are equal before the law. The humblest is the peer of the most powerful."[47] President George H. W. Bush, almost a century later, also protested, clearly too much, by stating that "[i]t isn't for the United States of America. We are not going to be divided by class."[48] Others, like William Henry, suggest that there is no shame in admitting to social hierarchy, and he unabashedly proclaims that "[a] superior culture organizes itself hierarchically."[49]

This "touchy subject"[50] is observable in the rules that regulate spatiality, territorial imperative and nonverbal communication and body language through the representation of the fictive African American servant. These servants govern relational tectonics, influence the processes of generalization and discrimination, and offer ways to conceptualize class.[51] Benjamin DeMott claims, and rightly so, that "the moral and social assumptions and the cultural and historical forces that nourish the concept of classless class, cannot be conducted without immersion in several modes of American evasion, contradiction, and fantasy."[52] Black servitude exemplifies and foregrounds these tendencies to dissimulate where class and caste are concerned.

Inextricably connected to the rules of class and caste are the consequences for deviation from or rejection of the rules. The principles are deep-rooted in American culture. They are bolstered by the Bible, which, for many Americans, provides particular guidance for the management of those who serve. Matthew 25:30 charges us to "[c]ast ye the unprofitable servant into outer darkness." Transgressions include violations of standards of conduct, resistance to authority and recalcitrance, challenges to the status quo by a servant, a disruption in the harmony of a situation, an inconvenience or loss-of-face experienced by a social superior, and other behaviors that denote unfitness. Most are met with swift and severe consequences for the servant. The repercussions for society in general are confirmed as well. There are rewards bestowed for appropriate behavior, and the punishments meted out for "crimes" range from ostracism and verbal chastisement to physical torture and death. These situations, which also surface routinely in retrospective literature, offer moral lessons for the reader, serve to both clarify and ratify a discernible social order, and affirm the need for that order.

Class and caste are but part of an observable social order that is manifested in the representation of black servitude. In a society preoccupied with physical attractiveness, the significance of personal appearance cannot be overstated. Physiognomy is an indicator and outward manifestation of intrinsic value and inner worth. Attire is a uniform that announces to the world the character of the wearer. A carefully delineated conventionalized system of observable external attributes gives clues and proclaims a complex of mental and ethical traits. Correspondingly, American retrospective fiction categorically offers characterizations of the sacred and the profane, of the desirable and the undesirable, of beauty and ugliness, goodness and evil, refinement and vulgarity, intelligence and ignorance through the representation of black servitude.

The relationship between veneer and value is unavoidable in a discussion about the defining characteristics of American society. It is possible to both predict and track, to a considerable extent, the inherent worth, the moral disposition and the commercial value of a servant or slave, and by extension, individuals in the wider social context, by reading the "visual" language of physical attributes that are intended as objective evidence and as a perceptible expression of distinctive, inherent qualities. Visual cues of physiognomy and attire engender the American aesthetic and substantiate the correlation between appearance and essence as a cultural value—what Annette Kuhn calls "bodily attributes as final arbiter of a basic truth."[53]

Color-consciousness, for example, underpins the moral and social value assigned to the different shades along the color continuum. The popular conception during slavery was that "mulattos were superior in intelligence to pure blacks. This superiority was attributed to the infusion of white blood."[54] Although Thomas Jefferson did not invent this point of view, he wrote extensively about it in *Notes on the State of Virginia:* "The improvement of the blacks in body and mind, in the first instance of the mixture with the whites, has been observed by every one, and proves that their inferiority is not the effect merely of the conditions of life."[55] The representation of African American servitude continually offers evidence to support this point of view; an ongoing legacy in attitudes and values. In "Black Women in Afro-American Literature," Barbara Christian discusses how the representations of the black mammy and the tragic mulatta figures in American literature demonstrate a (mis)apprehension of their realities. She argues that the representation of the mulatta serves as a means for white audiences to revel in their unarticulated guilt "in the ironic way that the guilty and powerful always delight in looking obliquely at their guilt," and the mammy figure, in addition to functioning as contrast to white femininity, offers a nonthreatening ideal of a slave that "is needed as an image, a surrogate to contain all those fears of the physical female."[56] The African American servant defines the parameters of feminine identity and value, especially through expectations of labor for black and white women, and the editorialized contrasts of physical characteristics of white mistresses and black servants and slaves.

Generalizations about size and shape, and the ways in which worthiness and unworthiness are often reduced to stereotyped stock characters and caricatures also enable the reader to assign value to the person represented. For example, deriving from generalizations on appearances are the slender, neat mulatto (industrious, provisionally refined), the large-bosomed maternal mammy with hair invariably concealed beneath a tidy rag (domineering but lovable), and the classy chauffeur in crisp livery with shiny brass buttons (efficient and obsequious), to name a few, which are eroticized and exoticized as objects of desire, contempt, amusement and fear. The representations of these servants provide significant information about how physical appearance and clothing are interpreted as evidence of moral, ethical and personality qualities.

Black servitude in retrospective fiction also draws attention to the vagaries of loyalty, the work ethic and delayed gratification. From the onset of American society, the moral benefits of hard work were espoused from the pulpits and in the writings of ministers, statesmen and philosophers. William Penn and Cotton Mather reaffirmed the tradition in the late sixteenth and early seventeenth centuries; they were followed by Benjamin Franklin in his *Autobiography* and other writings, and William Holmes McGuffey in his children's books, among many others. The idea of work in American society has always meant more than simply a way to administer to the practical matters of life, but has been considered an American virtue and the means by which one may edify the soul and improve character. Work was a sacred duty that allowed the individual to serve God and community.

African American servitude is a resource for demonstrating and cultivating as well as exposing the weaknesses and fallacies of the work ethic. It articulates, among other things, changing notions about the nobility and dignity of work. It draws attention to how the attending ideas of loyalty, religious duty and delayed gratification have also changed in a society in which the rewards for adhering to this ethic are increasingly reduced, or never existed in the first place, for so many. One of the guiding principles of the American work ethic is that there is a direct relationship between effort and achievement—a notion that conveniently disregards the overwhelming disparity in the material rewards for well-paid, poorly paid, and unpaid labor (slavery).

For example, contentment with slavery meant, for the slave, acquiescence to the status quo, a shoulder to the wheel and a reward in the Great Beyond.

Received Christian ethics provided a balm to assuage the pain of realization that toil would not alleviate hardship—a pain mitigated by the heavenly reward promised "In the sweet, by and by"[57] in religious doctrine, sermons and hymns. Delayed gratification for the unpaid slave and poorly paid servant invariably meant a compensation in the afterlife—considering that few earthly rewards were forthcoming for these workers. Among these few rewards was the satisfaction that a job was well done. Perhaps the most compelling motivation was to please an employer or master who not only had the power to provide an opportunity for the servant to fulfill his/her sacred duty in mortal life through work, but who also had the power to punish. To the habitually and perhaps deliberately unwitting slave owner, these behaviors would appear as the result of good training and discipline, loyalty and fidelity.

Loyalty and fidelity, however, are problematized by dependency. Frederick Douglass points out in his *Narrative* that slaves, who were routinely spied upon, gave the appearance of and paid lip-service to their own loyalties to their masters as part of their strategy for survival. This feigning of loyalty was a means to secure the meager trusts and rewards bestowed on the faithful, and was generally not the result of gratitude and affection, as was often imagined by the slave owners.[58] Slave owners were bewildered and insulted when slave "favorites," whom they assumed were contented members of the "family," ran away. Presumably, these slaves enjoyed congenial relations with their owners. When the slaves deserted their situations, their owners discovered that their servants did not feel respect and loyalty, but had strategically feigned deference to keep a job or situation. The owners could not understand that the slaves were not running away, but escaping. The perceived venality of slave defectors was a source of rage for owners and had the potential for deadly consequences. Slaves "who strongly disliked their masters might conceal their animosity. More often it erupted into disobedience and violence."[59] Not surprisingly, feigned deference is still part of standard operating procedures for servants.[60]

Faith in the work ethic as the basis of economic security and the means of respectability continues to be problematized, particularly for African Americans, because, as Cornel West argues in *Race Matters*, conservatives fail to acknowledge the

> innumerable cases in which black people do act on the Protestant ethic [. . .] [and] still remain at the bottom of the social ladder. Instead, they highlight the few instances in which blacks ascend to the top as if such success is available to all blacks, regardless of circumstances. [. . .] Such a vulgar rendition of Horatio Alger in blackface.[61]

In post–Civil War America, the values of the work ethic were presumed to apply equally across a diverse population. Clearly, the fallacies of the work ethic were a reality for those with restricted access to opportunity and a level playing field.

Perhaps paradoxically, the industrial revolution, which provided a higher standard of living for many Americans, contributed to the erosion of belief in the American work ethic as a system that guaranteed security and advancement for workers. In *The Work Ethic: Working Values and Values that Work*, David J. Cherrington explains that work for the early Americans was esteemed as noble, and that there was no distinction between the honor and dignity bestowed on honest work whether it was manual or intellectual. However, changes accompanying industrialization from the late nineteenth to early twentieth century had an enormous impact on faith in these principles. Some factors were the beginnings of alienation of the worker from the means of production and the products produced; the increase in leisure time, which resulted from mass- and over-production of goods; and the increased realization that "[m]ost people who made it to the top did not start at the bottom; they started much higher, with the advantages of wealth, family influence, and better education."[62] The concept of hard work as the means to personal progress and financial well-being and security was gradually and irrevocably, if subtly, undermined for many Americans. It was a system to which slaves could never aspire. Not surprisingly, the idea of loyalty and faithfulness was correspondingly eroded by a system that is governed by the belief that some forms of labor are more worthy than others and therefore some laborers more than others, where financial rewards are minimal or non-existent for those who perform the labor, and where the owner/master/employer is the worthiest of all.

Loss of faith in the work ethic, diminishing returns on the investment of labor, changing attitudes toward manual and nonskilled labor and a lack of respect for the laborer have created an atmosphere rife with "[t]hreat [as] the operative perception: threat to survival, savings, status, and self-esteem."[63] Interestingly, the fictive representations of African American servants and servitude often both reinforce and undermine the idea of the work ethic. They simultaneously exemplify the disparity between the extolled virtues of work and the exploitation of those workers who can derive little besides subsistence living, and, for some, personal satisfaction in a job well done. They make clear that very often there is not a direct relationship between effort and consequences, between effort and acquisition of the American Dream.

Gender issues—particularly where individuation, sexual identity, and the development or expression of selfhood are problematized both for and by servants—are also crucial. For example, as Gillian Brown observes in *Domestic Individualism:*

> Within [. . .] the home, the family, religion, sexuality, health—selfhood depends upon its severance from the world of work, a severance reflected in the individual's difference from her body. Idealized as independent of the vagaries of labor in the marketplace, individuality requires continual confirmation of impregnability. Self-dominion is accordingly secured in subordinating the body, the component of self all too untrustworthy for its labor history, its market service.[64]

Twentieth-century American retrospective literature offers an almost bottomless reservoir of examples of the African American servant as surrogate physical presence that makes possible the delegation of demands placed on the body of the mistress/master or employer.

These texts also, by suggestion or otherwise, hold up Christianity for scrutiny—its sensibilities and the pervasive (mis)appropriation of its tenets, the utility of paternalism and the role of expiation, absolution and redemption for individuals and the evolving national consciousness. The complex and multiple layers of meaning for each of these issues, and many others, such as cultural amalgamation, victimization and transcendence, are embodied in the representation of black servitude. It is a crucial function of African American servitude to draw attention to standards and values that, whether by deliberate design of the author or not, demonstrate both the long-ranging consequences of history and that the effects of the past are inescapable.

African American servitude in retrospective fiction is a rich textual source that enables both author and reader to (de)mythologize and rehabilitate cultural history. Through a close textual analysis of twentieth-century meditations on the past, as transmitted through African American servants—the agents, executors and purveyors of values and culture, and the conveyances for authorial wish-fulfillment—we may enlarge our understanding of the dynamics and complexities of national identity formation and character.

THE AFRICAN AMERICAN SERVANT: CULTURAL ARTIFACT AND AGENT IN PLACE

> *Whoopi Goldberg has whipped out tit for some disturbed little white kid in precisely two of her nearly two dozen movies:* Clara's Heart *and* Corinna, Corinna. *Yet the number seems higher. As her reward for being Hollywood's favorite Negress [. . .] Goldberg has been slowly molded into an all-purpose mammy.*
>
> —Ernest Hardy[65]

The Shame of Servitude: Stigma and Status

The above quote expresses such palpable outrage over what promises to be rather forgettable "B" movies—just two more in a string of films with Goldberg panned by critics and all but ignored by audiences. The continuing practice of representing African Americans as servants in films and on television elicits the outrage, indignation, disappointment and frustration of scholars, journalists and entertainers throughout the media, and defensive responses from those who play these parts.[66] Many African Americans are offended by the portrayals. Much of the distress over these representations can be attributed to a frustration over the perpetuation of stereotypical images and behaviors that dominate many of the portrayals; a justifiable sensitivity to the pandering of a negative fiction about a real people—the "fabulous images, neither entirely of this world nor of the realm of myth" that Sander Gilman describes in *Difference and Pathology*. As is most often the case with stereotypes, "[t]hese images never remain abstractions: we understand them as real-world entities"[67] that ultimately deny or obscure the individuality and even humanity of those who are members of the represented group.[68]

The African American represented as a servant, mammy or otherwise, evokes powerful emotional responses because they are a painful reminder of the legacy of slavery. Part of the abhorrence of fictive black servitude may also be directly attributed to the presumed state of mental servility as a necessary by-product or condition in which the servant defers or loses will, personality and identity. George Watson argues in "The Silence of the Servants" that this popular conception, which is promulgated in the products of culture, is both erroneous and limiting. As spectators and readers we are expected to suppose that "[t]o be a servant is to be servile through and through [. . .] and servility can become a habit of mind that destroys the soul." As a counterpoint to this type of representation Watson offers examples of the clever and talkative literary servant from two millennia to demonstrate that servants were, in fiction, and by logical extension, real life, more than the mere embodiment of the master's will.[69] Indeed. Even so, there are other unsettling aspects of representing the African American in a position of servitude.

In addition to the obfuscation of individuality and humanity, and the presumed state of mental servility for those who serve, is the troubling implication of limited options in life as the appropriate and predictable result of an inherent inability to do any better; that servitude is a suitable station in life for inferiors. The proliferation of African American servants in the products of culture is perceived as an affirmation that for African Americans servitude is part of the natural order of things; that in the hierarchy on The Great Chain of Being is a notch somewhere near the bottom designated for the African American as servant in perpetuity.

Also contributing to and inciting sensitivity to the figure/image of the fictive servant is the fact that servitude in general in American society is absolutely stigmatized. *Servant* is a dirty word, causing both pride and embarrassment for many of those who employ them, and humiliation and anxiety for many of those who serve.[70]

The maligning of servitude is a long-standing tradition in America. Frances Trollope wrote in 1832 about her difficulties acquiring a servant because of the stigma. In familiarizing herself with American methods for acquiring a servant, Trollope, who was visiting from England, discovered that she must call getting a servant "'getting help'; for it is more than petty treason to the republic to call a free citizen a *servant.*" Furthermore, this type of work was held in disdain even by the poorest girls, who would rather work for less and in appalling conditions in factories. Trollope finally finds a young woman who is willing to serve and who is so poor that she has but one dress. Yet, upon setting the terms of her employment this young woman says that her mother's slave, Phillis, will help her once a week with the cleaning. The employer/employee relationship between Trollope and her maid gradually deteriorates because this young woman, who wasn't accustomed to having dinner because of her poverty, was insulted that she was expected to eat in the kitchen. Trollope concludes that this woman has been ruined for servitude because of "having heard a thousand and a thousand times that she was as good as any other lady; that all men were equal, and women too; and that it was a sin and a shame for a free-born American to be treated like a servant."[71] However disdainful Trollope's maid may have felt about her status as a servant, imagine the status of a slave of a servant—the status of Phillis. There is no humbler or degraded "occupation" in American society.[72]

There are obvious distinctions and similarities between slaves (forced and unpaid servitude) and paid servants (including indentured), and specific values are attached to each of these categories of service. Each category is consigned to a specific place in the social hierarchy. In a society in which upward mobility is a highly prized matter and a guiding principle, volition, length of service, legal condition and color determine the social rank of the servant; thus, the lowliest status among servants is that of the black slave.

David Roediger points out in *The Wages of Whiteness: Race and the Making of the American Working Class*, that much of the opposition to the term *servant* was the result of the imprecise conflation of the word *servant* with *slave* from as early as the colonial period "right through Noah Webster's inconsistent distinctions between the two terms in his dictionary of 1828 and the tendency in the South to apply *servant* overwhelmingly to slaves in the antebellum years." Roediger argues that it is the association with blackness that made the term so objectionable: "in a society in which Blackness and servility were so thoroughly intertwined—North and South—assertions of white freedom could not be raceless." Household and farm workers increasingly became "*white workers* who identified their freedom and their dignity in work as being suited to those who were 'not slaves' or 'not negurs.'"[73] The nomenclature is a huge thing, directly affecting and affected by the value attached to those wearing the labels, and creating a distinction of personal value and esteem based upon color and legal status.

There is a beginning and an end to being a servant. The terms of employment are contractual and continue at the pleasure of both servant and master. A servant can quit an untenable situation at any time, or for no reason. Indentured servants and slaves do share a number of characteristics in common, such as extremely harsh working conditions, inadequate food, health- and life-threatening living conditions, and severe exploitation.[74] But for the indentured servant there was an end in sight; they could quit in time. The slave was a servant for life. The unfree black worker had a master. The free white worker had a boss or an employer, but could eventually become one. The difference between being a servant and being a slave has everything to do with class, color and state of freeness. Even so, voluntary servitude after slavery can in some ways be regarded as "forced" for so many black people because the only "choice" for employment, especially for most black women, was to continue in servitude.

Often ignored, misunderstood or maligned, these products of culture, fictive black servants, offer the criteria for assessing individual and group value and make visible and observable definitive social patterns and customs. The fictive servant assists the reader in interpreting some of the most consequential and common elements of valuation in American society, most prominently class, caste, color, ethnicity, physiognomy, dress and behavior.

Although many aspects of servitude have changed since Trollope wrote of her experiences, some things have remained markedly the same.[75] In her historical survey of domestic service, Judith Rollins observes that despite the changes in "its size, role, and composition in relation to changes in the larger political and economic spheres of the society," servitude remains ever

> grounded in stratification, it was always low in the class hierarchy, always composed of people considered inferior (by virtue of their unfree status, their gender, their geographic origins, their lower-class background, and/or their caste,

> race, or ethnicity), and always held in the lowest esteem by the overall society, including the domestics themselves.[76]

Negative attitudes toward servants and servitude in American society, across ethnic groups, are well-documented in numerous sociological and historical studies and surveys. In 1897 Lucy Maynard Salmon reported that her study of domestic work in 1889–1890 revealed that out of the twenty-four reasons women did not choose or want to choose domestic service as employment, the overwhelming reason was because of "[p]ride, social condition, and unwillingness to be called servants." It is a justifiable sensitivity to "this social position with its accompanying marks of social inferiority that, more than any other one thing, turns the scale against domestic service as an occupation in the thoughts of many intelligent and ambitious women whose tastes naturally incline them to domestic employment."[77]

A century later, Mary Romero faced considerable difficulty obtaining interviews with Chicanas who worked in domestic service for her project, *Maid in the U.S.A.* When she called to ask for interview appointments with domestics who had been recommended to her, she "was confronted with resistance and shame. The women expressed embarrassment at being identified by their work—as a 'housekeeper' or 'cleaning lady.'" Some of these interviewees expressed anger that Romero was conducting research on such a lowly occupation rather than studying lawyers and doctors, "'another occupation that presents *our people* in a more positive light'" (my emphasis).

The shame felt by these domestics, and their justifiable perceptions of the stigma attached to servitude, motivated many of these women to keep their work a secret from their neighbors, friends and some members of their own families. Even their children, completely aware of the stigma of servitude, often reported "that their mothers 'just did housework,' which was ambiguous enough to define them as full-time homemakers and not necessarily as domestics."[78]

In "White Mistresses and African American Domestic Workers: Ideals for Change," Annie S. Barnes reports that one of the subjects of her study feels strongly that the employer/employee relationship in domestic arrangements "has changed from social subordination to a relationship of equality with her employers. She becomes angry and adamant if one refers to her occupation as domestic or housework. To dignify her occupation, she created the Homemakers Enterprise Support Services, Inc." Furthermore, she discontinued the use of courtesy titles that both her mother and grandmother, also servants, had used, in an attempt to make her position as a servant seem more equal to that of her employers. Clearly, the efforts of this person are part of a "subtle rebellion to bring dignity to an important job that has long been stigmatized."[79]

The stigma of servitude has a lot to do with the very nature of much of the work itself. "[F]ood is not dirty, but scraps left on plates or smears on clothes are; shoes are not dirty except on the dinner table; clothes are not messy except on the floor, and so on."[80] It is considered humiliating to have to clean behind others—a significant aspect of servitude. The question, then, becomes: What can the fictive representation of those who perform what is considered lowly, disgusting and humiliating work lend to writers of retrospective fiction and their readers?

The African American servant in retrospective fiction identifies, defines and interprets the literary cues, cultural symbols, iconography, social schemata and historiocultural context which codify experience, organize perceptions and influence both cognitive and associative responses in the reader. The relationship of the African American literary servant to American culture is reciprocal. Fictive servants are at once artifacts/objects shaped or produced by the intention to represent American culture and history in a particular way, but they simultaneously act as *agents provocateurs* who effectively influence perceptions, and by logical extension, American culture. They are diagnostic tools, barometers of the sociohistorical condition or meteorological devices through which the reader may imagine the social climate of the moment. They explicate and disseminate cultural information and values, and deliver significant aspects of national identity and social consciousness. These purveyors of cultural information play a crucial role in concept formation and in the indoctrination of the reader to the most fundamental ethics of American society, in each case, according to the imaginings of the author.

Serving the Text: Elaborating Perceptions of Difference

In what ways does the representation of African American servants and servitude disclose or inter cultural information? What are some of the factors/elements employed by the author that ultimately fashion the African American servant as a reliable, or in some cases an unreliable, indicator of customs and values? In what ways does the representation define, critique, mythologize or revise American culture and/or the historical past? In what ways does the representation have relevance for current social and political concerns for the author? Why focus specifically on black servitude when servitude is not exclusive to blacks?

Ultimately, "[d]eep within the word 'American' is its association with race." Through these agents of culture we may discern what it means to be virtuous and what it means to be American—two notions that are sometimes conflated. The representation of African American servitude provides us with many clues to what it means to be an American; who or what constitutes a *real*, an *authentic*, a *good*, the *best* American. As readers, we are indebted to the proliferation of the African American as servant precisely because, as Toni Morrison explains, "the metaphorical and metaphysical uses of race occupy definitive places in American literature, in the 'national' character, and ought to be a major concern of the literary scholarship that tries to know it." This examination of the appearances, behaviors and circumstances of African Americans in servitude, and those in association with them, provides useful information about how Americanness is defined, constructed, perpetuated and enforced in American society and in the literature that explicates it. "The contemplation of this black presence is central to any understanding of our national literature and should not be permitted to hover at the margins of the literary imagination." I would like to suggest that the contemplation of this black presence, African Americans in servitude in this particular case, will also enlarge our understanding of national identity and character. It will elucidate the ways in which whiteness is conflated with Americanness, and how looking at blackness is a way of looking at whiteness. The figure of the African American servant delineates the rules of social engagement, precisely defining the limitations and circumstances under which "American" identity is constructed and maintained, or to which one is entitled to lay claim to being an American. Again, as Morrison points out:

> Race, in fact, now functions as a metaphor so necessary to the construction of Americanness that it rivals the old pseudo-scientific and class-informed racisms whose dynamics we are more used to deciphering. As a metaphor for transacting the whole process of Americanization, while burying its particular racial ingredients, this Africanist presence may be something the United States cannot do without.[81]

Certainly, an investigation of this presence is something a study of the black servant in retrospective fiction cannot do without. Although this investigation is not limited to African Americans as servants, they overwhelmingly constitute this population in literature, and they are perceived to do so in actuality.

Henry Louis Gates, Jr. writes in "Writing 'Race' and the Difference it Makes":

> Race, as a meaningful criterion within the biological sciences, has long been recognized to be a fiction. When we speak of "the white race" or "the black race," "the Jewish race" or "the Aryan race," we speak in biological misnomers and, more generally, in metaphors. Nevertheless, our conversations are replete

> with usages of race which have their sources in the dubious pseudoscience of the eighteenth and nineteenth centuries.[82]

In an attempt to quell the continuing furor over the meaning of race, the American Anthropological Association issued a "Statement on 'Race'" in 1998, which asserts that "it has become clear that human populations are not unambiguous, clearly demarcated, biologically distinct groups." This statement on race could not put to rest the "[n]umerous arbitrary and fictitious beliefs about the different peoples [that] were institutionalized and deeply embedded in American thought"; no statement could. In fact, a carefully worded proviso prefaces the "Statement" which makes clear that "[i]t does not reflect a consensus of all members of the AAA, as individuals vary in their approaches to the study of 'race.'"[83]

Still, inarguably, the term "race" is freighted with historical, social and political significance, despite the fact that many enlightened critics now believe that this term is losing both its importance as a generalization, and its emotional and social impact. This optimistic position may be premature. This purported lessening of "race" as a legitimate qualifier of difference is perceived as a result, in part, of the overwhelming scientific evidence that argues "that human genetic variability between the populations of Africa or Europe or Asia is not much greater than that within those populations"[84] and therefore calls into question long-cherished ideas about the values placed on racial difference. The term "race" has not been put to rest as a potent, unabating social construct; nor as an explanation for perceived profound difference—difference that translates into levels of value and that serves as an excuse for stereotyping, institutionalizing discrimination and oppression and as justification for racial hatred.

One has only to consider the implications of recent debates by scholars and intellectuals about affirmative action and reparations, as well as the proliferation of literature on racial difference and social consequence, to confirm that race is yet a hot issue, a viable concept for those with various social and political agenda.[85] It is certainly a tangible and vital concept for the average American, black or white. Perceived racial difference *is* a predominating concern in American society, and representation of black servitude manifests these concerns in its literature.

For some social scientists and other observers, the term "ethnicity" currently serves to mitigate, to some extent, what is perceived as the erroneous but pervasive application of "race." But "ethnicity" has taken its place, in many ways, as a garbage-can term that embraces every conceivable difference between groups of people who share common attributes, and reconfigures the differences into categories of distinction. "Ethnicity" employs as its constituents a mélange of culture, religion, geographic location, political affiliation, educational background, class or caste orientation, etc. This is an understandable effort to clarify or at least to provide a more comprehensive, and hopefully less derogatory, way to conceptualize difference other than by "race" alone.[86]

However, and Roger Sanjek says it best in "The Enduring Inequalities of Race," the trend to focus on ethnicity at the expense of race has had an adverse, modulating effect on the perception of the realities of racism. As a result of a shift of focus in the 1970s from race to ethnicity for many scholars in the United States,

> [t]he historic political and economic inequalities that underlie racial classification were underplayed. This, unfortunately, served a sinister agenda. A neoconservative glorification of ethnicity had been heralded in a widely read *New York Times Magazine* piece by Irving Kristol (1966), who asserted that African Americans were just another ethnic group working their way up the ladder like European immigrants. Glazer and Moynihan's *Beyond the Melting Pot* (1963) and Novak's *Rise of the Unmeltable Ethnics* (1971) also fueled this fire by portraying white ethnic groups as continuing to maintain cohesion and Old World cultural values for generations after their arrival as immigrants.

Of course race matters, and the historicized fictive African American servant has enormous metaphorical potential as an archetype for elaborating perceptions of difference and the values attached to that difference. "We need to understand how and why a ranked hierarchy of races has been put to such destructive uses, been affirmed 'scientifically,' been challenged repeatedly, and yet still dies so hard."[87]

Benjamin DeMott writes that

> [c]ultural materials of many kinds serve as the ground of analysis—movies, novels, cartoons, sculpture, poems, jokes, statistics, the language of "news," much more. The theme, however, remains constant: the need to bring difference alive, and the possibility of restoring our power to see others feelingly in their separateness and distinctness.[88]

The need to bring difference alive. Race complicates everything.

As agents for explicating real or perceived differences between "us" and "them," selfhood and otherness, Americans and others, black servants are useful constructs that elucidate perceived moral distinctions between members of the dominant culture and all others. They bring difference alive. This is often an attempt to either draw attention to and critique, or reconcile and make palatable, the reality of social dominance with the fragile nature of the idea of superiority.

The ostensible contrasts between the moral disposition of members of the dominant culture with all others routinely makes understandable the "enforced difference"[89] of a racialized society. For the authors under consideration in this book, in very different ways, the African American literary servant is essentialized and troped in a social context that demonstrates how the formation of identity, as an American, is significantly influenced by opposition-dependent referentiality, the "[d]ifference disliked is identity affirmed" notion that Barbara Johnson describes in "Threshold of Difference."[90]

I confront the usages of ethnicity and race in the relationships between literary servants and others in an effort to disclose the dynamics of self-validation and social valuation through the celebration of self and "same," and the abhorrence of difference resident in the American consciousness and national identity as envisioned by Warren, Doctorow, Johnson and Morrison.

African American servants whose duties bring them in physical proximity and/or personal, intimate contact with their employers, usually through the performance of personal service in the private domestic sphere, are the primary focus. Among these are housemaids, childcare workers such as mammies, wet nurses, nannies, the lady's maid to southern belles, washerwomen, chauffeurs, valets, manservants, butlers and loyal retainers of all sorts. Each of these categories of service has its own unique set of rules, limitations, parameters and expectations and have much to reveal about social hierarchy.

This book does not attempt to provide the "voice" of the servant, as if there could be any such thing, nor do I attempt to assess and/or critique the fidelity of the images to actual servants—the accuracy or purity of the representation. It does not engage in the debate over the evils of irresponsible, inaccurate representation in fiction writing—an irreconcilable quagmire of ideological expectations—except insofar as the "inaccurate" representations may serve the purpose of demonstrating the instructiveness of the fictive servant. Rhetorical effect and ideological purity or impurity are absolutely at the discretion of the artist/writer. It might be useful, therefore, to bear in mind that we are dealing with fiction. Yet, there is much to be discerned from inaccurate or untrue representations. As Bruce Robbins observes, "shamelessly nonrepresentational artifice [. . .] are thus not to be dismissed out of hand, but can be investigated as the site of unknown and perhaps surprising confrontations."[91] Some of the most compelling dimensions of these representations are the ways in which servants subvert our expectations and prefigure the destabilization of "accuracy" as a viable category. The representation, accurate or otherwise, has enormous metaphorical potential and connotative significance. It is the surprising confrontations and the construction, representation, observation and perception of them that fuel this investigation.

Representations of servants are liberally deployed throughout the products of culture—literature, opera, television commercials, film, etc. Perhaps the most salient reasons for a servant's presence in these works is that they are easily identifiable as symbols of wealth or financial well-being; "servants of life are themselves signs—signs of their masters' status."[92] They are also presented as the instruments of domestic order and harmony; they provide a contrast with or foil to the protagonists and sometimes with secondary or peripheral subject positions. They are often used in subtle and conspicuous ways to advance the plot—the "*servus ex machina* [. . .] who intervenes with superb and repetitive arbitrariness in plots exclusively dedicated to the destinies of his or her superiors."[93] They often provide comic relief; and, significantly, they are available and visibly perform a wide range of delegated tasks—they are there to work.

When I began this investigation I envisioned my task as an exploration of one or more of these dimensions of representation because fictively constructed servants are certainly more than a symbol of wealth; they are not simply "economically gratuitous [. . .] mere signs of money, itself a sign," or mechanisms by or through which work is accomplished. They are, in fact, material evidence of the complex values of American society.

Toni Morrison writes: "Readers and writers both struggle to interpret and perform within a common language shareable imaginative worlds. And although upon that struggle the positioning of the reader has justifiable claims, the author's presence—her or his intentions, blindness, and sight—is part of the imaginative activity."[94] I would like to suggest that as active participants in and observers of culture, we also struggle to interpret and perform through common language the shareable *real* world—and by language I mean any form or system of communication: the visual, the aural, and the sensory as well as the linguistic. Cultural conditioning predisposes us to interpret, perform, create and imagine a real world from the fictive. The world of the imagination offers meaning and order out of what might otherwise be chaos—a guiding principle, arguably the province, of artistic creation.

CHAPTER 2

WHAT MADE AMANTHA LEAN?

Racial Fanaticism in the 1950s and the Rationalization of Slavery in Robert Penn Warren's Band of Angels

The fathers have eaten a sour grape, and the children's teeth are set on edge.
—Jeremiah 31:29

The freedmen were not really free in 1865, nor are most of their descendants really free in 1965. Slavery was but one aspect of a race and color problem that is still far from solution here, or anywhere. In America particularly, the grapes of wrath have not yielded all their bitter vintage.
—Samuel Eliot Morison[1]

LEGACIES OF THE PAST

Slaves and servants in Robert Penn Warren's *Band of Angels* provide a frame of reference that exposes the visceral nature of color prejudice, the causes of white racial anxiety, the presumption of being human and American as "white," and the compatibility of all these elements with the idea of the inferiority and utilitarian nature of Negroes in antebellum culture—issues that were still rending American society apart in the early years of the civil rights movement, the period in which the book was written. My purpose here, if I may borrow from Dana D. Nelson's *The Word in Black and White*, is to uncover the

> "violence of representation" that occurs in texts about race, the oppressive reduction of the apparently infinite diversities among humans to an oppositional binary, always hierarchically figured. [. . .] The ideological figuration of "race" is structurally violent in its reductiveness, denying the perceptual evidence of multitudes of colorations [. . .]. At the same time, the notion of "race" is necessary for a certain kind of violence, established and promulgated to justify the domination of one group of human beings over another.[2]

Many issues about race and race relations in America are organized in *Band of Angels* around ideas about the Negro as utilitarian and best suited for servitude, both as slaves and servants, because of tradition, particularly in the southern agrarian culture, and presumably because of natural or divine design; a breed to be set apart except when in the performance of labor.

Posterity has not been kind to *Band of Angels*. In the words of biographer Joseph Blotner, it is "an ambitious failure and perhaps the least satisfactory of his novels."[3] Although *Band of Angels* has not fared well in the estimation of critics, and even of Warren himself, and is widely considered so problematic as to be unsuccessful, it is worthy of investigation. It offers significant insight into Warren's struggle to adjust his youthful positions on race relations and the appropriate place for black people in American society; a struggle that manifests itself in his work and in his life. Correspondingly, *Band of Angels* offers significant insight into the intricacies and confusions of the race and color consciousness of an entire nation throughout its history. At this, he does succeed.

Robert Penn Warren wrote *Band of Angels* during the Eisenhower administration, the period in which African Americans boycotted the segregated city buses in Montgomery, Alabama. The McCarthy witch-hunt hearings for communists were being broadcast into American homes. The Cold War was intensely and personally felt by Americans who feared the potential of Russian technology because American scientific efforts were eclipsed by the progress the Russians were making in the "space race." Warren traded one time of national turmoil for another. During the early 1950s Warren wrote a novel refabricating the antebellum South of the early and mid-nineteenth century—a period characterized and complicated by escalating contentions between North and South over slavery and other issues; John Brown's seizure of Harper's Ferry in an attempt to start a slave insurrection; uncontrolled land and railroad speculation; bank, factory and railroad failure; high unemployment, hunger and bread lines; and, Darwin's publication of the theory of evolution and the resulting public furor. This novel, set during the Civil War era, is the contested site for the disclosure of the complexities of white racialist consciousness, and the deployment and representations of blacks as slaves and servants is the strategy for disclosing this consciousness.

I am intrigued by Warren's penchant for "significant women characters [who] have sexual liaisons with men of power and wealth"[4] in all but one of his novels. Warren as author, and perhaps ultimately as grand puppetmaster, (mis?)appropriates a female persona in the character of Amantha Starr, the narrator of the story, through which he confronts and evades, obsesses about and dismisses social issues and their impact on personal lives, identities and national character. Amantha's confusions about race and race relations may suggest Warren's own struggles in this area. His intent is problematical in *Band of Angels*. His own changing ideas about race and race relations confound his purpose and the point of view of this text. Through Amantha's experiences, her reactions to and musings about them, the reader becomes acquainted with the author's imaginings of the historical moment, and perhaps more important, his imaginings (fantasies?) of what it was like to be a female of color in bondage as a sexual slave.

Warren explains the processes of writing historical fiction as succumbing to a state of mind in which creativity is governed by "the feel of the past, not the literal past itself. It is a mode of memories. It's the mind working in terms of memory. [. . .] The fiction writer's past is not provable; it *may* be imagined."[5] As readers, we are asked to imagine right along with Warren, who conceptualizes Amantha as she struggles to both imagine and deny herself as a slave and a "nigger"—her new status but not identity, after her father's death results in her being sold to pay the debts from his profligate lifestyle. What is especially interesting are the ways in which Amantha attempts to adapt to her changing circumstances and position herself both socially and psychologically. The ways in which she perceives slaves and servants before her own bondage, when she is a pampered, spoiled and neglected "white" child, and after, as the sexual slave of her owner, then finally as the "white" wife of a wealthy white military officer, reveals much about the intractability of social conditioning when it comes to race and color.

It is clear that Warren intended to fashion a protagonist who comes to terms with what she perceives as her own complicity in slavery and history. Yet, the preponderance of evidence offered to make apparent Amantha's culpability is at odds with her struggle to reconcile the contradictions in her own thinking. Therefore, Warren's tendency to make convincing the complicity of a victim of enslavement yields instead, and in spite of Amantha's assertions, an identity that is not only divided, but that suffers from multiple and complex fractures—none of which entirely heal. Amantha's coming of age is without maturity or insight. She simply finds a way to cope according to the dictates of the society in which she lives. Hers is an adulthood bought at the cost of self-delusion, an identity suppressed and denied out of shame and the desire to imagine herself as whole, as good and, most important, as white. Amantha struggles to free herself of a self-image tainted by racial heritage and by her experiences, those caused by sociohistorical forces and those of her own choosing. She achieves, at best, a fragile détente between the warring factions of her psyche. It is an imperfect coming of age that not only effectively mirrors the development and self-imagining of society, but can clearly be read as a fitting analog for American society.

The most perplexing thing to fathom about *Band of Angels* is the author's intent; a very troubling task because Warren, who had made radical revisions in his thinking about race by 1955, is absolutely effective in conveying the reasons for the conviction of black inferiority in white racialist thinking with almost imperceptible irony. It is easy to conflate the point of view of the text with Warren's more youthful ideas about race. Although Warren had changed many of his views by the time he wrote this text, it is conceivable that he had not resolved all his issues and conflicts. Is *Band of Angels* an attempt to exorcise or expurgate any residual attitudes or feelings from his earlier social conditioning? Perhaps. In any case, Warren wrote a novel that is a meticulous exposé of the rationalizations that made possible the oppression and consignment of people of African descent to slavery and servitude; rationalizations that also go a long way in explaining national, but most particularly southern, racial attitudes that had not significantly altered by the early 1950s. He accomplishes this by laying bare the raw dynamics of racial hatred through the graphically detailed disclosure of the psychological and social protocols that govern it. In doing so, Warren also, and perhaps necessarily in accordance with the traditions of the plantation epic, "rel[ies] on a culture of dissemblance [sic] and denial"[6] in his portrayal of race and race relations during the Civil War era. The gradual, and arguably almost indiscernible, dissolution of the idea of the Negro in a position of perpetual servitude is directly linked to the forcing of a nation, ready or not, to a new social order brought on by the catastrophic historical events of the Civil War and, one hundred years later, the civil rights movement; events that undoubtedly affected Warren deeply and personally.

Coming from the cultural indoctrination of his youth in Kentucky in the early 1900s to a more liberal, humanitarian and, importantly, practical point of view in middle age, Warren was in a position to diagnose and ventilate cultural complexities and offer insight into the fears and assumptions that drive racial fanaticism and color prejudice.[7] Therefore, *Band of Angels* does present "continuity for further exploration of the issues that had riven the country in the mid-nineteenth century and would come close to doing so again a hundred years later."[8] In this novel the past serves the present and is, I believe, a direct response to the radical racial turbulence of the early 1950s.

The fifty years preceding *Band of Angels*, Warren's first fifty years, were fecund ones for the nation. Almost every aspect of American life was affected by the continuing and burgeoning trends that characterize a modernizing society, such as demographic shifts from rural areas to cities and suburbs; transitions from private agricultural to corporate and industrial concerns; and shifts from manual to more mechanized, electronic and even computerized production. In the 1950s America was also undergoing a major adjustment in national identity because of global tensions, particularly those caused by the fear of communism during the Cold War, which was exacerbated by the McCarthy hearings, and, of course, the accompanying fear of nuclear war. But nothing threatened the well-being of the United States more than domestic racial conflict.

Although post–World War II prosperity made possible a higher standard of living for many Americans, racial inequality became the cause for war at home and asserted itself as an issue that would not go away without positive and progressive resolution, or the unceasing or total disruption of American domestic affairs. The America in which Warren lived as he wrote *Band of Angels* was one of stark contrasts. But because of postwar prosperity it was commonly mythologized and idealized in the products of culture as a place in which every (white) American who made the effort could advance, be happy and live well. As blacks mobilized and peacefully demanded their full rights as American citizens, maintaining the social status quo for many whites became not only a way of honoring the past, but was a determined resistance to change, a resistance that often led to violence.

If the number of lynchings is the bottom line for determining the intensity and purposefulness of racial hatred, then the 1950s pale by comparison to that of the late nineteenth and early twentieth centuries. The 1890s alone, for example, was a "reign of terror that resulted in a lynching in America on the average of once every two days. [. . .] [It was] a decade of blood and terror."[9] What made the 1950s seem so racially virulent and fanatical was the media coverage of the nonviolent resistance of civil rights proponents during protests, which was in great contrast to the crazed, ignorant, violent white racists and their leaders—whether a governor, a housewife or a dirt farmer with a rock in his hand leading an angry mob. Furthermore, black people were organized and united, had articulate leaders, had many more white supporters than ever before, including many public figures, and were clearly not going to back down.

Two significant issues under national review from 1905 to 1955 were lynching and segregation; this included some revision in the white public's attitude toward these injustices, and Warren was no exception. Warren grew up and lived for many years in the American South; a region in which the distribution and usage of every public space was governed by the rules of racial separation—waiting rooms and public transportation, schools, churches, cemeteries, libraries and hospitals, telephone booths in some states and even separate bibles required for swearing in witnesses in others.

The assumption of the racial inferiority of black people and, therefore, the need for segregation, were lessons learned early in life for the white southerner if social conditioning was to be effective and complete. Lillian Smith writes in *Killers of the Dream* that

> [t]he lesson on segregation was only a logical extension of the lessons on sex and white superiority and God. Not only Negroes but everything dark, dangerous, evil must be pushed to the rim of one's life. Signs put over doors in the world outside and over minds seemed natural enough to children like us, for signs had already been put over forbidden areas of our body. The banning of people and books and ideas did not appear more shocking than the banning of our wishes which we learned early to send to the Dark-town of our unconscious. But we clung to the belief, as an unhappy child treasures a beloved toy, that our white skin made us "better" than all other people. And this belief comforted us, for we felt worthless and weak when confronted by Authorities who had cheapened nearly all that we held dear, except our skin color. There, in the Land of Epidermis, every one of us was a little king.[10]

Furthermore, the enforcement of segregation was grounded in the need for a particular kind of hierarchy and "social order, [so that] white southerners chose geographic anchors, whether the imagined spaces evoked by narratives or the physical spaces recaptured through spectacle, literally to ground their racial identity within the mobility of modernity."

Prospects for equal access for black people were particularly bleak during the first three decades of the twentieth century, and not just in the South. "By the early twentieth century, whites were constructing modern racial identity [. . .] [as] a way to mediate the fragmentation of modernity and still enjoy its freedom." Segregation also enforced the ideal of white supremacy, the assumption being that "inferior spaces meant inferior people," and "[m]any southern whites believed that a permanent racial order and their own everlasting superiority had been achieved. Racialized spaces were meant to capture and identify blacks, not set them free from white control."[11] The ascendancy and boldness of white hate groups and the race riots in the major cities of the North and Midwest during the early twentieth century were warning signs that the country could self-destruct over race. The policies of the Wilson administration (1913–1921) bolstered racial division and disharmony. In fact, an official national policy of segregation, in which "all government offices, restaurants, and lavatories were segregated," was given a boost during this period. But, as Samuel Eliot Morison explains,

> [t]he real motive of the jim crow laws was to keep the black down and make him constantly sensible of his inferior status. That is why jim crow policy had so irresistible an appeal to the poor whites. [. . .] [T]hese lower-class whites of the South were a very unfortunate people—poor, illiterate, and diseased; but their feeling that the poorer of them was superior to even the most cultured Negro flattered their ego and assuaged their griefs. Custom, as well as the jim crow laws, compelled every black to address the lowest, dirt-eating redneck, hat in hand, as "Mr.," "Sir," or "Ma'am."

Despite almost unameliorating negative attitudes toward African Americans, and the individual state legislations and regional customs that operated continually to circumvent social and political progress, the federal government made some strides in advancing civil rights for African Americans during the Roosevelt administration (1933 to 1945). Although Roosevelt believed that African Americans were inherently inferior, his New Deal policies made some advances possible for black people. Segregation in Washington's federal offices was abandoned, the integration of the armed forces began and the appointment of many blacks to office, including in every new commission and bureau, was implemented. Roosevelt "insisted that in every industry, defense or otherwise, set up under the New Deal, blacks should receive an equal chance of employment. [. . .] [I]n 1946 there were four times the number of black federal employees as in 1933. Blacks benefited equally from New Deal projects [. . .] and the housing and other welfare programs." Furthermore, some labor unions, though few and far between, began to accept black membership. Subsequently, Truman, who was in office from 1945 to 1953, sometimes gave the appearance of being "sympathetic with the demands of blacks for a civil rights act to secure them their long-denied right to vote in the lower South, and at least diminish their other disabilities."[12] His policies were strategically part of his political effort to court black votes in the North.

The motives of both the Roosevelt and Wilson administrations were part of a political agenda that served complicated interests, and were not intended to be an acknowledgement of black equality. In any case, the federal government, however reluctant, incrementally but with steady deliberation was dismantling an old social order and replacing it with a more progressive one—against what were most certainly the wishes of the majority of its white citizens.

Almost concurrently, Warren was dismantling his ideas about the old social order as the changes were being implemented by the federal government.

The evolution of Warren's thinking about race made it possible by the time he wrote *Band of Angels* for him to have intimate friendships with some black people, as well as to champion the cause of civil rights.

But by the mid 1950s even the very marginal progress made in race relations in the country was seriously impaired by the question of what to do with America's children; how, against great and violent opposition, segregation in public schools would be abolished. The nation was in turmoil over *Brown v. Board of Education*, the Supreme Court's 1954 declaration that racial segregation in public schools was unconstitutional. "*Brown's* uncompromisingly radical rhetoric galvanized not just civil rights supporters but also civil rights opponents, ironically reuniting many white southerners increasingly divided by class and by the growing differences between rural and suburban white southern life," as Grace Elizabeth Hale points out in *Making Whiteness: The Culture of Segregation in the South, 1890–1940.*[13] The Jim Crow lines of demarcation between the races became battle lines, and black children were most often the little soldiers who crossed those lines amid the violence and intimidation of screaming hordes of angry white people, and who were innocently thrust, accompanied by military escort, into white schools seething with hostility.[14]

Although Warren was never a part of this class of southerner, and although he never lost his attachment to and love for the South and many aspects of southern culture, the more educated and worldly he became the more he differentiated from those who subscribed to a policy of oppression and abuse of those who were different, and who insisted on preserving racial hierarchy.[15] The climate of racial hatred in which America was embroiled when Warren was writing *Band of Angels* presented a dismal prognosis for progress, and was evidence that none had been made in the minds of those white people who seemed so fatally invested in seeing African Americans as inferior. As the federal government put forced desegregation into play, "the dark underside of the American Dream was unfolding, and it was a national nightmare. [. . .] As the bastions of segregation slowly began to crumble, southern whites unleashed a powerful backlash of hate."[16]

As a young college student and member of the Southern Agrarians in 1930,[17] Warren contributed to what is considered their manifesto, *I'll Take My Stand.* This book, as Louis Rubin describes in his introduction to the 1977 edition, "took for its title words from a song that had once been the anthem of a would-be southern nation whose very reason for being had to do with the desire to maintain and, if possible, to enhance Negro slavery."[18] Warren was eager to participate in the Agrarian project, a collection of essays on the social and economic philosophy of the group, which included the rejection of what were considered the dehumanizing aspects of industrialization and rampant consumerism. The book is also a celebration of the southern agrarian lifestyle, and a nostalgic yearning for the "good old days" in the South. In a letter to his friend and collaborator Donald Davidson, Warren volunteered for his subject: "The one I had in mind, is the essay on the negro [sic],"[19] he wrote. He fully understood that the controversial and potentially incendiary subject matter required special handling, confiding to his friends Allen Tate and Caroline Gordon that "[t]he negro [sic] is a delicate subject and one which could be most easily attacked; consequently, for my own good and the good of others, I can't afford to pull a boner in dealing with it."[20] The ease with which he objectifies African Americans is apparent in this statement.

In many ways "The Briar Patch," Warren's essay in *I'll Take My Stand*, expresses his agreement with much of Booker T. Washington's prescription for ameliorating the so-called Negro Problem, which included the idea that the industrial or agricultural, rather than liberal education of Negroes, was the correct strategy for that time. Warren writes: "Are some others [. . .] to be taught their little French and less Latin, and then sent packing about their business? If the answer is *yes*, it will be repetition of the major fallacy in American education and one of America's favorite superstitions."[21] Negroes have utility as a pair of strong hands and a strong back. Educating them for anything but manual labor was not only a mistake but a ludicrous joke. They were not ready/able to engage the higher brain functions required for a liberal education. Warren regarded "southern African Americans more as components of landscapes than as people."[22] There is nothing terribly surprising here about his position to uphold the status quo.

Interestingly, Warren did not confine his theory of gradualism in educational and economic strategies to blacks, which is an early indication that he was thinking in more comprehensive ways about status, class and race than many of his Agrarian colleagues as well as the general white population of his community. Rather than simply adhering to a strictly racial model, he believed in a more holistic approach for the underclasses, and that the same "principle applies equally well to the problem of white illiteracy." He acknowledged that "the fates of the 'poor white' and the negro [sic] are linked in a single tether. The well-being and adjustment of one depends on that of the other"—more a populist notion than a southern Agrarian one. What is more surprising, perhaps, is that Warren espoused views that were considered extremely radical for a conservative southerner; views that demonstrated some understanding of the plight of black people, such as that "[n]o blame is to be attached to the negro [sic] himself" for being a strikebreaker, because "[t]here is no good reason why he should fight the white man's battles if at the same time there is no proper provision for him in the system." He argued for the need for equal justice before the law for

Negroes, and acknowledged that "[a]t present the negro [sic] frequently fails to get justice [. . .]. It will be a happy day for the South when no court discriminates in its dealings between the negro [sic] and the white man." He also clearly understood the reasons that professional black men fled the South in great numbers; it was a place in which "restrictions confront him at every turn of his ordinary life." However, in terms of social equality and integration, Warren was absolutely in step with his white contemporaries, resolute that separation of the races was appropriate, and that it was best to "[l]et the negro [sic] sit beneath his own vine and fig tree."[23] In his own words, Warren called "Briar Patch" "a defense of segregation."[24]

Warren later claimed that he was never satisfied or comfortable with "Briar Patch." He explained that at the time his "position was exactly that of the Supreme Court. Equal, you see; 'different but equal' was the view of the Supreme Court and of 99 percent of the white people in the country."[25] Before the year (1930) was out, Warren wrote to Donald Davidson that "[t]he essay doesn't fill me with pride, but I hope that it will be harmless and will not look too shabby in the glittering array which I expect to see."[26] It is not perfectly clear whether Warren was more concerned about the quality of the piece or the ideas he had expressed in it.

As the civil rights movement played out in the media in the 1950s, white America was forced to confront the ugly realities of racial hatred and violence in glaring contrast to the self-evident, nonnegotiable humanity of nonviolent African Americans. Some hearts and minds were changed, including Warren's. In 1961 in *The Legacy of the Civil War: Meditations on the Centennial*, Warren's revulsion at the virulence of southern whites is apparent. He wrote:

> Does the man who, in the relative safety of mob anonymity, stands howling vituperation at a little Negro girl being conducted into a school building [. . . .] ever consider the possibility that whatever degree of dignity and success a Negro achieves actually enriches, in the end, the life of the white man and enlarges his worth as a human being?[27]

Clearly, Warren is light-years away from his pronouncements of "Briar Patch," in which he denigrated the liberal education of, and presumably what was perceived as the rapid advancement of, Negroes. The angry white crowds he witnessed at the schools targeted for desegregation were surely operating, on some level, with impulses that Warren understood, even though he deplored their methods and no longer shared their point of view. The white mob fears the possibility of dignity and the potential for success for the Negro. To what purpose is dignity and success for someone fit only to hoe, chop, clean or cook?

By September 1955, the year in which *Band of Angels* was published, Warren "would tell Ralph Ellison that by the time he had returned home after his Oxford years, he could no longer have written his contribution to *I'll Take My Stand*."[28] In an interview with Marshall Walker, Warren explained that he did not "begin to 'rethink' anything systematically. It was by accident." After his return to the rural South during the Depression he saw things

> more acutely than ever: first, from having to think about it during the years of absence, and then seeing this starvation—poverty that was coming on for whites and blacks and also certain aspects of the brutality of the system in its psychological way, which I'd been too young when I lived there before, or too stupid, to be aware of. So there was this long drift for several years of looking at that world again and seeing two [. . .] immediate kinds of degradation involved, personal, psychological, and spiritual degradation, plus poverty. [. . .] I had lived into the world now in a different perspective and a different age.[29]

Warren eventually "proved himself an incisive social historian and an especially perceptive and prudent chronicler of the Civil Rights struggle of the 1950s and '60s."[30] He supported the efforts of Martin Luther King, Jr., saying that he was "a great man, and that the sit-ins conducted according to his principles are morally unassailable and will win."[31] It eventually became a source of pain and embarrassment for Warren that he continued to be held accountable for "Briar Patch" long after he had changed not only his views but his life to reflect his new sensibilities. It has been difficult for critics to see "Briar Patch" as a youthful indiscretion.[32]

Although these factors cannot be considered a fool-proof prescription for enlightenment, I believe that Warren's many travels outside the South, his exposure to and participation in a more cosmopolitan lifestyle, and his extensive study at home and abroad all contributed to his changing sensibilities about race and race relations.[33] Most important, the fact that he was a sensitive and thinking man played a part in his changing opinions about race in spite of his earlier regional orientation, and cultural and social indoctrination. One way of looking at this evolution of thinking is in terms of the paradigm suggested by Grace Elizabeth Hale. Hale writes that a fissure developed between classes of Americans and some southerners with the increasing graphic publicity over the brutal lynchings in the South; and that

> [l]ynching, in this changing national context, stood more readily as proof of white southern barbarity. [. . .] More nationally oriented, middle-class, town- and city-dwelling whites increasingly found themselves unable to condone, for reasons of both public relations and principle, the deadly entertainments that

their more rural, more agricultural and working-class-oriented white brethren continued to support.[34]

Changes in attitudes about race in the 1950s owe much to the media. Warren grew up in a region in which a favorite pastime was the recreational lynching of black people. He was also certainly aware of the lynching of Emmett Till in Mississippi in 1953, and the media frenzy surrounding it. Pictures of his brutalized body that "depicted a misshapen head all the more horrible for the coroner's efforts to make the mangled corpse back into the boy" appeared in newspapers across the nation. The open-casket funeral, insisted upon by his grieving mother, in order to demonstrate to the whole world what white southerners had done with impunity to her fourteen-year-old child, created a horrific sensation for many. Americans then watched the trial as court officials "mistreated Till's mother," and

> [t]hey saw the bragging and confident defendants, the segregated courtroom, and the all-white male jury. [. . .] Americans with televisions witnessed reporters at the scene describe how the defense attorney in closing has admonished the jury: "every last Anglo-Saxon one of you has the courage to free these men." And this national audience also watched the acquitted murderers kiss their wives surrounded by the joyous celebration of other whites attending the trial. Americans saw a local white southern performance, naked and stripped of the niceties of New South boosterism, bare of the inflections so often spun by southern politicians and businessmen for that larger national audience. [. . .] As a result, television shaped a new collective out of many of its viewers.[35]

Warren later writes passionately about the tragedy of racial hatred and the bigoted southerners' use of what he calls the Great Alibi, the Civil War, as a way to excuse every violent horror, every moral failure. He takes to task those southerners who undermine anything of value in southern culture, and who have come to represent the South in the eyes of the civilized world with their ignorance, blood-lust, paranoia and refusal to change, which Warren regards as "part of the Southern disease"; the inability to face the necessity that society had to be reordered, including relationships, "because you *had* to have action or die."[36] Of the white southerner who refuses to acknowledge the true legacy of the past, and who threatens the possibility of a just and honorable future by clinging to a fantasy of southern and racial superiority, he writes:

> By the Great Alibi the South explains, condones, and transmutes everything. [. . .] Even now, any common lyncher becomes a defender of the Southern

> tradition, and any rabble-rouser the gallant leader of a thin gray line of heroes [. . .] pellagra, hookworm, and illiteracy are all explained, or explained away, and mortgages are converted into badges of distinction. Laziness becomes the aesthetic sense, blood-lust rising from a matrix of boredom and resentful misery becomes a high sense of honor, and ignorance becomes divine revelation. [. . .] He turns defeat into victory, defects into virtues. Even more pathetically, he turns his great virtues into absurdities—sometimes vicious absurdities. [. . .] And the most painful and costly consequences of the Great Alibi are found, of course, in connection with race. The race problem, according to the Great Alibi, is the doom defined by history—by New England slavers, New England and Middlewestern Abolitionists, cotton, climate, the Civil War, Reconstruction, Wall Street, the Jews. Everything flows into the picture. Since the situation is given by history, the Southerner therefore is guiltless; is, in fact, an innocent victim of a cosmic conspiracy.[37]

With *Band of Angels*, this novel of the Civil War era, Warren anatomizes the mindset of the recalcitrant, self-righteous southern governor on the steps of an all-white school; the snarling, angry white housewife in a shirtwaist dress at the doors of a schoolbus unloading black children; the white dirt farmer with a rock or lynch rope in his hand—ordinary southerners—showcased in the media of the 1950s. The prospects for the function and social status of African Americans during and immediately following the Civil War, in a culture radically altered by their emancipation, and the increasing social and political pressures to provide rights and protections for them under the law in an ongoing effort to bring them more closely to a fully viable American citizenship during the civil rights movement a century later, converge in *Band of Angels*.

Unraveling Point of View

Band of Angels begins with the following epigraph: "When shall I be dead and rid / Of the wrong my father did?"[38] The implication is, of course, that guilt is collective and that the sins of the father are visited upon succeeding generations. The only escape is death because the wrong cannot be obliterated; not by time or anything else. The reader may reasonably expect the text that follows such an epigraph to clearly define the "wrong," and that somehow it will be equally as clear that the possibility of expiation and redemption will be so negligible that death is the only escape. Not so for *Band of Angels*. Because the text is set in the deep slaveholding South and the narrator is sold into sexual slavery, one might reasonably anticipate, if not an indictment, then at least a critique of slavery, perhaps? Or a critique of the sexual exploitation of slave women, perhaps? Not so for *Band of Angels*. Might one reasonably have expectations for such an engagement of these issues because of the proclaimed changes in racial sensibilities of the author at the time of composition? "Aren't we," as Henry Louis Gates, Jr. says, "justified in being suspicious of a discourse in which blacks are a sign of absence?" Indeed. Is *Band of Angels* simply another example "from a literary tradition" in which "white males [. . .] represent blacks in their fiction as barely human, if they deem it necessary to figure blacks at all?"[39] Perhaps. These are deeply troubling issues. What was Warren hoping to accomplish in this text?

Band of Angels offers for consideration the carefully constructed emotional and psychological impulses that shape deeply ingrained ideas white people have entertained about black people. By the early 1950s Warren had altered his thinking about race and race relations to the point where he was confident enough to write this novel, in which the first-person narrator is a "white" black woman who is the child of a slave and a slaveholder; a woman tormented by her ambiguous social status, her value as a human being, and most of all, by her black blood. It is clear that Warren intended to create a sympathetic portrait of what may happen to an individual in a society driven by the rules of color and race, and in some ways he accomplishes this. But, what he truly achieves most noticeably, and perhaps most significantly, is a complex psychological profile of a "white" person, through the narrator's voice, caught in the agonies of attempting to reconcile deeply ingrained negative ideas about black people with new and very unfamiliar, more liberal and more tolerant racial attitudes.

Amantha Starr's palpable agony over being forced by her circumstances to confront her attitudes about color and class drives the narrative. I agree with Warren's biographer, Joseph Blotner, who writes that Amantha is "'the tragic mulatto' of drama and poetry, but she also serves as a focus for questions that often troubled her creator."[40] In this text, Warren demonstrates how the white southerner imagines himself as "guiltless [. . .] in fact, [as] an innocent victim of a cosmic conspiracy,"[41] often appears to give credence to the idea of southern white racial superiority through the characterizations of black people, and simultaneously ratifies servitude of many descriptions as the appropriate place for blacks in American society.

In spite of what appear to be good intentions, *Band of Angels* often appears to affirm the very notions about black people that Warren by 1955, both in his personal life and in his writing, was attempting to revise and transcend. Is it too generous to ascribe an agenda of enlightenment to Warren for writing such a book because of the evidence that supports his position on race at the time of its writing? Is he simply adept at the disparaging characterization of black people because of his familiarity with this type of thinking, or is it because he is still coming to terms with the idea of racial equality? Was writing

Band of Angels in some ways cathartic for Warren? A way in which to purge residual feelings about black people and race relations? In this act of ventriloquism, has he chosen a "white" black female to tell this tale of slavery and the South rather than a phenotypically black narrator because he can only imagine blackness through whiteness—clearly the crux of Amantha's identity crisis? Do the complex and multiplexing ways in which Warren grapples with the idea of the African American in a position of servitude—both as slaves and servants, and then also as free and nonservant—disclose an effort on his part to conceptualize a more human, humane and non-utilitarian designation for blacks? These questions haunt the attempt to unravel Warren's mission and point of view in this text.

In his essay "Why Do We Read Fiction?" Warren disclaims the function of fiction as "a mere substitute for anything else," and insists that "[i]t is an art—an image of experience formed in accordance with its own laws of imaginative enactment, laws which, as we have seen, conform to our deep needs." He also acknowledges that "the language is that of some individual man projecting his own feeling of life," and that "[t]he style of a writer represents his stance [. . .] toward the subject of his story." There are moments in this text in which one can hardly help but wonder what "deep needs" *Band of Angels* conforms to for Warren. We shall take him at his word in the effort to disclose his "stance [. . .] toward the subject of his story."[42]

I run the risk of being accused, as has been Maxwell Geismar, of having accomplished "a marvel of misreading," by pointing out that Warren created "practically an idyll of slavery in the Old South."[43] But it is plain to see in *Band of Angels* Warren's attempt to disclose the inherently flawed and contradictory thinking that makes it possible for white southerners to believe that God has willed slavery, that history dictates it, that man merely executes it. Furthermore, by continually juxtaposing the conditions of enslavement with "evidence" of black inferiority, Warren refabricates a slaveholding culture in which it appears that the enslaved are where they should be, and the enslavers are victimized by circumstances and history. *Band of Angels* offers, without editorial or critical comment, and with almost indiscernible irony, the representation of black people as supremely inferior, in such a manner as to say: Here's the proof. This is how they look, act and think.[44] True enough the whites are, actually, not anything to write home about in this text. But, they are offered as a contrast and overall improvement over the base, crude, lascivious, eye-bulging, butt-scratching, childlike, disloyal, ungrateful, weak, dysfunctional miscreants that most of the black people are portrayed as in this text—a people in need of close supervision and constraint; a people fit only for servitude. Finally, in *Band of Angels* the white man simply does the best he can, given all he has to contend with—the "good master" doing his paternalistic duty with the enormous and unasked-for burden foisted on him by God and History.

It is possible that Warren offers, in his confabulation of slaveholding culture, an exquisite example of what Toni Morrison calls the reflexive nature of the representation of the Africanist persona, which is "an extraordinary meditation on the self; a powerful exploration of the fears and desires that reside in the writerly conscious. It is an astonishing revelation of longing, of terror, of perplexity, of shame, of magnanimity";[45] it often appears to be the unwitting product of authorial wish fulfillment. Warren's exegesis appears to debunk the arguments that oppose slavery, and also challenges and subtly rebukes those who judge and condemn the enslavers. Is it also possible that this is part of Warren's strategy in blueprinting white racialist thinking? Perhaps.

Briefly, the story is this: Wealthy plantation owner, Aaron Starr, pampers and spoils his daughter by one of his slaves. Amantha Starr's mixed blood appears to be common knowledge to everyone except Amantha. Starr, who lived extravagantly and beyond his means, sends Amantha (as a teenager) to be educated at Oberlin. She is sent back to the plantation after his death and sold to help settle his affairs because she is a slave and, therefore, part of his estate. After being briefly passed through several business transactions, Amantha ends up in Louisiana with her master, Hamish Bond, a slave trader. Bond sets her up in his house in New Orleans as a "lady," and takes his time making her his sexual slave. Bond gives her freedom papers the day after their first sexual encounter and tells her that she may leave, but she decides to stay with him. Eventually, and during the Civil War, Amantha takes her freedom and lives, not to her satisfaction, in small and unprepossessing quarters until she marries a white man, Tobias Sears. At first Sears does not know that Amantha is not white, and she prefers it this way, especially because she finds it almost impossible to acknowledge, even to herself, that she is not white. After Sears learns of Amantha's racial identity, their relationship alters, and for several years they struggle with his alcoholism and adultery. They eventually find a way to live peacefully if not happily together. In the end, Amantha, who has been tormented by what she had seen as her father's betrayal, appears to find a way to rationalize what he did and did not do for her.

Interestingly, Warren appropriates the stylistic characteristics and rhetorical strategies of the slave narrative in *Band of Angels.* The slave narrative, usually narrated in the first person by the (ex)slave, typically chronicles the hardships endured as a slave and in the course of transition from slavery to freedom, whether as an escaped slave or a legally freed one. These coming-of-age narratives also often emphasize the strength and self-reliance of the narrator; the role of God and kindly people in the acquisition of freedom; and the life the narrator was able to make for himself/herself in freedom in contrast with their life as a slave. The intention of the slave narratives was not only to provide an autobiographical accounting of a life for posterity, but also to act as documents to enlighten white audiences to the evils of chattel slavery and to raise their moral sensibilities.

The slave narratives provide the information and horrific details that characterize slavery and the slaveholding culture, with an emphasis on the aspects of slavery that were absolutely contrary to Christian doctrine. These aspects include the separation of parents from their children, the sexual exploitation of female slaves, the physical depravation and brutality that result in ill health and sometimes in death, and so forth. The slave narratives were also a response to the denial of African humanity promulgated by both European and American scientists, philosophers and statesmen who claimed that for Africans there was "no true self-consciousness. [. . .] [A]bolitionists and ex-slaves conspired to break this resounding black silence by publishing the narratives of the ex-slaves."[46] The ultimate objective of the slave narrative was, of course, to persuade the reader that slavery was an uncivilized and un-Christian crime against humanity; the hope was that the reader would be moved to agitate for the abolition of slavery.

Yet, it appears that Warren makes a mockery of the slave narrative in that, while employing the rhetorical characteristics of the genre, its narrator generates not sympathy, but scorn; not an understanding of the horrors and injustice of slavery, but a rationalization for it; not a view of the slave as a victim, but as a co-conspirator in his/her circumstances; not pity, shame and outrage over the sexual enslavement and rape of black women, but the diminishment of this crime through the carefully constructed wantonness of the black female.

Band of Angels could not be anything but deeply cynical in its portrayal of race and race relations in America during the Civil War era. Within the beliefs that justify and rationalize slavery in this text are the perceived complicity of blacks with their condition of perpetual and deserved servitude; the conviction of the virtues of paternalism in general in slavery, which is embodied in the character of the "good" master Hamish Bond in particular, who has "kindness like a disease" (150); the perceived loyalty and fidelity of the female sexual slaves who "love" him; the venality and betrayal of the slaves who don't; the portrayal of the black woman as an object of desire and contempt; the consistently eroticized and loathed black male; the color-consciousness (worship of whiteness, abhorrence and repugnance for blackness); and, the definitions of femininity and beauty on which the protagonist/narrator, Amantha, obsesses. Furthermore, the hypocrisy of northerners and liberals, the quality and meaning of freedom for slaves and whites alike, along with continual references to everyone as equal victims of the perpetrator, History, are pervasive in the text. These issues beg attention in that while they may appear to simply offer an uncritical and romanticized reading of slavery and the slaveholding culture, they also illustrate the frame of reference required in the justification of the enslavement and abuse of people of African descent.

Perceptions about blacks are available for consideration through Amantha's deliberations about them, as far as she is able within the considerable limitations of her powers of discernment, and through the historical and cultural context provided in general. Very much present in Amantha's thoughts, and crucial to her coming of age, are her deliberations on the meaning of her identity and race, which Warren elucidates through an exposition of her attitudes about black slavery and servitude. Her obsession with color shapes her perceptions and valuations of herself and others, and dominates and disfigures all her relationships—a reflection of the color consciousness and nature of her society. Amantha ultimately functions as a telemetrical device, providing the details of her experience, acting as an interpreter of the historical moment. Through her mercurial and ambiguous identity and point of view, particularly where slaves and servitude are concerned, we may, through this tortured text, investigate many of the complex issues that drive ideas about race and that (mis)shape the moral sensibilities of individuals and, as a consequence, the social and legal traditions and policies of a nation.

Shared Complicity: Guilt and Denial of Causality

Who is responsible for American slavery? What are the predominating attitudes that perpetuate the idea of the appropriateness of African American servitude after enslavement? What are the causes of racial hierarchy and racial hatred? The refusal or inability to make a connection between great numbers of impoverished and un- or ill-educated African Americans, the living conditions and behaviors that often accompany extreme poverty and hopelessness, the economic and social conditions that cause such degradation and many other factors used to condemn black people completely elude the white racist mindset, whether in times of slavery, Reconstruction or the 1950s. The confusion and denial begins in childhood, when youth are indoctrinated, subtly but thoroughly, into the belief system. Lillian Smith writes:

> Neither the Negro nor sex was often discussed at length in our home. We were given no formal instruction in these difficult matters but we learned our lessons well. We learned the intricate system of taboos, of renunciations and

> compensations, of manners, voice modulations, words, feelings, along with our prayers, our toilet habits, and our games. [. . .] [A] terrifying disaster would befall the South if ever I treated a Negro as my social equal. [. . .] I had learned that white southerners are a hospitable, courteous, tactful people who treat those of their own group with consideration and who as carefully segregate from all the richness of life "for their own good and welfare" thirteen million people whose skin is colored a little differently from my own.[47]

Band of Angels equivocates between avowing that there is no real human agency for the horrors of human history and establishing a tentative accountability, which is both diffuse and inclusive—adroit and labyrinthine inclinations. The novel illustrates the peculiar mental contortions that both blame history and also use it as a reason to uphold tradition, while simultaneously disregarding historical context when it's convenient to do so. I agree with Forrest Robinson's assessment of the tendency to evade or deny causality that Warren demonstrates in his fiction. He argues that *Band of Angels*,

> Warren's first novel on racial themes, is a good index to his general treatment of these issues. Amantha Starr, the mulatto heroine, opens her narrative with the question, "Oh, who am I?" But having placed that issue in the foreground, Warren subordinates its painful racial implications to explorations of self-knowledge and identity. His inclination to have it both ways with the racial issue—to confront and at the same time to evade Amantha's question—manifests itself in a narrative that is throughout defensive on the score of race-slavery. Life on the plantation is happy, innocent, and free; black African slave traders are so brutal as to make American slavery seem a blessing; abolitionists are repressed, self-righteous hypocrites; and Yankees are cowardly opportunists. As to the ultimate responsibility for the evil in the world, *Band of Angels* stoutly refuses to lay blame. "Things merely happened," Amantha concludes, "that was all there was to it."

Warren repeatedly demonstrates in his fiction "[t]he contrary impulses to see and not see, to address painful racial problems and to turn away from them. [. . .] [T]he impulse to address racism and slavery is virtually always found in tandem with an impulse to sweep them from sight and mind."[48]

Psychological division was a continuing issue for Warren in his work, but it is in *Band of Angels* that he "for the first time merges his most durable theme, the search for personal identity, with the larger issue of national identity. A woman divided against herself conducts an agonized search for psychic unity within the resonant context of a nation divided against itself."[49] Her punishment for becoming a "black" person is so terrible that Amantha cannot see herself as whole and good without seeing herself as white. This is the mental dance between the confrontation and evasion of racial issues that Amantha goes through continuously in her effort to forge a solid center and identity that is white, or at least in some way raceless; it is an apt description of the inability of the larger society to truly address the bases of painful and debilitating racial problems. While it is possible, it is not entirely clear that Warren is critiquing the color line in this regard.

Although Amantha appears to have reconciled some of her conflicts and admits to a certain kind of peace in the end, the closure to her narrative rings false. She finds peace only through denial of who she is and what has happened to her. It is a peace of mind built on a fragile and fraudulent foundation of self-deception and on a refusal or inability to confront the truth. It is the very same fraudulent "peace," subsequently enjoyed by the nation, that the federal enforcement of civil rights legislations shattered a century later. That illusion of peace, based on self-deception and a society's refusal to confront the truth about racial hatred and its effects, continued to accommodate the oppression and lynching of black people in the 1950s.

Forrest Robinson notes that "[i]t was Lincoln's great wisdom, in Warren's judgment, to recognize 'a community in guilt—a complicity that belongs to the general human lot.' Guilt is even further extenuated in a pronounced tendency toward determinism."[50] In what may be an attempt to spread the guilt around in *Band of Angels*, Warren occasionally invokes, as a source of agency, the culture of the powerbrokers of the Civil War as the authority that creates or at least manages historical forces—undoubtedly with providential imprimatur. This can make one think that there *is* some accountability for those most in a position to control and influence the values, traditions and condition of the nation, particularly where slavery is concerned. In a rare acknowledgment of the powerful forces that have shaped her circumstances, Amantha does reflect on the power and dominance of what she sees as male culture, and she concedes that men have planned and ruled everything, over the ages, and probably over dinner. She struggles and fails to thrive against a backdrop of "victories and defeats, Chickamauga, Missionary Ridge, the Wilderness, Spottsylvania, Nashville [. . .]. Meanwhile [she] went back and forth to [her] shack of a schoolhouse while men killed each other and then tried to put back together the world they had knocked apart." Life goes on in an atmosphere in which Lincoln makes his appeal to states to return to the government, constitutional conventions revamp state policies to try to find a way to manage/circumvent the new status of Negroes, and "politicians sprang up like jimson weed" amid schemes, free whiskey and cigars (253).

But almost invariably, Warren diminishes, even obliterates the responsibility of the powerbrokers for the condition of the nation and for all the attending horrors suffered by those who are most affected by decisions and policies motivated by national commercial interests, and the exigencies of personal greed, by blaming those very victims of such a system of value.

Amantha, ironically (or perhaps not), is the primary spokesperson for the slave point of view. She promotes the idea of shared accountability for slavery through her repeated affirmations of the idea of her own complicity with statements such as: "I had been involved in the very cause of the world, and whatever had happened corresponded in some crazy way with what was in me, and even if I didn't cause it, it somehow conformed to my will," as if she had had any control over the circumstances of her birth, of being sold into enslavement, or of enslavement itself. Clearly, whatever had happened to the slaves was somehow a manifestation of their will.

It is true that Amantha does have some choices available to her and can exercise free will in certain instances, even as a slave, and she does manipulate some situations to her advantage. But manipulation for Amantha, manipulation for any slave, was one of the few tools for survival and empowerment in an almost powerless situation. The degree to which she should be judged for her choices cannot be determined without taking into consideration the context of the slaveholding culture in which she was raised as a "white" child, and the effects of her own enslavement on her character and state of mind; they are the consequences of her condition.

Although there are several examples in *Band of Angels* of the powerbrokers effecting change and pulling the strings, their authority and power are subject and subordinate to the whims of a nebulous, intractable, aggressive and unforgiving entity called History. Warren casts history, at times, as the absolute executor and curator of human experience, clearly intended to be regarded as an entity, by making it a proper noun. In this way, there is *no* human agency. History is the culprit, and therefore individuals need not accept responsibility for their actions. As Amantha says: "you do not live your life, but somehow, your life lives you, and you are, therefore, only what History does to you" (134). Amantha never distinguishes between holding herself accountable for her own actions and being the agent of circumstances completely out of her control—nor does anyone else. The entire relationship between cause and effect in *Band of Angels* is convoluted, illusory and even irrational. However, the relationship between cause and effect is also often convoluted, illusory and irrational in the white racialist mindset—which may or may not be the point Warren attempts to make.

In the products of culture, both romanticized whiteness and denigrated blackness are facilitated by exaggeration and misrepresentation. They perpetuate notions of an idealized southern past and thereby elevate and promote the idea of the supremacy of whiteness, which also ratifies the idea of African American inferiority. In significant ways *Band of Angels* contributes to this idealization, not only because of its ambivalence about accountability, but because of its vivid dramatization of black inferiority and fitness for servitude.

Undoubtedly, the ways in which history is manipulated and distorted in products of culture, particularly in the representation of the slaveholding culture, contributes to the overall confusion and denial about black enslavement "because its dramas have been so graphic, so violent, so perversely pleasing. White Americans generally have failed to see the ways they imaginatively 'live' in a metaphorical South, even as their relationship to the region has danced between the poles of attraction and revulsion." American films are a good example, such as *Gone With the Wind*, "a panoramic and technicolored national romance, a story of nation making."[51] Hollywood, "whose watery notion of reality has seeped deep into the bedrock of American culture," perpetuates a false history of race and race relations, and cultivates a flawed and damaging portraiture of African Americans. "Ever since D. W. Griffith blended history with racist romance in *Birth of a Nation*, the movie industry has pointed its cameras at sets resembling the past and steadfastly depicted the sensibilities of the present."[52] It was not until

> [t]he civil rights movement would force white southerners and other white Americans to see differently, at least for a moment, the South that white southerners lived in. Whether in return white Americans have or will ever fully understand the metaphoric South in which they "live," that reservoir of many cherished American self-perceptions, remains, even at the end of the twentieth century, uncertain.[53]

Similar to Hollywood plantation romances, Warren makes good use of African American servitude in *Band of Angels* as a way to draw attention to deeply held cultural values, particularly for the white South, and perpetuates a fantasy of the slaveholding culture. He catalogues with thoroughness prevailing attitudes, not only toward black enslavement, but also of racial hatred, the rationalization of which would not be complete without fingering God as the chief architect and engineer.

The notion that God has willed slavery is certainly not a new one; the antecedents for this thinking reach back into antiquity, and Frederick Douglass wrote about convenient misinterpretations of the Bible and commonly held views by slaveholding Christians in his autobiographical *Narrative* in 1845. The American slaveholders' position was that "God cursed Ham, and therefore American slavery is right," and that as a result "the lineal descendants of Ham are [. . .] to be scripturally enslaved."[54] One of the ironies here, of course, is that the curse put on Ham by his father Noah was that he would be a servant of servants. As Winthrop Jordan points out in *White over Black: American Attitudes Toward the Negro, 1550–1812*, "the question becomes why a tale which logically implied slavery but absolutely nothing about skin color should have become an autonomous and popular explanation for Negroes' blackness."[55] In any case, enough white people believed it, or at least found, without questioning, a convenient rationalization for the enslavement of black people in this interpretation of the Bible. By scapegoating God as the original perpetrator of the condition of slavery for black people, the responsibility of the slaveholders is thoroughly denied and shifts to the enslaved. Slavery becomes almost a personal issue for a reckoning between God and the enslaved.

In *Band of Angels* Amantha recognizes and identifies with this reasoning, having been conditioned by her culture. She concludes that her predicament must be her own fault for failing to pray, and takes responsibility for her fate, saying: "*So it was all my fault.* If I had then had the strength to pray, all would have been different, I would not be here now, in the house of the oppressor" (93, my emphasis). This thinking suggests that slavery is justified because the slaves deserve it; those enslaved are at fault because of some transgression against God, or because they are irrelevant to or ignored by God. As Ham erred in offending God and all his subsequent descendants were presumably cursed with blackness and servitude, so Amantha may reasonably assume that as a consequence for not praying she is cursed for offending a punishing God. She is doubly cursed because she is a descendant of Ham. At this early juncture in Amantha's life as a slave, and despite her repeated protestations about the injustice of it, the rationalizations for her enslavement make some terrible sense to her.

After her father's death, Amantha is forced to confront her mixed racial heritage when she is sold as part of the chattel in his estate. Up to this point Amantha doesn't know she isn't white, but the moment she hears it she recognizes the truth; all the inconsistencies, innuendo and whispers make sense to her in that moment. A new identity is formed, suddenly and by externals: she is nothing. Because of this revelation Amantha is forced to contemplate, for the first time in her life, what it means to be a slave—a piece of property without a soul; a nonperson. She has not previously given any thought to her attitudes toward her own servants and slaves. Yet, she is more aggrieved about having her status in life reduced from being "Little Miss Sugar-and-Spice" (65), as her father often called her, than about the condition of enslavement. At first she is, perhaps understandably so because of the rawness and newness of her situation, concerned only with what this new social status, or lack thereof, will mean for her: "I was a being without being, as though my inner experience reflected the abstract definition of the law, which called me a chattel, a non-person, the thing without soul, and I was suspended in that vacuum of no identity, in the numbness somehow aware of the pain that was being awaited" (62).

It is at these moments in the text, in which Warren demonstrates the agony of an enslaved individual who is acutely conscious of being regarded as a commodity, that it is most clear that he is making an effort to present a balanced picture of opposing points of view in the slaveholding culture—a slave point of view. But, and characteristic of this text, when she is deposited in the attic of her new owner, Amantha ponders whether she is being punished for being insensitive, or for lacking empathy for the suffering of poor black people, and the reader is invited to ponder right along with her. Is her enslavement simply retribution from God? She questions: "And with that thought a horrible question dawned. Was I here—oh, no, it wasn't I—but was I here because I hadn't felt sorry enough for somebody? [. . .] Was that the trouble? That I had never had belief and sympathy in my heart?" (63). These questions are answered, if somewhat obliquely. One may reasonably assume that black people, then, may be enslaved because they are nonbelievers, have an inherent lack of sensitivity to and empathy for others, and suffer from spiritual ineptitude—serious offenses to a punishing God. These are possibilities worth considering in *Band of Angels*.

Black Inferiority: Fitness for Servitude

At the core of white racial hatred and fanaticism lies the conviction of black inferiority. *Band of Angels* offers the justifications for black enslavement and the perpetuation of racial prejudice through a meticulously constructed representation of an inferior people; a people designed by nature for nothing better than servitude.

Most revealing is the depthless characterization of black people, first in Africa within their own culture and value system as heathens and barbarians and subsequently as marginally civilized and improved-upon in America in various capacities of servitude. In comparison to their circumstances in Africa, American slavery is, apparently, a character enhancement program. According to conventional southern wisdom

> "slavery was no disgrace to the owner or the owned." Blacks had arrived in America "savage," "without thought of clothes," "bowing down to fetishes," and "sometimes cannibals." Slavery not only Christianized the slaves but made them "the happiest set of people on the face of the globe—free from care or thought of food, clothes, home, or religious privileges."[56]

Even so, under the supervision of whites in America blacks still don't make the grade in a novel that endeavors to make sense of the rationalizations for slavery and racial prejudice.

Moral Disability, Cultural Deficiency

The "good master" Hamish Bond's rationalization for trading in slaves provides the rationalization for the enslavement of black people, period. He didn't make the situation, he just took his place in it. He offers the familiar argument that Africans are barbarians who betray and sell one another, and that they are an affront to a God who would be better off without them. The following graphic tirade, which bristles with self-righteous conviction, lists many of the assumptions white Americans have made about Africans and life in Africa. Bond says:

> Well, I didn't make the world that way. That's what I said to myself. It was that way a million years. They raided and warred back and forth, and cut throats and drank blood like buttermilk, and chopped off heads for some mud-post of a Bo-god, who is nothing but a human man-part [. . .] and if a British cruiser [. . .] put 'em in Liberia, where there was a free and civilized nigger country we fixed all up just like the Land of Liberty, those black Sons of Liberty passed their black brothers on to traders waiting on the border. It was all like that, and nobody cared, and don't let anybody tell you different, and if you took one of 'em off to pick cotton five thousand miles away, you did him a favor. [. . .] You'd do God a favor if you sunk that country under the sea. [. . .] I didn't make this world and make 'em drink blood. I didn't make myself and I can't help what I am doing. They drove me to it. (189)

Although Bond admits that something about the whole business wakes him up in the middle of the night, he apparently has no trouble going back to sleep; he stops short of real introspection and never acquires meaningful insights, admits to any wrongdoing or takes responsibility for his own actions. It is intrinsic to the psychology of the enslaver to shift the blame to the enslaved, and therefore, as Eugene Genovese explains in *Roll, Jordan, Roll: The World the Slaves Made*, they may still regard "themselves as Christians and human beings. [. . .] They could deny to themselves that in fact they did cause suffering and could assert that their domination liberated the slaves from a more deprived existence. Such a view demanded the doctrine of reciprocal duties implicit and sometimes explicit in their defense of their regime and their own lives."[57]

Bond's descriptions of the Africans and their behavior is as terrifying, bizarre and darkly comical as any of the most chilling scenes of black people in a

D. W. Griffith movie. In defense of black enslavement, the price of slaves to the "nigger-dealing [African] king" is only "brandy and beads and a rocking chair and a lady's feather fan, the ballroom kind, pink, and some striped silk shirts, [who] got together a file of bearers, hammock-men and stool-toters" (190).

There is also a blatant disregard for life in Africa; even the women are savage warriors and brutal killers.

> They didn't kill 'em quick. They killed 'em slow. They carved 'em with razor-work of the greatest tact and delicacy and left the deprived objects still crawling. This was extremely funny. They cracked open heads and dipped their ribbons and rigs and furbelows in blood and plastered more blood on the gun-stocks to stick cowrie shells in to keep tally on your killing. (196)

Because of his good breeding, Bond hesitates at first to defend himself when confronted by a female "savage," then comes to his senses because she was, after all, "a crocodile-hided, blood-drinking old frow, who had been in her line of business for twenty years, and I caught myself making allowances for a lady. She disabused me. She took a swipe at me with her razor-knife and got me in the right leg, a long, jagged swipe" (197).

The narrative luxuriates in the savagery and sheer barbarism of the Negroes—the butchery, human sacrifice, swilling of blood from calabashes; the African king's special sidewalks made of human skulls and body parts; razor-toting women; dancing, squatting, butt-wiggling, naked pickanninies—a rum-soaked, God-forsaken people. One must wonder if all this description by Bond (Warren?), which goes on for several pages, is intended to mitigate the subsequent horrors of slavery for a people who are apparently accustomed to living at such a bestial level. To top it off, consider Bond's graphic description of a surreal, nightmarish landscape in which missionaries are forced to dance in the midst of the horrors of this bloodthirsty culture:

> King David [. . .] was fanning himself now with the pink ballroom plume fan I had brought. They started dancing, if you call it that, two coast-fever skeletons sweating in black coats, doing a kind of slow shuffle in the tramped dust, with a lot of naked, hung-up black bodies and turkey-buzzards for a background, and naked pickaninnies paddling in the special mud, and the Wesleyites sweating and singing. "*Oh, let us be joyful, joyful, joyful, / When we meet to part no more.*" (195)

Even the missionaries are sickened by several days observance of Negro culture. Considering this, who could argue that slavery was not the better life? The enslavers were doing the blacks a favor. These are a people entitled to and qualified only to serve the lives of their betters, if that, and Bond's declaration that bringing the Africans five thousand miles to pick cotton is an improvement for them doesn't seem quite so unreasonable or inhumane.

In addition to the lack of loyalty and the level of venality that the blacks exhibit toward one another in Africa, is the lack of loyalty and regard they have for their masters, plantations and one another in America.

There are essentially two categories of black servants in *Band of Angels.* The first are those who have a clearly defined role as a slave, such as Dollie the house slave and Jimmee the horse groom; there is no ambiguity for them, they are clearly property. Dollie's loyalties lie with the slaves and she anticipates with glee their destruction of the plantation as the Yankees advance through the South. She has no conflicts or problems about her allegiance; the desire of the unambiguously oppressed is clear—burn everything. Dollie's is the voice of the restive slave yearning for the destruction of everything associated with their enslavement. Interestingly, she is characterized as childlike, stupid and "bulge-eyed," but she provides useful information about the state of mind and the activities of her comrades, and editorializes to elicit a response from Amantha:

> "Burn ever-thing," she uttered, in her breathless, bulge-eyed rapture [. . .]. Shore wish me down dar. [. . .] Word come dey grabben," she said. "Folks grabben. Grab and hit's yoren. Bust de barr'l and 'lasses in de street. Lay down in 'lasses and roll fer de sweetness. Stretch de mouf and pour rum down till hit come out both years lak a bung bust. Lay down in de alley and love-up and who gonna stop 'em? [. . .] burnen and dancen." (173–74)

But again, this description is not simply one of the enslaved rejoicing at the prospect of freedom. It is a description of the drunken, orgiastic, destructive revelry of a debased people let loose from the only constraints that could just barely civilize and humanize them—enslavement. The less ambiguous the status of the slave, the more disloyal and venal. That is, for those slaves who know they are nothing but property, the battle lines are clearly drawn; they fare the best when it comes to a clean, clear identity and purpose.

It is so-called kindness that confuses the "favorite" slaves, the second category of black servitude, in *Band of Angels.* It was this "kindness" that, presumably, confused many a slaveholder *and* observer of slaveholding culture. Eugene Genovese explains that

> the slaves also had, from the white point of view, incurred an obligation to be grateful. The white point of view, however, rested on a catastrophic misunderstanding. The slaveholders' rage over the desertion of their pet slaves and, less frequently, over that of their field hands usually included references to

> "ingratitude." [. . .] Northerners, including the sympathetic missionaries who went to the Sea Islands, could not understand the apparent lack of gratitude in the freedmen.

One northern journalist even reported that "[a] former Confederate soldier told him that the kindest and most benevolent masters had suffered the worst manifestations of their ingratitude."[58]

In *Band of Angels* the state of mobility, which masquerades as freeness, defines the second stratum of black servitude; by function, regard and legality the status of these slaves is often ambiguous. This category of favorites includes the female sexual slaves such as Michele and Amantha, and also that of Rau-Ru, the "adopted" African "son" of Hamish Bond, whose increasing and barely suppressed hostility is a source of bewilderment to Bond. The quasi-freeness of Amantha's status when she is with Bond contributes enormously to her identity problems, of which she already had many.

For Amantha, Michele and Rau-Ru, there is confusion and complexity in how they feel toward Bond, themselves and each other. There is gratitude, anger, sadness, affection, hate and rage. Their ambiguous status makes "choosing" loyalty to the master a complicated and difficult business. Interestingly, there is ample historical and anecdotal evidence to support the fact that many slave "favorites," those who were in closest association with and sometimes related to their owners, those who had the most material comfort and mobility and the mildest treatment by comparison to other slaves, "'those we loved best, and who loved us best—as we thought—were the first to leave.'" In any case, while there were certainly some slaves who stayed out of loyalty, many more stayed because they had no resources and nowhere else to go. Despite these obvious handicaps, "slaves 'in some cases have left plantations in a perfect stampede.'"[59]

In this text, Warren conforms to common notions of color coding and character in identifying the capacity for loyalty and the proclivity for venality by having Bond's mulatto and quadroon sexual slaves love and have empathy for him, while his black slaves, eventually including Rau-Ru, loathe and rebel against him. Rau-Ru's hatred and repudiation as his favorite and adopted son is the worst betrayal of all. In the end, Amantha chooses to return to Bond, and Michele casts her lot with Bond; a betrayal of her husband Jimmee and the other slaves. Rau-Ru is an anomaly; his refinement is the result of his special upbringing by Bond. In strict adherence to the hierarchy of value and moral capacity in the color-coding system, and the presumed inherent nature of black people in general, Rau-Ru, who is very black, reverts to savagery when he breaks free of Bond's influence and control.

Band of Angels seems to ask: Who could possibly blame any white person for regarding such beings, regardless of where they may be on the color continuum, as both culturally and morally inferior? Is Warren merely delineating the white racialist mindset on the idea of cultural and moral inferiority in these depictions? Arguably, this is an unself-conscious rendering of what he perceived as an accurate portrayal of blacks at least in slavery—their circumstances, behaviors and character.

Veneer and Value

Color and physiognomy are, of course, significant issues in social status in America, and often appear to be offered as further proof of black inferiority in *Band of Angels.* The privileging of whiteness, stereotypical depictions of blacks and blackness, examples of physical caricature and grotesqueness based on an implied comparison with whiteness, are pervasive in the text. Color consciousness and the exaggeration, emphasis and ridicule of black racial physiognomy, all of which are apparently further evidence of the degradation and unworthiness of black people, prove that servitude is the appropriate station in life for such a people who cannot, by decree of nature, conform to white standards of beauty and grace, and who may not, in fact, be fully human. It also explains, in part, the repulsion white racists have for black people. Warren carefully constructs and deploys both black and white characters along an established hierarchy of color that ranges, predictably, from the fairest—representing the best of everything from intelligence to beauty—to the blackest—representing the polar opposites—and through the gradations in between, on which the value of individuals may be determined by the place they occupy along the color continuum.[60] The lighter the skin, and correspondingly, the more Caucasian the features, the more human and valuable the individual. As Werner Sollors points out, the appearance of color is often attributed to "a crime or curse."[61]

Amantha Starr is obsessed with color and physiognomy. How could she be otherwise in a society clearly governed by these obsessions? She is a product of her white southern (American) culture, and typifies the general attitudes about color.[62]

From her early childhood Amantha demonstrates her awareness of the importance and superiority of whiteness and also how she has learned her lessons about female beauty. The white doll, Jessie, that she is given by her mammy, which used to belong to the deceased wife of her father, is so fine and elegant with its blue eyes that she doesn't feel worthy of it; no one is. Worship of this image of white, southern, female gentility and beauty becomes a lifelong obsession: "I remember the reverence with which I inspected the perfections. [. . .]

I was all but overcome by a sense of my own unworthiness. I felt that, somehow, it would fly to pieces, or evaporate instantly, from my crude reality" (6). Interestingly, the doll Amantha really loves is a battered one with a carved face on which the "lips were too generous" (11). Her aesthetics of acceptable appearance are clearly shaped and fatally defined at a very early age, at least in her recollection as an adult narrating the story. It is not clear whether Amantha, the child, attached any significance to the fact that the lips of her slave doll were not only generous, but *too* generous.

Amantha, who as a child does not know that her mother was a slave, asks her father why her mother is buried close to the house, and also whether or not her own mother may have had a doll such as Jessie. He squirms and overreacts to the innocent interrogation of a child, and resists being prodded to explain himself and his choices in life. The differences in the material quality of dolls is the difference between the social status of the owners. The white doll belonged to a white woman, and the doll that Amantha is entitled to is one fit for a slave. He is forced to tell her that her own mother (who was not his wife) probably did not have such a doll. Encoded within all his explanations of differences between the status of her mother and his dead wife are clues to Amantha's own precarious racial identity, and the differences in the status of white and black women. She begins to learn the rules of propriety and social spatiality, which are governed by something she understands but imprecisely, having to do with color.

Did slave children even have dolls? The point Warren effectively makes with all this black and white doll business is that a seemingly innocuous incident and a toy may in fact be extremely important. It marks the point in Amantha's life, a point that all children in a race- and color-conscious society must have, in which the awareness of color and physiognomy, and the values ascribed as inherent to physicality, are awakened and fixed.

We also get our first impression of Amantha's physical appearance at this point in the text, and discover that she is very light-skinned. Warren makes the white doll incident particularly crucial to Amantha's unraveling of who and what she really is, and this event resonates in her memory as an important piece in the identity puzzle. When her father refuses to let her continue to play with the white doll, an icon of white femininity and beauty, but tells her that she must take Bu-Bula, her crude, carved wood doll to bed with her, she does not have enough information to make sense of the situation; to understand her place in the scheme of things. She is too young to understand any of it, but the incidental facts remain with her and cause a vague uneasiness. She gets the message gradually and eventually; black is inferior. Although Amantha makes it clear that she loved Bu-Bula, and that she never really loved the white doll, she still worships the image of the white doll and its beauty, made even more special because it is elusive and forbidden to her. The unattainable whiteness represented by the doll becomes a defining force in the development of her self-image and self-esteem, or lack thereof, because she can never herself attain whiteness.

An incident occurs in which she is accidentally separated from her slave doll Bu-Bula, who has been left out in the yard during a terrible storm, and Amantha goes out to find her. Warren demonstrates, through the panic, terror and disorientation that she experiences at being separated from Bu-Bula the disorientation she must feel, on some level, because of separation and alienation from her true racial roots. Without having the information and ability to consciously articulate it, she feels the effects of being denied the truth about who and what she really is—a black child living a pseudo-white life. It is also possible that her attachment to this doll goes beyond the usual attachment children often have for a beloved toy, however raggedy and unattractive it may be. Bu-Bula has both white and black features. She is made by the plantation cobbler, the slave Shaddy, who gives the doll an interesting combination of features, which suggests that he is signifying about Amantha herself—a doll with black facial features and blond hair that denotes mixed race. Amantha may identify with this physiognomy. Interestingly, all the slaves at the Starrwood plantation appear to know Amantha's situation, but are prohibited by custom and potential consequences to speak of it. Shaddy, who is eventually sold (exiled) for inappropriate behavior with Amantha, did a bold thing in making Bu-Bula in this way.

Warren's configuration of Amantha's relentless fixation on whiteness is a detailed treatise on the careful indoctrination into color consciousness and the results of being completely lost in, to borrow Lillian Smith's term, the "Land of Epidermis."[63] At *Pointe du Loup*, Bond's plantation, Amantha dreams of being "lost in a world of white faces" (109).

On her wedding night to Tobias Sears, Amantha is enraptured by the white beauty of her husband: "He looked like the statue of a Greek athlete, and every muscle swelling strong and true in the white marble. For he was white and slick-looking, like marble. [. . .] setting his white feet down on the red carpet, coming toward me, smiling" (237). In the consummation of their marriage her mind is filled with the idea of absorbing as much of Tobias's whiteness as she possibly can: "I shut my eyes, and got his image into my head, and held it there [. . .] yearning toward an image, the brilliant whiteness, the beautiful whiteness, of that image that overhung my mind like a bright cloud. [. . .] There was the need to overcome, by the bright image, some coldness and desperation in myself" (241). In fact, Amantha scarcely thinks of her husband, even when he is sick and dying, without thinking of his chiseled features and white skin (336). His white body is both a beacon that guides her away from her own haunting blackness and a luminous metaphor for purity and goodness that stands between Amantha and darkness, literally: "*Oh, Tobias, Tobias,* I was saying to myself, wandering now in the dark, begging him to hurry and come to me, come to me, seeing him before me, bright in the dark, leaning at me, smiling with that benignity, his body white and glimmering in the dark" (292). Amantha needs, craves, consumes whiteness in order to feel whole and human. Her husband's true whiteness is a reminder to Amantha that her own is an illusion and a lie. She must borrow, by association, more whiteness than nature and circumstances have seen fit to allow her.[64]

Amantha, like the society in which she lives, is successfully indoctrinated into this belief system from the moment she is born. Her inability to accept the fact that she is black, because blackness is dirty, ugly, smelly, animalistic, stupid and ineffectual, is at the core of her self-loathing.[65] For example, in her dreams she holds her breath so that she "would not smell them," and the slaves in the hold "crowded around me, squatting on their hams like apes [. . .] all gabbling and leering, scratching themselves and laughing at me" (82). Her description of the slaves that Bond's neighbor, Prieur-Denis, is running are raggedy, black and glistening, big and burly, and have an oddly effeminate way in which they hold their chains: "eyes bulging white and rolling in the light of the flares, big awkward fellows, half crouching, near naked" (151). The questions the reader must repeatedly confront in this text, particularly in association with Amantha's visceral reactions to color and physiognomy are: What other purpose in life could such beings have other than to serve their social superiors? What other purpose could these particular representations serve in the text? Given his chang(ed)ing views about race by the time he wrote *Band of Angels*, is it possible that Warren was making a sincere effort to demonstrate the deleterious effects and the immorality of enslavement and racism by showcasing the pain and damage suffered by a recipient of it?

After she is sold, Amantha has the requisite experiences of being black, such as her first time being called a nigger. Her owner tells her not to worry, maybe things won't be too bad and she will end up with a fancy guy who will set her up nicely and use her for pleasure—not such a bad life, as he sees it. Each identifier that names her as *not white* threatens her racial virginity, and she descends more deeply into her new category as a slave and a Negro. But Amantha is a "special" slave, and doesn't sleep with the common ones, the ones who "have black or brown faces" (70), and who are quartered with the sheep and swine. She has special accommodations, but can take no real comfort from this. First, because her assessment of her accommodations is based on the standards to which she has been accustomed all her life. She criticizes the dingy and small space because she is still at this point thinking of herself as a lady and deserving better. She laments: "I wanted to cry out that I wasn't a nigger, I wasn't a slave, I was Amantha Starr [. . .] Little Miss Sugar-and-Spice. I could feel the pain of wanting to cry out" (65). And second, because the implications the trader makes about her new purpose in life are very distasteful to her. He says: "I am putting you in a cabin upstairs. Like you was a lady, mind you" (70), the implication being that she really isn't one. Amantha begins to understand what it means to be less than white and her vulnerability as a female.

Amantha also learns in her new circumstances as a slave how superior she is to the other slaves. In her assessment of the different classes of black people, she perceives correctly that mulattos are held in somewhat different regard than the other slaves. The people of mixed race in *Band of Angels* tread the line between black and white, realistically corresponding to the structure and expectations of the slaveholding culture. Examples of their falling short of being as good as white, as well as examples that demonstrate that their blackness is a liability, affirm the tenets of social hierarchy based on qualities of character, which correspond to gradations on the color continuum. Some are identified as lazy and lacking in natural vigor because of their black blood; the mulatto driver sleeps on the job in the hall. They are given the most peculiar jobs in the "gray area," negotiating the spaces between the white and black worlds, such as Amantha's "jailer" on the *Kentucky Queen* who is assigned to simply sit and watch Amantha carefully, to make sure that she does not throw herself overboard. The mulatto driver at the slave auction helps to organize things and drive the other Negroes. The soldiers of mixed blood who fight with the Federal Army are braver than the black-skinned ones because of their white blood—an affirmation of stereotypes of black cowardice. As Colonel Morton says: "You think Port Hudson proves niggers can fight. But look here, Captain, those weren't niggers. They are Louisiana *gens de couleur libres.* They've been free God knows how long. *They are people.* Take an average and every man in the outfit would be worth $25,000, cash and property" (243, my emphasis). They are mixed, therefore they qualify as people; valuable "people" worth $25,000 cash each, but people nonetheless. But the phenotypically black soldiers, referred to as "real gumbo blue-gums," are probably no different than the "toughs and aimless blacks" (243) who wander the streets, if not for the uniform and the supervision of white officers. Yet, those who inhabit the ambiguous space between white and black are clearly morally as well as socially ranked beneath their white associates and can be, but rarely so, in some ways inferior to certain black types, such as the mammy figures.

The mulatto women are sexually competitive and not to be trusted. Aboard a steamboat in transit to her new situation, Amantha is waited on by a mulatto woman who surreptitiously sizes her up and then verbally assaults her. But the old mammy she is put in the charge of, who is black and obese, is momentarily comforting and gives Amantha the best advice she can give—accept it, get over it. But, she then removes to her position as guard and closes off any possibility of emotional connection with the needy, terrified Amantha; she simply does her job. Amantha is repeatedly put under the charge and policing of other Negroes who regard her with curiosity, disdain or indifference—very rarely with empathy and concern. The representation of blacks with very specific color and physiognomical designations in various social positions and capacities of servitude is crucial. Through the accompanying editorializing about their individual value and character by Amantha and others, Warren effectively portrays body type as a visual cue and criteria that denote value and confirm societal standards.

Warren constructs, to great effect, significant comparisons between the social classes and functions of black and white women, and, predictably, makes evident the requirements for and value of those who serve and those who are served.

The reasons Amantha doesn't want to be a black woman, including the obvious one of being a slave, are embedded in her thinking. Typical of the culture in which she resides is the idea of black women as born to love the white children under their care. Warren demonstrates some awareness of the false assumptions made about the natural inclinations of black women. Amantha is aware that these women are destined to be ultimately rejected by those same children they have nurtured when they grow up and the affections of a black mammy become inappropriate and unwanted. These women are the worn-out, unappreciated, unattractive caretakers of other people's children. As she says of her own mammy: "Aunt Sukie, who was my black mammy, spoiled me because she loved me, for women like Aunt Sukie can live only by loving some small creature that they, in the accepted and sad irony of their lot and nature, know will soon grow up and withdraw, indifferent or contemptuous, even in affection" (4).[66]

Of course, the other major function of the mammy in *Band of Angels*, "the positive emblem of familial relations between black and white,"[67] is to provide food of a "libidinous richness" that springs forth "from the old barbarous simplicity and deprivation of the race, or from example of the master's indulgence" (28). It is inconceivable to Amantha that Aunt Sukie might harbor desires and aspirations beyond those assigned to her because of her race and circumstances. Here, Warren simply accommodates the southern mythology of black caretakers. These caretakers were conveniently referred to by "Southern orators" to show "a tender family feeling between the races with this image of interracial innocence." This idea of "being 'suckled at black breasts,'" as Catherine Clinton argues, still conjures up an erotic image, while simultaneously "reduc[ing] black women to an animal-like state of exploitation: Mammies were to be milked, warm bodies to serve white needs—an image with its own sexual subtext." Although Warren may have designed Aunt Sukie to play the traditional role of the exceptional, provisionally respectable black woman slave, "[t]he Mammy does not, by any means, validate the 'closeness' of the races." She is, in fact, simply another fictive construct designed to assuage white guilt and to feed the fantasy of selective inclusion.[68] Ultimately, Aunt Sukie is completely objectified as a "type" to Amantha—a type she would never want to emulate. Aunt Sukie is clearly a familiar type in the products of American culture.

Although the mammy is considered the perfect servant, happily foregoing autonomy for the sake of her white charges, she is not, cannot be, by definition and physiognomy, the feminine ideal for which Amantha yearns. Aunt Sukie sports the obligatory ample bosom of her "type"—warm, maternal, necessary. She has the power to comfort when "she would seize me and envelope me in the great, soft, spicy tide of her affection" (13). Aunt Sukie has the power to define Southern white femininity by contrast. Catherine Clinton explains, using perhaps the most familiar representation of the southern mammy and her relationship with her young mistress in *Gone With the Wind*, that "[t]he image of Mammy [. . .] [is] Scarlett's spiritual silhouette [. . .]. Scarlett's starched petticoats represent hours of Mammy's labor and Scarlett's wasp waist (a direct contrast to Mammy's girth) is a product of Mammy's tight lacing"—an act that underscores her function of actually giving shape to white females. Of course, the American observer of these products of culture that celebrate selective contrasts between black and white women, are experienced and skilled in interpreting these visual cues, and "have had their vision of the South, race relations, and even the entire panorama of our past shaped if not wholly defined by the movie business." American audiences, reading and viewing, are utterly seduced by this "perfect vehicle for exploring American dreams."[69]

Amantha has, in comparison to Aunt Sukie, the iconography of the white woman who is revered, cherished and refined by natural design. Amantha, like the society in which she lives, is utterly seduced by the idea of white femininity. This iconography of the southern white woman "emphasized the ideal of the southern lady as gracious, fragile, and deferential to the men upon whose protection she depended"; she was "delicate, she was to devote herself to charm and nurture," and her "obligation [was] to manifest piety, purity, chastity, and obedience." She was "shielded" and protected "from direct contact with the disorderly folks who populated the world beyond her household."[70] Consider Miss Idell, Amantha's father's mistress, a woman of dubious reputation. Even though she is less than a model of social propriety, Miss Idell is the portrait and definition of a beautiful, feminine woman in Amantha's mind, with her ruffles and roses and parasol with a silver handle. Miss Idell does not have an ample bosom scented from the work of the kitchen, but a "tight blue bodice defining the high richness of her bosom and the elegance of her waist," an ideal that carries for Amantha a "mystic virtue that infused all things honored" (22). She fully comprehends the morphology of beauty in her society.

The "Aunt Sukies" are never considered attractive, refined or desirable. This figure of the mammy has been explored extensively in the critical literature, and among the most cogent explanations of this persevering stereotype, as a distraction from and product of white obsession with black sexuality, is that of Elizabeth Fox-Genovese in *Within the Plantation Household: Black and White Women of the Old South.* Fox-Genovese explains that

> Mammy signaled the wish for organic harmony and projected a woman who suckled and reared white masters. The image displaced sexuality into nurture and transformed potential hostility into sustenance and love. It claimed for the white family the ultimate devotion of black women, who reared the children of others as if they were their own.[71]

In *Band of Angels* child-production is the one area in which the mammy/black woman is permitted to feel superior to white women, in that it ratifies the frail and feminine nature of the white female, and promotes the sexual and reproductive robustness and availability of the black female. In one instance Aunt Sukie explains to Amantha that the reason Aaron Starr's deceased wife had owned a pretty white doll, but had no children, was that she wasn't up to it. Aunt Sukie "shrugged with a heaving contemptuousness that flowed down from the shoulders to undulate the ample expanse of her bosom." Apparently Starr's wife had "no juice" (7); an interesting observation and an implied criticism of white women by the mammy.

As an adult Amantha recalls Aunt Sukie with affection, and in her reflections on the past, she summons up her mammy's bodily attributes, tactility and sense memory dominating the recollection. The feel and smell of Aunt Sukie's body were a source of comfort to the lonely child: "the warm, live, cinnamon smell of Aunt Sukie's bosom and armpits when she held [Amantha] to her" (25).[72] But after a seven-year absence away at school, Amantha returns to the Starrwood plantation to find her old mammy with "just the face of another very old Negro woman, the skin shrunken, losing its gloss, sagging off the bone, the toothless mouth fallen" (56)—a sad, decrepit woman who is a reminder to Amantha that she was at one time a "white" child. More so, I think, Aunt Sukie is terrifying proof of the fate that awaits a black woman in a society in which her beauty, youth and life are taken in service to others, to leave her like a bag of discarded bones and skin in the end. This is not the image or the status in later life Amantha would wish for herself; an image that feeds the fear Amantha has about her hidden genes, because she also sees her black blood as defilement and feels nothing but shame and repugnance at the idea that she is the child of a slave. She says:

> I saw myself, the stain of the black blood swelling through my veins—yes, I actually saw some such picture in my head, a flood darkening through all the arteries and veins of my body—no, a stain spreading in a glass of water. I saw myself for what I was, the half-caste, the child of the nameless woman, the slave child, the nigger gal Old Bond had cut down, ignorant, rejected. (227–228)

The disgust Amantha feels toward blackness is fueled by her fear that her suppressed biological traits might find visible expression and reveal her secret heritage to the world. As Amantha gets older she feels the necessity, indeed, it *is* a necessity considering the false status she enjoys as a white woman, to tame her increasingly crinkling hair, which she tries to control by pulling it back "as tight as possible to *correct* its crisp curliness" (26–27, my emphasis).[73]

The idea of the defiling power of black blood resounds through *Band of Angels*. Warren foregrounds a deeply hidden fear that resonates, perhaps subconsciously, in the white racialist mindset, particularly in the South—the fear, given all the racial mixing in the slaveholding culture, of the possibility of some black ancestry, a suppressed "one drop" that then necessitates an assertive, aggressive "whiteness" as an overcompensation for the shame of secret defilement.

Warren clearly intended the reading and reception of Aunt Sukie as positive—to represent the best of her kind (black, female, servant). She seems a safe bet as representations go in this racially charged society—both fictive and real. The very predictability of this figure, however, seems a denial of her full humanity—she is a stock character. Yet, Warren discloses the bleakness of her life in old age, which demonstrates an uncharacteristically sensitive and even radical literary treatment of the plight of such a caretaker. This is one instance in which Warren elicits empathy in *Band of Angels*, and successfully calls attention to the being behind the "type."

However, Amantha's perceptions and assessments of the unattractiveness of blackness extends beyond her misapprehension of and repugnance for black femininity. She repeatedly links black physical attributes with crude, coarse behavior as well as with limited intelligence. In her early life, Amantha, whose clothing and appearance are that of a wealthy white child, constantly makes physical comparisons. The slave children she plays with have "popped-out bellies glistening below the level of the abbreviated singlet, their only garment, standing with the thumb of one hand stuck in the mouth, and with the other scratching, in lofty indifference, the little black belly or private parts" or "bare backsides and chunky little unsteady black legs, chunky as sausage" (20). As a teenager she has a tendency to be extremely derisive in her descriptions of black people—blacks who have caused no offense, and are most likely unaware of her existence or her race (which is not readily apparent), and certainly are unaware of her cruel observations. She either states or implies a contrast to her superior self, a habit of consolation. It is a way to validate the degradation of blacks and explain away the mistake of her own degradation:

> I was envious, in recollection, of that Negro who had long back escaped to Oberlin to show to a bevy of gaping, prissy, pious-tongued girls the scarce-healed cicatrice on his flesh where the terrible fangs of reality had slashed. [. . .] I felt hatred for that Negro sitting under the lamp, exposing his precious arm. Who was he, ignorant, stupid, unwashed, wall-eyed, afraid? In recollection I caught the sour smell of his rags. (124)

There are examples, too numerous to mention, of Amantha's hatred for black people in general, and particularly for black physiognomy. But one that truly resonates with her detestation of blackness is the following incident, in which Amantha recoils at the touch of a friendly young black slave girl's hand; her reaction is spontaneous, visceral, full of loathing. Her description of coarse hair and the foulness she associates with it are evidence of the contempt and abhorrence she feels for those who have the physical characteristics she despises. Amantha also makes numerous references to bulging eyes; they denote imbecility to her.

> Suddenly, I thought I was going to faint. A nausea assailed me, a frightful sense of defilement, not just defilement of the hand seized and pressed on that coarseness of hair, but a total defilement, a crawling foulness on my scalp, a pricking of skin down my spine, a twitching revulsion to my last nerve-end. And I heard my voice crying out, "Don't—don't touch me!" And I had jerked my hand away, and was standing there with it held in the air before my gaze. I was staring at its whiteness. Yes, it was white. (250)

The question is, of course, what is Warren doing here? If Amantha's consciousness is to represent white southern perceptions and attitudes, she does so effectively. Amantha appears to function as a vehicle, in this particular instance, through which such a mindset is laid bare. However, after her initial response to the physicality of the black child, Amantha is stung to remorse when she hears the child crying because of the brutal rejection. Warren demonstrates, in this rare moment, some capacity for understanding and change. Arguably, shame and regret would not be typical reactions under such circumstances.

As Amantha develops a growing awareness of the conditions of slavery—and it is in these brief, glancing moments of introspection that the reader has an opportunity to consider the injustices and terrors of enslavement in *Band of Angels*—it is in these rare moments that Warren presents a more comprehensive and balanced view of the slaveholding culture. But these moments are few and fleeting, and are continually circumvented or undermined by a reminder of the degradation that *must* be inherent in the natural state of being a Negro. As Amantha waits in the steamboat cabin, she recalls what she has heard about the Middle Passage, which at first appears to be an indication of a developing consciousness about enslavement and what it truly means to have one's freedom taken away, and she contemplates suicide.

She has a moment of relief when she thinks about her mother as beautiful and calm, but then remembers that "*she was a nigger*" (75). Her mother's face disappears because Amantha can no longer derive comfort from the image of what she now knows is a nigger mother and, therefore, has no further use for the idea of her; the fantasy is obliterated forever. This response makes perfect sense considering Amantha's social indoctrination. In constructing and enforcing the idea of white supremacy, children learn early in life to romanticize whiteness, and "God and Negroes and Jesus and sin and salvation were baled up together in southern children's minds and in many an old textile magnate's also,"[74] as Lillian Smith describes it.

Considering her views on blackness, as well as the secret life she lives as a white woman, Amantha's relief that her children turn out to be phenotypically white is also understandable. For Amantha, the absence of blackness equals beauty and safety. She is stunned over her husband's decision to join the Freedman's Bureau after the war because she had fantasized an escape to a new life in Massachusetts, and equates safety and peace with kind strangers who have blue eyes. She imagined herself there with her silken-haired children at her knee—a very revealing description of Amantha's idea of paradise, especially considering that her eyes are brown and her hair is curly and coarse by comparison (259).

Warren demonstrates powerfully, through Amantha's agonies over color, the damaging effects of being race- and color-struck. However, there is not a single instance in which black physiognomy is presented with neutrality in this novel—it is denigrated, loathed, pitied or eroticized, sometimes simultaneously. Amantha's point of view is that of the white racialist tormented by the idea of blackness and makes terribly real the fear and loathing that enables the consignment to slavery and servitude, as well as the rejection and abuse of black people, which appears to be so natural for white people who think in this way. It may be that Warren is attempting to demonstrate the intransigent power of racism through Amantha. One thing is certain: Amantha is ultimately salvaged and redeemed through her total embrace of whiteness, her denial of her black blood, and her refusal to hold accountable those race- and color-conscious individuals who were responsible for her predicament. In *Band of Angels*, they are not to be blamed.

In Defense of "Rape": Sexuality and the Female Slave

No investigation of the intricacies of white racialist thinking in this text would be complete without considering attitudes toward black women, particularly where sexual matters are concerned. The representation of black women in sexual slavery in *Band of Angels* is most troubling, but entirely conventional. Warren makes liberal use of all the stereotypes and conventional assumptions about black women, and he uses them in ways that not only appear to support the justifications for their enslavement, but also the violence and rape to which they are subjected. In addition to this, in corruption of historical fact—black women were the victims of white male sexual aggression during and after slavery—Warren makes two female sexual slaves, Amantha and Michele, agents of sexuality; they are sexual aggressors who desire their master, Hamish Bond.[75]

If we take Warren at his word that his thinking about race had altered dramatically by the time *Band of Angels* was written, then it may be conceivable that these representations of the complicity of black women in sexual slavery are part of an agenda to disclose a flawed way of thinking about these situations—at least it requires some consideration. It is possible that in Warren's zeal to map out the white racist mindset that he creates, instead, what appears to be a ratification of those ideas. In order to dismiss or rationalize the sexual enslavement of black women, it is necessary to have a thorough misapprehension of the circumstances of enslavement and the dynamics of consent in power relations; it is necessary to have an inability to see the humanity and vulnerability of these women. Ultimately, in *Band of Angels* sexual enslavement is not violation or forced servitude at all.

Harriet Jacobs, whose *Incidents in the Life of a Slave Girl* chronicles the horrors of sexual intimidation and violence against young, even pre-adolescent female slaves, possessed the certainty of self that gave her the strength to attempt to resist and eventually escape her tormentor. For obvious reasons, there are few examples of affidavits or depositions by slave women who wrote of their own sexual experiences, but what we have available to us through *Incidents* and other slave narratives that address these situations are a number of recurring similarities that define the master/female sexual slave dynamic, which complicate and make Amantha's behavior almost incomprehensible.

Typically, the female slave would be introduced to the concept of sex by the master, his male relatives or friends, or the white overseers or other white workers on the plantation as she began to show evidence of physical maturation. This would occur in the form of veiled suggestions, lewd descriptions of a sexual nature to innocent ears, explicit invitations. Sometimes gift-giving or promises of favors, as a bribe, would accompany any of these gestures. In all cases, even those that masqueraded as a courtship ritual but were in fact a twisted aberration of the respectful wooing proffered decent white women, the slave girl ultimately could be raped with impunity at any time. The illusion of consent obviated the need for forced sex, and was based on the idea that the black women wanted it to happen. The white male could then maintain his self-delusion as a decent person.[76] Of course, for some white males in the slaveholding culture no illusion was necessary; the violence and terror of forced sex was desired.

Warren does not follow the established pattern of child seduction and rape that was endemic to slaveholding culture. Instead, Amantha's initiation into sexuality is actually at the hands of the black cobbler, Shaddy. Further proof of Amantha's, and by extension the female slave, complicity in sex is the fact that despite her general aversion to blackness, Amantha has an attraction to black males, which she demonstrates from the time she is a small child, and her descriptions of black men are very erotic.

Amantha recalls the making of her beloved doll, Bu-Bula, by strong, competent dark hands; the fashioning of an artificial being out of wood with a knife excites her, as it would almost any child. Her encounters with Shaddy in the shadows of the workshop are vaguely sexualized. He holds her and bounces her on his lap, and tells her of "sweet recollection, or dire pains and punishments, or thrilling strangenesses." He lures her with tales while she watches him make things with his "peculiarly deft" hands, tickles her on his lap, and sometimes just holds her quietly and tells her tales of a crazy man who eats little girls and scrapes out their brains to eat, all the while asking for more kisses and hugs from Amantha. The entire relationship has an unwholesome quality about it. She admits, "But I wanted to be scared," "and he made like he was going to eat me, baring his old yellow teeth, and grabbing my stomach with all five fingers of one hand, while with the other hand he held my back. I screamed with delight" (14). She is innocently aroused by the experience and by the sound of his voice.

It is not perfectly clear whether Shaddy is merely a nice old guy paying attention to a lonely child, or if there is some illicit activity taking place. For Amantha, "everything would become his voice with its mixture of lulling comfort and secret excitement" (13). But apparently Amantha's mammy, Aunt Sukie, believes that Shaddy plays inappropriately with Amantha, and, as Amantha's protector, warns him off:

> She just looked quiet at Shaddy, and said: "That chile gittin too big, you to fool her up that a-way." [. . .] And he gave me another grab and jounce to make me scream and demonstrate my willingness for the pleasure. [. . .] "Yeah," Aunt Sukie was saying [. . .] "I knows you. And doan you reckin I doan know yore goins-on down yander. [. . .] In yore little ole work-place, down the barn-shed." (14–15)

Memory regression distorted by time, actual experience or autosuggestion? Dream or fantasy? Amantha is not sure if her recollections of the past are actually true, but she does know that she had a "mysterious attraction" to the old Negro—and he to her. As she reflects back, she is convinced that Shaddy did love her, and she feels responsible for his sad fate. But she does, even in her complicated recollections of her relationship with this man, admit that he was evil and bitter, as well as kind and loving. She has trouble separating fact from fiction in this relationship. She also acknowledges her own accountability in the situation:

> I remember, and to a degree even now, relive, the feelings that accompanied the scene, my guilt at telling on him (the fact accomplished or contemplated, or perhaps put into my head by his pleading), my resentment for that moment when he had shaken my world to shadow, my mysterious attraction toward him and his terrible tales and lulling voice, my gratitude for Bu-Bula, my natural and childish desire to enjoy the love he proffered me, a desire not quite canceled by the present revulsion. For, I am sure, Shaddy did love me, in his own sad, confused, bitter, lonesome, evil, and kindly way. (18)

The emphasis on Shaddy's illicit conduct with Amantha, as well as her admissions of culpability in retrospect as an adult, shifts the reader's attention from the most common circumstances of sexual initiation for young slave girls; from the hands of white men, to a black man and his somewhat willing young victim.

Amantha's powerful attraction to black men, albeit against her own will and better judgment, also points to her sexual proclivity—a proclivity that makes her fair game for sex. *Band of Angels* equivocates between a repugnance for and a fascination with black physiognomy, most particularly when it comes to black men.

Typically, Warren uses animal imagery in the descriptions of black people, especially the men, such as the "big, fine-looking old Negro, blue-black and shining in the face, with a long black coat and a red neck-scarf, and a voice like a melodious bull" (35). Amantha dwells on the physical prowess of Michele's husband, Jimmee, who grooms the horses. His voice reminds her of the "darkies" back home. Although he shows signs of age and wear, his strong youthful body does not escape Amantha's notice; her descriptions are detailed and sensual: "His shirt sleeves were hacked off high up so that I could see the bare arms, lightly but strongly muscled, like a strong young boy's" (100), and also, "the slick brown curve of the shoulder, bright-filmed with sweat. And I was aware in a cold, fascinated awareness that I had the impulse to reach out my hand and touch that shoulder" (102). Although Amantha is aroused by Jimmee's physique, she is also offended by his attraction to her; she feels revulsion at admiration from a Negro—one who has the audacity to remind her that she is also a Negro. Her sexual awakening begins first as a child with Shaddy, and then with Jimmee, a Negro not of her social class. She is completely confused and not a little disgusted as much with herself as with Jimmee.

Her description of Rau-Ru, Bond's "adopted" African "son," on their first meeting illustrates her attraction to him:

> I don't know what I had expected, certainly not the lithe figure [. . .] the face of preternatural blackness, like enameled steel, against the white of the loose blouse. For an instant he stood there, and I saw that his eyes were wide, large, and deep-set, his nose wide but not flattened, the under-lip full, if not to the comic fullness favored in the make-up of minstrel shows of our day, and the corners of the mouth were drawn back so that the effect of that mouth was one of arrogant reserve and not blubbering docility. A mustache of a few hairs hung wispily down below the corners of the mouth, in a kind of ambitious boyishness. (118)

She also fantasizes about touching Rau-Ru's (Lt. Jones) scarred flesh, which echoes her fascination with the scars of the escaped slave at Oberlin, as well as with Bond's leg wound. It is possible that Warren intends to demonstrate that these visible manifestations of pain and damage are denied Amantha because her scars cannot be seen. Her husband's insistence that she not dwell on Lt. Jones/Rau-Ru's scars, perhaps because it was rude to do so, is instructive to her in that it tells her that scars are a private matter best left concealed and unacknowledged:

> And I saw it in my mind, the healed-up scars, great corded scars, rough as hemp rope, rough as oak bark, black with gray scaling, humping out, interlacing

> mathematically on the bare, black flesh. I could just feel how rough that surface would be if you ran a finger down it. "Rough as oak bark—oh, it was terrible what they did." Tobias' fingers had gripped my shoulder, quite hard. "Darling," he was saying, "I am quite positive that Lieutenant Jones does not wish to dwell on it. We all have new problems now." (271)

Amantha is depicted as a sensualist with complicated and perhaps idiosyncratic sexual needs. It is not surprising that such a woman would be amenable to a sexual situation, such as that with Bond, in which she could give free reign to her powerful impulses, and, therein, subjugate her innocent accomplice—her owner, her master. As a black woman, she simply cannot help herself.

Many of the critics of this text absolve the white southern male of sexual predation and any wrongdoing because Amantha is regarded as bad news for men; she is a seducer and destroyer. Amantha starts this career as a destroyer of men as a child, when she is "responsible" for Shaddy being sold off—the selling of a slave a rare occurrence on her father's plantation—because of his inappropriate (possibly sexual) relationship with her. Although he has actually been strung up by his ex-slaves, including his adopted African son, Rau-Ru, Hamish Bond does not wait for his executioners to kick the cotton bale from beneath him, but leaps to his death when he sets eyes on Amantha. Bond is, in a sense, killed by Rau-Ru, who, it turns out, has harbored a secret desire for Amantha and jealousy toward Bond all those years. Charles Prieur-Denis, Bond's neighbor, is struck down by Rau-Ru because he has attacked Amantha. Rau-Ru must flee his comfortable life, which affords him a certain amount of power and respect, because he has hit a white man in Amantha's defense. Amantha's husband Tobias is secretly tormented into alcohol and adultery and eventually self-exile because of her race secret. The super-religious Quaker Seth is haunted by the idea of Amantha, considers her fair game and falls from grace after he tries to force himself on her when he discovers that she has Negro blood—the temptress!

It is true that Amantha's status as a victim is both complicated and diminished because she is the narrator. The reader is privy to the fuzzy thinking, contradictions, weaknesses, immaturity, lack of insight, prejudices and whining of this character; qualities of a plaintiff that a prosecuting attorney in a rape trial today would try to conceal from a jury; qualities that can also sway a reading audience to suspect the complicity of the victim. That she is "a tiresome character whose frail sense of discrimination puts the trivial and the momentous on a single egocentric plane," or that she is "a nagger, a spoiled, petulant woman who refines a talent for manipulating men"[77] are not sufficient grounds for denying her very real experience or for discounting the possibility of rape.

Admirable qualities or an attractive disposition are not, of course, criteria for determining whether or not a rape has occurred.

But in the critical literature about this text, Amantha's status as a rape victim is continually up for review. There are three recurring questions: Did Bond rape Amantha? Did she *choose* to be Bond's mistress after their first sexual encounter? Is Amantha a manipulative seductress, and their sex, therefore, simply the consummation of a relationship between a man and a woman? That these questions arise, considering the circumstances, is evidence enough of how little is understood about rape, the dynamics of enslavement, and the dubious and low regard in which black women are held. Amantha's designation as a sexual servant is simply in accordance with the society in which she lives; a society that "divided women into two classes: ladies, always white and chaste; and whores, comprising all black women (except for the saintly Mammy)."[78] In *Band of Angels* it is clear that sexual servitude is a natural and fitting occupation for black women.

In order to work through these issues we must consider the context of slavery. Is sex between master and slave ever really consensual? Is there any such thing as a willing participant in a power relationship, especially when one is actually the property of the other? Should it not be considered rape because Amantha herself does not really condemn Bond or leave him when he offers her freedom? These are significant issues, with which, I believe, Warren grapples in this text.

On Amantha's first night in Bond's house she doesn't get completely undressed for bed, but simply removes her dress and shoes. She awaits Bond's first approach in the night, and for the first time confronts the facts of life for a female slave. Waiting in the night for her master she does not, understandably, reflect back on her own parents' relationship and the fact that she is the product of such a union. In the description below, which effectively shows how fearful and sick a powerless teenager must feel in such a situation, it appears, at first, that Warren is setting up a scene in which the appalling act of slave rape is made evident. Amantha recalls:

> And all the time I was straining for some sound within the house. [. . .] Well, I had steeled myself. I knew what to do. If that man came through that door, I would fling myself from the balcony, and die on the stones. [. . .] Yes, I would do it, and my breath, at the thought, came quick and shallow. Somehow, I almost longed for that wild, vindictive, vindicatory leap. [. . .] I sat up in the bed. I heard it tap out the shriveling of time, of distance, with a torturer's deliberation. I held my breath. Then the blackthorn stopped, and I couldn't stand it, not to breathe. Then from the floor below I heard the faint sound of a door closing. (96)

Bond does not enter Amantha's room on this or many other subsequent nights; during this period she discovers that her function as a slave is not considered work. Michele, her predecessor, tells her that "work" is not in her job description; there are many others for that. Work is, after all, a mental or physical effort directed toward the production or accomplishment of something. It produces some sort of tangible output or object for which compensation is typically awarded. It is a job, employment, a trade or profession that is the means of livelihood. The obvious irony here, of course, is that forced sex for survival purposes precisely fits the description of work. But the idea of the sexual slaves' function as "work" is thoroughly denied in this text, most particularly when Amantha is set up in the pseudo-status of a "lady" with nice accommodations and attire. The most insidious implication here is that the black woman craves sex, therefore, although these women are completely objectified as sexual objects, they are seen to be gratuitously compensated for fulfilling their own sexual desires. There is no "work" here; there is consent and pleasure for all concerned. There are no victims. So, Amantha and Michele embroider together in a pleasant room by a shady window, the sounds of other slaves "working" in the kitchen provide the background music to their tasks. Amantha observes a colored man currying a horse in the yard and begins to understand her rank and the "privileges" attached to it; she and Michelle are set apart from the other slaves. But they *are* meant to serve, in a different way.

When Amantha experiences a moment of peace and forgetfulness she immediately feels guilty and evil—considering her new circumstances. Here is the situation as it finally happens:

> A young girl, storm-drenched and storm-scared and lonely and confused in a foreshortening of time, is disposed on a bed by an aging man, who utters her name like a groan, and gently and bloodily does that thing to her, and she cries out. I had almost used that foul word that old Mr. Marmaduke, back in Kentucky, had used in his prediction of my fate. I would have used it in some impulse to spit upon and spurn that aging man and the young girl on that bed, but something forbids. (134–135)

Why does Warren have Amantha tell of her "impulse to spit upon and spurn" not only Bond but also herself? Does she simply express anger and disgust at being forced to participate and now see herself as dirtied or corrupted? Or, is Warren suggesting that she is equally responsible for this situation and that her awareness of this causes the self-disgust? To make matters more confusing, although the language describing this situation and Amantha's response to it clearly shows that it was an act of violence, Warren then shifts the agency of the act to History; he has Amantha relieve Bond of all responsibility for the rape. She says: "It is, in other words, History, and what you are is an expression of History, and you do not live your life, but somehow, your life lives you, and you are, therefore, only what History does to you" (134). They are both simply part of the historical moment and momentum. Who and where she is, and what Bond does to her without her consent, are not only expected but appropriate. She refuses to judge herself (lonely, young, confused) or Bond (aging, needy, gentle) when she says:

> Well, the young girl is adjusted upon the bed, but how is what happens to her connected with some late conversation of bankers that same night in New York City, wreathed in the spicy smoke of cigars and eye-glittering with French brandy, or connected with the sweat-cold nocturnal death-fear of a politician abed in Washington, or connected with a grim-jawed old man, seated by the candle in a farmhouse in Maryland, not far from Harper's Ferry, who lifts his eyes from the Holy Writ and moves his lips stiffly in prayer, panting for the moment when the old blood-drenched fantasy will whirl again before his eyes and justify all? (135)

As usual in this text, there are victims denied, as well as victimization to spare, as Amantha not only absolves Bond of any wrongdoing, but views him also as a victim. She begins the process of rationalizing the rape—and it is History, not Bond, who has raped her—when she cries: "Oh, who is whose victim? And the hand of Hamish Bond laid to my side, and the spreading creep and prickle of sensation across the softness of my belly from the focus of Hamish Bond's sandpaper thumb, and the unplaiting and deliquescence of the deep muscles of things were as much History as any death-cry at the trench-lip or in the tangle of the abatis" (135).

What Amantha's critics read, and what may appear to be her complicity, may be a way for her to avoid facing her own helplessness. Is Warren's attempt to make Amantha's notion about historical causality a deliberate deflection of her real circumstances? Perhaps, but it follows a pattern of commonly misunderstood responses to rape. A rape victim often uses any means or explanation at her disposal as part of a survival strategy; a psychological mechanism that may help her to keep from feeling fully the degradation of her life and self. To what extent Warren considered this is unknowable, but it should be considered as a possibility.

Still, Amantha's response to Bond, and to the rape, is in no way represented as a Stockholm Syndrome type of situation, in which a victim or hostage begins to identify with and develop an empathy for their captor or abuser.[79] At first, this may appear to be the case, because in the aftermath Amantha feels a delayed sense of honor about what has happened to her and even a sense of tenderness as she watches Bond sleep; it seems a purely mechanical and oddly obligatory reaction. But, Warren goes so far as to have Amantha kiss an old wound on the sleeping Bond's leg; a shocking display from a young girl who has just lost her virginity under such circumstances. What is this but evidence, not of compliance, but of actual complicity? This act suggests that he, too, is wounded and a victim of circumstances and is in need of consolation, and that Amantha understands, and that it's all right. What is going on here? Gratitude? Identification with her captor? An expression of moral degradation? That Warren has Amantha do such a thing suggests that she is a willing participant; it is never suggested that she does not really have a choice in the first place.

Amantha acquires a sense of power when she is able to feel that their "relationship" is somehow consensual and that it is love, which is a common rape victim response. It also gives her critics permission to blame her. When she first awakens, Amantha feels "feebly but dutifully" a sense of having been violated, but confesses that she did not feel violated when she was supposed to feel it, during the act itself. This admission appears to somehow make the rape more palatable; to make it simply an unfortunate act or event that failed to register as a violation at the time it occurred because it was not, in fact, a violation. If she did not feel violated until she had time to think about it, and realize that it was the expected and decent thing to do to respond in such a way, then perhaps it wasn't such a terrible thing after all. Never mind that had she not been in this situation as a piece of property in her master's house, she may have made other choices that would not include having sex with this man. Amantha is so pliable the next morning after the first rape, that she waits to see how he will "define" her with the first glance or word: "But I do know that I suddenly leaned over and kissed the scar, and as I did so, my heart was flooded with tenderness. What I mean to say is that, according to my recollection, it was not the tenderness that made me lean to kiss the old wound. The tenderness came after I had leaned. But what made me lean?" (136).

What made Amantha lean? I think that the reader is compelled to consider the possibility that this text suggests that desire and inherent moral ineptitude made her lean. One of the popular assumptions about rape is that, regardless of the circumstances, the victim must clearly demonstrate an unwillingness, or at least a reluctance, to participate. Because we see Amantha's mental wafflings during the event, and her rationalizing after the fact, many critics are uneasy with defining the act as rape. One critic writes that "[a]t first reading, Amanda [sic] Starr appears to be the victim of circumstances. [. . .] Yet, the truth is she is victimized more by her own false assumptions than by acts perpetrated upon her by others." That "Manty's own attitude is also responsible for her condition of servitude. [. . .] Her bondage is of her own making." This critic goes so far as to say that Amantha was really asking for it from Bond. During a storm

> Manty is rescued by Hamish and clings, quivering, to his chest, her face pressed "into the security of his shoulder and neck." [. . .] Manty is a child no longer, and Hamish is not her father. Her actions awaken desires in Bond, and she is put to bed in quite a different manner. [. . .] Her actions lead to complications that she fails to foresee (or, perhaps, to complications that she subconsciously desires).[80]

Another argues that "Amantha's most serious victimization is self-inflicted, and because she caresses her injuries for so long, her healing takes more than twenty years."[81] What is a reasonable time limit for recovering from such trauma? What these critics and others who share this view fail to acknowledge is that Bond has bought Amantha precisely for sex, and for no other reason, and his power is absolute. Could she say "no"?[82]

Amantha is very young, inexperienced, fearful and naïve in a strange place away from all connections and the protection of others. Lucy Ferris correctly points out in "Sleeping with the Boss: Female Subjectivity in Robert Penn Warren's Fiction," that Amantha, "like many rape victims [. . .] hoodwinks herself into believing that the act of violence was an act of love, at the same time employing the means she does have at her disposal to survive, physically and emotionally."[83] One can understand how a young girl in these circumstances would feel a need to translate the violation into an act of passion or love to keep from feeling sullied, devalued and helpless. But in the larger context of the story, outside of Amantha's consciousness, there are no recriminations, no judgments of Bond. Yes, he does demonstrate that something is going on with him the next morning, but it appears to be more discomfiture and embarrassment than remorse.

Why might Bond feel embarrassment or discomfiture considering that he has bought her as a sexual slave and has the legal power and social approval to do with her whatever he may choose to do? There are a number of possibilities. Perhaps Warren attempts to demonstrate that in spite of social sanction, which make Bond's conduct routine and even acceptable, Bond still apprehends that he has committed an offense, on some level. It is also possible that he is squirming a bit under what may be Amantha's judgment of his sexual performance—being a considerably older man. She may be a slave, but she is also female—a female who may not be free to voice her opinion, but who has one nonetheless. Warren doesn't give the reader much to go on in this respect. But, Bond does offer Amantha her freedom after this incident, which she rejects. She says:

> Then I knew that I must have been smiling at Hamish Bond, but with some kind of shy, tremulous appeal. [. . .] Then, all at once, his face lighted in that strange way that, as I have already said, reminded me of sunlight breaking through cloud on a craggy landscape. "Well, Manty," he said, grinning, "well, I'll be darn." (138)

In this instance, Warren clearly attempts to set the stage for a budding affection and romance by demonstrating Amantha's willingness to participate. Her tremulous smile does not signal a defeated or fearful resignation or acquiescence, but reciprocal desire. I agree with Catherine Clinton's assessment of such circumstances. She writes:

> The sexual dynamics of southern race relations are fundamentally ignored in this speculation. Consent would never be more than a minor factor in a society where slaveowners maintained despotic rule. The slave female, for example, could not give herself "freely," for she did not have herself to give: she already belonged to the master. To imagine that "falling in love" might be a decisive element in the formula is a sentimental rather than analytical assessment of such interracial unions.[84]

Bond's magnanimous gesture of offering Amantha her freedom may be a maneuver to deny the wrong he has done to her. It is not possible to determine to what extent Warren understood the psychology of rape. We, as readers, can only look at the ways in which he has constructed the circumstances and responses, of both the perpetrator and the victim, and try to make some sense of his intentions within that context.

How Warren has Amantha respond is not unusual in such circumstances and states of mind. Ironically, Amantha does not and probably cannot really confront the rape issue herself, but very clearly sees herself as a victim of almost everything and everyone else: her father, Shaddy, the abolitionist Seth, Rau-Ru, a fellow slave girl Dollie, Bond, her husband Tobias, her father's mistress Miss Idell, slavery and freedom. Warren may demonstrate, through Amantha's occasional capacity for transferring responsibility for what she suffers in life to everyone and everything else, the way in which she diffuses and absorbs the shock and grief she must feel but must repress. But it is just as possible that Warren is simply consistent in her characterization as petulant, self-absorbed and self-pitying. In any case, her decision to stay with Bond makes some practical sense, and it is fairly clear that Warren is making a point about the necessity of a black female under these circumstances to be practical and realistic about her prospects in the world. She is, after all, a teenager and has no real experience of living entirely on her own (at Oberlin she was closely supervised), she has no other familial or friendly connections in the world and Bond has ruined her chances for respectability. Perhaps most important, as Lucy Ferris argues, "Manty cannot get on board the steamer [. . .]. [She] cannot accept the freedom spread out before [her] because [she does] not yet possess the certainty of self which freedom demands."[85]

It is Amantha's refusal to leave Bond when he offers her freedom that causes so much consternation from readers of this text. The nature of the relationship between Bond and Amantha after the rape, and then her subsequent refusal to leave him when given the chance, is often misapprehended. For example, it is argued that

> [f]or the first time she senses, though she cannot or dare not articulate them, the psychological dimensions of slavery, the ambivalent satisfaction in comfort, secure with a master who is more like her father than a new lover. If Hamish Bond does not quite make her the "Little Miss Sugar-and-Spice" that Aaron Pendleton Starr did earlier, he is just as careful to protect her against the world and is extraordinarily solicitous of her ladylike desires.[86]

Bond may protect Amantha from the world, but who protects Amantha from Bond? How can Bond be perceived as fatherly, considering that he brutally rapes this teenager?

There is even an observable dearth of understanding of Amantha's predicament from "the feminist camp," which Lucy Ferris argues has "thus far [. . .] avoided attacking Warren directly [. . .]. Has Warren, they might ask, succumbed [. . .] to the central male fallacy regarding rape, i.e., that it is an act of male passion elicited by the siren's song?"[87] In assessing both Amantha's conduct and Warren's intentions, it is absolutely necessary to consider the vulnerability and absence of choices for someone in her position. As Elizabeth Fox-Genovese explains, when "a slave woman and her master confronted each other, the trappings of gender slipped away. The woman faced him alone. She looked on naked power."[88] Bond is neither lover or father. The creature comforts and the pretense of being a "lady," like any white southern woman living in luxury, is a cruel sham and serves only to add to Amantha's confusion about her identity, her value as a human being and her place in the world.

After Amantha decides to remain with Bond, and has had time to process what has happened to her, she comes to quite a different conclusion about him and her circumstances. She confronts Bond and accuses him of freeing her when it was too late, meaning after he had raped her. He does admit that it was too late, but that the gesture was better than nothing. His "kindness" was a torment to her, and she wishes he would beat her so that she could, at least, know how to feel. Bond's brutality toward Amantha escalates and he rapes her again, this time with more roughness and force because for the first time she resists. Finally, with any pretense at romance and consideration stripped away, Amantha feels the full degradation and danger of her situation as she had not been able to before.

With the images and thoughts of Bond's confession about his past as the captain of a slave ship and his brutal treatment of his former fiancée still reverberating in her mind, Amantha is frightened and confused and ceases struggling against him; but her response is purely out of terror and resignation. She says: "it was like he hated me. [. . .] It was as though there was a confusion of the terrible things he had told me, burning and screams at night, but somehow I was wickedly involved in it, making it come true. But I was extremely frightened. I cried out, I was so frightened" (203). In this instance, it appears that Warren is making it clear that this is rape. It seems clear that Amantha is in the process of learning how to fulfill her role as a sexual slave, and that she finally has no illusions about Bond's feelings toward her; she is figuring out the difference between rape and consent. At this moment, she is completely aware of how unfree she truly is, even as she tries to fathom her role in slavery and her culpability. It would seem that Warren, at this point, is making Amantha's victimization clear.

When Amantha is finally able to leave Bond to try to find her own way in the world, whatever that effort might bring, her confusion about him is not so easily ameliorated by his absence. Because she misses Bond, it is easy to conclude that she has exaggerated her fear of and disgust for her relationship with him. One might reasonably think that her impulse to go back to him not long after she has been freed is based on fear of the unknown. The security and material comfort of the knowable world of Bond's plantation, *Pointe du Loup*, whatever she may be subjected to there, beckons to Amantha in her new circumstances, which offer terrifying uncertainty to the single, unprotected very young woman on her own during a time of civil war. But if Amantha is tempted to return to Bond because of this, she also recalls, this time without the romanticizing of a young girl trying to pretend that she is loved, the "violence that made my heart stop" (209) that she felt after Bond's confession about his past as a slave trader, and she is able to confront the fact that she doesn't really know who Bond is. This knowledge appears to help her establish the critical distance necessary to accurately assess her situation as violation, and she feels the shame and fear she could not feel in the beginning and resolves to lock her door. Amantha appears to experience a new level of awareness; one in which she has a greater sense of self and self-respect. But true to form for this text, Amantha's self-awareness and her possible status as a victim are not only short lived, but perhaps do not exist at all.

What is so disturbing about this entire situation is that it turns out, finally, that Amantha's misgivings about being with Bond are based more on the fact that during her stay with him she has managed to put herself in a different category than the "filthy niggers" (215) Bond has had sex with on the slave ships and elsewhere. In her mind, she is not one of them. When he becomes rough with her and she is not in the mood for sex, and she finally realizes that in Bond's eyes she has no function different from that of the African women on his slave ships, she becomes infuriated. As it turns out, she is not as outraged and devastated by the fact that she is forced to have sex with Bond, as she is outraged and devastated that Bond does not truly distinguish between her and these other sexual slaves. She says: "Then I cried out, 'Oh, I know—I know—it's just you want to make a nigger of me—that's what you want—a nigger—a nigger—like those niggers you had, off yonder in Africa—oh, you want to make me filthy like them!'" (215).

What this means is that as long as Amantha can imagine that she and Bond are a couple, and that she can choose to have sex or refuse him, then the sex is all right. But if she is handled roughly and forced, then the illusion falls away, and she needs the illusion to continue in the game. The fact that Amantha appears to desire Bond, despite everything that he has done to her, ends up supporting the idea that the female slave is not a victim, but is a sexually interested woman. She not only wants to have her master, but on her own terms. It is a blatant ratification of the notion of the sexual wantonness of black women—women not deserving of respect or consideration.

To further substantiate the complicity of slave women is the relationship between Bond and Michele, the quadroon sexual slave who Amantha replaces. Michele and Bond were together for years until he decided he needed to marry a respectable white woman. He offered Michele freedom, as he says, "to sort of make something up to her, [but] she wouldn't do it. She said she would lie down at the door" (200). Michele, like Amantha, refuses to leave Bond when he offers her freedom. Who, therefore, can then blame him? As Winthrop Jordan has pointed out in his chapter entitled "Fruits of Passion,"

> by calling the Negro woman passionate they were offering the best possible justification for their own passions. Not only did the Negro woman's warmth constitute a logical explanation for the white man's infidelity, but, much more important, it helped shift responsibility from himself to her. If she was *that* lascivious—well, a man could scarcely be blamed for succumbing against overwhelming odds.[89]

There is no acknowledgment in *Band of Angels* that slave women in this position have been spoiled/soiled. In reality, slave masters robbed these women of any prospects for respectability in the white world, if they could pass for white, and they were sometimes subjected to repercussions in the slave community after becoming sexually experienced and "tainted" by their masters. Their position as "free" women can only be an illusion and a fantasy after they have been sexual slaves. The decision of a slave woman to remain in or return to such a situation can obviously be based on these factors. But, Warren takes great pains to show that both women care for and desire Bond, which is finally the only explanation for their refusal to give him up.

In *Band of Angels*, the black female sexual slave simply cannot give up her master because she is sexually capricious and lacking in virtue. The complicity of these women with their sexual bondage, and their power to ruin men, is made clear. After years of being on her own and then of being legally married to a white man, Amantha, like her predecessor Michele, still desires Bond, and returns to his house just as Rau-Ru is about to kill him. But Bond, waiting to be hanged, and before he leaps to his death, finally to be free from his "self-torturing kindness," expresses in his last words his bitter regret at being "[a]ss deep in niggers" (324). He specifically tells Amantha that this includes her; the greatest insult imaginable for Amantha. A kind man, indeed. To the last, and in spite of the rare moments in which it is possible to see the victimization of slave women in these situations, *Band of Angels* ratifies the idea that it is the black female slave who desires her master, and that he is just a victim of her desire. For Amantha he was "a dream I had to have and cling to" (163). Bond is the victim; his only escape is death.

Michele also returned to Bond after she had left, and after years of being married to a black slave. According to Jimmee, Michele's husband, she willingly slept with Bond after he returned upriver old and sick: "yeah, all that-air time, sweet to me, and all 'twunce she crawl out my baid. Yeah, him come back to the country, upriver, ole lak a ole man, ole and sick to lay down, and she crawl out my baid, just up and go to him, she lay in his baid. [. . .] Ole son-a-bitch Bond,' he said, and spat" (312). Jimmee and the other male slaves acknowledge this weakness on the part of the slave women, and wish that they had hung Michele naked with Bond because of her assumed betrayal of them—a voluntary defection to the Big House. They are, in fact, so overwrought that Michele chooses to return to Bond that they seem to have concocted a story about her taking up with some white bushwhackers and betraying the slaves. There is no evidence whatsoever of this, but they guess this is what she is doing. Once again, a black woman, a mixed race black woman, is blamed for things going wrong and the betrayal and ruination of men. Even the male slaves recognize the truth in this. To underscore the point, Amantha also betrays the black slaves. When caught with the black renegades, Amantha avows she is "not nigger" (332) and lies about Rau-Ru, saying that he had forced her to come with him. She then lets herself off the hook for the lie, telling herself that they were condemned men anyway. But the truth is, add a kidnapped "white" woman to the equation and things can always get worse for a black man during slavery—someone in Amantha's position would have surely known this. Amantha seems to take some comfort in the idea that she acted out of reflex and not out of fear. To Rau-Ru and his comrades, this would be a moot point. Is this a moot point to Warren?

In characterizing both Michele and Amantha as slave women who choose to stay with their master because of deep personal attachment, sexual desire, lack of virtue, Warren makes use of the long-held notions of the black female as a succubus, a seducer of innocent and vulnerable men who then become captives under their spell. Ironically, it is Miss Idell, former mistress to Amantha's father and Amantha's secret tormentor, who frankly points out the attraction some white men have for black women. She advises Amantha to not worry about telling her husband, Tobias, the truth about her race: "a little dash of the dark brown. [. . .] A lot of men like it, you'd be surprised" (290). Other than this very rare admission of the white male's attraction to the black female, *Band of Angels* focuses on the black female as a powerful seductress.

This attitude has its roots in the earliest years of contact between Europeans and Africans, as Deborah Gray White explains: "Unaccustomed to the requirements of a tropical climate, Europeans mistook seminudity for lewdness. Similarly, they misinterpreted African cultural traditions, so that polygamy was attributed to the Africans' uncontrolled lust."[90] Winthrop Jordan also writes extensively about this phenomenon, which extends back hundreds of years:

> By the eighteenth century a report on the sexual aggressiveness of Negro women was virtually *de rigueur* for the African commentator. By then, of course, with many Englishmen actively participating in the slave trade, there were pressures making for descriptions of "hot constitution'd Ladies" possessed of a "temper hot and lascivious, making no scruple to prostitute themselves to the *Europeans* for a very slender profit, so great is their inclination to white men." And surely it was the Negro women who were responsible for lapses from propriety: "If they can come to the Place the Man sleeps in, they lay themselves softly down by him, soon wake him, and use all their little Arts to move the darling Passion."[91]

Band of Angels substantiates the notion of the libidinous black female as sexual aggressor, and by doing so relieves Bond, and all others who sexually violate their female slaves, of any responsibility for their actions. Clearly in this text, as well as in prevailing popular mythology about the hypersexuality of black women, the women want it and, therefore, deserve it. In fact, the female slaves in *Band of Angels*, particularly the ones of mixed blood, are so lustful and desperate for their master's sexual attentions that they maintain a running competition between them, with one notable exception—the mammy figures.[92]

Amantha receives information about arrangements for and hierarchy of sexual slaves, which is based on age and color, through her first contact with Michele, who is "probably a quadroon." It appears, although the explanation has been given in French to Michele, that Bond has bought Amantha to displace Michele, who is about forty-five; another clue to Amantha of the precarious nature of her status. They size each other up: "Clearly, however, he was defining me and my condition; I caught the secret surprise on the woman's face [. . .]. [T]he eyes were [. . .] very steady in their gaze upon me" (91).

Elizabeth Fox-Genovese describes the dynamic of the relationships between women in the slaveholding household as being controlled by "the premier custodian of their own specific and different subordinations," and that "[w]omen were bound to each other [. . .] not in sisterhood, but by their specific and different relations to its master."[93] *Band of Angels* repeatedly exemplifies this dynamic. When the slave trader, Mr. Calloway, explains to Amantha that he must fatten her up for sale value, he defers to his mulatto Jillie, who clearly feels threatened by Amantha, for ratification of the market for voluptuousness. Possessiveness and desire for this crude slave trader almost brings Jillie to violence against what she views as her rival. This portion of the text, so graphic in its depiction of the sexually hungry black female, is worth presenting here at length:

> "Got to put some meat on yore bones. I don't sell niggers by the pound, I sell 'em by the lump, but a juicy lump shore fetches more'n a scrawny one. Ain't that so, Jillie?" With that he gave a commendatory whack to the young mulatto woman's near rump, at which attention she grinned and gave a slight upward hitch of the flattered part of the lump that was herself. "Yeah," he continued, "Jillie cost me plenty. But I wouldn't take nigh double right now. But you"—and he leaned over me, "you better eat the grub and git some meat on." [. . .] Jillie shut the door after him, then turned decisively back to me. She took the tray off my lap. "Starve, and be damned to you," she said. She set the tray down and leaned over me. "Git some meat on," she mimicked, "yeah, but you won't have nuthin lak this!" And she slapped herself on the rump, jiggling herself. "Yeah," she was saying, "he lak what I got—" And she slapped and jiggled, "Yeah, he laks somethin to really wrap round him, yeah—and ain't no good rollin them big eyes at him—yeah, I seen you roll 'em—but listen! [. . .] White ner no, I cut yore thote. [. . .] I'll tell you what you done. You

> try to make him take a shine on you and not sell you. But he sell you. Yeah, you think you whiter'n me, but you ain't, you jes nigger too. Yeah, and he gonna sell you, and some feller buy you, and what he do, what he den do?" She leaned at me, and asked quite calmly: "You know what he do to you, some feller?" [. . .] "Yeah, and I show you—nigger, and think you so white, yeah, and I show you." There she stood, swaying in her obscene pantomime, hands clutching and weaving the air, her red *tignon* slipping off her head to the floor, her hair coming loose, her face slick and damp in the rays of the gas jet. (80–81)

Is Jillie simply protecting her own interests by warning Amantha away from her master? Or, is this a classic representation of the highly sexed, seductive "Jezebel" black woman who is conscious of her sexual power? According to Fox-Genovese the "Jezebel"

> explicitly contradicted the image of Mammy and that of the lady as well, although, like that of Mammy and unlike that of the lady, it presented a woman isolated from the men of her own community. Jezebel lived free of the social constraints that surrounded the sexuality of white women. She thus legitimated the wanton behavior of white men by proclaiming black women to be lusty wenches in whom sexual impulse overwhelmed all restraint. The image eased the consciences of white men by suggesting that black women asked for the treatment they received.[94]

Fathoming Warren's intent here is difficult. True enough, as some critics point out, there were slave women who were seduced by the idea of special attention, and "the thoughts of silks and satins and jewelry lured such women." It is easy to hold these women to a standard of "virtuous" conduct if one does not consider that they lived in a social context that not only failed to acknowledge the very concept of virtue for them, but that was designed to destroy it. These women were trying to survive, and often currying the master's favor, or attempting to avoid disfavor, were part of a strategy for survival. There were negative consequences for these particular women, and far-reaching sexual consequences for black women in slavery in general:

> in order to ease the burdens of slavery, they made themselves available, they only fulfilled the prophecy of their lustfulness, which in turn made it more difficult for other black women to reject the overtures made by white men. While slave women became the easy prey of profligates, justification for their exploitation came from the lips of some of the South's leading statesmen. This was particularly true after Northern abolitionists questioned the moral health of Southern society, a society that degraded and exploited a class of its women and ignored the involvement of its male youth with women alleged by

> Southerners themselves to be immoral. Rather than fault themselves, some Southern spokesmen blamed black women.[95]

Realistically, how much power did slave women have to reject the overtures made by white men? These women were often, after their masters were through with them, replaced by other female slaves or white wives, or both, as is the case with Michele. Subsequently, many of them were sold out-of-sight/out-of-mind because they were an affront to the wives of the slaveholder, especially if they had had children by him.[96]

It is true that all Bond's relations with women are deeply troubled. He hates his mother; a pretentious hag in his memories of her. He actually never marries, and has revengeful "sex"/rape with his innocent, chaste white fiancée. He is brutal in the act, then dumps her, and she is forced to go into a convent. He admits to having wronged her, although he clearly does not see himself as the rapist he really is; but he is able to see somehow that what he did was wrong because she was white, beautiful, aristocratic and pious—and, she didn't like it. She likes it even less when he refuses to marry her, and these are the clues he apparently requires to help him see that he has done something wrong. He seems to relish relating this tale to Amantha:

> "I'll tell you this," he added after a little. "I did that girl a wrong. I did her what they say is the worst wrong you can do a nice, young, respectable, Catholic, priest-loving, beautiful, aristocratic Creole girl, and I did it to her the first chance. She was cold as ice, and suffering like a martyr. But me, I was cold, too. I did it in cold blood. I was cold as arithmetic, and I did it like I was doing sums. It was something it looked like I had to do, to wind up some business. It was like a revenge. But I don't know for what. She had never done anything to me. Then I told her I wasn't going to marry her. She went to a convent. She was that kind." (201)

This type of behavior makes it more than ironic that Bond is repeatedly referred to as having "kindness like a disease" (176); a strange kindness considering his history as an enslaver, his treatment of this innocent woman who had agreed to marry him, his lack of compassion for and patience with his mother, the appropriation of Michele and Amantha for sexual purposes and his capture and defilement of the African female cargo on the decks of his slave ship. In fact, his track record with women marks him deeply problematic at best, a misogynistic sociopath at worst.

Warren draws attention to the defilement of women within the slaveholding culture in general. Yet, Bond's treatment of women corresponds directly to the value allotted them, both as women and as human beings, by virtue of their placement on the color continuum. Their innocence and chastity or culpability and decadence are ratified on the basis of race. He understands that his treatment of his white fiancée was wrong. He has some vague sense of having taken something from both Michele and Amantha, but thinks that money and an offer of freedom when he is done with them will make it all right. Clearly, they do not suffer the same loss as his Creole fiancée; their virtue has a monetary equivalent. For the African women on his slave ship he has not even the most fleeting sense of pity or wrongdoing; the idea of feminine virtue being entirely incompatible with black African women. Although it is true that Bond's relations with all women are deeply troubled, this does not in any way make his treatment of his sexual slaves, including the African women on his ship, seem any less horrifying. His penchant for sexual violence against women finds an uncensurable outlet—the female slave. He may and does give free reign to his sexual impulses with impunity in a society and in a text that denies that these women are victims and that insists on their complicity with and desire for their masters.

The conduct of female slaves in *Band of Angels* is an affirmation of racial inferiority and degradation—a significant dimension of the rationalization for oppression. They must, as Jefferson would have it, be "removed beyond the reach of mixture."[97] There is no place in decent, white society for such beings other than enslavement.

Paternalism and the "Good" Master

"Southern paternalism," as Eugene Genovese puts it, "like every other paternalism, had little to do with Ole Massa's ostensible benevolence, kindness, and good cheer. It grew out of the necessity to discipline and morally justify a system of exploitation." A significant component of racism in the American slave system was the prevailing belief that black people lacked the capacity to govern themselves and to grow into independent maturity; therefore, it was not only justifiable and necessary but humane for them to be under the supervision of their superiors. Paternalism in slavery was said to be a kindness, a system of protective custody and nurturance of the weak, uncivilized and limited, a practical and compassionate response to black inferiority. Presumably, this paternalism ensured the well-being of the slaves, providing for their basic needs while denying them rights and responsibilities they were incapable of appreciating and managing. It was said to be a mutually beneficial arrangement that "defined the involuntary labor of the slaves as a legitimate return to their masters for protection and direction."[98]

Paternalism, considered a good thing by slave holders, is ultimately presented as a good but complicated thing in *Band of Angels*. In this text, God wills slavery and History (probably as an agent of God) dictates it. But prominent among the rationalizations for black enslavement is that black people are demonstrably inferior, and the southern white man simply does the best that he can given all with which he must contend. For the most part he is benevolent, a "good master" and man who has a heavy burden to bear, and rises to the occasion. It is the nature of the master's relationship with his slaves that determines goodness and decency. A good master in *Band of Angels* is one with paternalistic inclinations.

Goodness and decency are relative in this text, and are determined by the ostensible intent of the enslaver. The criteria that determine where a master may be ranked on the brutality scale are quite specific. Factors of goodness and decency include a willingness to accept the burden of mastership, concern for the well-being of inferior creatures and their level of material comfort, reluctance to beat or whip slaves except in extreme cases where it is deemed warranted (intransigence and disciplinary purposes) and the amount of pleasure derived from being an owner of human beings. These are the reasons that the likes of Aaron Starr and Hamish Bond may be considered kind and good masters. The fact that they are enslavers is irrelevant.

Amantha's father is a good master in that he is a "humane man" who "didn't believe in whipping. He took the view that, if you had to whip a nigger, the nigger wasn't worth keeping anyway," and "selling your people was against his principles" (17). This distinguishes him not only as a good master but as a good man with the best of intentions. Starr has affection for Amantha, his daughter by a slave woman. He looks after her and plays with her when she is a child, and sends her to Oberlin for an education when she is older. He is not in the habit of selling off his slaves; they may feel secure of their future on his plantation. Hamish Bond looks after Rau-Ru. He offers Rau-Ru and Amantha their freedom. He never whips them. His slaves jubilate upon his return to the plantation. There is every indication that Bond is considered a benevolent slaveholder who governs his properties and people mostly with a benign indifference, at least until the threat of insurrection, which becomes increasingly evident with the approach of the Yankees.

Bond's delusions about himself as a good enslaver may be a metaphor for the delusions of the slaveholding culture in general. He sets himself above the average slave owner. His superior management of his own slave ship gives him a sense of pride and comfort. He is, in his self-assessment, humane, organized, clean. He is proud that daily he hosed down the decks of his slave ship and never considers that he is, in fact, literally washing away evidence, white-washing the traces of his crime. He does not think of the horrors that awaited his human cargo at auction and afterward (188–189). Each near-admission of the wrong of slavetrading is undermined by the supposed complicity of the Africans themselves, as those horrific descriptions presented above of Africans misbehaving in Africa attest. The continual sparring and feint between notions of who is to blame and who isn't, dominate this text.

Warren makes an observable distinction between "good" and "bad" slave owners; moral relativism, circumstances and complexity being reasons, if not justifications, for what is a very sensitive issue for many who do not condemn, out of hand, everyone who participated in or benefited from slavery. Bond's explanation for the jubilation at any master's return is that the master is perceived as better than the overseer, who is "always a hellion," and also that he can fix things up. Their effusions and jubilation ratify for Bond, and for the reader, the notion that he is a good and appreciated master. The Negroes are where they belong and are doing what they were designed to do, things are as they should be, all is right with the world. Interestingly, the slaves have been given rum to celebrate the occasion of their master's return, which may explain their extreme response (140). But this scene raises the question apologists often ask about slavery: Can slavery be so bad if the slaves don't object?

Paternalism is a system that both promotes and is defined by "[s]outhern masculine conventions," ritualized, "displaced brutality" and violence. Presumably, in southern culture the "toleration of male violence responded to the perceived exigencies of governing a troublesome people," which also served to reinforce identification. It is an ideology fraught with contradiction. The paternalism in *Band of Angels* "invokes a specific metaphor of legitimate domination: the protective domination of the father over his family. The invocation of the metaphor does not guarantee the benevolence of those who exercise the domination, but it does signal a distinction between the principles that govern domestic relations—including relations with unfree laborers—and those that govern the polity."[99] The idea of legitimate domination is unquestioned in this text, and an uneasy stupefaction presides over the consciousness of Bond and others as they try to fathom the resistance or recalcitrance of slaves, the ungrateful wretches, who clearly do not accept their lot in life. The enslavers in this text are presented as fundamentally moral men in the grip of culture, tradition and the historical moment. Within these contexts, they are models of propriety. This point of view mirrors that of apologists who are comfortable with absolution on the basis of relativity and who advance the argument that the individual is simply a product of his or her time and culture. This position seems specious considering that many slaveholders themselves, including Washington and Jefferson, knew that slavery and their participation in it was immoral.[100]

Warren frequently juxtaposes some of the most dreadful aspects of slavery, such as the selling of human beings, with southern decency. Yes, there were decent white folk in slaveholding culture, *Band of Angels* repeatedly reminds the reader. The Sheriff who is responsible for turning over Aaron Starr's property to a creditor tries to make Amantha remember papers that will establish her free status, which he is certain must exist. Without attempting to look, Amantha knows that no such papers exist, and that her father has not seen to her future. Some of the mourners are outraged and saddened, and ask the creditor for time to raise the money to keep her from being sold, but he is intractable. This poignant and sentimental parting shot is indelibly engraved in Amantha's remembrance of white southern decency:

> the vision seized in my last backward glance, as our rig wheeled off down the drive: the great trees, the white gleam of the house beyond, as in shadow, the group of people under the trees in the foreground, a gentleman kindly assisting Aunt Sukie to rise, one lady with head bowed and hand pressed to her face as though weeping, or as though she could not bear the sight before her, another gentleman forward from the group of black-clad mourners, his right hand lifted after us in a gesture of command, his mouth open to utter a call. (62–63)

This is very interesting because the general "one drop" consensus meant that a person with any Negro blood, regardless of their phenotype, was considered black. That these people, especially in the slaveholding South, should be so upset that Amantha is treated as property is fantastical. Amantha was just one of many slaves in the same position—their response, although remotely possible, is contrary to custom and protocol.

The paternalistic impulse is so completely a part of the dominance hierarchy in slavocracy that even Amantha, because of her perceived "rank" by association with her master, has no trouble distinguishing herself from the Negro hordes and imagines herself as an agent for benevolence and an appropriate subject for adulation. However, although she is adept at playing the plantation mistress and revels in her superiority over the slaves, and particularly over her rival Rau-Ru, Amantha also suffers the psychological turbulence and ambivalence of the slave who must pretend to be a free person, but who is, in fact, obligated to be obedient and play a role in a drama scripted by the needs of the master. As James Justus argues: "When she is with Rau-Ru [. . .] she senses herself in his terms, as the slave who has been raised to a special status only by the grace of the master." But Rau-Ru, who has acquired insight about his true position as a slave favorite, makes it his business to spoil Amantha's illusions about her status, and serves as a reminder of what and who she really is—a piece of property purchased for sex—and that they actually have much in common:

> Although his manner is not insulting, his nominal respect is tempered by an unspoken assumption that they are equals and that their equality is relative to Bond's pleasure. Both Amantha and Rau-Ru finally come to hate Bond not because he is a cruel master but because he is an indulgent one whose liberality further blurs the meaning of slavery and freedom. Framing precise definitions of these terms, which would thereby define her self, is Amantha's lifelong ambition and the source of her frustration.[101]

Yet, like Bond, Amantha appears to need the adulation of her social inferiors to shore up her sense of self and make palatable her domination of the slaves; an indication that on some level Warren is aware of the fragile and flawed nature of her self- righteousness. As plantation mistress Amantha easily conforms to the elitist role of one who enjoys her special status and power over her inferiors. Fox-Genovese, in her indictment of white females in the slaveholding culture, writes:

> Slaveholding women were elitist and racist. With some pain I am compelled to express my considered opinion that, in some essential respects, they were more crudely racist than their men. [. . .] Life would be easier if we could dismiss them as oppressive tyrants or exonerate them as themselves victims of an oppressive system. We cannot. By class and race, they were highly privileged ladies who reveled in their privilege [. . .]. They were women who owned [. . .] slaves in a world that increasingly recognized slavery as a moral evil and a political danger.[102]

But Amantha's easy adjustment to the role of plantation mistress has another dimension; she attempts to recapture her "white" identity through the pretense that she is entitled to play this role.

In *Band of Angels* slaves are the beneficiaries of paternalism, not the victims of it. The insular world of *Pointe du Loup* seduces Amantha and she feels guilty because she doesn't want the peaceful life there interrupted, even if it means the continued enslavement of "all those black men," who in her mind are away in distant places and not at *Pointe du Loup* "where this easy rule of kindness like a disease did not prevail" (150). It doesn't register with Amantha that all the black people at *Pointe du Loup*, including herself, are not free either. The fact that they are all taken care of with "kindness" appears to be a ratification of the benignity of the institution.

But, realistically, loyalty is always problematized by dependency and slavery. "The slaves impaled their masters on the central point of slaveholding hegemonic ideology—the dependency relationship." Bond is mightily invested, as are many slaveholders, in believing that the slaves adore him, and he truly believes that at least, by comparison, he is a good master—all the more reason for his complete incomprehension and bewilderment at the knowledge that Rau-Ru hates him even though he has raised him as a son and probably loves him. Bond tries to explain his own goodness to Amantha: "'I've been respectable a long time. I've owned a lot of niggers. [. . .] I've always tried to treat them fair. [. . .] None of 'em ever hated me. [. . .] Except,' he said, 'for Rau-Ru. [. . .] You're right, he was the one shot at me. And he had least reason. [. . .] And I raised him the best I could. Like a son. I swear it. [. . .] Yeah, I reckon that's why he hated me'" (199–200).

It may be possible that Warren is attempting to show the fallacies and failings of paternalism, but he succeeds in demonstrating the ingratitude of the slaves. The rejection of the father/son bond by slaves is a result of the weight of history brought to bear on such relationships. As Justus notes:

> Metaphorically it is related to "paternalism," the attitude that turns the pejorative master-slave arrangement into an honorific father-child relationship. By extension, the father is also generalized as the Past, as History. Amantha feels raped by History, which is another way of saying she has been ill-used by her father as an object of little worth. And, by further extension, the sins of the father are linked to philosophical enslavement of the will, a pietistic doctrine that drains the present generation of real purpose.[103]

The rejection is a natural by-product of a relationship based on dominance; "paternalism rested precisely on inequality. The masters desperately needed the gratitude of their slaves in order to define themselves as moral human beings. The slaves, by withholding it drove a dagger into their masters' self-image."[104] Extreme and unwholesome complications and confusions arise from the need of masters to feel loved by their property.

The paternalistic dimension of slavery is fully embodied in the Bond/Rau-Ru relationship. Rau-Ru is known as Bond's "free nigger," and because of his favored status with Bond enjoys special consideration and treatment throughout the community. His mobility, material comforts and obvious genuine regard for Bond appear to be evidence, in this text, of how slavery can be beneficial to some. Yet, as Genovese argues,

> [i]nherent in this doctrine were dangerously deceptive ideas of "gratitude," "loyalty," and "family." Inherent also was an intimacy that turned every act of impudence and insubordination—every act of unsanctioned self-assertion—into an act of treason and disloyalty, for by repudiating the principle of sub-

> mission it struck at the heart of the master's moral self-justification and therefore at his self-esteem. Nothing else, apart from personal idiosyncrasy, can explain the ferocity and cruelty of masters who normally appeared kind and even indulgent.[105]

Interestingly, Amantha feels left out and jealous of what she perceives as the father/son relationship between Bond and Rau-Ru, but on reflection realizes that Rau-Ru is, what? "[*T*]*he favorite slave.*" She tries to sort out and understand what words mean, how they have changed and become charged with new meaning under her yet unfamiliar circumstances of enslavement:

> Then he had stepped toward Hamish Bond, had seized his right hand, bowed over it, and to my astonishment, had kissed it. No, that wasn't what he did, I suddenly realized. He had touched his brow to the back of the hand. He straightened up, and Hamish Bond grabbed him by the right shoulder—this with Hamish Bond's left hand—and with his right hand slapped Rau-Ru's left shoulder in the immemorial gesture of fatherly affection. [. . .] And all at once I felt cut off, outside, displaced. I was not, after all, the favorite. (119)

The peculiarities of the ranking system in enslavement are not yet entirely comprehensible to her. Amantha wonders what will be the appropriate way to introduce her—as a slave, as a, what? It is a delicate situation, one of which both Rau-Ru and Bond are also conscious.

Rau-Ru is also a *k'la*—a trusted slave who is confidant. Bond describes the *k'la* as something even closer than a brother or a son; he is alter ego, part of yourself. This "special slave [. . .] the one you tell your secrets to" (200) is forced to play this role. They do not choose, but have their lives appropriated for what is perhaps one of the most difficult and demeaning aspects of enslavement and servitude, most often a role played by house slaves: forced personal intimacy and the pretense of friendship with someone who owns you, or to whom you are beholden for your life or livelihood.

The *k'la* have been known to lay down and die when their masters die, and their intimacy is considered so binding and absolute that they are sometimes killed when the master dies. Clearly, the *k'la* is not considered a separate being in his own right, but merely an extension of the master's will and even consciousness. He is killed, perhaps, because the master must be buried whole, and the *k'la*'s existence is not only indistinguishable from that of the master, but is otherwise irrelevant. Perhaps more important, he may be killed because he is not trusted by blacks or whites and there is no place for him in the world without his master. Rau-Ru may be the adopted "son" and the *k'la* of Bond, but he is also most certainly a servant and slave because he has no choice in the matter;

everything he is and does is at Bond's pleasure. He does not consent to enslavement. His rebellion against and rejection of Bond is the only way he can claim his own life and rewrite his identity. Nevertheless, in this text the *k'la*'s ingratitude and disloyalty to someone who saved his life and treated him well becomes evidence of moral inferiority and ultimately supports the idea of the moral superiority of his master.

In some ways Warren effectively demonstrates that the bogus father/son relationship captures the illusory nature of an arrangement in which certain liberties may be parceled out by the masters to suit their own needs and underscores the "equality" pretended to by the owners. Yet, situations in this text that show how hierarchy and rules govern spatiality between classes and races are also examples of the easy benevolence and unself-conscious goodwill of the masters. These situations were controlled and manipulated by those with the power to do so and could cause chaos, frustration and rage in the mind of the unfree person, such as in the case with Rau-Ru. For example,

> [Rau-Ru] would sit long hours with Hamish Bond in the study at some business. (Unlike Jimmee, or the other slaves, when he appeared before his master, he was always invited to sit. And I recall now that they used to say that Jefferson Davis, at his place up in Mississippi, had his Isaiah Montgomery sit with him.)

Jefferson Davis did not sit with Isaiah Montgomery; he "*had his* Isaiah Montgomery sit with him" (120, my emphasis). In other words, "his" property was *made* (forced) to sit with him—an important distinction. Amantha (Warren?) naïvely imagines the appearance of relaxed social propriety in these circumstances to be one of reciprocity, honor and affection bestowed on the slave. She is incapable of apprehending subtext, the unspoken but clearly understood fiat that obligated the servant to sit with the master for hours. Could he say "no"?

Bond's repeated characterization as "kind" is a challenge to work through, both in the text and its criticism. How may one reconcile the notion of kindness with someone who has a history such as Bond's with women and slaves? Perhaps the key is Rau-Ru, who hates Bond, despite his "kindness." He comes to understand the nature of Bond's paternalism and that his selectivity in dispensing favor is a trap that disguises a true state of bondage; it is a state that also undermines the suffering of the other slaves. This understanding becomes his saving grace and allows him to reclaim himself and his life. Rau-Ru attempts to enlighten Amantha about the role she plays in this revelation and encourages her to admit the contradictions she feels for Bond because of his "kindness." She is unable to do so (270–271). Ultimately, the reader may be unable to do so. The continual buttressing of kindness and paternalism in this text reinforces the idea that it is an inherent and necessary part of the infrastructure of slaveholding culture.

Warren's portrayal of southern paternalism in *Band of Angels* is decidedly defensive. The South may be paternalistic, but it is meant for good. On the other hand, Warren casts the North as corrupt and hypocritical, and in no position to judge something about which it knows little. The text begs the question: Which is worse?

Enslavers are criticized by Amantha's schoolmates at Oberlin and she, as the representative of "the fascinating evil from below the Ohio River," is forced to judge her father according to their principles and culture. She is also a beneficiary of "black sweat" (29). But the abolitionists are sanctimonious and deceptive, and hide behind religion while they do their dirty deeds. The pious northerner Seth is a manipulator and meddler, and tries to rape Amantha when he finds she is a Negro. A certain Mr. Taylor, postmaster, "a godly man," "president of the Seventh Commandment Association, editor of the *Oberlin Evangelist*, and a stout crusader for the strictest laws against libidinousness" (46), gets his servant girl pregnant and has an abortion performed on her. Taylor, the pillar of abolitionist society, steals money both from his job at the Post Office and from the operating money for the *Evangelist*, and engineers the lynching of a young man. Worst of all is the behavior of the Federal troops, which include some black troops:

> When Federal troops—Connecticut—stripped black men of the uniform on the streets of New Orleans. When at Ship Island the Federal gunboat *Jackson* fired directly into the black troops it was sent to support. When the Negroes aimed to take over the country, it was theirs. When Federal troops scoured the country—black troops, sometimes—to seize Negroes for conscription, and the Negroes ran for the woods and swamps, and they shot them like beasts for running. When they broke contracts and the crops rotted in the field. When the lessees of confiscated land—men come down to make fortunes—drove off the old, the children, the sick, not to feed them. When the scum and adventurers came, when they sold them the red-white-and-blue sticks to set in the ground and claim land. (249)

It would seem that the North does not do well by its Negroes.

Northerners, even when well-meaning, are also naïve, delusional and hypocritical about the prospects of uplifting the degraded and deprived Negroes. The dedication and hard work of the northerners and abolitionists to advance the causes of slaves and former slaves are to no avail. Amantha's white husband, Tobias Sears, is, presumably, in a unique position to assess the worthiness and prognosis for Negro improvement because he had commanded the Negro Corps in the army, worked for the Freedman's Bureau after the war, and was married to a woman who was the child of a slave. Tobias is, in the end, a hypocrite and a fraud who denounces blacks as a lost cause, and fools those who intercede on their behalf. After years of effort, Tobias feels nothing but bitterness, race hatred and disgust at himself for having once believed in the advancement of black people. In the end, Negroes are a disappointment.

Tobias chastises Amantha for paying the most "foul-smelling old coon the All-Father ever let live" when he had not done the work for which he was hired: "'Yes,' he [Tobias] was saying, 'you have to pay that violet-scented son of Ethiope and then get down on your knees and beg him. It was for this we bled and died. Hooray for William Lloyd Garrison, Harriet Beecher Stowe, Abe Lincoln and me'" (357). Tobias repudiates "niggers," aligning himself finally and totally with whiteness. Blood wins out; racial solidarity is all. He begins to drink, and lets fly the casual use of the word "nigger" as he pleases (365–366, 368). His greatest source of shame is that he ends up a "Brother to coons" (373); a fitting comeuppance for his hypocrisy and his stupidity in believing that blacks were worth saving in the first place. According to this text, in comparison to the deceitfulness of the North, southern slaveholding culture is, at least, open and honest about what it is doing.

By explicitly showcasing the moral failings of the North, Warren makes clear the rationale white southerners use in defending their right to manage their own affairs, race-related or not, without interference from the outside—be it northern or federal government. That Tobias Sears comes to the bitter realization that Negroes are not worth the trouble is evidence that outsiders are simply slow to figure out what the South has always understood: Black people are both different and inferior. Racial separation and black subjugation not only make sense, but are necessary.

These guiding principles of the slaveholding South survived through the mid-twentieth century. The observable regret over the failure of paternalistic ideology to elevate the miserable and ungrateful Negroes in *Band of Angels*, and the corresponding inability of the resisters to desegregation and black civil rights in the 1950s, are related by the impulse to both subordinate and control those people considered to be inherently inferior, by any means necessary.

After slavery, there was no further need for the rationalizations of paternalism. Blacks who were struggling for security and autonomy were increasingly considered competition for jobs, land and other resources and were, as a result, perceived as a threat. The conceptualization of them as helpless children fell away, but the idea of their inferiority did not. The belief that one might behave in almost any fashion toward these inferiors and remain a decent and moral human being survived the emancipation of the slaves and continued to gather strength, momentum and conviction through the twentieth century as white southerners showed resourcefulness and innovation in establishing new ways of exploitation and abuse.

It is possible that Warren, considering his social and political sensibilities in the 1950s, intended the deterioration of the *Pointe du Loup* household as the harbinger of the demise of a way of life—a metaphor for the falling apart of the nation. The recalcitrant, inscrutable and silent slaves and the deterioration of *Pointe du Loup* not only mark the end of an era, but also demonstrate and predict the probable fate of an entire nation if it does not come to terms with the race-slavery question. When things begin to really get out of hand, Bond orders a whipping, something unheard of at *Pointe du Loup*, and creates a spectacle by making all the slaves watch. His paternalistic practices cease, and the facade of his "kindness" begins to crack and fall away in proportion to his way of life being threatened. With each punishment he is "forced" to administer in the face of growing insurgency, the self-delusions become more apparent. Paradise fades away as the servants get sloppy in their tasks—a true indicator of approaching calamity. The jollity of the slaves on Saturday night changes; it doesn't last as long, and there is complete silence afterwards as though something is brewing:

> *It was the small things that began to go wrong at first.* They were so small that you scarcely noticed them, like the scorched meal [. . .] things like the broken dish, the tracked-in mud in the hall left on the floor, the tardiness when the horn blew for tumble-up time, the horses half-curried, the jollification fading away early on Saturday night, the sudden silence after the singing and juba.
>
> *Bigger things began to go wrong.* [. . .] Hamish was sure one of his horses was being run at night, off to God knew where and for what. (165, my emphases)

The language in this passage invokes the climate of the 1950s and 1960s in the South; Negroes are acting up and are out of control. For whites, the threat of paradise fading away also occurs in the 1950s and "things begin to go wrong" (165), particularly for southerners who fear the changes demanded by the civil rights movement as the nation once again attempts, in a major way, to come to terms with the race question. The civil rights movement, like the Civil War a hundred years earlier, marked the end of an era; both periods were similarly distinguished by the growing dissatisfaction of black people with the status quo and the fierce resistance of whites.

One passage in particular stresses the similitude of the two periods, which may be read as metaphor: "The new hands bought from Charles didn't seem to learn anything, despite all Hamish could do. One of them died. He just lay on his back and kept looking up at the rafters of the infirmary and died" (165). Literally and figuratively, a black man gives up enslavement in exchange for freedom (death), which corresponds with the civil rights workers who put themselves at great risk to give up a status of forced subservience and social inferiority for freedom (equality).

"An Innocent Victim of a Cosmic Conspiracy"[106]

Warren repeatedly demonstrates his awareness of the need for both reconciliation and resolution in sources as varied as his essays on fiction, his works of fiction and poetry and in the epigraph that opens *Band of Angels*. He attests that catharsis occurs in the reader through the resolution of conflict and acknowledges that we actually crave resolution: "we wait in suspense to learn how things will come out [. . .] not only about what will happen, but even more about what the event will mean"; and that resolution of the conflict of the story creates an "exhilarating sense of freedom." In fact, he even goes so far as to claim that "good fiction"[107] offers reconciliation. Reconciliation and resolution in *Band of Angels*, if in fact there is even such a thing, makes this position seem extremely ironic.

In recalling the true story that inspired him to write *Band of Angels*, Warren said that "what made the story stick in [my] mind for some years was the questions it did not answer. This affectionate father, who had done so much for the happiness of his children, who certainly had never profitted and had no intention of profitting from ownership—why had he not set them legally free? A stroke of the pen would have done it." Joseph Blotner, who writes that "Warren had determined to write a book that would answer these questions," believes that this mission was accomplished and that the story has a "happy ending." He holds that "[t]he donnée of the book—why had Amantha Starr's loving father not provided papers freeing her?—drove the plot, and the question was answered in the novel's last pages."[108] But, was it really?

Warren sincerely grapples with this problem, but his conclusions seem more the product of generous, wishful thinking on behalf of the men who fathered children by their slaves (a common practice) than anything else. Amantha's father's failure to provide for her in his will is both comprehensible and predictable within the context of slavery. It was necessary for the white southerner who fathered children by his slaves to deny any wrongdoing so that he could maintain a sense of being a good and Christian person who was faithful to his culture and heritage. Winthrop Jordan explains that for the white slaveholder who impregnated his slaves

> [i]nterracial propagation was a constant reproach that he was failing to be true to himself. Sexual intimacy strikingly symbolized a union he wished to avoid. If he could not restrain his sexual nature, he could at least reject its fruits and thus solace himself that he had done no harm. Perhaps he sensed as well that continued racial intermixture would eventually undermine the logic of the racial slavery upon which his society was based. For the separation of slaves from free men depended on a clear demarcation of the races, and the presence of mulattoes blurred this essential distinction. Accordingly he made every effort to nullify the effects of racial intermixture. By classifying the mulatto as a Negro he was in effect denying that intermixture had occurred at all.[109]

Band of Angels suggests that the neglect of an affectionate white father of slave children to free them or give them some legal protection in the event of his death, may be attributed to a number of reasons having nothing to do with denial. It is hard to imagine that situations such as these were simply oversights, such as is assumed in the case of Aaron and Amantha Starr. Such a man as Starr would have to know the society in which he lived and his daughter's status in it. Although Aaron Starr pampers and spoils Amantha as a child and does not deny her relationship to him, he could not bring himself to do the one thing that would provide protection for her, because it would be an official declaration and proof of his failure to "restrain his sexual nature." His inability to reconcile his responsibility toward Amantha with his need to deny that he had violated standards of decency, or perhaps even committed a moral crime, left Amantha completely vulnerable—so strong is the desire in enslavers to deny personal responsibility and wrongdoing in order to feel like a decent human being; so strong is the desire in this text to make such a position understandable.

In an effort to absolve if not explain away Aaron Starr's conduct, Warren has Amantha reconcile her father's neglect and the resulting trauma she experiences in her life with her memories of the man she had actually known, and she decides that he did love her. In order to reach this conclusion, she must imagine and rationalize what the reasons must have been for his failure to provide protection for her after his death: he was not expecting to die so soon, he was afraid to hurt her with the truth, and so forth. By doing this, the disinherited, unacknowledged child is able to make peace with his memory. In the end she determines, "No, he hadn't betrayed me" (374), and because of the catharsis accompanying this revelation can believe that there is nothing to forgive; he had, after all, done nothing wrong.

Forrest Robinson argues that Warren refuses to acknowledge southern responsibility for the past because, ultimately, he denies any wrongdoing. He writes:

> The crime is ours, but it is not ours alone, and it is not our fault. Warren arrived at this paradoxical position, I have argued, because he could neither fully deny nor fully accept the burden of his own Southern past. He made peace with that past, if peace it really was, by continually and variously accepting and denying responsibility for it. His stance was not unlike the one he ascribed to Jefferson Davis, who "would accept no pardon" for the crimes laid by Yankees at his door; "for pardon could be construed to imply wrongdoing and wrongdoing was what, in honor and principle, he denied."[110]

At one point in the story Amantha, upset at Rau-Ru's apparent lack of gratitude, denigrates him to her husband, but Tobias explains that he understands Rau-Ru and doesn't expect or want gratitude; he works for reasons other than to receive the gratitude of those he helps. The point, he says, is "to be able to live with oneself" (272). This simple statement helps Amantha begin to heal from the trauma and confusion of her life, even if it does not help her to reconcile racial identity conflicts. In fact, she never comes to terms with her racial heritage, and can find peace only in denial and subterfuge. Finally, she manages to live with herself without torment; not with forgiveness and expiation for those who had wronged her, but by denying that they had, indeed, wronged her. Instead, she forgives herself:

> *To live with oneself:* The words seemed, in a strange, bright way, to be healing a wound, a wound in me. Then I saw them like a bright miraculous unguent laid over the weals and humped, corded scars of the black back. As soon as it was laid on, the scars were gone, simply gone. The back was there with its unmarked sheen and molded musculature. I felt purified somehow, forgiven. (272–273)

In one symbolic self-blaming, self-reflexive gesture, "*To live with oneself,*" Amantha, a victim of slavery, manages to erase the material evidence of enslavement and the suffering of slaves by imagining the disappearance of whipping scars on a black back.

In an interview that he conducted with himself some twenty-five years after *Band of Angels* was written, Warren wrote the following:

> A. I don't think the problem is to learn to live with the Negro.
> Q. What is it then?
> A. It is to learn *to live with ourselves.*
> Q. What do you mean?
> A. I don't think you can live with yourself when you are humiliating the man next to you.[111]

Warren is a complex man, and the evolution of his thinking about race and race relations is an indication of that.

Warren felt relief when he left the South to visit or to live in other places. He said: "I know what the Southerner feels, going out of the South, the relief, the expanding vistas. . . . But I know what the relief really is. It is the relief from responsibility . . . the flight from the reality you were born to."[112] It has been suggested that "years away from the South [. . .] intensified Warren's attachment to other motives of the Agrarians, most profoundly a subtle but pervasive fear on their part of their personal displacement in the South, of their becoming rootless, or placeless, in short, exiles in their own land." He may "have been affected by emotions associated with *depaysement*, or the yearning for a lost homeland."[113] But, ultimately, it is the "yearning for a lost homeland," the idealized planter aristocracy culture that vanished with the emancipation of the slaves, that presides incontrovertibly over this narrative.

If one charts Warren's ideas, from his early contribution to the Southern Agrarian manifesto, *I'll Take My Stand* (1930), with its commitment to white, conservative southern values and traditions, including segregation; to *Segregation: The Inner Conflict in the South* (1956), in which he "figures prominently [. . .] as a narrator and character who dramatizes his own moral struggle, and the South's, in the early days of the civil rights movement" and that "depicts a growing dynamic tension between past and present, and the desire to preserve the heritage of the past weighed against the moral imperative of the need for change and justice in the present"; to *Who Speaks for the Negro?* (1965), in which Warren grapples with "the tension between pragmatism and idealism, free will and determinism; the meaning of identity, the individual in the modern world, the burden of history and the future of American democracy"[114] one can see an attempt at resolution and reconciliation of deeply held values rooted in the traditions and culture of the South, with opposing ideals that affirm the humanity and equality of black people. The tension created by this conflict of conscience resonates in *Band of Angels.* I am in agreement with Christopher Metress who writes that, finally, Warren became "too unreconstructed for the liberals, too reconstructed for the conservatives."[115]

There is considerable evidence that Warren was ultimately successful in resolving much of what had clearly been a moral dilemma for him—the race question—by his death in 1989. But we must take him at his word, when assessing the text that he wrote in 1955, that "[t]he style of a writer represents his stance [. . .] toward the subject of his story" and that fiction is an "imaginative enactment [. . .] [that] conform[s] to our deep needs."[116] It may be true that this story is told through a narrator almost universally considered to be unequal to the task, even by Warren himself, who admitted that "[t]here's not enough richness and depth in the experience of the narrator—at least, it isn't brought out." I agree with Warren that "it isn't brought out."[117]

That he could have written a book in which the protagonist, the narrator no less, is subjected to lies and betrayal about who and what she is from her father, enslavement and rape at the hands of her owner, abandonment and betrayal from her husband and so on and make the claim that the problem is that "there is not enough richness and depth in the experience of the narrator" is very revealing about Warren's inability, at this stage in his thinking about race, and perhaps about women, and certainly about black women in particular, to fully grasp the *significance* of Amantha's experience. It reveals that Warren was unable to fully understand the psychological and emotional consequences of her experience; to fully understand the devastating and far-reaching consequences of slavery not only for all black people, but for the nation as well; to fully understand the consequences of racism for the racist.[118] The narrative execution of the white racialist mindset in *Band of Angels* is absolute; this Warren does effectively, whether deliberately or not. But "Warren's failure lies in [. . .] allowing Manty to set the stage for a story he is unwilling or unable to tell."[119] Ultimately, the text must stand on its own merits; as readers we can only deal with what we have before us, not with what might have been. As it stands, Amantha as a character often upholds, and as a narrator delivers, the mythologies that defend and even celebrate the slaveholding culture and the consignment of people of African descent to enslavement by virtue of their inferiority.

In the end, it is Warren's unself-conscious portrayal of Amantha's treatment of her own servants, as a free, married "white" woman during and after the war, that ultimately ratifies the presumption of white superiority and the appropriate place for Negroes in American society. She feels resentment at having to make and serve coffee to her husband and Lt. Jones (formerly Rau-Ru), because her servant Mathilda, a former slave, is "off duty by this hour" (272). There is a beginning and ending to Mathilda's workday, as well as on the demands made of her; she has time and a life of her own. Times are changing. Amantha performs this small task "quite calmly" (272), but clearly with reluctance not only because it is servants' work, but with resentment because she has to serve Rau-Ru.

The point here is subtle but clear; the world is apparently out of joint when a "white" woman must serve a black man. Amantha, the former slave and now married "white" employer, is acutely sensitive to and feels diminished by anything she must do because a servant is not available, even something as mundane as answering her own door. She feels magnanimous in "giving the servants freedom from noon until the next morning" on Saturdays, but bristles with offense when Seth Parton, a former friend from Oberlin, comes to visit on one of these days and "stepped across the threshold, ignoring me as though I were a flunky" (282).

In a later incident, after being absent for days without letting anyone know where she is, Amantha stops at home in a torn and filthy condition. The black cook, who is shocked to see her, tries to comfort her and pass along information about Tobias. Amantha is characteristically rude to the cook at first, angry that her servant has stepped out of her place to question her presence there. She mistakenly thinks that the cook is signifying something about her status, and "rejoin[s] tartly, 'why not?' As though defending [her] right to be here at all" (335). She casually mentions that the cook has a black face, apparently affirming a qualification for her occupation and station in life.

Interestingly, Warren may have constructed an unconscious, self-reflexive gesture made by Amantha, which may be evidence of some level of consciousness about the wrongness of dominance hierarchy in her society and her "stolen" place in it by virtue of physical approximation of "whiteness." In spite of her sense of superiority over both slaves and servants, Amantha fears and dreads their judgment of her. When Tobias needs to convalesce and Amantha must move, she pays the servants well and dismisses them. They took their secret assessments of her and "whatever knowledge they had of [her and] sunk without a trace into the dark, teeming tide of their lives" (337).

One of the greatest fears for the slaveholder was that there would be divine retribution for the enslavement and oppression of black people—as Thomas Jefferson wrote in *The Notes on the State of Virginia:* "I tremble for my country when I reflect that God is just."[120] Is Amantha's wish, then, posited as the ultimate wish for white American society—that those who were consigned to slave and serve would simply go away and "s[i]nk without a trace into the dark"? (337). A dream of repatriation, as Jefferson and many others held, perhaps? Is there some form of remuneration or even magic that would make it possible to quietly dismiss both the slaves and the secrets of the past?

Perhaps Warren intended to write a novel about the South and the effects of slavery that was balanced, realistic and progressive. This would mean, of course, that all the slaveholders could not be evil, all the northerners morally fastidious, all the slaves virtuous, all the white women paragons of impropriety and unattractive and all the black women beautiful and chaste. No one would expect this or would want to read it. *Band of Angels* does exhibit considerable sensitivity in some regards to the experience and realities of those who are enslaved, such as in the case of the dejected elderly mammy figure Aunt Sukie, the rage felt by Rau-Ru at the dubious nature of his relationship with his master and, to some extent, the disgust and terror experienced by the young Amantha when she is raped by her master.

But, Warren also systematically divests enslavement of its sting, to put it mildly, and invests the slaveholders and their culture with an almost unassailable dignity and rightness. These are the impressions that resonate and endure most vividly in *Band of Angels*. Warren plays fast and loose with history, manipulating it to make southern (but not northern) white people, at the least, as much victims as are blacks in the slaveholding culture.

In 1961 Warren wrote about the southerners' persistence, which he had come to recognize as a failing, in seeing themselves and their history as "guiltless [. . .] [and] innocent victim[s] of a cosmic conspiracy." Ironically, in *Band of Angels* Warren makes the white slaveholder "an innocent victim of a cosmic conspiracy"[121] in that he both overturns the historical and anecdotal evidence of slavery by using the slave narrative technique to tell the story and structures the narrative in such a way as to elicit empathy, if not sympathy, for paternalism and slaveholding ideology. He details the barbarism of blacks in Africa and emphasizes crude, uncivilized, disloyal and licentious behavior in America. He spreads the blame for slavery between History and God, and even the enslaved themselves. He frames Amantha's initiation into sexuality at the hands of a black slave when she is a child with her willing, though confused, consent—therefore, she had already lost some of her innocence when she was sold into slavery. Of course, such a thing was possible, but such initiations were customarily the province of a white male who had power over the female slave. He makes the slaveholder, Bond, the victim of lynching by blacks—the absurdity of this at a time in which the lynching of black people was recreational and also functioned as an outlet for racial hatred.

Warren asserts that fiction gives us the "pleasure of entering worlds we do not know and of experimenting with experiences which we deeply crave," and that it "can give us pleasure without any of the painful consequences, for there is no price tag on the magic world of imaginative enactment."[122] Warren may have been experimenting with experiences for which he deeply craved a deeper understanding, thus the reason for his choice of narrator. Considering his stance on race when the novel was written, this makes some sense. His foray into the ideologies that underpin white notions of black enslavement and servitude may have also been intended to shed some light on the injustice and obsolescence of this thinking. By exposing, in *Band of Angels*, the white racialist mindset that distorts the facts of history and disregards standards for ethical and moral behavior toward black people in order to accommodate social policy based on greed and fear, Warren makes clear, deliberately or not, the doctrine of racial hatred to which he was exposed as a young person and that continued as a challenge for him; a doctrine that fatally shaped the habits of mind of white racists, and that continued to stoke the fires of racial fanaticism in the South in the 1950s.

Still, we do not have the luxury, as readers or as a nation, to use Warren's own words, of "[getting] off scot-free with something which we, or society, would never permit in real life." A fiction that undermines and distorts the exploitation, degradation and even annihilation of a people contributes to very "painful consequences"—the perpetuation of an ideology that makes the oppression comprehensible and acceptable in the first place. The "price tag" for such an "imaginative enactment"[123] is no less than the division of a nation grounded in the rationalizations and denial of one group, and the frustrations and rage of another.

CHAPTER 3

A WASHERWOMAN WREAKS HAVOC

Moral Reckoning and the "National Soul" in E. L. Doctorow's Ragtime

All day long I'm bustin' suds
Gee my hands are tired
Washin' out these dirty duds . . .
Sorry I do washin' just to make my livelihood
Cause the washwoman life it ain't a bit of good.
Rather be a scullian, cookin' in some white folks yard.

—Bessie Smith

Testifying before a Senate committee, the American banker J. P. Morgan warned, "If you destroy the leisure class, you destroy civilization." Asked later by reporters to identify the leisure class, he said, "All those who can afford to hire a maid."

—John Kenneth Galbraith

Go forth into the streets where the rich dwell, before the palaces of your dominators . . . and make them tremble.

—Emma Goldman[1]

WRITING IN THE HISTORICAL BLANKS

Why would E. L. Doctorow choose a Negro washerwoman as the means for explicating the national temper and the values of a society? A common notion about most of the characters in *Ragtime* is that "Doctorow's figures are essentially passive units impinged upon by social and economic forces,"[2] and that he uses historical personages to examine "the impact of large historical forces on the lives of common people."[3] Undoubtedly, but *Ragtime* does much more than this. A significant aspect of this text is that large historical forces and ordinary people are symbiotic and have a reciprocal, if not necessarily equal, contingency. Doctorow states in "The Beliefs of Writers" that "[h]igh seriousness in literature is attached to the belief in the moral immensity of the single soul."[4] *Ragtime* examines and even celebrates the potentialities of ordinary people and, in particular, the solitary person on large historical forces—among these people the washerwoman and domestic servant, Sarah. It is true that these individuals are buffeted about by external forces they cannot control, but even within such a context some are resourceful and resolute and act in ways that accommodate their own lives, sensibilities and agenda. These seemingly powerless individuals, such as Sarah, become forces that are ignored at the peril of an entire society. They are, at the least, the means by which suppressed social and political issues are brought to light, are sometimes able to effect change or even progress and quite often create havoc and anarchy in the face of denial or resistance.

One cannot possibly underestimate or understate the significance of metaphor and symbolism in *Ragtime*. There is scarcely a person, place, thing or action that does not conjure up multiple and complex layers of meaning. Each of the characters is a representation and a critique of a particular "type" of person and mode of thinking; this is most likely the reason Doctorow does not give names to the upper-middle-class white family's characters who are referred to only by their position in the family, such as "Mother" and "Younger Brother." Doctorow situates this family in New Rochelle as representative of the economically successful class, and also uses its dissolution, metamorphosis and transmutation as a way to think about America as a nation in progress; a society struggling to come of age. It is, in the beginning of the tale, a family in which each person knows and plays a traditional, predictable role. It is a family seemingly untouched by and uninterested in the problems outside its world of carefully manicured lawns, bay windows and striped awnings.

Briefly, the story is this: The mother in an affluent white family in a suburb of New York discovers a live Negro baby buried in her garden. She takes responsibility for the care and convalescence of both the mother, Sarah, a young washerwoman in the neighborhood who has become emotionally ill from the experience, and the child. The baby's father, a professional musician, Coalhouse Walker, Jr., shows up and begins to court the resistant Sarah, a process that takes many weeks of patience and perseverance. Upon leaving the family's house one day, Coalhouse is harassed by the local volunteer fire department and not allowed to pass, and his beautiful new automobile is vandalized and then desecrated with human excrement. Coalhouse demands justice from the local authorities, without success. Knowing that he will not marry her until the matter is resolved, Sarah attempts to intercede by approaching a political candidate, is mistaken for a threat and killed. Sick with grief, Coalhouse's determination to get justice—restitution of his car and punishment of the offenders—turns into a fatal obsession; he takes matters into his own hands. On one terrible night of retribution, Coalhouse and his friends attack the fire department and several people are killed. He holds J. P. Morgan's library hostage in New York and makes his demands. The city is at a standstill and a nation looks on while negotiations are conducted. Coalhouse is finally killed as he surrenders to the authorities. His and Sarah's child is informally adopted by the white suburban mother.

When the outside world encroaches upon this insular suburban family through the introduction of the black washerwoman into their lives, issues having to do with race, class, gender roles, sexuality, powerlessness, human dignity, justice and individual responsibility—issues heretofore having no particular relevance to them—begin to tear the family apart. The events and circumstances by which this idealized family, clearly a metaphor for American society, is reconfigured are the direct result of the presence and actions of Sarah, and a new family emerges out of the remnants of the old one, with the welcomed inclusion of racial, religious and ethnic Others. Although the larger society continues almost unabated in the aftermath of Sarah's terrible death and the ill-fated rebellion of her fiancé, the suburban family at the end of *Ragtime* is an idealized family of a different sort, an American polyglot with a different set of values and inclinations.

E. L. Doctorow flatly denies that he is a historical novelist. In fact, in an interview with Bruce Weber, he says, "if you ask am I a historical novelist, I say no. Am I a political novelist? No. Am I an ethnic novelist? No. I'm a novelist." Doctorow even appears at times to further dissociate himself from the term, claiming that "[t]here are always characters in the books that do the writing [. . .]. I like to create the artist and let the artist do the work."[5] When asked if *Ragtime* is historical, Doctorow responded: "I call *Ragtime* a novel."[6] Nevertheless, the reviews and critical literature about Doctorow's work overwhelming make the assumption that he is both a political and historical novelist, and repeatedly in numerous interviews Doctorow is persistently questioned by incredulous and genuinely puzzled interviewers who cannot reconcile his protestations with the knowledge of his having written what appears to be a historical progression in his work that forms "a continuous examination of

American history" from "the late nineteenth century [. . .] [to] contemporary America."[7]

The facts of Doctorow's life—his background, his politics and social concerns—all point to a sensibility that presides over his work, not like a disinterested disembodied voice, but very much like an invested, ethical, refined awareness. Doctorow "has been described as a 'radical Jewish humanist' in sensibility, and he is proud of the label, even telling one interviewer that 'if I was not in that tradition, I would certainly want to apply for membership.'" Born the son of immigrant Russians in 1931, Doctorow grew up in a working-class family in New York that valued reading, particularly of a political and philosophical nature; works such as those by Herbert Spencer, Jack London's "prophetic radical" *Iron Heel* and *War of the Classes* and the "rationalist critique of the Bible" by Robert Ingersoll. He was a child who at the age of ten or eleven was given Thomas Paine's *The Age of Reason* by his grandfather. Doctorow's interest in social and ontological matters continued as a young adult.[8] Although he majored in philosophy at Kenyon College, the influences of which resound through his work, Doctorow also insists that novelists are not philosophers.[9]

If not a philosophical, political or historical novelist—then what? Doctorow explains that it is his interest in injustice that motivates him. He says: "If I'm a leftist, it's because, as I think of them, the Ten Commandments is a very left dogma. What is just? What is unjust? That's where it all begins for me. But I tend not to accept any modification of the word novelist."[10] It is his interest in the nature of justice that causes him to write back into the historical record, by way of his fiction, the likes of an obscure washerwoman and the catastrophic, cascading effects her circumstances have on an entire society in *Ragtime*. His writing is a counterpoint that challenges conventional perceptions and the received history that historians have sanctioned and written because "[t]hey had written out of existence the history of black people and women and Indians and Chinese people in this country,"[11] as Doctorow himself puts it. Doctorow claims fiction as the medium in which to write back in the erased and to examine, among other issues, the nature of materialism, inhumanity and justice. Although Doctorow resists "any modification of the word novelist,"[12] he does describe himself as "a Cold War writer," and attributes some of his creative impulses to an effort to draw attention to the social and economic issues that were important during this period. In an interview with Bill Moyers, he says:

> I published my first book in 1960. My whole life as an adult writer has occurred during the conditions and terms of the Cold War. It's been a very peculiar experience for all of us. Part of it, of course, is the bomb and the rise of a

> militaristic culture that must be fed with money, money, money to keep it going. This has eroded our national identity terribly. It's certainly one of the things I've tried to talk about as a writer one way or another, metaphorically or explicitly.[13]

Doctorow has a "concept of history as imagery [. . .] as a resource for writing," and as a way to express his "[interest] in how our past is responsible for us as we are now."[14]

Ragtime is, therefore, an elaborate dance between the historical and the imaginative. It is also a dance between dissolving social boundaries and the attempts to keep them in place. In this cautionary and allegorical tale Doctorow conveys the feeling of the historical moment in his depiction of early-twentieth-century America as a time of unprecedented industrial growth and unexamined, uncritical patriotism, and strategically foregrounds a postcard-perfect picture that corresponds to Hollywood films that celebrate this era with nostalgia.[15] He seeks to disable our naïve fascination with the past, which is based on "our sense of the innocence of the dead—the innocence of their ambition and their vanity and even their murderousness."[16] Unlike much historical fiction that sentimentalizes society and obfuscates causality in the past, *Ragtime* does not absolve the dead. This text identifies them and holds them accountable because, as Doctorow says, "nostalgia is an inadequate self-deluding emotion. Usually you feel nostalgic for what you never experienced or for what you only have the illusion of having experienced. It is the disposition for nostalgia that *Ragtime* mocks."[17]

Doctorow, in fact, begins *Ragtime* in a mocking tone with a fanciful description of the era of Theodore Roosevelt, when there were

> parades, public concerts, fish fries, political picnics, social outings, or indoors in meeting halls, vaudeville theatres, operas, ballrooms. [. . .] Trains and steamers and trolleys moved them from one place to another. That was the style, that was the way people lived. Women were stouter then. They visited the fleet carrying white parasols. Everyone wore white in summer. (3–4)

It was a time of almost total self-absorption, self-centeredness and obliviousness to social problems for those who enjoyed economic prosperity; a time when "[t]here were no Negroes. There were no immigrants"(4).[18] It is clear that Doctorow is demonstrating that this insular world, unpolluted by racial and ethnic Others, is a state of mind; an idealized one that does not reflect the historical reality of American multiplicity at that time. Lawrence Levine explains in *Highbrow / Lowbrow: The Emergence of Cultural Hierarchy in America*, that "the multiplicity [. . .] at the turn of the century, if not a new phenomenon, was more complex, more intricate, more varied, more immediate and undeniable."[19] It is this intricate multiplicity and complexity of social context that Doctorow confronts in *Ragtime*.[20]

Systematically, "Doctorow exploits our stereotypical conception of the good old days only to break down our complacency."[21] As a counterpoint and contrast to a romanticized version of early-twentieth-century America, he presents the corrupt and hypocritical underpinnings of this society, which are knowable to the general public only if "[o]ne read between the lines of the journals and gazettes" (5).

The burgeoning urban populations of this degenerate age gave rise to "[t]he urban boss," most often a shady and unscrupulous character who wielded enormous power. As Richard Hofstadter points out in *The Age of Reform: From Bryan to F.D.R.*, this boss was

> a dealer in public privileges who could also command public support, [who] became a more important and more powerful figure. With him came that train of evils which so much preoccupied the liberal muckraking mind: the bartering of franchises, the building of tight urban political machines, the marshaling of hundreds of thousands of ignorant voters, the exacerbation of poverty and slums, the absence or excessive cost of municipal services, the co-operation between politics and "commercialized vice"—in short, the entire system of underground government and open squalor that provided such a rich field for the crusading journalists.[22]

There were gross inequities in labor and millions of people were unemployed. Children were a cheap, uncomplaining and disposable form of labor. Police brutality attempted to keep workers from organizing. A wealthy man in *Ragtime* proclaims that "the laboring man would be protected and cared for not by the labor agitators [. . .] but by the Christian men to whom God in His infinite wisdom had given the control of the property interests of this country. If all else failed the troops were called out" (45) to crush civic unrest.[23]

Publicly, Theodore Roosevelt proclaimed the need for inclusion and harmony for all Americans, at least for all white Americans. In a speech he made to the Knights of Columbus, Roosevelt said: "There is no room in this country for hyphenated Americanism. [. . .] The one absolutely certain way of bringing this nation to ruin, of preventing all possibility of its continuing to be a nation at all, would be to permit it to become a tangle of squabbling nationalities."[24] Privately he expressed the prevailing attitude of many white Americans. "In 1906 he wrote to one correspondent: 'Now as to the Negroes! I entirely agree with you that as a race and in the mass [they] are altogether inferior to the whites.'"[25] In this social climate in which they were held in such low regard, black people were still being lynched with impunity.

E. L. Doctorow wrote *Ragtime* in the wake of the Watergate scandal and the subsequent convictions of powerful members of the Nixon administration. During this period the United States evacuated troops, civilians and refugees from Vietnam; student protests and civic unrest made the front pages of newspapers; the United States experienced the highest unemployment since 1941; and OPEC put the squeeze on its customers by raising the prices of petroleum yet again. Doctorow reconfigures early-twentieth-century America and offers a state-of-the-union report from the past: high unemployment, child labor, dangerous and unhealthy working conditions, monopolies, trusts and robber barons. In this historiocultural context J. P. Morgan has his servants place laurel wreathes on the heads of his illustrious guests, and a black washerwoman buries her live baby in the garden of an affluent white family.

Doctorow deploys the black washerwoman and maid, Sarah, to unwittingly influence personal and local events, attract the attention of the nation and to disclose many layers and contradictions of early twentieth-century American society. This is really standard operating procedure for Doctorow, who uses fiction in a way "that can accommodate a revisionist and imaginative history of modern America, one that can unpack the mythology of American life and at the same time encompass the moral fate of the American people."[26] Through Sarah's characterization and fate, and the responses of those caught up in the events that unfold around her, we are invited to consider the complexities of a nation coming of age, and the mythologies of American morality.

It has been argued that as readers "we are invited to wallow in the ultimately bogus revolutionary zeal of the novel, siding with the 'oppressed' while we luxuriate in Doctorow's re-creation of the cars, clothes, furnishings and *mores* of an unregenerate capitalist age."[27] Perhaps. But, wallowing aside, is this not a legitimate way in which to draw attention to the politics of class, race, politics and justice? Doctorow writes in *Ragtime:* "There seemed to be quotas for death by starvation. There were oil trusts and banking trusts and railroad trusts and beef trusts and steel trusts" (46), and the fabulously wealthy who controlled them fetishized the poor in the poverty balls they gave to raise money for charity. "Across America sex and death were barely distinguishable" (5); the wealthy Harry K. Thaw beat his wife with extreme brutality and pleasure. *Ragtime* bears witness to the power of privilege, and the complicated consequences, if any, for unbridled greed, lust, violence and indifference.

I am in complete agreement that *Ragtime* is no less than "a massively cynical indictment of capitalist, racist, violent, crude, crass and impotently middle-class America."[28] It is "less a novel about American history than a novel about perceiving this history and of translating it into a sense-making fiction by emplotting it with the help of poetic strategies and by rendering it intelligible through 'images [which] are what things mean'."[29] Doctorow brings this complex and disparate society to life in *Ragtime* through splicing the lives and circumstances of a Negro washerwoman with the unscrupulous capitalists of this era, and thereby forces the reader to witness, judge, learn.

A Washerwoman in the Ointment

Why a Negro washerwoman? Why someone who does laundry and domestic work, an innocuous and seemingly insignificant person, to be the catalyst for such enormous upheaval in the family, and ultimately, in the larger community? Why choose someone who is on the lowest rung of the socioeconomic ladder by virtue of her lowly occupation, race, gender, poverty, her status as a mentally ill unwed mother, someone who is clearly incapable of comprehending the role she plays in this situation? The life of a washerwoman is one of virtual powerlessness and without prospects. Consider the circumstances for someone of Sarah's class and position.

As an epigraph to her chapter entitled "The Domestic Does Her Job," Phyllis Palmer uses a letter written to Eleanor Roosevelt in 1937 from a certain L. G. H. of Fort Worth, Texas, which is worth including here because of the light it sheds on the debilitating, dismal, invisible, disrespected and almost impossible life of a washerwoman. This servant writes:

> Mrs. Roosevelt can [you] help take to or organize something that will cause these dear housewives who we work for will realize we are human even if we are a Black race. . . . We do laundry for the family whom we work and have to pay to get our laundry done . . . don't have time to work for ourselves or even to cook a decent meal of food at home for our husband untill [sic] Thursday evening [when] we get what is called one evening out of a week, get off at 2:30 P.M. stores close at 3:30 P.M., a very short time to shop, clean our own house, cook that one decent meal at home.[30]

That this woman would take the time and have the nerve to write to the wife of the president of the United States for help is an indication of the extent of her desperation. According to Jacqueline Jones in *Labor of Love, Labor of Sorrow: Black Women, Work, and the Family from Slavery to the Present*, "urban black women had to rely almost exclusively on wage-labor in order to provide for their families or supplement their husbands' income. Most of these women [. . .] toiled either as domestic servants or laundresses,"[31] and the word *toil* is no exaggeration. Faye Dudden reports that "[l]aundry work was the most onerous part of housework, and housekeepers were eager to delegate it to a domestic or a laundress. [. . .] Employers sometimes put the laundry out to a laundress to placate their other servants. [. . .] Families who hired no other domestic service turned first to a laundress."[32]

> The arduousness of this type of work, and the contempt with which middle-class whites regarded manual labor of any kind—especially cleaning (whether floors, clothes, or infants)—meant that laundering was the province of black women exclusively. Washerwomen ranked highest on the "racial exclusion" scale, even higher than domestics, in the Cotton South by the late nineteenth century.

Being incredibly vulnerable, and needing this work—none other being available to them—for the very survival of their families, washerwomen were notoriously exploited. "Mistresses advertised for a laundress to do a week's worth of washing, but then presented her with three times that amount—apparently freshly soiled—to launder for the agreed-upon wages. Some women promised but never delivered pay raises, while others insisted that the servant perform additional work for the white woman's neighbors for one day's pay."[33] Quite often, and apparently according to long-standing tradition, washerwomen would very often not even be paid. In "The Problem of Payment" Dudden writes that

> In the 1860s Anthony Trollope remarked on a tendency he perceived among Americans to run up bad debts to their servants. In England, he wrote, there was a presumption that "failure to pay one's washerwoman was the mark of lowest insolvency, quite apart from the inability to pay a merchant"; but in America the washerwoman and the merchant were "about equal game." In 1855 the managers of the charitable Rosine Association of Philadelphia reported receiving complaints from domestics who had been denied their wages. A Philadelphia alderman told them of receiving "frequent applications from women who had been domestics in families, to institute suits for the recovery of wages from their employers."[34]

There was no legal redress for these women.[35] The tradition of exploitation of washerwomen continued in the early decades of the twentieth century. Women in domestic service were often forced to "give up their children [. . .] leaving them with relatives, boarding them, or binding them out" or leaving them in an orphan asylum because employers did not want their domestics to have their attention and time divided between their own families and the family of the employer. Unmarried servants who became pregnant, sometimes by their male employers, were forced to give up their babies to keep their employment (a possible explanation, along with post-partum psychosis, for Sarah's panic response after the birth of her child) or turn to prostitution.[36]

Isolation and loneliness were also significant aspects of the life of a domestic worker, particularly if she lived in. Presumably, this was the case for Sara. For domestic servants "[t]he combination of adjusting to a new culture and climate, working long hours, and not living near any other black people was difficult. Employers sometimes exacerbated the problem by discouraging their employees from going out or deliberately impeding their efforts to make contact with the black community."[37] Interestingly, although Sarah lived for months with the family in New Rochelle, "[n]obody knew Sarah's last name or thought to ask. Where had she been born, and where she lived, this impoverished uneducated black girl with such absolute conviction of the way human beings ought to conduct their lives?" (215). Also, Sarah is not forthcoming about her background; she is a cipher to the family that takes her in. "As far as they knew she had no family nor any friends from the black community in the downtown section of the city. There was a settled society of Negroes there but also, on its margins, a transient element. Apparently she was a transient and had come by herself from New York to work as a servant" (181). Sarah was most likely seeking to escape to a more stable life, one that regular employment could support.

When the combination of isolation, extreme overwork and severe exploitation, which contributes to the physical and mental deterioration of washerwomen, is considered, then Sarah's state of mind is more easily understood. Insanity, in fact, is an occupational hazard for black female servants. Dudden reports that

> laundry was extremely heavy work and it involved exposure to dampness in all sorts of weather, so it was suited only to the fittest and strongest women. These few cruel occupational alternatives took a great human toll. It is probably significant that most of the black women admitted to New York State asylums for the insane, 80 percent of whom were domestic servants, presented medical histories of overwork, illness, financial disaster, family problems, and physical exhaustion.[38]

The general reader of *Ragtime* may not be expected to know of the dreary and oppressive details of the life of a washerwoman or domestic servant. However, it does not take much imagination to conceive of the lowly social status of someone who hand-washes other people's dirty clothes for a living, and to at least imagine some of the hardships imposed by extremely low pay and very hard work. The legendary blues singer Bessie Smith makes it clear in "Washwoman Blues" that she would "rather be a scullian cookin' in some white folks yard / I could eat a plenty / Wouldn't have to work so hard."[39] Who would do this kind of work if they had another choice?

It may be true, as Bruce Robbins argues in *The Servant's Hand: Fiction from Below*, that novelists generally may have no real interest "in conveying anything historically precise about domestic service. This disparity between art and life is observable from the very beginning of the novel."[40] But Doctorow, I think, relies and plays on the social status and common perceptions of washerwomen and domestic servants to great effect—the art of *Ragtime* exploits life precisely to explicate and critique history as well as to both admonish and rewrite some of the received history about early-twentieth-century America. *Ragtime* examines the nature of kindness, compassion and accountability, and the consequences of hypocrisy, greed, racism and indifference within the context of this servant's relationship with a white suburban family as a way of drawing attention to how these factors have an impact on the larger society.

Doctorow admits that he has a mission as a writer to raise the moral sensibilities of his readers. In an interview he explains that it is not the writer's place to save society, but that

> you feel that somehow, you might inch things along a little bit in a good way toward civility, toward enlightenment, and toward diminishing the suffering. But you don't want to get too pompous about that. Really what you do is distribute the suffering so it can be borne. That's what artists do. [. . .] If you or I read a book, and we learn about someone else's life and torment, to the extent that that book is effective and good, we will be participating in that character's suffering. Presumably, when we close the book, it will give us an enlarged understanding of people we don't usually think of looking at. We are at the level, the depth, of the universal. In others we see ourself. So fiction really enlarges our humanity.[41]

A washerwoman is certainly someone many people wouldn't think of looking at. But with *Ragtime* the reader, along with the white suburban family, is invited to enlarge their understanding of the plight and prospects for someone like Sarah. *Ragtime* also offers ways in which to consider the present, and a possible prognosis for the future—a more responsible, inclusive and just present that will help to ensure a future that will live up to Doctorow's liberal ideology. That, as Doctorow asserts, "of course is what writing about the past is all about: you are really writing about the present."[42]

Doctorow arrived at the idea for the character of Sarah from a true story related to him by his wife some years before he began to write *Ragtime.* There was a maid in their New Rochelle neighborhood who had a baby and buried it in a garden. Doctorow says:

> I knew when I heard this I'd use it someday. I found myself using it in *Ragtime.* Suddenly there was Mother discovering the little brown newborn in the

> flower bed. There was Sarah coming to live in this house with this baby. Obviously, she would have tried to kill her child only from some overwhelming despair or sense of betrayal.[43]

An easy case can be made for Emma Goldman or Coalhouse Walker, Jr. as radicals in *Ragtime*. But Sarah is also a radical figure in that she is clearly the embodiment of how, as Doctorow says, "radicalism is a part of the picture, in the sense that we're all implicated in our relationship to the political extreme in our midst."[44] The criteria for growth and the growing pains that ensue from change for both individuals and American society are explicit in this text. Even when Sarah is ill and most passive she has an enormous impact on circumstances, and she unwittingly becomes the catalyst for regression, destruction or growth. Each individual who comes in contact with her must choose to either accept her as a fellow human being in great need and come to her aid, or refuse the opportunity to help; but she cannot be ignored.

Sarah's voice is rarely heard; her thoughts, even less so. Although she takes the initiative in certain circumstances and seems to operate on some powerful, internal impulse to control or influence certain outcomes, she is, perhaps ironically, most powerful as an object to be acted upon. The objectifying of Sarah differs greatly, however, from the "literary marginality" typically ascribed to servants, in which "[t]he maid parallels the mistress as the 'foil' that brings out the 'elegance' of the jewel, as the indistinct 'background' that sets the upper-class foreground in sharper relief. [. . .] As in centuries of literary tradition, she appears by the grace of a hierarchical parallelism that brings her out of invisibility only within a frame that excludes most of her subjectivity, routine, plans, destiny."

Doctorow does quite a different thing with Sarah. She is herself a jewel and beautiful in her own right. Indeed Mother, who "was awed by her beauty" (215), often appears to serve as a foil or background for Sarah's elegance and beauty, and the "hierarchical parallelism"[45] we come to expect in the representation of the literary servant is set on its head with the complete disruption of domestic routine and tranquility and the sociospatial distribution which seems to both emanate from and accommodate Sarah's needs in the white home.

A Patriarch Deposed

At the beginning of *Ragtime* the family is headed, in the traditional sense, by Father, the owner of a fireworks and flags company who goes on extended explorations to the North Pole and elsewhere. Father's life has been one of privilege; educated at Groton and then Harvard, where he read German philosophy. His father had made his fortune during the Civil War, then gradually lost it. But Father, an astute businessman, rebuilt it. Father is a proper gentleman and reserved in his interactions with his family. He shakes his little son's hand before embarking on a trip to the Arctic with Peary that will last for months, and kisses his wife goodbye on the cheek. He is "at first depicted as the embodiment of the unexamined pieties of his day, benign capitalism and patriotism, which—as we seem to learn—mask exploitation, racism, and sexism. He is a manufacturer of the signifier of these illusions, the American flag, which draws credulous immigrants in ships to New York Harbor."[46] The dark eyes of the thousands of immigrants on a ship passing by deeply disturbs Father for a moment—the convergence upon America of dark Others causes a quaking in his soul, but he is able to console himself with the thought that they are all potential customers for his business.

When he returns from the North Pole to find a nearly catatonic colored woman and her baby living in his home, he feels at first shock, and then excluded and disoriented—something he never felt on his excursion to the Arctic:

> When Father returned to New Rochelle he walked up the front steps of his home, passed under the giant Norwegian maples and found his wife holding a brown baby in her arms. Upstairs the colored girl was withdrawn. Melancholy had taken the will out of her muscles. She did not have the strength to hold her baby. She sat all day in her attic room and watched the diamond windowpanes as they gathered the light, glowed with it and then gave it up. Father looked at her through the open door. She ignored him. He wandered through the house finding everywhere signs of his own exclusion. His son now had a desk, as befitted all young students. He thought he heard an Arctic wind but it was the housemaid Brigit pushing an electric suction cleaner across the rug in the parlor. (123–124)

An important part of Sarah's function in the text is to foreground various moral options for responding to someone in need. Father utterly fails to comprehend the necessity for compassion, and Sarah's prominence in family affairs and her impact on their lives causes his extreme discomfiture. One of the many reasons for his unease is that Sarah has lost the invisibility of a domestic mechanism and the anonymity expected and typically required of servants. She forces everyone to confront her humanity.

In her discussion, "Invisibility, Consciousness of the Other, *Ressentiment*," Judith Rollins, who posed as a domestic worker for her research, writes of the occasions when her various employers behaved as though she weren't there. They would have very personal conversations in her presence, turn the heat down to 50–55 degrees in the dead of winter when they left the house, and lock her in the house when they left without telling her. Rollins does not interpret these actions as "intended insults." Rather, she sees them as casual and not calculated: "they were expressions of the employers' ability to annihilate the humanness and even, at times, the very existence of me, a servant and a black woman." This she attributes to an aspect of racism in which people of color "are more easily perceived by whites as invisible or non-human than are other whites."[47] David Katzman also advances this argument in *Seven Days a Week: Women and Domestic Service in Industrializing America.* He writes that

> [o]ne peculiar and most degrading aspect of domestic service was the requisite of invisibility. The ideal servant [. . .] would be invisible and silent, responsive to demands but deaf to gossip, household chatter, and conflicts, attentive to the needs of mistress and master but blind to their faults, sensitive to the moods and whims of those around them but undemanding of family warmth, love and security. Only blacks could be invisible people in white homes.[48]

This dynamic of the willful blindness of white employers and the resulting invisibility of black servants has its roots in a slaveholding culture that demanded the appearance of total deference and anonymity from its slaves. To see was to scrutinize, to assess was to judge. A device of domestic labor need not, dare not have and exhibit such power. bell hooks writes that

> [a]s fantastic as it may seem, racist white people find it easy to imagine that black people cannot see them if within their desire they do not want to be seen by the dark Other. One mark of oppression was that black folks were compelled to assume the mantle of invisibility, to erase all traces of their subjectivity during slavery and the long years of racial apartheid, so that they could be better, less threatening servants. An effective strategy of white supremacist terror and dehumanization during slavery centered around white control of the black gaze. Black slaves, and later manumitted servants, could be brutally punished for looking, for appearing to observe the whites they were serving, as only a subject can observe, or see. To be fully an object then was to lack the capacity to see or recognize reality. These looking relations were reinforced as whites cultivated the practice of denying the subjectivity of blacks (the better to dehumanize and oppress), of relegating them to the realm of the invisible.[49]

Sarah is certainly silent, having been struck mute because of the trauma she has experienced, but because of her condition she is anything but invisible or responsive to the needs of the household. In fact, her vulnerability puts her in a position where "warmth, love and security"[50] and especially understanding are required from her employers and their entire household for her survival and recovery. Furthermore, the baggage Sarah brings with her is complicated and heavy. Her problems create a mess for the family to clean up and make right—a symbolic reversal of functions for these classes and categories of people. Father, along with the rest of the household, is forced to acknowledge and respond to their servant's needs. As a result of this rupture in and destabilization of the predictability of established expectations and appropriate behaviors, Father loses his frame of reference for how to relate properly.

His inability to change with the times and adapt to the new circumstances that the black washerwoman brings into his home is the direct cause of his estrangement from his family, and in many ways causes his demise. At first the family just survived and continued as always in Father's absence, but on his excursion to the Arctic he stayed away too long. Gradually he has become obsolete in his own home, his family has begun to thrive and a subtle shift in power takes place. Social boundaries completely dissolve for everyone in the family except Father. His refusal to come aboard the new situation, which includes a sick black servant and her baby, with acceptance, grace, understanding and compassion mark him as an outsider, an Other in his own family, and creates a permanent emotional and moral chasm between them. For example, Mother acknowledges and approves of the ritualized courtship of Sarah by Coalhouse Walker, the musician father of Sarah's baby. In striking contrast is Father's condescension and hostility, which offend Mother, who rebukes him—the first time she openly criticizes him:

> She said to Father I think what we are witnessing is, in fact, a courtship of the most stubborn Christian kind. Father replied Yes, if you can call a courtship what has already produced a child. I find that an unkind remark, Mother said. There was suffering, and now there is penitence. It's very grand and I'm sorry for you that you don't see it. (181)

But the real litmus test for the quality of Father's humanity is how he behaves after Sarah is killed. When she tried to get the attention of a politician in a campaign crowd "[h]er arm was extended and her black hand reached toward him [the politician]. He shrank from the contact" (219–220). It is suggested that her hand may have been mistaken for a weapon, and she is struck down with such brutal force as to crush her sternum and ribs. The entire event is a metaphor for the oppressed seeking justice from someone in a position to make a difference, only to be met with contempt, rejection and violence. Sarah's black hand mistaken for a gun may also underscore the fear of black violence and retribution—a recurring theme and concern in the story. Although Father is sorry for Sarah's death, his mission is to turn the clock back; to get his family and homelife back to a place in which he is in control, to a time when "[t]here were no Negroes" (4). There is no place for a brown orphan in his vision of a good life.

The contrast between Father's and Mother's response to Sarah's death makes clear the two opposing points of view of the dominant social issues in the text. Father represents the conservative, disinterested and obsolescent; Mother the more liberal, humane and progressive. The family is shattered and haunted by Sarah's death and "sat at the dinner table. Mother held the baby in her arms," and her body language eerily recalls Sarah's as she holds the brown baby. "Without realizing it she did not now expect ever to put the child down. She felt the touch of his tiny fingertips on her cheek" (241). Mother's refusal to put him down, especially in her own mind, alarms Father and indicates to him that she has made a complete commitment; she has bonded with Sarah's child for life, and he worries that their own lives are forever altered and out of control because of it. Instead of giving Mother time to grieve and heal, he blames her for playing a role better left to Social Services, and a subtle but fatal shift occurs in their relationship. He rails: "You took her in without sufficient thought. You victimized us all with your foolish female sentimentality" (241). Mother's response is to assess him carefully, and he suffers in her estimation. She realizes that Father will only be satisfied if she abandons the baby and pretends that they and their lives have not been changed.

Increasingly impotent in his own household and familial relations, Father rebels in his own way. His new state of mind is one in which he is critical of Mother's appearance (she has begun to look matronly and he has lost his physical attraction to her; he takes pleasure in making her cry). The polite reserve which had heretofore governed their relationship is finished. All this he blames on her championing Sarah and her baby. Perhaps not so ironically, Father's flag and fireworks business produces, albeit without his knowledge and consent, and by his own brother-in-law, the materials from which the bombs are made for Coalhouse's rebellion; a metaphor for his attitudes and ideas that have become unacknowledged incendiary material in his own home, and by extension, the attitudes that cause social upheaval in the greater society.

Because of Sarah, Father is forced to confront the perceptions and delusions he has enjoyed and perpetuated about himself; the huge disparity between what he thinks he is and who and what he really is. This can easily be read as a prescription for a nation in civil crisis; a society unable or unwilling to see past self-mythologizing to reality. Father had thought himself an improvement over the preceding generation: openminded, progressive, liberal about the prospects for Negroes. He was self-congratulatory in his thinking that "there was no reason the Negro could not with proper guidance carry every burden of human achievement. He did not believe in aristocracy except of the individual effort and vision. He felt his father's loss of fortune had the advantage of saving him from the uncritical adoption of the prejudices of his class" (265). But as his brother-in-law Younger Brother puts it to him when they have an altercation about Coalhouse and Sarah, he is apparently a man who has never had his principles tested. When they are tested, his bewilderment becomes increasingly apparent, and his responses are reactionary, self-indulgent, self-defeating, entirely fruitless.

What happens to Father in *Ragtime* is symbolic and mirrors what is happening simultaneously to the nation in the early twentieth century. A healthy and positive outcome is entirely dependent upon facing difficult situations and making just and humane decisions; on these grounds this individual and the nation will either stand or fall. The parallels are obvious.

Father is a prosperous individual in a wealthy and powerful country. He has traveled (conquered, exploited) the most remote regions of the world without, as Younger Brother puts it, having learned anything. Yet, he has lost control of his own household (country). It becomes clear that economic strength, success and recognition on the global stage are not enough when the most festering domestic social problems are not correctly identified and addressed. Although Father is conscious of and sensitive to his wife's changed and disapproving opinion of him, he cannot progress in his thinking, and will be judged wanting for posterity. His estrangement from his young brother-in-law, who regards his values and standards as selfish, shortsighted and dangerous, suggests how he and people of his class will be judged by generations to come. All of Father's relationships are affected by his inattention and lack of understanding and care. He has also neglected his own son; not showing him respect or demonstrating a real interest in him. Most significantly, he has not fulfilled his obligation to enlighten and prepare the next generation, but offers, instead, the pitiful legacy of passing the torch of narrow-mindedness and self-absorption by default. He is forced to acknowledge that he is turning into his spiteful father; he is, in fact, no improvement over past generations. He has not evolved.

Father's obliviousness to relationships and issues that demand consistent, positive and aggressive action from him is a symptom, a bad habit, and a warning in this cautionary tale. Even during the family's retreat to the shore he becomes distracted and bored and begins to reengage with his business affairs back home. He literally and figuratively doesn't want to get in the swim but plays billiards, completely unaware of what this recidivism will cost him. His conduct foretells the end of a marriage and a way of life. In this way, Doctorow offers a vivid and powerful metaphor for the unstoppable forces of changing times and what it takes to change with them—the necessity of putting aside obsolescent and socially unproductive attitudes and behaviors to make way for a progress grounded in justice and compassion.

Suburban Matron, Moral Compass

In the beginning Mother, a competent homemaker, is a desexualized matron who is vaguely dissatisfied, but resigned to a life that is abundant but somehow incomplete. While her husband is on an extended excursion to the North Pole, Mother takes to reading political treatises by Emma Goldman. She is transformed into a socially conscious, sexually awakened woman who has demonstrated her business acumen in running the family company, which stands up to Father's scrutiny and grudging approval when he returns from his exploration. During the early years of the Progressive Era, women began to mobilize in their own interests in women's clubs and other organizations and to agitate for social and political reform and equality, including suffrage; Mother struggles with her own sense of powerlessness. She "felt deserted by the race of males" (75). Her frustration is caused by the fact that Father, although a good provider, does not pay attention to what is important to his family and what goes on in his own home. Her isolation is a metaphor for those who are neglected or abandoned in America, which includes women, while those who are purported to be in charge, caring for things and responsible, are self-absorbed and in the pursuit of adventure, pleasure, self-aggrandizement and, most of all, money. As Father has abandoned the home front, so has the nation abandoned its responsibilities for the well-being of all its citizens.

Early progressivism witnessed many efforts to align public and legal policy with moral sensibilities in the wake of the excesses of the Gilded Age. This is evident in the works of social workers and reformers, philanthropists, journalists, novelists and assorted intellectuals.[51] Yet, there were many issues, particularly where equal rights for women and civil rights for blacks, immigrants and other minorities were concerned, that were grossly neglected, if not outright opposed. The situation was ripe for change, and the language of precipitous crises, conflict resolution, expiation and redemption that Doctorow employs in *Ragtime* to both destroy and rebuild the family, with Sarah as the catalyst, is infused with symbolism and meaning for the larger cultural context.

In the garden Mother and her Irish servant girl literally dig up Sarah's baby. In a much larger sense, we find out later that she has, indeed, "dug something up" (77)—the "Negro Problem." Mother represents the capacity for change. She is emotionally available and receptive to this problem, and acts as appropriately as she can to correct the situation. She wonders and cares about what would have happened if she had not heard the cry at all; evidence of her humanity and developing social conscience. Without having experienced it herself, she understands the consequences of not being aware of and responsive to dire need, and assumes responsibility, even against the advice of the doctor and the policemen. Significantly, her little son silently observes his mother's actions, and learns from her example. The cries of the brown baby from underground are almost literally the cries of Negroes and others of the American underclasses; those who are being buried alive by neglect, oppression and injustice. Their cries are muffled by the deliberate design of those in power, who refuse to acknowledge their claims and the need for political and social change, and by the apathetic, who feel that it is all of no concern to them, and who are, therefore, equally guilty.

Mother's moral disposition and her social consciousness become one and the same, and she becomes a symbol for human decency. The formula for decency is a simple one in *Ragtime:* pay attention and take appropriate corrective action. Mother permits her comfortable and uneventful life to be touched and disrupted by the misfortune of the Negro baby and mother. She cannot rely on her husband or brother, who are both gone. Her father is senile. She has no one to make order out of the difficulties she has taken on or to make decisions. But one can see her evolving sensibilities as she looks out the window and reflects, perhaps for the first time, about the washerwomen who empty out into her neighborhood each day from the trolley and the other workers who travel from parts unknown into her community to provide goods and services. Doctorow's self-proclaimed purpose of providing for readers "an enlarged understanding of people we don't usually think of looking at" is clearly at work here. Mother's ability to get out of herself and operate "at the level, the depth, of the universal"[52] makes these anonymous workers become real to her; they now have a human face to which she can relate—that of Sarah's. At night, Mother sits by the bed of her sleeping son and thinks.

In her family, Mother becomes the moral compass and authority who hands down to her own child a new social consciousness, and ultimately she evolves because of her willingness to confront difficulties responsibly and with compassion. It is her treatment of Sarah and the brown baby (as he is referred to in the text, but not by the family) that cultivates in her son the capacity for compassion and responsible conduct. After Sarah's death, "Mother kept the baby in her room. She would no longer take him downstairs. She enlisted her son to watch over him when she had to see to something" (257). Her sensibilities and responses are held in sharp contrast to those of Father and provide the means to compare the nature of immoral intransigence, apathy and unregenerate self-interest with that of humanism.

In evaluating Mother's extraordinary conduct one may reasonably wonder if, because of her almost unself-conscious altruistic tendencies, she is intended to be regarded as saintly, or at least as a person of extreme moral constitution. But Mother is quite ordinary in her needs and concerns and disposition in every sense. This is, I think, the whole point. That is, anyone may, and should, find it possible and within the realm of normalcy to make the moral decisions that Mother makes.

Typically, the white female employer/black female servant relationship is a complex one, fraught with subtleties and driven by the rules of race and class. Understandably, "the often-cited 'closeness' between women of the two races—at times both mothers about the same age—was more illusory than real."[53] "Even when the employer was extremely benevolent, class and race still profoundly separated mistress and servant."[54] In *Maid in America* Mary Romero describes the typical accounts that domestic workers give of their relationships with their employers as ones in which deferential behavior was a way to affirm the superiority of the employer.

> In their accounts of emotional labor, domestics expressed an awareness that deferential behavior was the result of their employers' desire for status. Employers could simply have asked domestics to engage in deferential behavior, however in almost all cases they manipulated appearances and structured the interaction, which introduced a great deal of tension into the relationship when employees resisted accepting an inferior status.

The climate that usually dominated the employer/employee relationship was shaped by the fact that

> [m]ost domestics were not from the same racial or ethnic group as their masters or mistresses. Domestics frequently worked alone but not without supervision. They were expected to complete the demanding routines and labor-intensive tasks of housekeeping under the critical gaze of mistresses. Speedups, ceremonial cleanings and rituals of class deference were demanded of domestics.

As a result, "[i]ntense cultural, racial, religious, and class conflicts were played out in the private sphere of the mistress's home. Racial and cultural differences between employees and employers were so apparent that the 'servant problem' became synonymous with more general social conflicts over ethnicity, race, or religion."[55]

The potential for maternalism is also a factor in these relationships, the "concept related to women's supportive intrafamilial roles of nurturing, loving, and attending to affective needs. [. . .] The importance of the employer's being female in affecting the position, tone, and dynamics of the relationship cannot be overestimated." As Judith Rollins further explains, "[t]here is little doubt [. . .] that servants provided psychological validation of class differences between women. [. . .] [T]he presence of the deference-giving inferior enhances the employer's self-esteem as an individual, neutralizes some of her resentment as a woman, and where appropriate, strengthens her sense of self as a white person."[56]

Clearly, Mother's relationship with Sarah is extraordinary and complex. Almost every aspect of her behavior and responses to this desperate black woman is absolutely contrary to the socially approved conduct of the period and for her social class. She becomes more than a benefactress to Sarah and her baby—she becomes a friend. The cross-border identities that Mother and Sarah acquire, and the borderland that they create together in *Ragtime*, has an absence of both paternalism and maternalism, of deference and servility. Mother and Sarah "worked together on her [Sarah's] wedding dress" (215), and are able to achieve an uncommon level of kinship and affinity not usually seen in the domestic/employer relationship.

The development of a cross-border identity, that is, the incorporation both consciously and unconsciously of qualities, characteristics, tastes, behaviors, points of view, moral (re)positionings and many other dimensions of another culture into one's own personae and psyche, is a significant and perhaps inescapable by-product of a society that includes more than one race, religion or ethnicity and is in the process of evolving into heterogeneity. The cross-border identity may take many different shapes as a result of a greater sensitivity and sense of possibility and freedom, without fear, to difference. Affecting the appearance of having acquired certain traits of the dominant culture is also often employed as part of a survival strategy for social inferiors. For example, African American slaves and servants sometimes behaved ingratiatingly and paid lip-service to certain values and ideals as a way to assuage the fear of difference or Otherness an employer/master or mistress may have been experiencing; an effective tactic for maintaining job security or life itself.

According to David Wellman, individuals or cultures that are open to the inclusion of alien or foreign factors are cross-border entities in the making. He suggests that this openness and fluidity offers new ways to reassess cultural identity:

> In border cultures identities are not discrete and finite entities. They are plastic and open-ended; as much dynamic constructs as inherited facts, as much strategic responses to the present as an immutable series of practices

> and beliefs derived from the past. Border cultures produce identities that are neither singular nor static. In these locations, multiple cultural identities are invented, and people slip in and out of them without being called upon to renounce their initial identifiers. In this context, identity is achieved and inclusive. It is learned through the process of taking on and shedding the roles required to participate in complicated cultures. Border peoples trying on new and different identities learn that identities can be changed. They find out that one is not completely bound by bloodlines, nationality, or occupation. The roles they try on, the cultural practices they learn to perform, teach them how to be multicultural. They learn how to be culturally competent actors in multiple cultural contexts. Border cultures therefore contradict conventional sociological wisdom. They fracture received categories. The discovery of border cultures calls for a reformulation of sociological theories of cultural identity.[57]

In *Ragtime*, Sarah's cross-border identity is in the making and minimal as she emerges from her nearly catatonic state and begins to reconnect with the outside world. Her status has been promoted from washerwoman to patient in the affluent white home. It is Sarah who takes the initiative to begin housework and to move freely through the family's home as she becomes healthier, clearly an exercise of volition and autonomy not expected and probably not approved of for servants. But, it is actually Mother and her little son who most noticeably acquire characteristics that alter their fundamental suburban middle-class sensibilities because of Sarah in their lives. Mother works alongside Sarah, assumes responsibility for Sarah's child after she is killed and develops an appreciation for rag music. Both Mother's and Sarah's self-definition, identity and status alter as a result of their paths crossing and their ability to embrace difference. This is possible only because of the absence of paternalism in Mother, and the absence of deference in Sarah. Together they create, not a demilitarized zone with a suspension of hostilities, but a safe and viable place in which each also retains her cultural identity. Gloria Anzaldúa describes such happenings as a "racial, ideological, cultural and biological cross-pollenization, an 'alien' consciousness [which] is presently in the making. [. . .] It is the consciousness of the Borderlands."[58] Sarah and Mother create something new when they come together; a nonthreatening place, a borderland in which they both can heal and grow, and their personalities, characters, dispositions and outlooks on life are irrevocably altered as a result.

In the dissolution of social boundaries in the household, even the spatial arrangements normally designated for separation of family and servants is modified for Sarah's benefit. Sarah occupies the attic space during her illness, which was not an uncommon arrangement for servants considering that most of the middle-class homes constructed during this period were made specifically to accommodate live-in servants, and the space allotted was remote from the family area. Deborah Fairman Browning writes that

> [t]he architectural configuration of the Victorian house was, in part, a reflection of the desire for a front and back stage. But the complete physical separation of servant and employer living spaces, the conflation of work and living space for domestics, and the quality of life those spaces afforded reflect a middle class investment in maintaining a material, and indeed psychological, distinction not just between employer and employee, but between middle and working class. The wealthier the household the more the architectural separation between servants and employers. They could buy privacy.

However, the visitations of Sarah's fiancé, Coalhouse Walker, are almost inconceivable in a time when "servants could not have visitors," as a rule, except under the close supervision of the mistress of the house, and those visits were most often confined to the kitchen. "Essentially, class boundaries were preserved through architectural and material boundaries."[59] Yet, as Sarah begins to recover and is courted by Coalhouse, Mother permits them both to violate the sociospatial requirements designated by traditional cultural codes and even the physical construction of the homes that made separation of employers and servants easier to regulate. For many weeks Coalhouse is admitted to the family's parlor where he takes tea and plays rag music on the piano. Eventually Sarah relents and joins them in the parlor, but "Mother insisted that the members of the family excuse themselves so that the courtship could go on in privacy" (186). All this for a black servant when the rules of Jim Crow, albeit de facto for the most part in the North, governed the usages of public spaces, and, by custom, private spaces.

Although it may seem that Mother makes all the concessions and does all the giving, her relationship with Sarah is mutually beneficial in ways that may not be immediately apparent. By constructing their relationship in this way, Doctorow mitigates the idea of social and moral responsibility as simply burden, and demonstrates the potentially reciprocal nature of such arrangements in which the interests and welfare of all concerned may be taken into account.

Mother receives certain benefits from her relationship with Sarah besides the personal satisfaction that comes with being humane and living correctly. Father is wrapped up in his own interests and oblivious to the emotional needs of his wife, both he and Younger Brother are gone most of the time, her father is senile and her son is a young child. Sarah provides companionship for Mother, who is lonely and whose life doesn't include many satisfying relationships, and this is no small thing. Judith Rollins writes that

> [i]ndustrialism created, along with the proletariat, the "housewife," the women removed from their economic sphere and solely responsible for home and family maintenance. And these new middle-class housewives of the nineteenth century created the market for widespread use of domestic servants. Might the servant have been needed to mitigate against the isolation of such women as well as for practical maintenance?[60]

Normally, "[t]he relationship of emotional labor is in no way reciprocal. Employers expect to be consoled; the inherent power relation of employer-employee means that middle-class white housewives have little fear of rebuttal, retaliation, or disparagement."[61] Yet, for Mother and Sarah the support is reciprocal. They provide comfort and companionship for one another in a world that appears to be, at turns, hostile with or absent of males.

Interestingly, Mother changes in profound, observable ways in addition to her rising social consciousness. During his trip to the North Pole, Father had sex with an Eskimo woman. He is wracked with shame and remorse, and feels filthy to return to his wife. But there is a punishment in store for him that he could never have imagined. His retribution from God is a sexually interested wife. She is more bold, less sexually modest. Is it implied in *Ragtime* that this is because of the presence of the Negro woman in her house? Does the presence of a woman who is believed to be driven by animal passions because she is black (the proof is in her giving birth to an illegitimate child), awaken in Mother her own sexuality? These are possibilities to consider. But the changes in Mother's sexual demeanor are likely more attributable to the confidence she acquires from being in charge and discovering that she is good at it. Making the tough decisions, becoming aware of her own competency in business and at home foster a new self-awareness and strength that allows her to develop more of her total being, including her sexuality.

Reconfiguring America: A New Family, A New Generation

Generational conflict looms large in *Ragtime.* Coalhouse Walker represents the new, not servile and nonservant Negro; Younger Brother represents an aspect of the younger generation of white Americans who are ready to make changes at all costs and who will join ranks with the oppressed in the name of justice; and Little Boy represents an idealized state in which the expectation and acceptance of change is natural—he moves with ease into and through new circumstances.

Younger Brother is driven by a new set of social rules and assumptions that are played out not only in his involvement with Coalhouse's rebellion, but in his relationship with Sarah. In fact, his expanding social awareness may be directly attributed to his relationship with Sarah. He is able to see her not as the social embarrassment, burden and inconvenient servant, as does Father, but as a human being he can relate to and admire. Younger Brother thinks of Sarah as a displaced African queen who would be considered graceful in some other place—but not in early-twentieth-century New Rochelle. This troubled, lonely and isolated person, who is emotionally disconnected from the suburban world and family in which he finds himself, is looking for love, meaning and purpose in his life. Younger Brother and Sarah have an unspoken connection and affinity; they seem to understand one another. He is somewhat estranged from the older people in his family, and her fiancé is an older man. "And that was why he followed her into the kitchen and she confided to him the news of Coalhouse's vow not to marry until he had his car back" (216).

It is Younger Brother who lays into father, who he has decided has no moral understanding of Sarah's and Coalhouse's situation and who has threatened to "deal" with Coalhouse if he comes to their house. For the first time, he is referred to in the text not as Younger Brother, but simply as Brother, and it is clear that he has come of age when he points out Father's hypocrisy and literally stands up to him. He represents a more socially conscious way of thinking. It is evident in this encounter that Father, representing an old school of thought, is completely and fatally clueless. Everything that is wrong with Coalhouse's situation actually represents the sorry state of affairs in race relations in American society, and comes piercingly through in Brother's exquisitely metaphorical tirade:

> Are you going out to find him and shoot him? he said. I'm going to protect my home, Father said. This is his child here. If he makes the mistake of coming to my door I will deal with him. But why should he come here, Brother said in a goading tone of voice. We did not desecrate his car. Father looked at Mother. In the morning I will go to the police and have to tell them this murdering madman was a guest in my home. I will have to tell them we are keeping his bastard child. Younger Brother said I think Coalhouse Walker Jr. would want you to tell the police everything you know. You can tell them he's the same Negro maniac whose car is lying at the bottom of Firehouse Pond. You can tell them he's the fellow who visited their own headquarters to make a complaint against Will Conklin and his thugs. You can tell them he's the same crazed black killer who sat by the bedside of someone who died in the hospital of her injuries. Father said I hope I misunderstand you. Would you defend this savage? Does he have anyone but himself to blame for Sarah's death? Anything but his damnable nigger pride? Nothing under heaven can excuse the killing of men and the destruction of property in this manner? Brother stood so

> abruptly that his chair fell over. The baby started and began to cry. Brother was pale and trembling. I did not hear such a eulogy at Sarah's funeral, he said. I did not hear you say then that death and the destruction of property was inexcusable. (242–243)

Doctorow makes clear that the fashioning of a new, more humanistic society requires sacrifice and cannot be achieved without growing pains. There are, of course, consequences for opposing the status quo. Mother's protectiveness of the brown child and her grief over Sarah's death rock and eventually ruin her marriage. Increasingly, Mother is out of control. On an extended holiday in Atlantic City "[t]o the consternation of the hôtelier she had taken to having the child at her table in the dining room. Father gazed at the little boy with grim propriety" (308). Father's resentment of Sarah's child, and his unceasing and accelerating insinuation into his family life in such a public way, is silently observed and judged by Mother, who is undaunted, and who does not in any way curtail her open interactions with the child. She takes as much pleasure in the baby's first steps as she would a child of her own; in fact, they have clearly become mother and child. As Mother's awareness increases, she becomes more tender towards those around her, including the new black maid, and especially toward Sarah's child (292).

Clearly, this situation is allegorical:

> [Mother's] face was radiant. She stepped aside and walking down the hall, holding the hand of the housemaid, was Sarah's child in his nightshirt. He tottered and swung against her skirt, righted himself and looked at Father in triumph. Everyone laughed. We can't hold him Mother said. He wants to walk everywhere. The boy knelt and held out his arms and the child shook his hand free of the housemaid and lurched toward him, picking up speed as he went, outracing his instability and falling happily against the boy's chest. (269–270)

The Negro baby (the oppressed and downtrodden) learns to walk under the care and concern of Mother (an ordinary person with a conscience). Little Boy (the younger generation, carefully taught and influenced by his conscientious mother) welcomes him without question and with open arms. Symbolically, the child takes his first steps down the hall toward the family, holding the hand of the Negro housemaid. This child is a link between classes and races; his race and class status have, in fact, been erased. With little assistance the child is on his own two feet and not only does not need, but does not want, help from anyone. Literally, the younger generation, black and white, fall "happily" into an embrace of one another.

At the shore Mother and Father hire a chair, which is sometimes pushed by a porter (the underclass responsible for holding them up and moving them along). "They could be hired too without a man" (291). It is possible to get along without the subjugation of others. Sometimes Little Boy likes to push them in the chair: "he loved that best of all, for then he pushed the chair with his mother and father seated in it and he could direct it as he would, at whatever speed, without their feeling the need of instructing him" (291). In keeping with the spirit of the text, this scene suggests that it is the younger generation that will take the initiative to lead the parents to a new place, without any interference or support from them, and perhaps even against their will.

Even so, and characteristic of this text, there is a reminder of the social realities of the day, and Doctorow uses African American servants to facilitate the reality check. In this case, established spatial propriety still governs the physical arrangement of black servants in public places; it is, after all, 1907. At the beach the "Negro woman," the maid, is separated from the family "some yards away" (288). But in keeping with the point/counterpoint configuration of social and traditional constraints, as opposed to a new and different, perhaps better, but in any case inevitable social reconfiguration, is the placement of the children.

In contrast to the public positioning of the black maid away from the white family is the absence of physical barriers between the children. The younger generation in the newly configured family—black and white and immigrant—play together oblivious to social demarcations, propriety and carefully observed physical spatiality of the adults: "The boy and the brown child studied the tiny crabs that buried themselves with a bubbly trail in the wet sand" (288–289). And while it is true that the rules for young children are typically not nearly as rigid as for adults (even the children of slaveholders often played with young slaves), Doctorow develops a relationship between Little Boy and Sarah's child that is clearly fraternal. Little Boy is the protector, teacher and big brother to the brown baby. Little Boy is diametrically different from his father—more politically and socially aware. He is a thinker, not just a taker. He "treasured anything discarded. He took his education peculiarly and lived an entirely secret intellectual life. [. . .] In his mind the meaning of something was perceived through its neglect" (131), which goes a long way in explaining his attachment to both Sarah and her child.

Little Boy accepts without question or hesitation an immigrant Jewish girl as his closest playmate and new sister, and a Negro baby as his little brother. This quietly intelligent, observant child, understood by some to be the unidentified narrator of the story, is regaled with stories of transformation from Ovid by his grandfather. He perceives the possibility of renewal through continual transformation, that "the forms of life were volatile and that everything in the world could as easily be something else" (132–133).[62] Little Boy has a tendency to assess things and people according to their impermanence and instability: "It was evident to him that the world composed and recomposed itself constantly in an endless process of dissatisfaction" (135)—the province and apparently a major motivation in the writing of retrospective fiction, and perhaps in the writing and rewriting of history itself.

Sarah is the object of feminine beauty in the fantasies of Little Boy, who thinks of her as a displaced Nubian princess-turned-slave.

> The boy was attracted to her more and more, and to her baby. He played gently with the child and there was solemn recognition between them. The mother sang. She sewed her wedding costume and tried it on and removed it. Underneath she wore a shift which rose to her hips as she pulled the white dress over her head. She saw the boy's honest and attentive regard of her limbs and she smiled. (216)

Sarah's relationship with Little Boy is friendly and familial, and she contributes to his development and outlook. But the scene in which she changes her clothes in front of him is a cause for reflection about her didactic function in both the text and in the family. Typically, "[d]omestics could be a source of information about aspects of adult life that parents alone might have been incapable of conveying. They regularly introduced young children to the facts of class and race," and some would argue sex as well.[63]

Robert Coles argues that "servants in wealthy households teach young children about the existence of people less fortunate than themselves and cause them to assume that they are entitled to make use of those less fortunate. In effect, servants reconcile the young to their privileges." This is clearly not the case in Little Boy's relationship with Sarah. Sarah's very presence makes the world outside his home more comprehensible to him and sensitizes him to the plight of others outside his secure world. They are at ease with one another, and the class and color differences do not seem to operate when they are together. Mother's willingness to allow Little Boy to freely associate with Sarah is a far cry from the mothers who feared that servants were a bad influence on children in that they might not take good physical care of them, might endanger them through carelessness or neglect, or even "administer opiates or punishment for crying. They were notoriously supposed to impart fears and superstitions to young children," and were assumed to influence children with their own bad manners and morals.[64]

The seemingly innocent encounter, in which a servant disrobes to her underclothes in the presence of a young boy, raises many questions about Sarah's function as an object of eroticism and desire in *Ragtime*. Although the scene seems to demonstrate that both Sarah and the boy are entirely at ease with one another, and there is no apparent prurient intent in including such a scene, it still may strike a dissonant chord, and one might well wonder what to make of it. Is Sarah's behavior appropriate? Is this simply the unself-conscious expression of someone who is completely comfortable and familial? If so, would an older sister get down to her underwear in the presence of her little brother in this time and place? Or, is she functioning as an emissary of the "nether world" of servants as described by Peter Stallybrass and Allon White in *The Politics and Poetics of Transgression?* In the chapter "The Maid and the Family Romance" they discuss the role of the servant (especially female servants) in ushering middle-class children into sex, or at least the idea of sex, and examine "[t]he connection of the bourgeois boy's desire to a woman of low social status and to dirt"[65]—a notion that has enjoyed popularity as common knowledge for centuries.

But, this is no striptease. This carefully constructed scene in which Sarah sings happily as she sews and Little Boy plays with her baby actually resonates with a simplicity and innocence that belies any notions of sexual impropriety, or even of sexuality at all. This younger generation, composed of black and white, servant and social superior, denotes friendly familiarity, nothing more. Their conduct is not shaped or constrained by prevailing attitudes and traditions, which are completely immaterial to their situation and sensibilities.

Long after Mother and Father had become estranged and Father has perished at sea, Mother marries again. Tateh, her new husband, is a Russian Jewish immigrant street artist and socialist turned Hollywood filmmaker. Their children complete the newly reconfigured American family in which the rules of race, class, ethnicity and gender are completely collapsed: Tateh's beautiful silent daughter; Mother's Little Boy; and the Brown Boy, the son of Sarah. It makes sense that Sarah's son, like the members of the white family, is never named—his humanity in this situation is a given. There is no particular need to differentiate him from his foster sister and brother; he represents a new type of person in a changing America—a person who just happens to be a Negro. This is monumental. Tateh's girl and Little Boy take Sarah's child, no longer a baby, on their excursions. "In the afternoons they played in sight of the beach umbrellas, collecting sticks of wood and shells, walking slowly with the little brown boy splashing after them in the ebb tide" (301).

> Their desire for each other's company was unflagging. This was noted with amusement by the adults. They were inseparable until bedtime but uncomplaining when it was announced. They ran off to the separate rooms with not a glance backward. Their sleep was absolute. They sought each other in the morning. [. . .] [Tateh's daughter] had relieved herself in wooden outhouses

> behind the tenements. The tails of rodents had curled about her ankles. She knew how to sew with a machine and had observed dogs mating, whores taking on customers in hallways, drunks peeing through the wooden spokes of pushcart wheels. He [Little Boy] had never gone without a meal. He had never been cold at night. He ran with his mind. He ran toward something. He was unencumbered by fear and did not know there were beings in the world less curious about it than he. He saw through things and noted the colors people produced and was never surprised by a coincidence. A blue and green planet rolled through his eyes. (304–305)

The family unit, arguably the foundation of civilized society, is redefined in *Ragtime* along terms that have only to do with the human connection between individuals; a connection identified, unquestioned and embraced by the younger generation. Their differences make no difference. Literally, a fresh and verdant world full of possibility awaits them.

Explicating the Historical Moment: Social Context and Black Servitude

Sarah is represented primarily as a guest and patient first, and only provisionally as a nurse and maid in *Ragtime*. Doctorow problematizes family dynamics by utilizing Sarah as a catalyst for the dissolution of the original family unit and the reconfiguration of an "alternative" family. The enormous influence this African American woman has on the fate of this one family, and ultimately on the police force, the wealthiest of powerbrokers and the entire city of New York is extraordinary and outrageous. Washerwomen were considered the very lowest echelon of women workers and, arguably, the most powerless and downtrodden segment of society. According to Jacqueline Jones this arduous work, which was almost exclusively the province of black women, was held in contempt by their middle-class employers:

> laundering [. . .] hardly paid a woman a reasonable wage for her considerable expenditure of energy. Most women made no more than a couple of dollars a week for work that was exceedingly heavy and hot. [. . .] A woman would usually collect clothes on Monday from two or three families. She set up a large pot in the yard of her house and instructed the children to help her draw water. The clothes had to be boiled in the pot, scrubbed on a washboard, rinsed, starched, wrung out, hung up, and ironed. (She had to pay for the starch and soap out of her own meager earnings.) On Saturday she would deliver the clothes and, she hoped, collect her money. A customer's complaints that her new wash powder had eaten a hole in his shirt, or that she had lost a

> sock, resulted in his refusal to pay for the entire week's load if she was lucky, her imprisonment if she was not.[66]

The typical circumstances a woman in Sarah's position faced were oppressive and degrading: "Domestic service recapitulated the mistress-slave relationship in the midst of late nineteenth-century industrializing America. [. . .] It thus served as a tangible reminder of the days of bondage. [. . .] Moreover, service made manifest all the tensions and uncertainties inherent in personal interaction between the female members of the two different classes and races."[67] Therefore, Sarah's inclusion as a pampered guest and patient in the home of a wealthy white family is almost too unreal to imagine. But the representation of this washerwoman turned domestic servant has considerable utility, for Doctorow and for the reader, in that it both underscores and ratifies the African American in the capacity of servitude while simultaneously undermining or even negating what must have been the social realities for someone in Sarah's position at the turn of the century.

Of course, we must remember that we are dealing with fiction, a product of the imagination, and Doctorow emphasizes this point in an interview in which he explains his philosophy of composition as a writer of fiction; everything is fair game. In his vision Doctorow complicates Sarah's lowly social status. Ultimately, her tragic fate is juxtaposed with the indelible portrait of compassion and tenderness she receives within the adopted family; a portrait that resonates after her brutal death, which allows the reader to imagine kinder and gentler associations.

What are we as readers to make of Sarah's circumstances in *Ragtime?* Is this an atypical family with extraordinarily sensitive, caring and moral individuals? May the reader conclude that it is only those in power and with authority who deny, oppress and destroy? May we read the adoption of Sarah and her child as a typical act of kindness that could be expected at this period of time from someone in Mother's position? Or, are we not to raise these questions in the first place, but accept the situation as entirely plausible under the circumstances?

I believe the text itself begs these questions and insists that the reader contemplate the plausibility and probability of such a situation. The multiplexing interactions and relationships between this servant and her child and her employers may have been difficult if not impossible to conceive of and construct in the early twentieth century, the period in which the story takes place, but not for a writer with a progressive late-twentieth-century social consciousness who has lived through the civil rights era of the 1950s and 1960s, and who has witnessed, firsthand, the forced desegregation of a nation.

Sarah's presence and predicament are useful in drawing attention to a number of social problems, such as inter-ethnic competition and class and race conflicts of the larger society. The immigrant/Negro conflict is played out in the behavior of the Irish maid after the black washerwoman enters the household. Faye Dudden writes that

> [h]istorians have noted that immigrants tended to drive blacks out of the skilled trades and much unskilled work. [. . .] Some evidence suggests that a similar displacement occurred in service, where it may have been particularly pronounced because co-workers had to eat together and often sleep in the same room, as well as work together. European travelers noted the difficulty or outright impossibility of having black and white servants together on the same staff. As white immigrants put blacks in a distinct minority, the employer who wished to take the line of least resistance would simply hire an all-white staff.[68]

But, not so Mother. Her impulse is to do the right thing rather than simply obey the rules of racial solidarity. Her priority is to restore Sarah's health and to care for the unfortunate baby.

At first, the Irish maid is helpful, following Mother's lead. Eventually Brigit succumbs to confusion, resentment and anger about her own status. Although they are both servants, Brigit has to work while the black woman languishes in the attic, and she cannot adjust. She loses respect for a formerly respectable white woman who now takes care of a black child, becomes disrespectful and appears to be setting herself up to be fired. To Brigit, Mother's behavior is inappropriate and violates the rules of conduct for her class and race.[69] Eventually, Brigit simply leaves. As Sarah begins to show outward signs of healing, she begins to take an interest in her baby and takes up the responsibilities of servitude. Mother enjoys the fact that Sarah cleans the house as if it were her own, and realizes that it is patience, time and effort that have made the difference. But, the immigrant Irish servant has, in fact, been displaced by a black servant making manifest the fears of her class.[70]

In significant ways both servants and immigrants, particularly when they are in physical proximity in this text, are utilized to illustrate changing times and how the boundaries of social propriety and between classes are breaking down, the results of which are often confusion. It is suggested that one of the reasons the family's Irish maid has a change in attitude, from helpful and respectful to recalcitrant and neglectful, is that times are changing, and that she is simply a young person who resists the social constraints and expectations of her class. After all, Father "saw it everywhere, this new season, and it bewildered him. At his office he was told that the seamstresses in the flag department had joined a New York union" (124), and his response, characteristic of many of those who are financially and socially secure, is both bewilderment and disdain. Social boundaries, class distinctions and individual function are disrupted and are undergoing perplexing and profound changes. When J. P. Morgan "stepped out of his limousine the car robe fell around his feet. One of the several bank officers who rushed out to meet him disentangled the robe and hung it over the robe rail on the inside of the door. The chauffeur thanked him profusely" (157). Harry Houdini has an automobile accident outside the family's house, and he is welcomed into their home. This immigrant enters the living room and is loud, animated and full of charm. However, his "driver [who] was in livery" (9) waits for the overheated car to cool down, while Houdini is shown hospitality and courtesy in the house, in spite of Father's disdain for immigrants. "[T]he car was parked correctly," that is, in its proper place in the street with the chauffeur, who is correspondingly in his proper place. Yet, "Houdini climbed in the seat next to the driver and waved" (11) as he rode away. Although Houdini employs a driver, he clearly does not maintain strict spatial boundaries to designate their positions of employer and servant.[71]

Lawrence Levine describes a common response by people of Father's social class at the turn of the century to the encroachment of the Other, as one in which there was

> an escape into Culture, which became one of the mechanisms that made it possible to identify, distinguish, and order this new universe of strangers. As long as these strangers had stayed within their own precincts and retained their own peculiar ways, they remained containable and could be dealt with. [. . .] But these worlds of strangers did not remain contained; they spilled over into the public spaces that characterized nineteenth-century America and that included theaters, music halls, opera houses, museums, parks, fairs, and the rich public cultural life that took place daily on the streets of American cities. This is precisely where the threat lay and the response of the elites was a tripartite one: to retreat into their own private spaces whenever possible; to transform public spaces by rules, systems of taste, and canons of behavior of their own choosing; and, finally, to convert the strangers so that their modes of behavior and cultural predilections emulated those of the elites—an urge that [. . .] always remained shrouded in ambivalence.[72]

But none of these solutions are really available to Father; a retreat into a private space is impossible because his home, his refuge, has been invaded by the Other, immigrant and Negro, aided and abetted by the rest of his family with Mother at the helm. For Father, there is no place to hide.

Even Coalhouse Walker is permitted, or at least has forced his way without much resistance, into an area that wouldn't welcome the likes of Fire Chief Willie Conklin, the "dumb Mick" (251), and his Irish compatriots, who are considered poor white trash, ignorant and drunken. Conklin is resented by all the other municipal authorities and citizens for his part in creating the situation with Coalhouse in the first place. Father's class consciousness is aroused as much by the intrusion of Conklin into his life as he is by Coalhouse's and Sarah's intrusions. He is appalled at Conklin's familiarity:

> Father felt demeaned by the man. Conklin spoke to him differently from the way he addressed the policemen. His diction improved. His assumption of social equality was galling. It's a tragic thing, Captain, he would say. A tragic thing indeed. Once he actually put his hand on Father's shoulder, a gesture of such alarming brotherhood that it felt like an electric shock. (251)

An interesting contrast to Sarah's status with the white family is that of the other African American servants in the text, what little we know of them. There is absolutely no personal information about these other servants. They are entirely backgrounded in the story performing their tasks, fulfilling their professional domestic obligations without any particular attention being paid to them. Yet, their very presence and the functions they perform draw attention to the status and utility of black people in American society at the turn of the twentieth century. For example, after Sarah is killed a wet nurse is brought in to nurse the inconsolable brown baby—an almost incomprehensible event. This is undoubtedly rare; hiring a wet nurse to accommodate the child of a servant. But it is also clearly a necessity if the child is to remain in the home, and cannot be read as an indication of progress or changing times. The wet nurse is simply there to perform a needed domestic function, and her presence underscores the fact that Mother will go to necessary lengths to keep Sarah's child in her home and under her care.

Servants are also a bandage solution for the huge problems the family faces, yet, they cannot do without them. After the Irish servant has left and Sarah has died, Mother's appearance and health deteriorates without domestic help. She is also under pressure from state authorities to turn the brown baby over to "one of the excellent asylums" (257); she refuses. Even today, the presence of a black child in an all-white family may arouse curiosity. In early twentieth-century *Ragtime* such an arrangement causes a circus in the family's neighborhood. The appearance the family's situation gives to the neighbors is appalling to Father—the impropriety of it! Sightseers drive up and down their street to get a glimpse of the family with the brown baby. Their lives fall apart, as Father sees it, because "Coalhouse ruled" (258). After being accused of stinginess, Father relents and hires two live-in servants and a gardener. The family takes on a Negro housekeeper not only to give Mother some relief, but to serve as a smokescreen for the brown child; to assuage some of the curiosity of the neighbors and, of course, the media (Coalhouse's rebellion is the story of the day for the press).

During a vacation to Atlantic City "[t]he housekeeper would stay with Mother at the shore. She was a stolid, conscientious Negro woman who would provide, in addition, the obvious and erroneous explanation for the presence of a brown child in their party" (272). The housekeeper also becomes their laundress, and has actually been employed to perform both duties at the shore, but she is in no way a true surrogate for the beloved Sarah. "Mother was wearing a white ensemble. The laundress held Sarah's child" (277), a poignant recapitulation of happier times.

Coalhouse Walker, Jr.: The Inscrutable Non-Servant

One of the most interesting aspects of *Ragtime* is the characterization of Coalhouse Walker as *not servant, not servile*, which causes extreme confusion for the family, as well as for many critics of this text, who misapprehend his personality and his motives. There are those who think that Walker is simply a man who wants his car back.[73] Others are mystified at "the nature of Coalhouse Walker's involvement with Sarah. Both his character and his motives are mysterious. One does not know precisely why he acts as he does."[74] In a society in which, by virtue of his color, Coalhouse is reasonably expected to be a servant, with appropriately deferential demeanor, he is, instead, out of place in his society. He is not a servant, and it is precisely his refusal to *be* subservient in his attitude that marks him as an anomaly, an embarrassment and a problem, first in the New Rochelle family, and then for the larger community.

Coalhouse's clothing, appearance and demeanor mark him as someone sure of his own worth; he is not shy or self-effacing in his attitude, but self-assured. "When Mother came to the door the colored man was respectful, but there was something disturbingly resolute and self-important in the way that he asked her if he could please speak with Sarah" (179). Mother tells him to wait at the back door during his first visit, but finds him in the kitchen looking at his child in the carriage, which was a family heirloom. She is upset at first that Coalhouse has entered her house without permission, because she is still at this point working through the appropriate boundaries for these Negro people, particularly a black male, in the new circumstances of her life. The proper place for Sarah is in the attic. The proper place for the brown baby is in the kitchen. The proper place for Coalhouse is on the back porch.

Motivated by her growing love for Sarah and the baby, however, Mother quickly comes to understand that her ideas are based on an old and clearly useless set of assumptions and traditions. She decides to play matchmaker, and begins to invite Coalhouse into the parlor for refreshments, relaxing the socially prescribed boundaries. Father intensely dislikes the idea of *serving* tea to "The Negro," as he calls Coalhouse, a reversal of the natural order of things in which Coalhouse would be serving them. Mother is forced to try to educate Father on the appropriateness of it, using Roosevelt's having Booker T. Washington to the White House for dinner as an example of changing times. Coalhouse has conducted himself in a polite and gentlemanly way and offered himself as their equal, therefore Mother can't see anything wrong with extending this courtesy. Coalhouse is not deferential but comfortable and correct in their home, an attitude that Father despises.

When Coalhouse plays ragtime music on Mother's piano the entire family is transfixed. This uncommon, foreign element tinged with beauty has found its way into their lives and consciousness. Strangely, the music is not out of place; and, perhaps, neither is Coalhouse, Mother decides. He is fit to both court her charge, Sarah, and to sit in her parlor and drink tea. Social barriers erode faster than Father can adjust, and his resistance to change becomes increasingly apparent. Coalhouse represents the undoing of class and race signifiers, which along with Sarah's presence causes much upheaval in the white family's life. These interlopers have the potential to undermine and cause disorder in, and even the dissolution of, social structure based on class and race. In fact, Coalhouse's casual and self-assured obliviousness to the effects of his intrusions mock and threaten pretensions to social superiority, which Father has enjoyed without question.

Coalhouse is referred to as The Negro, which is all he is to the white firemen, the authorities and to Father—a mere specimen of his "kind." He becomes the representative of all the struggling, oppressed, disrespected, potentially insurgent Negroes of America. In fact, for the general public Coalhouse is so thoroughly objectified and representative of his entire race that when the newspapers can't find a picture of him, they simply substitute a photo of Scott Joplin. Apparently, any Negro will do. Coalhouse's presence in the New Rochelle neighborhood is a threat to established social boundaries. What happens to Coalhouse is a metaphor for what has happened (is happening) to American blacks. David Emblidge writes that

> [t]he embattled Negro, drawn into upward mobility through imitation of high white culture, is beaten down for racist fun by white trash; the system of jus-

> tice, even when used in the Negro's defense by white bourgeois sympathizers, does no good; the Negro turns radical and threatens to destroy white private property representing the social and financial success no longer available to him; everybody except the Negro and his revolutionary colleagues wonders why; the Negro is caught and killed.[75]

But Coalhouse's resorting to violence becomes increasingly understandable as justice through legal channels eludes him.

Father does not respond well and never adjusts to Coalhouse's visits to Sarah in his home. During his visits Coalhouse brings the family up to date on his doings, assuming they care. Father resents what he perceives as Coalhouse's "airs" and is sick of the whole business, probably because Coalhouse does not affect any of the obsequious and deferential behaviors Father is accustomed to seeing in the only Negroes he has contact with—those who serve him. Although Coalhouse is aware that his appearance of material success is an affront to white people (199), "[a]pparently it did not occur to him to ingratiate himself in the fashion of his race" (202), and "[i]t occurred to Father one day that Coalhouse Walker, Jr. didn't know he was a Negro" (185)—a notion that is completely disconcerting to Father, and apparently to many readers of this text.

One very striking thing in a good deal of the scholarship about *Ragtime* is that the critics who take on this aspect of the book believe, as does Father, that Coalhouse Walker does not know he is a Negro; they simply do not know what else to do with him. In fact, one critic writes that "it is unlikely that Father would have any real objections if only the black man recalled he was a Negro. But everything about Coalhouse's manner suggests that he is unaware of his blackness."[76]

How must a person act to demonstrate an awareness of his or her blackness? Without stereotypical behaviors as a frame of reference, these observers of black people assume that the person has no self-awareness and is completely insensible to their own color—the very reason they are reviled and subjugated. Apparently, the rules and expectations that govern the performance of certain behaviors, which will affirm an awareness of blackness, must also affirm an awareness of inferiority. Ingratiation, deference, submission, self-disparaging humor, ignorance, a show of a lack of intelligence and, most of all, servility are all very useful indicators of self-knowledge that one is a Negro. Father's unselfconscious racism assumes that Negroes must know themselves to be what they are perceived to be by white people, and that they should act accordingly.

Coalhouse doesn't act like a man who knows that there is something "wrong" with him. He knows he is a Negro, he simply does not feel diminished by that fact. It would seem that it is precisely because of his "personal talent and dignity, his stylishness and quiet bearing [which] mark him as 'uppity'; [that the] vandalizing of his car is not just a joke on the part of the volunteer firemen, it is also a lesson in reality," according to Arthur Saltzman. The lesson that Coalhouse must learn, and that we as readers must be reminded of, is that "[t]he Negro, no matter how qualified or well-mannered he may become, can only hope to be tolerated as a second-class citizen in White America. In fact, because the system of justice is designed to protect the ruling class, thereby ceasing to function when a Negro seeks to share in its benefits, not even second-class status can be guaranteed him."[77]

One critic writes that "Walker lives in a volatile world where racism exists, but he refuses to recognize it," and that "[s]ymbolic of his desire for an unchanging world which reflects his own view of reality is his persistent demand that his Model T be restored to 'just the condition it was.'"[78] It is almost inconceivable that a black man living in early twentieth-century America does not recognize racism; Coalhouse does. But he refuses to conveniently step aside and assume the servile, and therefore knowable and acceptable, position that would accommodate the expectations of his collective audience—Father, New York City officials, Fire Chief Conklin, the mass media of his day and some critics of this text. He demands that his car be restored, not because of his "desire for an unchanging world," but because he is attempting to force the world to change, and because he is entitled as a human being and an American to this simple request for justice. He stands up for his rights; something Emma Goldman understands when she says of his conduct that "the Negro was tormented into action" (321–322). Furthermore, Coalhouse Walker is a representation of a radical, and the radical left, according to Doctorow, is always faced with the difficulty of mobilizing what are generally a fearful and resistant population behind them. Doctorow says "it's so much easier for the right to command mass support, because it does not attempt to reform. It does not attempt to answer the needs of people, alleviate their miseries and their terrors. All it has to do is confirm them in their fear and their hysteria." Coalhouse Walker is, therefore, the perfect foil for the establishment and the political right. His need for and insistence on justice, and his refusal to simply go away, forces both those in power and ordinary people to confront the possibility of having to make adjustments in their thinking and behavior. Walker "confirm[s] them in their fear and hysteria."[79]

No servant, he—at least not in the usual sense. Unwavering commitment and loyalty; scrupulous management and keeping track of funds; stealth and cunning; study of the enemy's reactions through a careful scrutiny of the media; uniformity in dress for solidarity and unity; courtesy and deliberate gravity in the bunker; sharing of responsibilities, including the housekeeping and chores, constitute the culture of "Coalhouse," as Coalhouse's comrades have come to think of themselves collectively. With their prescription of insurrection for justice, they are committed revolutionaries. Coalhouse is indeed a servant in the cause of justice for his people, as he explains to Booker T. Washington when he comes to persuade Coalhouse to give up his quest because he is making all Negroes look bad. Coalhouse replies:

> I have always stood in admiration for you. [. . .] It is true I am a musician and a man of years. But I would hope this might suggest to you the solemn calculation of my mind. And that therefore, possibly, we might both be servants of our color who insist on the truth of our manhood and the respect it demands. Washington was so stunned by this suggestion that he began to lose consciousness. (326–327)

But Booker T. Washington, arguably the advocate of black servility, is as incapable of identifying with Coalhouse Walker's mission as are the policemen who have their weapons trained on every window and door of Morgan's building in which the revolutionaries are barricaded. As Doctorow says, "[i]t's much easier to terrify people and confirm them in their rigidity than to say—look, there are other ways we can do this. [. . .] The left, the radicals, have always been easily isolated and made objects of terror."[80] This, along with his shame about the choices Walker has made, which he feels are a negative reflection on every decent, law-abiding black person in America, make Washington an adversary rather than a supporter. He laments: "Every Negro in prison, every shiftless no-good gambling and fornicating colored man has been my enemy, and every incident of faulted Negro character has cost me a piece of my life. What will your misguided criminal recklessness cost me!" (325–326).

Although many critics find Coalhouse as inscrutable as do Father, Washington and almost everyone else, the text is very clear about Coalhouse. Tactical retreat for appeasement and survival is unacceptable. He refuses to stand down because he is a servant of justice for his people.

Coalhouse functions as a symbol of black virility and power, and is the very source for fear of white emasculation in *Ragtime*—the diminished capacity by comparison, or fear of competition, with black men. In a rare moment of self-examination Father is able to consider the possibility that he is simply jealous of Coalhouse. He

> wonder[s] if his dislike for Coalhouse Walker, which had been instantaneous, was based not on the man's color but on his being engaged in an act of courtship, a suspenseful enterprise that suggested the best of life was yet to come. Father noted the skin mottling on the back of his hand. He found him-

> self occasionally asking people to repeat to him what they'd said. His bladder seemed always to demand emptying. (248)

At the height of Coalhouse's rebellion, the words of the distressed colonel express the fear of black male sexuality and suggest a rationalization for racist attitudes and policies—the emasculation of the powerful "nigger" male. By "cut[ting] off his balls" (317) the country will become safe once again. This is a thinly disguised excuse for wholesale extermination, which deflects the real issue—suppressing autonomy and obliterating black male sexuality—which is conflated with violence, power, desire and forbidden and envied sexual pleasure. The colonel fears that if they don't decisively obliterate Coalhouse, then "every nigger in the country [will be] at your throat!" (317). Washington wasn't wrong about the impulse of white people to see each negative example of black behavior as representative. If Coalhouse were white and his crimes the same, the fear would not be that every white man would "be at your throat." This fear suggests the belief that, given the chance, black men are simply waiting to annihilate white men. Although the fear of the potential for black male violence is clearly grounded in an understanding of the dynamics of injury and reprisal, the position and posturing of the authority figures in this text fall short of an admission of guilt or accountability. It does, however, demonstrate an awareness that on some level Coalhouse's frustration and rage are justifiable, or at least understandable, to those very people who are in a position to grant him justice, but refuse to do so.

The text begs the question: What to do with this not-servant/nonservile Negro man? Predictably, the authorities resort to blaming the victim, manipulating circumstances for damage control, and ultimately pass the responsibility for the outcome of the situation to someone else. For Father "[i]t seemed like such a foolish thing to have happened. It seemed to be his [Coalhouse's] fault, somehow, because he was Negro and it was the kind of problem that would only adhere to a Negro. His monumental negritude sat in front of them like a centerpiece on the table" (212). Father's assessment of the deteriorating situation leads him to decide that it's time to take matters into his own hands. He will bribe the firemen, if necessary, to get the car restored. "I will make them see they are dealing with a property owner of this city, Father said. If that doesn't work I will quite simply bribe them. [. . .] I will pay them money. I will buy them off" (217). Father only understands throwing money at the problem to make it go away. His solution represents an outmoded and ineffectual way of dealing with social problems, particularly The Negro Problem.

But Mother understands that it is the principle of the situation, the disrespect that Coalhouse has been subjected to, that needs amelioration. Mother's solution takes into account the legitimacy of the grievance and respect for the complainant. Clearly, black anger is comprehensible to people like Father. But his response, and that of the authorities, unlike Mother's and Younger Brother's, is to think of ways to kill Coalhouse, or at least to flush him out. They toy with extreme solutions; maybe poison gas would work, even if it would kill everyone on the East Side. But while they plan their terrible and short-sighted solution to the problem of this out-of-control Negro, "coon eyes" (318) watch their every move.

Creating a Constituency: Liberal Humanism and *Ragtime*

Emily Miller Budick in *Fiction and Historical Consciousness* correctly names Doctorow's work the "moral fiction of history [which is] intended directly to effect social and moral change."[81] Doctorow states:

> We started off from the point of view of property, including slaves, and by means of the use of capital—as it discovered technology and was invested in technology—worked our way into a rather generous, prosperous society that was able to ignore the terrible decimation of working people and of minorities in order for it to achieve what it achieved. A kind of social and political blindness came along.[82]

Ragtime makes the connection between American prosperity, the ascendancy of technology and the social and political blindness that is its by-product, and the disposition of those classes of people who make such a system possible because of the support roles they play. But most important, for Doctorow, "[t]he big story is always the national soul—who are we, what are we trying to be, what is our fate, where will we stand in the moral universe when these things are reckoned? That's always the big story."[83]

Coalhouse Walker and Sarah are the only primary fictional characters in *Ragtime* who are named, because "these characters represent ideas and American values." In this way, Doctorow makes clear that all of American history, current and future, will succeed or fail, will "turn" on what happens to the likes of Sarah and Coalhouse. By naming Sarah and Coalhouse, Doctorow draws attention to their humanity; white people's humanity is a given. Sarah and Coalhouse are not just part of the "Negro Problem," they are individuals. Barbara Cooper writes that the other fictional characters "are not uniquely developed people; instead, they are people like any of us."[84] Although it is not clear who is included in Cooper's category of "us," that, I think, is the whole point. Everyone plays a part and has a responsibility for how things turn out.

Ragtime is a portrait of a society driven by gross materialism and acquisitiveness; a society in crisis struggling toward and simultaneously resisting a more comprehensive and inclusive identity and agenda. Doctorow places the towering figures of American business and industry in a context in which we are not accustomed to viewing them—as they actively engage with their servants and those who they believe should be serving them, such as Coalhouse Walker.

J. P. Morgan holds a banquet for the greatest business minds of his age. He is a lonely man who hopes to find a kindred spirit among his celebrated guests. Morgan is sorely disappointed to find that they have nothing in common, nothing of interest to say to him or one another. They are shallow, silly, socially inept, gross. "Rockefeller startled him with the news that he was chronically constipated and did a lot of his thinking on the toilet. Carnegie dozed over his brandy. Harriman uttered inanities. [. . .] How they appalled him. [. . .] But the pomposity that had accrued with their wealth persuaded them that perhaps these ridiculous vines held some significance" (160–161). The wives are vacuous, boring, unattractive, eclipsed by their husbands' greatness. Still, he marks the moment of their coming together with the laurel leaves, forces ("ordered") his servants to play along with the charade of paying homage to these people and has a photograph taken to capture the precious moment for posterity. It is clear to Morgan, and to the reader, that these men may be gifted at making fortunes, but their relevance beyond this is questionable.

On the other hand, the silent and invisible servants who prepare and serve an extraordinary meal are the epitome of efficiency and competency. Their viability is valued and is not questionable, much as one would value the parts of a well-oiled machine. "The service was magical, two of Morgan's house staff making dishes appear and disappear with such self-effacement as to suggest no human agency" (166)—the resonating presence of the unacknowledged class of Americans who are invisible to those they serve.

Morgan possesses hordes of cultural treasures of the Western world. His acquisitiveness and sense of ownership for art, artifacts, antique manuscripts and intellectual properties extends to the scholars who explicate it for him. "My scholars," or "[m]y private staff of Egyptologists," as he refers to them, are nothing more than servants to him. They furnish him with information to satisfy his curiosity, expand his knowledge and excite his vanity. Their presence and the service they provide comforts him with the knowledge that he is not alone in the universe, and that there have always been a few extraordinary individuals in every age, including himself, who are superior to all others of the species—really a species unto themselves, who will lead mankind to the next phase in human evolution.

In Europe, Morgan is completely oblivious and unchanged about what had happened in New York on his property.

> [Morgan] debarked at Cherbourg, the incident of the mad black man in his Library quite forgotten, and made his customary way across the Continent, going from country to country in his private train and dining with bankers, premiers and kings. Of this latter group he noted a marked deterioration in spirit. If the royal families were not melancholic they were hysterical. They overturned wineglasses or stuttered or screamed at servants. He watched. The conviction came over him that they were obsolete. (355–356)

As the world of privilege and gentility deteriorates, royalty screams at their servants—the last vestiges of civility disappear as a way of life is threatened. The treatment of their servants is a barometer by which to calibrate the changing social conditions of an age that is passing away. The gene pool has gone to seed for European aristocracy, and they seek to flee a Europe that has increasingly little use for them. They offer their possessions, wives and children in exchange for money (356–357). The deterioration of aristocratic European civility and the certainty of its obsolescence are intended as a harbinger and cautionary note for America. The dissolution of the ruling houses of Europe foreshadows the dissolution of the "aristocracy" and the ruling classes of America—the J. P. Morgans and Fathers.

Doctorow is often accused of going too far in his use of history in *Ragtime*, that he actually exploits history to suit his own agenda and that "[t]he very fantasy on which the novel depends is opportunistic and history is a shtick."[85] But Doctorow is completely unabashed about his uses of history. He believes that "history shares with fiction a mode of mediating the world for the purpose of introducing meaning, and it is the cultural authority from which they both derive that illuminates those facts so that they can be perceived. Facts are the images of history, just as images are the data of fiction."[86] It is the facts and images of history, real and imagined, that accommodate Doctorow's exploration of injustice in *Ragtime*. He is, as Frederic Jameson describes him, "the epic poet of the disappearance of the American radical past, of the suppression of older traditions and moments of the American radical tradition: no one with left sympathies can read these splendid novels without a poignant distress that is an authentic way of confronting our own current political dilemmas in the present."[87]

Ragtime is a portrait of a society in conflict and crisis. "[T]he point of view, in political terms, is that history, especially the American brand, is far from a progressive evolution toward peace among men. The book is an indictment of the recurrent malignancies of spirit beneath the period's chimerical technological progress and social harmony."[88] Younger Brother listens to the terrible music of a train moving forward, a parody of the sounds of a society struggling to advance. The metal grates where the two cars are joined, much like disparate groups, come together, but not without "screeching and pounding. [. . .] It was a suicide rag" (198). Perhaps coming together is impossible, and will cause the death or destruction of everything in the attempt. Progress may, in fact, be an illusion; the repetition of the sounds of ragtime music and of the mechanical parts of the train echo the human tendency to repeat history with the same regularity and predictability of a wheel turning, or the repeated refrains of a ragtime song.

But Doctorow's use of the past also offers ways in which to consider not only alternate realities but alternatives. He is clear about his mission to raise the consciousness of his reading audience when he says, "I know that a book can affect consciousness—affect the way people think and therefore the way they act. Books create constituencies that have their own effect on history, and that's been proven time and again. So I don't see that distinction between facts and art."[89] He presents a challenge to writers to confront important issues when he says that "[l]iterary life in the present is, by comparison [to the 1930s], decorous. It's very quiet today. Is it because our society is sunlit and perfect? Are all our vampires staked through the heart? Or have we, as writers, given up our presumption of the authority of art, of the central place of the sustained narrative critique in the national argument?"[90]

Ragtime engages the national argument, and, through the personal social dynamics and historical consequences that surround a single black washerwoman, offers both illumination and a prescription for staking the vampires of racism and classism through the heart. *Ragtime* may be a fantasy about how things might have been or should have been, if only. It is very clear in this story that there is always the potential for other outcomes, the ubiquitous "what if" that carries with it the idea of choice. The promise of progress, or the threat of failure and destruction, is always contingent upon forward thinking and moral sensibility.

CHAPTER 4

"EVOLVE OR DIE"

Rewriting "the Disfiguring Hand of Servitude" in Charles Johnson's Middle Passage

The moment the slave resolves that he will no longer be a slave, his fetters fall. He frees himself and shows the way to others. Freedom and slavery are mental states.

—Mohandas K. Gandhi

Freedom is not something that anybody can be given; freedom is something people take and people are as free as they want to be.

—James Baldwin

Liberty means responsibility. That's why most men dread it.

—George Bernard Shaw[1]

COUNTERMANDING "THE OVERLY DISCUSSED VICTIMIZATION OF BLACK PEOPLE": A PHILOSOPHY OF COMPOSITION[2]

Self-reliance and self-determination loom large in Charles Johnson's writing, both critical and creative. His position on self-determination has its roots in the way he was raised by conscientious and hardworking parents. They encouraged Johnson to become educated and to work hard at honest work (his father found a summer job for Johnson as a garbage man when he was in college), and this goes a long way in explaining Johnson's views about the possibility and necessity for self-reliance and creating one's own opportunities regardless of social context and obstacles.[3]

Johnson's father held several jobs to make ends meet, including doing chores for an elderly white couple. His mother was a cleaning lady and his grandmother worked as a cook at a Northwestern University sorority. Johnson writes with no small amount of justifiable pride about how even individuals who have the appearance of being constrained or trapped by social class, economics and race are able to transcend their circumstances and make a different and better reality for themselves. In an autobiographical essay, he describes the ironic, but perhaps not so surprising, turn of events that started the child and grandchild of people who were employed as servants on the path of upward mobility and self-actualization. He writes of his mother:

> And she brought me along with her since she couldn't afford a baby-sitter. I remember her telling me that the sorority's chapter said no blacks would ever be admitted into its ivied halls. There are two great ironies in this story. The first is that my mother brought home books thrown out by the sorority girls when classes ended, and in those boxes I found my first copies of Shakespeare's tragedies. The other irony is that decades later in 1990 Northwestern's English department actively (and generously) pursued me for employment by offering me a chair in the humanities, which I declined.

Johnson received an honorary doctorate from Northwestern University in 1994, and dedicated it to his mother and grandmother. In his commencement address he stated that he "devoured" the discarded books his mother rescued "with the pleasure, the delight, the wicked knowledge that the girls of Gamma Phi Beta would never be able to say they knew something their cleaning woman's son didn't know."[4] He learned early in life from his parents' example the importance of education and personal growth, and that "[t]he only person responsible for someone's intellectual life is that person. [. . .] We should read as much as we possibly can from all cultures. It's that simple."[5] It is through his early reading of the books provided by his mother—a wide and eclectic selection ranging from Christian mysticism, Rilke, Richard Wright, Defoe, yoga, Victorian poetry, dieting and flower arranging, to books about American theatre and painting—that Johnson's imagination was fired and his love of learning was secured.[6] In the preface to *I Call Myself an Artist: Writings by and about Charles Johnson,* editor Rudolph Byrd describes Johnson as a messenger, one who is concerned with "our collective health and identifies fully with such a vision of renewal and power." Johnson is clearly a believer in both the power and the obligation of the individual to transcend circumstances, and, resounding through his work, fiction and otherwise, is a call to self-actualization. Perhaps most illustrative in *Middle Passage*, for which he received the National Book Award in 1990, is a summons to "evolve or die."[7]

In *Middle Passage* Charles Johnson deploys the sassy, irreverent reprobate, former slave and servant Rutherford Calhoun to draw a fresh kind of attention to some of the social issues relevant to the 1830s, the period in which the story takes place. Perhaps most important, *Middle Passage* offers a critique of unresolved social issues, especially for African Americans, from that period up to the time the book was published in 1990—particularly where self-reliance and self-determination are concerned. Johnson accomplishes this through a very particular and controversial representation of African Americans in a position of slavery and servitude, which could easily be considered unlikely, even radical (some might say retrogressive), for an African American writer.[8] Ultimately, *Middle Passage* suggests that what is commonly perceived as the legacy of enslavement and servitude for African Americans, the "disfiguring hand of servitude" (179), need not be disfiguring at all, and can in fact be, if not motivational, beneficial.

Briefly, the story is this: Former slave and self-described drunk, womanizer, petty thief, liar and all-around low-life Rutherford Calhoun sows his oats and squanders his freedom in 1830s New Orleans. He runs up a considerable debt to the black godfather figure, Papa Zeringue. In an effort to escape a blackmail marriage to Isadora Bailey, a New Orleans schoolmarm formerly from Boston who has paid off his debts to Papa, Rutherford stows away on the slave ship *Republic*, which operates in the text as a metaphor for the American republic. During his term on the *Republic* Rutherford begins to comprehend, through the example and culture of the Allmuseri Africans who have been taken on board as cargo for enslavement in America, and through the examples of the females in the text and his own brother Jackson, the "unity of Being" (65).[9] Unlike the slaves and servants in both *Band of Angels* and *Ragtime*, it is through his ruminations about servitude and learning value through service to others that Rutherford finds and validates his own humanity. As a reformed individual, and because of his experiences in slavery and servitude, Rutherford becomes an improved and healthier human being ready to take his place in the world.[10]

Middle Passage has been execrated by critics such as John Haynes, who reads it as "romantic racism," and who are concerned, perhaps justifiably so, that "black readers may feel that the dark night of the Middle Passage has been exploited simply for effect."[11] Richard Hardack argues that "Johnson systematically develops [. . .] slavery only as a *form* of slavery: that is, as a metaphor with almost exclusively psychological and metaphysical, rather than historical or political, consequences." Perhaps most scathing of all, he suggests that "[l]ike Michael

Jackson, Johnson seems intrigued with the idea of an unfixed, hybrid, fluid, actually morphing tissue of multi-colored skin, while all the time denying that race even exists as a category."[12] Hardack and Haynes are not alone in this criticism.

The humor Johnson employs on such a serious subject is also a cause for consternation for some critics. He constructs characters and situations, often fantastical and humorous, that are designed to challenge and ultimately destroy erroneous assumptions about race. "I think that's what fiction ought to be about," he says. "It ought to be about getting beneath those sedimented meanings, all the calcified, rigid perceptions of the object."[13] Some critics believe Johnson is successful in this respect, such as Daniel Scott, who writes in "Interrogating Identity: Appropriation and Transformation in *Middle Passage*" that this text "asserts racial identity as a hybrid, active process of being that reads and interprets itself and the culture that surrounds it. It is this identity that Johnson holds as a means to a larger, humanistic 'end': the liberation of perception, the opening up of epistemological perspective and of ontological meaning, not just for African-Americans but for all people."[14] Molly Abel Travis would agree with this sentiment, and writes that "Johnson's rhetorical audience is composed of those African American writers and critics who make racial resentment the primary determinant of their aesthetic endeavors. [. . .] [But] Johnson feels that such a response is retrograde in the 1990s and should be replaced by an aesthetics and a politics of cultural synthesis."[15]

One might reasonably wonder about Johnson's novel approach to such serious subjects as, among other things, slavery and the Middle Passage, particularly the comic aspects of this text, which includes an impudent and brazen narrator who manages to find humor in most situations (e.g., "The whole Middle Passage, you might say, was one long hangover") (36). Rutherford even recounts some of his experiences as a slave child with humor. The protests are worthy of consideration, but would anyone care to argue that humor didn't exist for slaves? And Rutherford's humor is most often both self-defensive and self-disparaging, biting and ironic, and showcases his wit and considerable powers of observation and understanding of human nature, as well as his growing apprehension of himself. As Wolfgang Binder points out in "Uses of Memory: The Middle Passage in African American Literature,"

> Johnson does not in any way trivialize the terrible burden which represents middle passage, but he dilutes to some extent simplistic, woodcut-like dichotomies. In his ironic, playful way, the author claims, as did Robert Hayden, with all due *caveat*, America as "the nigger's home." His novel is thus also a celebration of survival, of mitigated, tongue in cheek heroism, of remembrance, growth, belonging, and life.[16]

In all fairness, as a significant part of his narrative strategy in *Middle Passage*, Johnson makes apparent the horrors and injustice of slavery. He painstakingly depicts the moral consequences for American society, using everyone aboard the *Republic*—crew, officers, Africans and Rutherford Calhoun—and details the conditions, the cause-and-effect paradigm one might expect in such a tale. In fact, Johnson is particularly adept at explicitly chronicling the contexts of physical and mental slavery that make visible, and to some extent understandable, the ambient conditions that may give rise to antisocial, immoral and self-destructive attitudes and behaviors, particularly for those who are or have been enslaved.

Accompanying the humor are the deleterious effects of slavery, and the humiliating and catastrophic consequences for slaves are carefully catalogued. The horrors of kidnapping aside, the brutality and inhumanity the Africans are subjected to on the *Republic*—a ship distinguished by filth and disease (literally and figuratively), pederasty, storms, crew mutiny and a slave uprising—are graphic and appropriately horrifying, Johnson having researched for seventeen years to make the context realistic.[17] The ears of dead Africans are slashed off and preserved in oil to be used as proof-of-purchase seals for investors, ensuring some remuneration for the ship's captain when he is unable to deliver a live African for trade. Everyone on board suffers from running sores and dysentery; the food, what little of it there is, is insect-infested; putrefying bodies litter the hold and deck, some of which end up being food; children and women are raped as a matter of course; there is humiliation, ridicule, torture, branding and castration. The chaos of crew mutiny and slave insurrection makes terrible sense in this floating nightmare on the high seas.

Behaviors normally considered character flaws are shown to be expedients in the American slaveholding culture, a place that "was a battlefield, a boiling cauldron. It created white rascals [. . .] black ones [. . .] hundreds of slave lords, bondmen crippled and caricatured by the disfiguring hand of servitude" (179). Rutherford's moral corruption, his stealing, lying, feigned ignorance and stupidity and shifting loyalties are all, in fact, strategies for survival, part of his "racial savvy" (28) necessitated, one might reasonably conclude, by the conditions of forced servitude and powerlessness. In his explanation for why he steals, for example, Rutherford discloses the relationship between the severe physical deprivation and disrespect endured, and the resulting psychological toll experienced by the enslaved. The slave is perpetually in a totally demoralizing situation in that, not only being subjected to the obvious wrong of being deprived of liberty and autonomy, all that the slave receives is in the dubious form of "charity." This so-called charity causes humiliation and ratifies the powerlessness and lowly status of the recipient. Rutherford explains in detail the potential crippling effects and consequences of severe deprivation and degradation:

> As a boy I'd never had enough of anything. [. . .] [D]uring the leaner years, suppertime: watery soup and the worst part of the hog and so little of that that Jackson often skipped meals secretly so I could have a little bit more. If you have never been hungry, you cannot know the *either/or* agony created by a single sorghum biscuit—either your brother gets it or you do. And if you *do* eat it, you know in your bones you have stolen the food straight from his mouth, there being so little for either of you. This was the daily, debilitating side of poverty that no one speaks of, the perpetual scarcity that, at every turn, makes the simplest act a moral dilemma.

Rutherford goes on to explain the scarcity of adequate clothing and the humiliation of wearing hand-me-downs inherited from his master, Rev. Chandler, and some "pious" friends. He has inherited more than old clothes and boots that smell of the original owners; he is forced to speak the language of his oppressors. It would be completely understandable that the demoralizing and depressing conditions of enslavement could produce an individual full of rage, who had little or no regard for the rules of a so-called civilized society. Rutherford acknowledges this: "Ah, me. The Reverend's prophecy that I would grow up to be a picklock was wiser than he knew, for was I not, as a Negro in the New World, *born* to be a thief? Or, put less harshly, inheritor of two millennia of things I had not myself made?" (47).

As a young child Rutherford decides that he has two choices: "If you are born on the bottom—in bondage [. . .] outright sedition or plodding reform." He chooses to be a barn burner, swear, refuse to keep himself clean, associate with bad company, fight, steal, lie and destroy things—all "small acts of revolt—blows against the Empire" (114). He tells sarcastic lies, always second-guessing what people want to hear as a way of controlling the situation and putting himself at the best advantage for self-protection and manipulation of others. He lies for effect, for fun, for secret observation of the responses of others to it. An accomplished manipulator, it is his birthright as one born into servitude. It gives him what little pleasure and power he can have, if undetected, with impunity. He says of a conversation with the mutinous crew of the *Republic:*

> they thought I was lying. Which I was. As a general principle and mode of operation during my days as a slave, I always lied, and sometimes just to see the comic results when a listener based his beliefs and behavior on things that were Not. But don't judge me harshly; it was one of the few forms of entertainment bondmen had. (90)

Through Rutherford's experience Johnson illustrates how these small acts of defiance are often a slave's only amusement and opportunity for self-empowerment; to have some effect, impact and control over their environment and life; to exercise the human right of volition.

Johnson creates, in Rutherford's rationalization for stealing, a vivid psychological profile of someone teetering on the edge of sociopathy but who, because of his self-awareness, is still capable of making different choices. Stealing is not just the means to get what he needs or what he wants; it is like the lying, simultaneously part of a survival strategy and an act of defiance. Theft, after all, is an ameliorating balm for the powerlessness, humiliation, frustration and rage of the enslaved and oppressed. It alleviates stress and in his idleness gives Rutherford something to do with his hands. It is a sensual ritual choreographed and "balletlike" that he performs with practiced and prideful skill. He touches everything in someone else's home to taint it, is aware that the people he robs will feel violated and is completely conscious of and thrilled at being the violator. He confesses that it was "as if I were slipping inside another's soul. [. . .] [I]t broke the power of the propertied class, which pleased me." It is, he says, "the closest thing I knew to transcendence" (46–47, 46). It is also the by-product of being a Negro in America; he was born to it.[18] At this early point in Rutherford's life it appears that his circumstances have shaped his character.

In his need to have some sense of power in his life, Rutherford also does more than steal from his victims. His naughty practices in the private quarters of his victims are part of his power play. Knowing that these deeds will cause, at the least, domestic strife and most likely fear and terror gives Rutherford the satisfaction of knowing that he has some negative effect on the lives of the class of people who have stolen and have complete control over his life. Sometimes, when he breaks-and-enters, his purpose is not even to steal. Instead, he leaves his "usual signatures of defiance: pooping amiddlemost a local politician's satin pillow, for example, or fabricating for his wife—some blue-blooded snob—a love letter from their black chambermaid [. . .] or simply scrawling on their parlor wall in charcoal from their hearth, as I often did, 'I can enter your life whenever I wish'" (48). It is a chilling concoction of foreboding mischief for pleasure. It is guerrilla warfare. It is a storm warning.

Johnson also offers other contexts for assessing Rutherford's antisocial behavior by demonstrating the power of parental example, even within the context of enslavement, particularly when the example is a negative one. Riley Calhoun, Rutherford's father, attributes his own irresponsible conduct to the exigencies of being enslaved—he has been infantilized and emasculated:

> "Looka how we livin'," he'd say. "Looka what they done to us." You couldn't right blame a colored man for acting like a child, could you—stealing and sloughing off work when people like Peleg Chandler took the profits, and on top of that so much of their dignity he couldn't look his wife Ruby in the face when they made love without seeing how much she hated him for being powerless, even with their own children, who had no respect for a man they had seen whipped more than once by an overseer [. . .]. Each time Da talked like this, checking off cankers and cancer spots of slavery on his porch in the quarters, the other men listened, [. . .] their eyes rage-kindled and drifting away to old angers of their own. (169–70)

One might think from all this that this text is offering a justification or vindication for antisocial, criminal and even pathological behavior in some African Americans because of what they have suffered in the past and continue to suffer as blacks in America. Not so. Although, ostensibly, Johnson's purpose may appear to be to cultivate understanding, and he provides the explanations and contexts to do so, he in no way permits denial of personal responsibility for the slaves or servants in *Middle Passage.* This is the notion that drives this text.[19]

Middle Passage is not simply a seafaring action-and-adventure tale about a feisty young free black man in early-nineteenth-century America who takes to the sea to escape a needy woman and a gangster. It is the theater in which many of the strongly held and deeply cherished values of its author are played out—the "*human* values"[20] that Johnson believes are not situational- or time-dependent.

It gradually becomes clear that Riley Calhoun, who becomes a runaway slave and abandons his family, represents those black people who use the crime and effects of slavery as a reason to abandon responsibility and to not move forward in life. Rutherford reflects that they have become a fiction and have fictionalized themselves, sitting around reminiscing about the good old days in an idealized Africa when, as Riley puts it, "'[w]e was kings once,' [. . .] (and neglecting to add that in his tribe his own family was not royalty but instead the equivalent of Russian serfs or Chinese coolies)" (170). Riley's "misspent manhood," Rutherford tells us, was focused on fighting with his family and fellow slaves out of frustration and the inability to make some meaning out of and have some purpose in his life. Increasingly, Rutherford "had to listen harder to isolate him from the We that swelled each particle and pore of him, as if the (black) self was the greatest of all fictions" (171).

This is Riley's legacy to his sons: a wallowing in self-pity; fantasizing about a place and past that are not really his to claim; using his enslavement as an explanation and an excuse for doing whatever he pleases regardless of the consequences to himself or others.[21]

The renegade Allmuseri African, Diamelo, also functions as an example of an enslaved black person who exploits the idea of his enslavement and uses it as a reason for failing in life. Prior to his capture in Africa, Diamelo was not a pillar of his society, but a cowardly, lazy and drunken lecher who had no love or interest in the culture and traditions of his people and was held, justifiably, in low regard. Capture and enslavement gave him a cause on which to blame all his failures. He cleverly shifts the focus from his own shortcomings to his circumstances. He is, in fact, able to rally his people around him, and "it was not so much his stature that sometimes swayed and stoked up the others when he spoke as the purity of his racial outrage. This he kept close to him like a possession [. . .] a point of reference that made every event prior to his enslavement pale by comparison." His enslavement became "the most significant, the most memorable, even the finest hour of his life, a memory to safeguard and strengthen" (153). Being forced into servitude becomes the defining moment for Diamelo, and he gives himself and others enslaved permission to relinquish all sense of accountability.

> Diamelo found his long-delayed focus: Ebenezer Falcon [the *Republic's* captain], a true (godsent) devil to despise. A dragon so exquisite in his evil that Diamelo, never a boy to impress his people by his skills or social contributions, discovered no one spoke of his flaws and personal failings when all their lives were wreckage. He had but to breathe one two-syllabled iambic word, *Falcon*, to hold their ear and magically control their emotions. [. . .] But a champion must keep his dragon alive. It must not disappear. (154)

His latent embracing of his people's culture is sadly amusing and fanatical, and in its extremeness entirely misses the point and the spirit of their philosophies and their ways. He would lead them to their doom. Nevertheless, his fervor, however "opportunistic" or "false" (154), inspires a fearful, lost and vulnerable people too easily swayed by passionate rhetoric. According to Johnson's prescription for both literary and social progress, it is time to put the dragon to rest.

Johnson does not shrink from stressing in his work the moral and social values he holds dear and sees not only as a significant part of what used to be at the heart of black culture and tradition, but as the salvation of black people today. He writes:

> *human* values. Call them conservative, if you like, but once we dispense with labels they will be seen simply as the formula for successful living at any time. They are: a strong work ethic, self-reliance, delayed gratification, discipline, an appreciation of the individual, a commitment to education, dedication to

> one's family, marital fidelity, a respect for life, the capacity for self-sacrifice and religious piety. (my emphasis)

In *Middle Passage* Johnson imagines a slave history that offers possibilities for diverse experience and outcomes for a single individual, one person against enormous odds, who learns the "formula for successful living at any time,"[22] and who transcends what could have been fatally disabling circumstances to become a more whole human being and member of society. Johnson appropriates some of the most salient features of the slave narrative genre, the coming-of-age tale narrated by the subject, with an emphasis on how Rutherford comes to terms with the external world as it is and finds his own place—a transmutation forged under the duress of slave life, life as a free black man in early-nineteenth-century America and during the Middle Passage.[23]

Like real-life slave narrators, the fictional Rutherford Calhoun knew forced servitude firsthand, and uses that experience to explain, among other things, many aspects of social hierarchy and injustice in America. Significantly, one of the prevailing characteristics of slave narratives is the emphasis on the determination and self-reliance of the former slave. It is absolutely clear that Johnson intends to make the point that many slaves and ex-slaves prevailed and progressed under the worst of circumstances. From this truth the reader may conclude that quality of life and character are ultimately determined by the individual; it is a matter of perception and choice. At first, it appears that Rutherford will fall through the cracks, but his willingness to acknowledge his own responsibility to himself and others saves him. His very understandable explanations for the antisocial behavior of his childhood and youth (stealing, lying, laziness, selfishness, arson, etc.), are, in the end, convenient excuses for not trying hard enough, for not taking responsibility. In this coming-of-age text Rutherford must confront his own failures as a human being and as a man. He must acknowledge that within *any* context, even as a slave or servant, one is required to do the best they can; that there are certain nonnegotiable rules of decent conduct that must be subscribed and adhered to; that self-absorption and selfishness is always a choice; that the "unity of Being" (65), connectedness to and cooperation with others, is a significant part of the formula for being whole. Most significantly, Rutherford must admit he has mismanaged his freedom and has no one to blame but himself for his failures. This insight is clearly instructive for the reader, and it also begs the question: Is *Middle Passage* a critique of and commentary about how black people have squandered freedom and opportunity? I think so.

However, in addition to critiquing black experience and response, Johnson also hopes to fill what he perceives as a black literary void; the absence of "genuine philosophical black literature," and in this way draw attention to the social and cultural issues with which he is most concerned. He credits his interest in the "'philosophical novel'" to "personal taste [which] ran toward Sartre, Malraux, Herman [sic] Hesse, Thomas Mann, Ralph Ellison, Voltaire, and Herman Melville—the world-class authors who understood instinctively that fiction and philosophy were sister disciplines."[24] Johnson states in "Philosophy and Black Fiction":

> Because all conception—philosophy—is grounded in perception, there is no reason, in principle, that we cannot work through the particulars of Black life from *within* and discover there not only phenomena worthy of philosophical treatment in fiction, but also—and here I make my wildest claim today—significant new perceptions.[25]

He even goes so far as to admit that "[a] great work of fiction has the same importance to me as a great work of philosophy."[26] Although he relies heavily on his training in philosophy and history to construct his narratives, Johnson, like E. L. Doctorow, does not define himself as a historical novelist. In fact, he denies it categorically, and "hope[s] no one ever mistakes me for an 'historical writer.' That's never been my intention."[27] His method and intention is to glean from the past and synthesize from diverse sources of inherited knowledge for the purpose of "understand[ing] what others have brought to the rendering and disclosure of the subject." His borrowing from the past serves a larger purpose, as he explains:

> Any sense that other human beings have made out of the world, any sense that they have pulled out of this universe of non-sense as Merleau-Ponty would say, any judgments—all that is what we have inherited as human beings. And in a way, that's how I have to write. [. . .] We are perpetually indebted to our predecessors for that. It's not something I can ignore or something I can abandon. I may come upon a disclosure of the object that's different from anything that's come before, but I think it's predicated on all that came before. In the same way, I don't think you can get the Einsteinian universe without first the Newtonian universe. It's all a long conversation, and the writer does not come into this discussion *ex nihilo*, born with nothing behind him.[28]

Johnson is unabashedly on a mission to reinterpret black experience through artistic representation. He encourages other African American writers and is himself committed to disclosing the enormous complexity and diversity of experience, most particularly African American experience. He rails, in fact, against what he perceives as the self-stereotyping and narrowly constricted view of black people and black life being perpetuated and insisted upon by black artists. In "Philosophy and Black Fiction" he states, in the strongest terms:

> Clearly, the menagerie of Black caricatures and clichéd situations so popular today in Hollywood, so frequent in trashy fiction—the motor-mouthed dandy, two-faced preacher, hopheads, the spiritual African, ball-busting women, meek Christians, blind Caucasians, fiery Black social activists, all those frustrated, butchered lives—fail, fail utterly to express authentic ways of seeing [sic] (And let us assume there *are*, can be, authentic Black ways of seeing). We wonder, What Lord, are Black artists doing? Our *interpretation* of our experience, as Ishmael Reed has written in numerous articles, has become rigid, forced into formulaes; it does not permit, as all philosophically (and aesthetically) genuine fiction must, an efflorescence of meaning or a clarification of perception. We have so stylized our sense of the Black world [. . .] Black life, in fine, has become a frozen gesture, a one-dimensional style of being. How can we, then salvage Black fiction from calcification?[29]

Although, as Johnson points out, "[i]mage control has been the aim of black fiction—and perhaps its problem—from the very beginning of black literary production and was sounded as a specific goal," he acknowledges the reasons for this tradition in African American writing, such as the enormous burden for black nineteenth-century writers, for the "free, literate population was staggering—to lead the antislavery effort, counteract the ideology of racism, and prove themselves worthy of equality."[30] But, he calls now, and rightly so, for a new approach that will rewrite and transcend the constricted images in black fiction that appear to be "so stamped with *sameness* they seem to be the product of a committee, not an individual consciousness grappling with meaning."[31] As Travis acknowledges, his "aesthetic project [. . .] [is] to transcend the material and political conditions of history through artistic production/construction."[32]

In *Being and Race* he asserts that "we find meaning in flux [. . .] we find, I am saying the black world *overflowing* with meaning, so rich and multisided that literally anything—and everything—can be found there, good and bad, and one of the first choices of the writer is to be immersed in this embarrassment of rich, contradictory material."[33] He continuously reiterates that "Black life is ambiguous, and a kaleidescope [sic] of meanings rich, multi-sided, and what the authentic Black writer does is despoil meanings to pin down the freshest interpretation given to him. This is genuine fiction."[34]

Johnson offers a prescription for ameliorating this problem of narrow and most often negative self-definition, stifled creativity and blighted representation. "We" must start over, and throw out all preconceived notions of what it means to be black, and learn to "describ[e] without prejudice what has not been seen, or seen so deeply before," and then be certain that "this look at Black life—stripped in the first stage of all Black particulars, purified or irrealized such that it now stands before us as an instance of all experience [. . .] of its type—exhibits traits that illuminate our theme. Surely, it must."[35]

Therefore, in *Middle Passage* black experience is not monolithic. To name a few examples: Papa Zeringue is a powerful and wealthy black gangster in 1830s New Orleans. Rutherford, a sharp-witted renegade slave and then servant, and his brother Jackson, ostensibly an "Uncle Tom" type, are erudite and somehow strangely autonomous within the constraints of forced servitude. There are many more. Part of Johnson's objective as a writer is to create what he sees as "the ultimate moral fiction," and the disclosure and celebration of multiple and multiplexing perspectives is for him both a narrative strategy and a moral endeavor. In explaining his objectives, Johnson stresses that

> [e]very major character [. . .] is a character of evolution and change. They are not the same at the end of the book as when we first saw them. [. . .] Everybody is in this situation of process and change. Everybody is being forced and pressured, as the main characters are, to move forward in their lives, to have their perceptions changed, to react differently in different situations. That would be the ideal novel. What I want is the process novel where everybody mentioned is a main character in the process of evolution.[36]

It is conceivable that in his own work Johnson attempts to reveal the complexity and diversity of African American experience while simultaneously downplaying—without, presumably, undermining—the significance of racism in American history and society. Some critics make a case for this interpretation of his work, including Jonathan Little, who writes in *Charles Johnson's Spiritual Imagination:*

> One of Johnson's central aesthetic strategies involves the imaginative transportation of the self into the other. [. . .] [H]e urges writers to transcend their own limited perspectives and embrace as many different perspectives as possible to avoid racial and regional parochialism and to encourage interracial understanding and, perhaps, cross-cultural empathy. This is a fundamentally romantic impulse that stresses the mysteriously transcendent power of art.[37]

Johnson does acknowledge the difficulties for such an empathetic, imaginative transport. He writes: "perhaps we can never know others. Phenomenology aside, perhaps all we shall ever know are the workings of our own nervous systems. But real fiction *tries*. [. . .] Surely we don't wish to limit knowing to direct perception only. History, journalism, biography involve, rightly or wrongly, a suspension of disbelief not unlike fiction's own."[38]

This attitude makes possible the literary creation of a former slave and servant as the writer of a controversial and what can easily be perceived as flawed history and representation. On the slave ship *Republic*, Captain Falcon asks Rutherford "to be my eyes and ears. [. . .] No matter what becomes of me, I want others to know the truth of what happened on this voyage" (146), and he inherits the captain's log. In this way, Rutherford becomes guardian and curator of the past. What is significant here is that he (and Johnson) gets to write history the way he sees it—filtered through his own experiences, imagination, point of view and agenda. In all fairness, it is clearly intended to be regarded, in accordance with Johnson's own convictions about multiple realities and perceptions of reality, only as *one* possible history.

Consequently, there is a most unusual (some might argue ludicrous) trajectory in Rutherford's life in conspicuous contrast to that typical of Africans transported to the western hemisphere through the Middle Passage.[39] In fact, it may be argued that Rutherford, as a free black person, embraces slavery by deliberately stowing away aboard a slave ship bound for Africa, working as an unpaid laborer on the ship (a free black man who works for free), and openly declaring that "what lay ahead in Africa [. . .] was [. . .] far worse than the fortune I'd fled in New Orleans" (1), foreshadowing his disappointment when he reaches Africa and discovers corruption and African complicity in the slave trade. These possibilities make sense in light of Johnson's notions about reconfiguring experience and consequences and suggest the need to work backward or start over with a new mindset about how to respond to the experience of enslavement. It is clear that Rutherford doesn't belong in Africa and has no real connection to it, which "makes any lasting return to Africa impossible and irrelevant."[40]

Although Rutherford's tenure as a slave comes to an end, he continues to flounder and appears lost and ungrounded, or perhaps grounded in all the wrong things as a freed man, and it becomes clear in the novel that "free" is a relative term. Rutherford, for example, is a slave to the impact of his past experiences but also to his poor choices in life to which he is habituated and committed. The text also emphasizes the unwholesome effects of other kinds of "slavery." These forms of slavery may be equally as debilitating to an individual and a society: a slavishness to inherited assumptions about race, gender, experience, individuality, identity and the inability to acknowledge diversity of character and experience in all contexts, including slavery and the slaveholding culture. Most significantly, despite his lament about the conditions of his childhood as a slave, Rutherford eventually acknowledges that even the oppressed have the power to make moral choices; that slavery and freedom are, most of all, perceptual.[41] This understanding is crucial to his metamorphosis, and is, again, instructive to the reader.

Rutherford Calhoun is the perfect example of a black person in America with almost every conceivable reason to be angry and despairing. Without condoning his behavior one might still understand if he had continued his youthful path of petty crime and dissipation because of his life circumstances. He was born into slavery, his mother died when he was a child, his brother assumed the role of surrogate parent when their father abandoned them on the plantation. He is a black man in 1830s America—which just about says it all in terms of what he was up against in life. But *choice* is the operative word for Rutherford, in *Middle Passage* and in Johnson's philosophy of life and art. Rutherford comes to realize that he makes his own reality. This he learns from the Allmuseri, the Africans who have been captured and are being shipped on the *Republic* to America to be enslaved.

For Rutherford, like other characters in Johnson's fiction, "there is a progression from ignorance to knowledge, or from lack of understanding to some greater understanding [. . .] a moment of awareness, an epiphany if you like, a place where the character is smashed into a larger vision under the pressure of events."[42] Johnson's opinions about black status in America and his prescription for progress may be easily construed as "boot strap," a term he resists. It is understandable why Johnson may be viewed as insensitive or blind to the harsh realities of being black in America, because he is given to making statements, such as in his essay "The Second Front," that "our predecessors [. . .] who despite the overly discussed victimization of black people early in this century, found ways [. . .] to 'make a way out of no way.'"[43] However, he perceives, correctly so, that there is a receptive audience for his message. In 1995 Johnson wrote in the introduction to *Oxherding Tale:* "younger black and white critics, were eager to move beyond protest fiction and the literature of gender and racial victimization, which was beginning to ossify by the mid-1980s, and turned to the novel as a springboard for broadening their discussions of blackness and Being. To them I am eternally grateful."[44]

Rutherford is no victim. The difficult circumstances of his former life as a plantation slave and all-purpose servant in/on the republic/*Republic* are turned into advantage. He comes to understand his status as a black man in America in more worldly terms, from a global historical perspective. Most significant, his changing perceptions of servitude and service are crucial to his progress in life and to his moral evolution. By constructing Rutherford in this way, Johnson demonstrates that perpetual degradation does not have to be the legacy of servitude, forced or otherwise. He offers, instead, the idea of diverse outcomes and the possibility of purpose, viability, humanity and transmutation. As Daniel Scott puts it, Johnson makes Rutherford "black but he is not found to sit on one or the other side of an artificially imposed and enforced racial, social dichotomy."[45] He evolves not only in spite of forced servitude, but because of it. Johnson, through Rutherford Calhoun, makes a solid case that the "hand of servitude" need not be "disfiguring" (179). However, in *Middle Passage* those who serve and those who are served are held to a completely different standard.

Selective Culpability: Benign Diversity in a Slaving Society

In *Being and Race* Johnson writes:

> Poor writers or wealthy ones are told they cannot truly cross class boundaries. Black writing rarely, if ever, attempts to reconstruct the complexity of the world as seen through the eyes of a richly detailed three-dimensional white character, or of other nonwhites (native [sic] American, say, or Asian), and who can doubt these days that male writers worry, as well they should, about authentically presenting a female point of view?

In his determination to show complexity and diversity in African American life and character, and in keeping with his intent to demonstrate the nonmonolithic nature of experience, black or white, Johnson offers in *Middle Passage* unlikely and perhaps even preposterous characters in different capacities in the slaveholding culture. This is arguably a consequence of his thinking about the limited utility of "direct experience [. . .] [as] the raw stuff of creative writing." Instead of conforming to the notion that a writer writes most effectively when he or she is writing from the informed position of experience, Johnson promotes the primacy of creative conceptualization in the act of writing, and that "great literature resolves [. . .] problems of viewpoint and epistemology by emphasizing the fact that literary art is at its best when it is a sumptuous act of imagination, invention, and interpretation."[46]

Captain Falcon makes a special request of Rutherford Calhoun: "Give me a hand here, Mr. Calhoun. I hope you can see that I trust you. I need a colored mate to be my eyes and ears once the Africans are on board. Same with the crew. I want to know what each man's thinkin'" (57). Rutherford becomes both agent-in-place and interlocutor in a macabre minstrelsy, ferreting out, interpreting and moderating, not only for Falcon but for posterity, the motives and objectives of those in power; rendering them in his narrative, if not generally inoffensive, then ultimately benign.

Consequently, the world Johnson creates in *Middle Passage* is extraordinary and far-removed in many significant and unusual ways from the direct experience of being enslaved as evidenced in slave narratives and other historical documents. Most noticeably, it is a world that is almost deracialized and peopled with some characters who operate almost completely outside and apparently without the influences and contamination of racial consciousness. The first mate aboard the slave ship *Republic*, Peter Cringle, is an educated, sensitive aristocrat who is oblivious to a black stowaway casually calling him by his first name—this at a time when absolute deference was required of black men, when even eye contact or erect posture was often considered an insolence worthy of severe punishment or death. In a pub in New Orleans a friendly and helpful white cook, Josiah Squibb, shakes Rutherford's hand without hesitation, asks this black stranger about his troubles and buys him a drink. One might reasonably consider these situations improbable. But, are they absolutely unimaginable within the huge context and infinite possibilities of human interaction? *Middle Passage* requires a willingness to modify assumptions based on what are social constructs—class, race and even the perceived historical moment—in order to discern the author's methods and intentions.

Perhaps made the most familiar by romanticized versions of slavocracy in American film, fiction and popular mythology is the "kind" slave master—and *Middle Passage* has its own in the reluctant, "good" slave master, the Reverend Peleg Chandler. He is "a fair, sympathetic, and well-meaning man" (111) who educates Rutherford and his older brother Jackson. Rutherford acknowledges that "[t]hough a slaveholder, Reverend Chandler hated slavery. He'd inherited my brother and me from his father and, out of Christian guilt, taught us more than some white men in Makanda knew, then finally released us one by one" (8). Chandler's extensive knowledge of history, the Bible, mythology, philosophy, music, the sciences and classical literature "he passed along to his servants, the Calhoun brothers, when we attended to him" (111). Arguably, part of the motivation for educating them was that Chandler was rather isolated and lonely, having no family of his own, and their considerable erudition afforded him some intellectual companionship. Chandler was able to hold forth on anything from van Ruysbroeckk's *Flowers of a Mystic Garden* to Thomas Aquinas to Bach's *St. Matthew Passion* and be assured of receptive and comprehending ears.

Rutherford is generous in his assessment of Chandler, who, although he supposedly hated the "Peculiar Institution," never saw fit to free his slaves until he was old and dying—not an entirely unknown practice in slavery. He got good use of them before setting them free. But the inescapable point being made in *Middle Passage* is that there were benevolent slaveholders; those who had slaveholding thrust upon them against their wishes and better judgment, and who had a real fondness and maybe even familial feelings toward their slaves. Most of all, evidence of Chandler's "kindness" is that "Jackson stayed, more deeply bound to our master than any of us dreamed" (8)—a situation that bears some resemblance to many situations in sentimental plantation fiction.[47]

The most extreme example in *Middle Passage* of a complex yet ultimately benign white character in the slaving business is that of the *Republic's* captain, the bigoted suicidal pederast Ebenezer Falcon, who frankly admits that "generally speaking, I don't like Negroes either. [. . .] [They] don't think too well, or too often" (30). In time, Falcon establishes an intimacy with Rutherford that appears to disregard race—but, only after Rutherford proves himself worthy by demonstrating his intelligence and "loyalty" to Falcon. Falcon comes to trust Rutherford, arms him with a weapon to protect himself on the voyage home, gives him valuable information about how to survive the intrigue on the ship, calls him a friend, confides in him, flounces around naked before him, shares the food off his plate with him—with the same fork—and eventually entrusts the ship's log to him (46, 53–58, 94–95). In fact, Rutherford begins to suspect that Falcon has taken a fancy to him, "wondering if in a single fantastic evening I had become Captain Ebenezer Falcon's shipboard bride. [. . .] His courtship of me, for so it must be called, began the night Falcon caught me rummaging through his cabin" (46).

Perhaps most preposterous is that Rutherford admires Falcon's exploits and ideas; this "empire builder" who represents American imperialism in the world, who plunders religious shrines and takes what he wishes from one end of the globe to the other, is, to Rutherford, a genius. Rutherford rhapsodizes, even gushes about the daring and success of this one-man imperialist machine bent on conquering the world, or, at the least, acquiring its material riches. He is, as Rutherford says admiringly, "a patriot whose burning passion was the manifest destiny of the United States to Americanize the entire planet. Really, I wanted to take off my hat in his presence. [. . .] *Never mind that his sins were scarlet. He was living history.* [. . .] I was, as I say, impressed" (30, my emphasis).

The slave ship *Republic* functions as both a metaphor for and a microcosm of American society, and accordingly Falcon's physical stature of a dwarf may be seen on some level to represent the moral and ethical statures of the masters and leaders of the American republic in general—stunted in their development by unrestrained self-interest and greed. But Johnson also gives the enslaving business and the imperialist impulse an unusual and outrageous twist, which ultimately undermines this reading as a possibility. Rutherford, a former slave and a servant, is an apologist for imperialism and all its attending horrors because he comes to understand empire building as a cry for attention, and regards its participants as vulnerable and pitiable. He concludes that "this above all else did Captain Falcon and his species of world conquerors thrive upon: the desire to be fascinating objects in the eyes of others" (33). The adulation or revulsion felt by those who observe their conduct, or who are victims of it, is all one and the same—it is simply the attention the empire builders crave that matters most. In *Middle Passage*, Empire building is ego-nourishing and therapeutic for these sad subjugators, and this must be taken into consideration. As Johnson himself has said: "during the so-called 'peculiar institution,' black and white [. . .] are living in a system that is a lie but adjusting to it as best they can as human beings."[48] In such a view, wealth, power, domination and the means by which they are acquired are almost incidental.

Rutherford is clearly not naïve; his admiration is without irony and completely genuine. Is this part of Johnson's attempt to add dimension by avoiding the simple, easy and predictable demonization of such a character as Captain Falcon? Is this an effort to offer the possibility of an alternative reality and point of view regarding imperialism and the "Peculiar Institution," as well as their consequences? Could this be part of Johnson's attempt to demonstrate black individuality and the singularity of perspective of just one former slave, purposefully avoiding a predictable response from someone who could easily and justifiably regard himself as the victim of such exploits and of such a man as Falcon? Is Johnson deliberately seeking to countermand the "overly discussed victimization of black people"[49] by having a former slave and servant celebrate the people and practices that have caused so much human suffering? Arguably, yes, to all of the above. But he goes very far, indeed, in making these points.

Johnson's phenomenological perspective, in his philosophies of both composition and life, has a direct bearing on the construction of the likes of Rev. Chandler, Cringle, Squibb and Falcon. He has borrowed, it seems, from philosopher Herbert Spiegelberg's "Phenomenology through Vicarious Experience," which Johnson outlines in *Being and Race*, and employs the practice of imagining "other lives" according to the following prescription:

> (1) Using imagination and the techniques of variation, we try to occupy the real place of the other and view from this standpoint the world as it is present in all its texture, limitations, and possibilities. (2) In transporting ourselves in this manner we must divest ourselves of our own historically acquired peculiarities by adopting as much as we can of the other's viewpoint. We must quit the familiarity of our own lives momentarily to experience this. (3) After this transposition we move back and forth between the other's perspective and our own, comparing evidence, collating profiles, criticizing the other's perspective for what it lacks, and, according to what we find, amending our own.[50]

According to this prerogative Johnson attempts to locate the reader into the personal circumstances and consciousness of these particularly imagined participants in American slaveholding and/or the slave trade. He has, in fact, said that it is his job as a writer to "get me out of the way," and that "[o]ne of the hardest things to do when writing is to let the world come singing through our words. The world in all its richness, ambiguity and complexity. [. . .] [W]e must 'suspend' or 'bracket' our own pettiness and bias so these people can come to life on the page."[51] Although it may not have been Johnson's explicit intent, the result is a text that appears, in part, an attempt to evoke understanding and even sympathy for those judged by history, or at least by many, to be criminals and villains.

Simultaneously, continually and ironically, Johnson moderates the idea of black victimization in American slavery and servitude in *Middle Passage* by extending the field of observation to a global and historical one. There is blame enough to spare for slavery in general in this regard. This includes the "Arab trader Ahman-de-Bellah, whose first caravan of captured Negroes from eight, maybe nine tribes, was herded in Bangalang" (46). Everyone is in on the game; it is all a matter of commercial interests and profit motive throughout human history. There is the long history of slavetrading in which "the barracoons [. . .] built by the Royal African Company in 1683—one of several well-fortified western forts always endangered by hostile, headhunting natives nearby, by competing merchants, and over two centuries residents at the fort had fought first the Dutch, then the French for control of Negro slaves" (44).

We are reminded in *Middle Passage* that even blacks were involved in the slave business, such as "Owen Bogha, the halfbreed son of a brutal slave trader from Liverpool and the black princess of a small tribe on the Rio Pongo" (44). Rutherford is stalked in an African bazaar by black Africans who may kidnap him and sell him into slavery amid the cheering of the throngs as the coffle arrives from the interior.[52] In fact, the Africans are so terrifying, and their potential for violence is so great, that on the *Republic* Ngonyama, one of the rivals for Allmuseri leadership who understands this potential, tells Rutherford: "I worry less about your captain now than how Diamelo can sway my people" (137). Papa Zeringue, the black American gangster in New Orleans, is partner in the slave ship *Republic*. Zeringue buys and sells slaves from Africa, but is described as a "Race Man to be admired" for "those who did not know the full extent of his crimes" (198). Rutherford lists Zeringue's finer qualities: he is a patron of the arts, invests in his community and brings financial power to blacks, never sells real estate "back to white men," although he certainly has no compunction about selling into slavery black people to white people, or for enslaving black people for his own purposes. Rutherford ponders:

> Could evil such as his actually produce good? Could money earned from murder, lies, and slave trading be used for civic service? [. . .] [F]reedom was property. Power was property. Love of race and kin was property, and if the capital in question was the lives of other colored men . . . well, mightn't a few have to perish, in the progress of the race, for the good of the many? (198–199)

Although Rutherford blackmails Papa with the truth about his participation in the slave trade, and Papa is most likely given a thrashing for it by his henchman and laundress, Santos—not a real reckoning or retribution for his crimes—this question of expediency for a greater good, even when it involves slave trading, is never really answered. That the end outweighs the means remains a very real possibility.

Johnson comes perilously close to explaining away agency and accountability for American slavery by demonstrating that slavery is a routine occurrence and part of human behavior across time—many other societies are equally culpable in the bartering and usage of human beings—greed and power-hunger being part of the human character and condition. This text seems to ask: Why, then, should white America be singled out and held to a particular standard of judgment for enslaving blacks? In fact, Rutherford Calhoun, in his dawning comprehension of the exigencies and magnitude of historical global commerce, goes so far as to say of the slave ship *Republic* that "[s]uddenly the ship felt insubstantial: a pawn in a larger game of property so vast it trivialized our struggles on board" (150). In *Middle Passage* it is clear that African Americans have no special claim to suffering and oppression. In the larger global and historical context, countless other people and targeted groups have suffered as much and more. Therefore, victimization from slavery and servitude are not reasons or even good excuses for not doing better in life, for doing well. Acknowledging this is, as Rutherford demonstrates, the first step toward transcendence.

Johnson writes in an article, "Accepting the Invitation," which is introduced by the subtitle, "Charles Johnson suggests that we take to heart Benjamin Franklin's challenge: Democracy is an invitation to struggle," that according to "Buddhist terms, we must [. . .] use the means of the relative-phenomenal world to reduce suffering for we are part of the relative-phenomenal world. But suffering will continue, despite our best efforts, until all of us experience [. . .] enlightenment and liberation."[53] It is never remotely suggested in *Middle Passage* that the slaves did not suffer. In fact, Johnson is meticulous in detailing the suffering of the slaves. However, and ultimately, suffering is the portion of humanity; it is part of the human condition.

It is incumbent upon those who are enslaved or oppressed to "make a way out of no way"[54] in this text. Although Johnson has stated that during slavery both "black and white [. . .] [are] adjusting to it as best they can as human beings,"[55] he is noticeably selective about assigning responsibility and blame. The black characters in *Middle Passage* do not receive the same consideration for their transgressions and failures.

Rutherford is ultimately held accountable for creating his own reality and transcending his social context as a former slave and servant—the crux of this tale. The ne'er-do-well Rutherford must gain a holistic, worldly understanding of his enslavement, and he must choose to be a servant on the *Republic* before he chooses to serve *the* republic or himself—presented as the logical sequence in his development into maturity and full citizenship in the human community. However, even though the immoral and criminal Falcon's experience and conduct is graphically presented, and it is also placed in a larger context as is the slaves', it is ultimately minimized and even explained away. He is, after all, under a great deal of pressure. Falcon confesses that he has investors with specific expectations, and that he has promised to deliver a considerable return on their investment, no excuses acceptable. In addition to being "a patriot" and "living history" (30) for his plundering and pillaging, Rutherford lets him off the hook very easily for his responsibility and participation in slave trading. Rutherford confesses: "I pitied him too, for his incompleteness. I pitied him, as I pitied ourselves, for whether we like it or not, he had changed a people simultaneously for the better and worse" (143–144). Most significant, he ponders: "But was Ebenezer Falcon telling me that he, at bottom, was no freer than the Africans?" (147). Although Rutherford raises the question, he is also offering this as a possibility for consideration.

"Evolve or Die":[56] Rewriting the Social Contract

Middle Passage is an exposé of the power and ineluctability of transformation—for individuals and for the American republic. Johnson uses the idea of inherited forced servitude as a way to draw attention to a number of social issues that are most affected by or in need of transformation.

Consigning the overall perspective of a fictional work, and especially equating that of the narrator with that of the author of the text, is a perilous undertaking fraught with obvious and understandable objections.[57] Nevertheless it appears that Johnson almost inhabits the mind and personae of this former slave and voluntary servant—a character who is ultimately devoid of most of the recognizable elements of this type of fictionalized figure. This may be for the purpose of holding forth on his own literary and social concerns and ideologies, as many writers do. Multiple and alternative points of view are also offered. For example, Rutherford appears at first to simply illustrate and revisit, but then challenge and reshape stereotypes of the black male.

Also prominently featured are the dynamics resulting from compulsory association between different racial and cultural groups, and what this means in terms of identity, power and hierarchy. The tensions between the desire for a true synthesis, sometimes regarded as a value or objective, and fear of change, contamination and obliteration of culture and/or self through amalgamation, plays out dramatically in the relationships between the Allmuseri, Rutherford Calhoun and the crew of the *Republic*.

Most significantly, Johnson reconfigures the idea of black servitude and offers an alternative rethinking of this crucial part of African American experience in such a way as to countermand the idea of victimization—an issue of immense relevance to Johnson in much of his work. It is clear that *Middle Passage* is intended to challenge the presumed disabling and immutable damage that accompanies notions about black slavery and servitude, as well as the mindset that keeps the pain associated with these circumstances alive, unresolved, debilitating.

In many ways this text, like *Band of Angels* and *Ragtime*, is a response to what is happening at the moment of its writing. During the period in which Johnson wrote *Middle Passage* the United States experienced two terms of a right-wing president, Ronald Reagan. In accordance with an increasing climate of political conservatism, Reagan was determined to, among other things, substantially dismantle the social welfare programs that had been implemented during preceding administrations. The Reagan era was distinguished by its commitment to undo much of the progress made for workers, education, consumer protection, environmental issues, women's rights and civil rights for blacks.[58] George H. W. Bush carried the torch of Reagan's policies with extreme gusto, to the extent that their administrations, commonly referred to as the Reagan-Bush years, are a period in American history that catered shamelessly to the rich, and exacerbated the burdens of the poor. It was a period in which the prospects for social and economic progress for African Americans was, once again, in serious question. (Has it ever *not* been in question?) There was also a prevailing and politically self-serving assumption and convenient delusion, an idea then gaining currency, that all social inequities had been rectified by the Civil Rights Law of 1964, that black people were like other ethnic/immigrant groups and were merely participants on a level playing field.

Consequently, a combination of political and social factors contributed to the urgency to accelerate and secure African American economic independence: the knowledge that economic support from the federal government was no longer a certainty; the waning of liberal support because of compassion fatigue, prevalent after the death of Martin Luther King, Jr. and the subsequent disintegration of the civil rights movement; and, the predictable yet incalculable impact of white conservative backlash after the civil rights movement. External support was in decline. It became increasingly clear that in spite of the realities for African Americans—high unemployment, lower test scores for school children, what appeared to be an irreducible number of low- and no income families, an escalating rate of imprisonment particularly for black males, high infant mortality, lower life expectancy, etc.—that African Americans were on their own.

The rhetoric of politicians and social theorists exuberantly stressed the need for personal responsibility and self-reliance—determination, clarity of purpose, hard work, decency and service to self and others, all incontestable values not unknown to black people—as the best solutions, the *only* solutions for the social and economic problems that besieged African Americans. This rhetoric conveniently ignored the impact of centuries of oppression, neglect, race-based hostility and government-sanctioned, institutionalized discrimination.[59]

One might reasonably conclude, after reading *Middle Passage*, that Charles Johnson is one such critic and observer. Consider, for example, the following anti–affirmative action speech by Captain Falcon, ostensibly for Rutherford's benefit, on the need for individual excellence, and the problem of illiterate Negroes getting college degrees. Negroes aren't "ready":

> "I believe in *excellence*—an unfashionable thing these days, I know, what with headmasters giving illiterate Negroes degrees because they feel too guilty to fail them, then employers giving that same boy a place in the firm since he's got the degree in hand and saying no will bring a gang of Abolitionists down on their necks. But no,"—he looked pained—"not on my ship, Mr. Calhoun. Eighty percent of the crews on other ships, damn near anywhere in America, are *incompetent*, all because everyone's ready to lower standards of excellence to make up for slavery, or discrimination, and the problem . . . the *problem*, Mr. Calhoun, is, I say, that most of these minorities aren't ready for the titles of quartermaster or first mate precisely because discrimination denied them the training that makes for true excellence—ready to be mediocre mates, I'll grant you that, or middlebrow functionaries, or run-of-the-mill employees, but not to *advance* the position, or make a lasting breakthrough of any kind. O, 'tis a scandal on the ships I've seen, and hardly the fault of the poor, half-trained Negro who hungers like anyone else these days for the glamour of titles and position." [. . .] I almost saw his point. (31–32)[60]

This petulant outburst, a diatribe really, which has no real relevance to the social realities for blacks, slave ships, the American republic or any other historical context in the 1830s is one example of many in *Middle Passage* in which Johnson appears to exploit long-standing and contemporary issues, and pushes the boundaries of time and place in order to make a point.

Johnson, as much social theorist and philosopher as novelist, argues in "Second Front" that

> even in the face of staggering racial oppression (beside which today's bigotry pales), and despite the lack of opportunities in the first half of this century, our elders in the pre-civil rights era raised strong, resourceful sons and daughters; their intention—their personal sacrifices and life-long labor—was to prepare their offspring for the chances they themselves were denied. Black men today can do no less.

For Johnson, the "enem[ies] within" the black community are pathological cynicism, anti-intellectualism, disparagement and disdain of "square," hard-working, honest people along with the celebration of "hard dudes" and the "bad nigger" who is "too cool for the room" and the conviction that achievement and knowledge are "white" and a sell-out. He points out that black leaders and heroes such as Martin Luther King, Jr., Malcolm X and Frederick Douglass all embodied the virtues of self-reliance and service to one's society. They believed in hard work and acquiring an education, and were on paths of enlightenment and personal evolution. His conviction:

> I am convinced as never before that after the great civil rights legislation of the 1960s, which ended legal segregation, and in today's increasingly conservative climate, whatever renewal and progress black people in America can hope for must come from *within.* This is the second "front" mentioned by King, which even he could not speak too loudly about in the sixties because he and others feared that discussing the health of our culture would only give ammunition to the enemies of integration. But we have neglected this question for too long. We need to talk about it now. Moreover, we need to *act* on it by recapturing old and developing new cultural practices worthy of the great sacrifices, intractable wills, dignity, and deep-plowing faith of our ancestors.[61]

Instead of being disdained, excellence must be restored as a value and an objective in black society. It is, in fact, a common theme in Johnson's writing, the reviled black middle-class professionals who do seek excellence, and who

> have been the subject of belittlement by members of the black underclass, the white liberal media, self-appointed radical spokespersons, by some novelists, by academics black and white and now, it seems, by foreigners too. In their judgment the black middle-class is not "black" enough. It doesn't take four

> years of college to see that there is a whopping amount of racism involved when someone insists upon identifying black American life with the social pathologies of the ghetto, with the scatological, sex-obsessed language of Eddie Murphy in his "Raw" performance, the offensive comedians on HBO's "Def Comedy Jam," or with the nihilistic lyrics on rap recordings by Ice T and 2 Live Crew.

One of the major points Johnson makes in *Middle Passage* and in his other writing is that degradation and failure are personal, in spite of the historical or social conditions that may give rise to it. The failure to embrace individual responsibility, a significant part of which means to reject a self-definition of victim, will result in the perpetuation of mediocrity and the paternalism that denies and encourages it—impediments to excellence, true equality, social progress and acceptance, full and deserved citizenship and moral evolution. Johnson attributes the current difficulties with excellence within the black community to the popularization of a spirit and temperament of defeat and low expectations; that "built into black culture since at least the 1960s [. . .] [is] an attitude that sneers at hard work, good citizenship, and traditional morality! Our crisis, if we presently have one—and I believe we do—is fundamentally one of (ethical) values and (social) vision. [. . .] [W]e must invest as much energy in cultural house-cleaning as we do in political activism."[62]

Rutherford becomes a counterpoint to the stereotypical black male after he evolves, mirroring his brother Jackson (who is a stereotypical "Uncle Tom" figure, with an explanation), and functions as an example of how an individual who has every reason to fail, and who subscribes to defeatist thinking and the degrading behaviors that accompany it, can reform and turn his life around. Before his metamorphosis, Rutherford exemplifies the defeatist attitude Johnson identifies in the black community today. For example, it is true that Rutherford, like other slaves, is cut off from traditions and values because slavery has severed him from his African roots, and, because he has been abandoned by his father, he has no ancestral frame of reference. He, therefore, believes that he is at a disadvantage and suffers from this absence of history and culture. He complains bitterly to Cringle: "I don't even know who my father *is*. Mine was never there to expect anything of me, or to make me expect much from myself. I *have* no family traditions to maintain. In a way, I have no past, Peter. At least that's how I've often felt. When I look behind me, for my father, there is only emptiness" (160).

But Cringle corrects him on his perception of things, and schools him in the advantages of not being connected to the past—it is a form of freedom itself. It is a fresh start in a life unencumbered by the success and failures of one's forefathers; a life in which one needn't worry about measuring up to or letting anyone down—a point of view that is often a significant driving force in the immigrant experience. You can't inherit mistakes or be judged about things you have not yourself done. "[Y]ou're luckier—and freer—than you know" (160). Culture and tradition do not determine or guarantee character.

By contrast, the Allmuseri Africans, whose culture and traditions are ancient, and precisely defined, become thoroughly corrupted by their experiences on the slave ship. When they become disconnected from their past and traditions they become morally disoriented and fall from grace. Their core beliefs are compromised by murder, and they are forever changed. A guiding principle for the Allmuseri is that what a man imagines and thinks, he becomes; that thought and desire are powerful manifestations of the heart's true intent: "What came *out* of us, not what went in, made us clean or unclean. Their notion of 'experience,' I learned, held each man responsible for his own happiness or sorrow, for the emptiness of his world or its abundance, even for his dreams and his entire way of seeing" (164). Accordingly, it follows that because the Allmuseri relinquish tradition, culture and character, and respond to the harsh circumstances on the *Republic* with mayhem and bloodletting, they may simply be manifesting what they truly are beneath the rituals and practices that seem, at first, so enduring and inviolable. Or, they may represent the actualization of negative potential when behavior is governed by a disregard for consequence. Either way, Johnson suggests that culture is not exactly superficial, but tenuous and contingent, very vulnerable to external pressures and that extreme vigilance is required to maintain a "way of seeing" (164), as well as a way of being.

The ephemeral nature of culture and identity is a concern for Johnson, and comes up repeatedly in his writing. In the introduction to an edition of *Proverbs*, he writes of that book in the Bible, "it is a two-millennium-old blueprint for the staggering challenge of living a truly *civilized* life. Culture, we realize after reading *Proverbs*, is an on-going project. We are not born with culture. Or wisdom. And both are but *one* generation deep."[63] In "Second Front" he again states that "culture and civilization are but one generation deep. Yes, they can be lost in a mere twenty years. The blink of an eye. They are not givens."[64]

Henry Louis Gates, Jr. has a different take on the probability of such a radical transformation, as the Allmuseri experience suggests, during such a short period as the Middle Passage. He argues in *The Signifying Monkey* against the possibility of "complete annihilation" of cultural traits during the Middle Passage and even goes so far as to state that annihilation "would have been far more remarkable than their preservation." He does support the idea of revision, and that "[s]lavery in the New World, a veritable seething cauldron of cross-cultural contact, however, did serve to create a dynamic exchange and revision among numerous previously isolated Black African cultures on a scale unprecedented in African history." He argues, however, that obliteration of identity, culture and values could not occur during the time period and simply because of the impact of the Middle Passage:

> The African, after all, was a traveler, albeit an abrupt, ironic traveler, through space and time; and like every traveler, the African "read" a new environment within a received framework of meaning and belief. The notion that the Middle Passage was so traumatic that it functioned to create in the African a tabula rasa of consciousness is as odd as it is a fiction, a fiction that has served several economic orders and their attendant ideologies. The full erasure of traces of cultures as splendid, as ancient, and as shared by the slave traveler as the classic cultures of West Africa would have been extraordinarily difficult.[65]

Whether or not the Middle Passage experience could so quickly and radically change a culture such as the Allmuseri's may be unknowable, but the possibility of it serves Johnson's objective of demonstrating the power of choice. The idea that every act has consequences and is part of a cosmic equation that must be balanced is central to this text. The choice must be made to evolve or die. Fear of cosmic retribution may be a motivation, but behaving differently and correctly is always possible.

Progressive, positive transformation in *Middle Passage* is both a moral imperative and a strategy for survival. Questions that bedevil the interrogation of this text, in respect to transformation of self and culture, and that require continuing consideration because of the complex and contradictory nature of the representation here are: Is Johnson successful in disclosing new and different perspectives and representations, without suggesting a deliberate contrast to stereotypes? In his effort to transcend "the calcified, rigid perceptions of the object"[66] does he, in fact, end up doing precisely what he hopes to avoid by invoking the opposite of what he represents by inference? Is it possible to present such an unusual representation of a former slave and servant without denying harsh historical realities and their inescapable consequences for the majority of black Americans? Has Johnson effectively made the point that the presumed consequences of slavery and servitude are, in fact, "escapable," and that it is time for a new perspective? Johnson continually plays against assumptions about race and race relations; in his effort to step outside a predictable "circumscribed notion of race,"[67] does Johnson promulgate unrealistic expectations of personal power for the truly powerless? Is there, in fact, any such state as absolute powerlessness?

Questions such as these often seem deliberately fractious or completely elusive in the text. Johnson's unconventional representations and the questions raised by his work inspire some critics to describe him as conservative—a word presumably meant to suggest backward, insensitive, narrow-minded, even racist. Molly Able Travis suggests that what she perceives as Johnson's conservatism may constrict his notion of cultural synthesis. She argues:

> Johnson's [method] is transcendent in terms of race and seems to me politically conservative. At the 1991 conference of the National Council of Teachers of English, Johnson spoke of the dangers of multiculturalism, expressing the fear that our literature as well as our cultural lives will be "balkanized" into separate spheres. To support his position of cultural synthesis, he quoted Martin Luther King along with Allan Bloom and Dinesh D'Souza. It is at this point that I pause. Has Johnson discovered the fourth way, with cultural synthesis coming after segregation (rejection), assimilation (introjection), and cultural separatism? Or is Johnson's notion of cultural synthesis simply another form of assimilation in which the dominant culture swallows up marginalized cultures?[68]

Perhaps. But even so, in spite of what appears to be an inclination to hold blacks to a separate standard in *Middle Passage*, Johnson offers a prescription for growth and for wholeness, for transformation and evolution that applies to all individuals and societies alike. This seeming contradiction may be part of his effort to demonstrate the free-floating complexity and inclusiveness of his phenomenological and ontological take on human history and individual experience.[69]

The filth and disease on the *Republic* are clearly metaphors for a diseased American society in *Middle Passage*, particularly where slavery is concerned. They demonstrate the symbiotic relationship of all members of society, as well as the necessity for progressive transformation, which is posited as the cure. Any disorder or corruption, however small and seemingly insignificant, spreads rapidly and disturbs the ecological balance of the community. As conditions on the *Republic* worsen it is often unclear who gave what disease to whom because the conditions are so terrible and everyone is sick. But most important, after a point it doesn't matter who is responsible for causing the situation, they are all, literally and figuratively, in the same boat. They suffer from constipation and fatigue, "Black Vomit," tetanus, boils and chancres, sores oozing pus and blood, typhus, worms, scarlet fever, insanity, lice, eczema, distemper, scabies and scurvy—the conditions and diseases they are able to identify (155–156). Most of the diseases are highly contagious and are caused by uncleanness. In this way, Johnson makes the point that when a society is infused with corruption, when all are wallowing in filth, everyone is a potential carrier of or recipient for disease. No one remains unaffected or uninfected. Yet, when the eight-year-old orphaned Allmuseri girl Baleka falls ill, the ship's cook suggests it is she (who is most likely the victim of sexual molestation) who has infected at least some of the crew, and tells Rutherford, who has become her protector, "I think she give all them boys somethin' when they was heah" (108), a rare admission of the ease at which victims are often blamed.

Whatever the culpability for moral corruption or disease, the prescription in *Middle Passage* for cleansing and curing the filthy and sick ship/nation begins with the acknowledgment of evil and taking responsibility. Then, it may be possible to exorcise the consequences of slavery and other social injustices. The acknowledgment that "[t]he master's house must be dismantled" (154) begins the process of moving forward.

Karmic Debt and the Cost of Metamorphosis

Johnson employs the idea of karma and karmic debt, and applies it to nations as well as individuals in order to demonstrate the dynamics of cause and effect in transformation and evolution. The enslaved Allmuseri are an example of what can happen if social wrongs and oppression are not addressed—their insurrection is the consequence of seriously neglecting problems on/in the *Republic*/republic. Even so, they have a karmic debt to pay even though their grievances are real, their cause just. America also has a karmic debt to pay, which comes in the forms of civil war, continuing race-motivated oppression and violence and the potential for complete self-destruction. The Allmuseri must pay for their bloodletting by demotion on the evolutionary scale and will be subjected to billions of rebirths in order to become human once more. The American republic must pay for its crimes against humanity with many generations of retribution to pay back and achieve transcendence over its past.

Correspondingly, the mysterious cargo in the hold of the ship is a metaphor for transformation. Rumors abound that the huge crate, which is not registered in the ship manifest by Falcon, contains "an African god" (100), "the Missing Link" or "a nearly extinct lizard, maybe intelligent," a shape-shifter or perhaps even a UFO (67). It is "Loki and Brer Rabbit" (102), at once. In any case, it "has no business in our world" (63). One thing is certain: almost everyone in the crew is transformed when they are lowered down to "feed" it—although we are also told that it requires no food. Among the possibilities for what the mysterious cargo may represent is the secret, unacknowledged historical and social "baggage" below the surface of the *Republic*/republic, like the slaves chained beneath the surface of the ship, which has the power to transform and destroy. The mysterious cargo represents unacknowledged potential, the capacity for change. It is mysterious not only because it can't be clearly seen or defined, but also because of the possibilities for multiple outcomes. It makes clear that out-of-sight/out-of-mind may be an injurious practice for individuals, and a dangerous policy for the *Republic*/republic. The failure to address the crimes and problems of a society, such as the enslavement and oppression of human beings, will stunt the evolution of the society as a whole, and it will not preclude a reckoning.

During the storm, the crew in desperation throws cargo overboard to lighten the load, but not the crate which contains the mysterious cargo, signifying not so much their inability, but their unwillingness, to excavate and destroy this burden. They blame the Africans for the storm, demonstrating, perhaps, that those who are enslaved and oppressed on/in the *Republic*/republic are easily blamed for society's ills. The storm, which may be equated with the Allmuseri insurrection, is one possible result of their condition, but only one possible response. The Allmuseri themselves acknowledge alternatives to insurrection, after the fact.

Confronting the baggage beneath the surface is also necessary to the coming of age and moral evolution of individuals in this text. Nothing observable happens to Falcon where the crate is concerned because he is suicidal and needs only his own death, which he eventually gets. For him, the mysterious cargo is a "witty conversationalist" (101) and worth something on the open market as an Allmuseri god, which is his only concern. The same holds true for the Allmuseri when they "feed" the mysterious cargo, most likely because their culture is so self-contained that they require no modification or external sustenance, and transcendence is already written into their creed and way of life. But, the cabin boy Tommy emerges from his confrontation with the mysterious cargo in an altered state. He comes back speaking languages he has never heard, swaying to music only he can hear—clearly out of his mind (68). Although this may seem tragic; it works to his advantage. Tommy's madness finally motivates the first mate Cringle to take this vulnerable child under his protection and shield him from Falcon's sexual abuse. When Rutherford confronts the mysterious cargo, he sees his father Riley, imagines his father for the first time not simply as a villain but as a human being and is therefore able to begin to come to terms with his abandonment issues. This is one of the last steps he must take in his journey toward maturity and transcendence. The point is that by confronting the mysterious cargo, Rutherford, like Tommy, is transformed and gets what he needs most, despite the cost.

Cost is always a concern in *Middle Passage*—and cost/benefit analyses and ratios are in continual attendance with ideas about transformation and the requirements for evolution. One of the by-products of transformation in *Middle Passage* is a "cruel kind of connectedness" such as exists between the Allmuseri,

Falcon and Rutherford. They are all changed "for the better and worse" (144), but changed forever, nevertheless. An atmosphere of doom presides over this text simultaneously with the hope of redemption and evolution, because trepidation and revulsion—major reasons for resistance to a social evolution—are often grounded in fear of racial and cultural amalgamation. A prophetic and apocalyptic vision of the collision of cultures is an unrelenting undercurrent from which arises the rather potentially negative by-product of disorientation. Rutherford's head reels from the ethnological mix of things in Falcon's cabin, which make him "culturally dizzy" (142). Much more devastating, the Allmuseri are corrupted by their exposure not only to the conditions on the ship, but to the culture of the crew. Yet, this part of transformation, the cross-cultural acquisition of traits and perspectives, is suggested as a necessary part of evolution, which is a symbiosis and annihilation of what are often erroneously regarded as part of a core self, as sacred. It is replenishment and a way to stave off limitation and stagnation caused by sameness and lack of diversity, much as can happen in the gene pool of small isolated communities. If there is no evolution, what results is chaos, regression, destruction—still, all forms of transformation.

Captain Falcon represents the white American mindset bloated and stymied with self-interest and weary with contradictions about race. The fear of the dissolution of boundaries between racial and religious groups is embodied in Falcon's dying "nightmare" (144), a prophetic vision of a world of multiplicity and horror that rivals any rendering of Hieronymous Bosch, of what Falcon perceives as an inversion of the natural order of things—ironically, the corruption of "normalcy" and "moral" and "ethical" behavior. In this nightmare Falcon imagines the complete disintegration of "civilized values and visions of culture" (145), which is both the product and result of racial mixing to the point where racial groups are indistinguishable. It is a new world where white children may become slaves, where venereal diseases, domestic violence, civil unrest and wholesale poverty are all part of a society in which Mudmen, yellow men, Jews and women have exceeded proscribed limits and have taken over. It is a global society designed by and consisting of rubbish—absurd, chaotic, damnable—a world in which "Hegel was spewing from the mouths of Hottentots" (145), which makes Falcon shudder with fear and repugnance.

Concomitantly, the Allmuseri slaves share some of the same fears, fears based on the inevitable reconfiguration of identity and values as a result of contact with other groups and that amalgamation is contamination and a diminution of what they believe they are. Yet, the Allmuseri are already themselves the product, the very beautiful and ancient product, of eons of amalgamation. "About them was the smell of old temples. Cities lost when Europe was embryonic. [. . .] Physically they seemed a synthesis of several tribes, as if longevity in this land had made them a biological repository of Egyptian and sub-Saharan eccentricities, in the Hegelian equation—a clan distilled from the essence of everything that came earlier. [. . .] [T]hey might have been the Ur-tribe of humanity itself" (61). They are, in fact, the essence of amalgamation.

> Once they had been a seafaring people, years and years ago, and deposited their mariners in that portion of India later to be called Harappa, where they blended with its inhabitants, the Dravidians, in the days before the Aryans and their juggernauts—"city destroyers"—leveled the civilization of Mohenjo-Daro overnight. Between 1000 B.C. and 500 B.C. they sailed to Central America on North Equatorial currents that made the voyage from the west coast of Africa to the Caribbean only thirty days, bringing their skills in agriculture and metallurgy to the Olmec who, to honor these African mariners, stamped their likeness in stone and enshrined in song their prowess as warriors. Specifically, their martial-art techniques resembled Brazilian *capoeira*. Over time these elegant moves [. . .] had become elements in their ceremonial dance. (76–77)[70]

Their metamorphosis is still in progress because evolution does not have a fixed objective and end; it is an ongoing process. Even so and most ironic, the Allmuseri regard amalgamation as a denaturing, a coming apart or breakdown of unity and a descent into a terrifying plurality. It was their "vision of Hell. And that was where we lived: purgatory. That was where we were taking them—into the madness of multiplicity—and the thought drove them wild" (65). Correspondingly, what America has in store with the continued infusion of the Other, particularly because of the slave trade, is a polyglotism. Always present is the idea that the transformations Falcon fears have already been set in motion and are the direct result of imperialism, slavetrading, commercial interests. Rutherford ponders:

> the Africans, I realized, were not wholly Allmuseri anymore. We had changed them. I suspected even he [Ngonyama] did not recognize the quiet revisions in his voice after he learned English as it was spoken by the crew, or how the vision hidden in their speech was deflecting or redirecting his own way of seeing. Just as Tommy's exposure to Africa had altered him, the slaves' life among the lowest strata of Yankee society—and the horrors they experienced—were subtly reshaping their souls as thoroughly as Falcon's tight-packing had contorted their flesh during these past few weeks, but into what sort of men I could not imagine. No longer Africans, yet not Americans either. Then what? And of what were they now capable? (124–125)

Yet, in *Middle Passage* a society must modify its notions about identity and individuality if it is to survive and evolve. Culture and history are fluid; they are process, not product. The nature of individual identity, if there is even such a thing, is elastic and variable and revision is mutual and reciprocal, even if unwanted. Most of all, transformation is inevitable, and fear and resistance are not barriers but only temporary obstacles to revision. Metamorphosis—the evolution, the revision of identity of a nation or an individual—is the certain outcome of exposure and contact with other cultures, ideas and peoples. This is what happens to Rutherford Calhoun, the Allmuseri and the crew on the *Republic.* A guiding principle in this novel is that resistance to change must be confronted and disarmed, because transformation will occur regardless of individual intention, because "the mills of the gods were still grinding, killing and remaking us all, and nothing I [Rutherford] or anyone else did might stop the terrible forces and transformations our voyage had set free" (125).

A Prescription for Survival: Embracing Mongrelization

Johnson regards racial identification as an erroneous and defunct social construct—a bad habit in need of reassessment. The notion of racial identification is central to the engagement of transformation and identity in *Middle Passage*. Mongrelization, polyglotism and transformation are already givens.[71] Criticism of Johnson's point of view is abundant. Timothy Parrish charges that Johnson "imagines African-American identity to be irretrievably mixed with other American identities, a happy mongrel."[72] Richard Hardack argues that Johnson "[i]n paradoxical but consistent ways [. . .] undermines the category of race, and ultimately racial surfaces, to construct both black and white identity."[73] But Johnson is resolute in his idea that "[t]here is only Being, which holds within itself spirit, mind, and body without our limited, racial, parochial, and self-interested distinctions," and that he has "always seen myself first and foremost as an American, because it is impossible to separate out black people from this nation's evolution." [74] He explains his objectives in *Being and Race*, and attempts to dispel some of what he perceives as a misreading of his authorial intent:

> Doubters may object that it is racially impossible to strip themselves of their own historically acquired traits. Many black writers claim they cannot imagine what it is like to be white, that all they know is the "black" experience. For my money, this objection is sheer laziness. I will also say such objections are based on a very circumscribed notion of race. We can, I think, trash such objections quickly by noting that in a country as genetically mongrelized as America it wouldn't be unthinkable to scrap racial nature altogether.[75]

This kind of thinking makes possible the creation of a postmodern identity for Rutherford. He is a black man who does not identify himself with, and who is not identified with, the Africans. Rutherford is an American, not a black American; he is the "Cooked Barbarian" (153). In fact, it can be argued that he "takes a non-essentializing view of race: Just because he shares skin color with the Allmuseri, he is not automatically joined with their culture. In other words, Calhoun wishes to deconstruct the simple bond of color [. . .]. To this end, Calhoun attempts to mesh with the white crew, to blend in with the civilization of white America."[76]

Finally, and understandably, Rutherford's identity is tied to the only place he has known as home; his homesickness and longing are for the America that enslaves his people and rejects him, the America he loves in spite of himself.[77] It is a place "where allegiances are sound, where Calhoun believes he is capable of knowing where he stands."[78] As he "desperately dreamed of home," while on the *Republic* in the aftermath of the mutiny and storm, he recalls how "it was a battlefield, a boiling cauldron [in which] bondmen [were] crippled and caricatured by the disfiguring hand of servitude" (179). Yet, there is no place he would rather be:

> I desperately dreamed of home. [. . .] Nay, the States were hardly the sort of place a Negro would pine for, but pine for them I did. Even for *that* I was ready now after months at sea, for the strangeness and mystery of black life, even for the endless round of social obstacles and challenges and trials colored men faced every blessed day of their lives, for there were indeed triumphs, I remembered, that balanced the suffering on shore, small yet enduring things, very deep [. . .] weird, upside-down caricature of a country called America, if this land of refugees and former indentured servants, religious heretics and half-breeds, whoresons and fugitives—this cauldron of mongrels from all points on the compass—was all I could rightly call *home*, then aye: I was of it. There, as I lay weakened from bleeding, was where I wanted to be. Do I sound like a patriot? Brother, I put it to you: What Negro, in his heart (if he's not a hypocrite), is not? (179)

Nevertheless, Rutherford is, in spite of his newfound allegiances and clarity about where he fits into the scheme of things, "often merely the *tool* of others,"[79] a servant if not a slave.

Johnson explains in *Being and Race:*

> the enduring truth that if we go deeply enough into a relative perspective, black or white, male or female, we encounter the transcendence of relativism. [. . .] Why is this so? Because what we have, from the standpoint of phenomenology,

> are not different worlds but instead innumerable perspective on *one* world; and we know that, when it comes to the crunch, we share, all of us, the same cultural Lifeworld—a world layered with ancestors, predecessors, and contemporaries. To think of this world properly is to find that all our perspectives take us directly to a common situation, a common history in which all meanings evolve.[80]

Consequently, in *Middle Passage* race, color and class are false distinctions. Rutherford's representation ultimately denies slavery and servitude as racial signifiers, as fate, or as future. Ultimately, the text asserts that rather than physiognomical determinism, that rather than being defined and debilitated by the social crimes of the past (namely enslavement), that in spite of fear of loss of self and culture, a society must, like the Allmuseri, transform and evolve and become "a clan held together by values" (109). Although polyglotism and mongrelization are already demonstrable fact, embracing and promoting this reality is a moral imperative that will ensure survival.

Moral Evolution through Constructive Servitude

In *Middle Passage* Johnson makes a solid case for African American servitude, forced or otherwise, as other than a disfiguring experience and status in life. He showcases the ways in which servitude may contribute to moral evolution. Johnson brings this about by completely collapsing into one concept the idea of slavery and servitude as caretaking—concern, and positive and aggressive action on behalf of the well-being of others—a concept that ultimately means "service to others." In his reassessment and reconfiguration of African American servitude in *Middle Passage*, almost everyone on the *Republic*, but most particularly Rutherford Calhoun, comes to understand the value of service according to this definition.

In Rutherford's reassessment of his early life he eventually comes to regard his experiences as a slave as a moral training ground of which he didn't, unlike his brother Jackson, take advantage when he had the opportunity. Part of the process for acquiring a new attitude toward his past is that he has to acknowledge what he had been up against. As a child Rutherford received no real encouragement to rise above his thieving and rebellious impulses, to do better for himself and to do right by others. He received constant criticism and the expressed belief of those closest to him that he would never amount to anything, and that he had no real value as a human being. This fueled his anger and reinforced a negative self-image. His response was to be the best reprobate he could possibly be. On the *Republic* in crisis, he rises to the occasion because he has gradually learned the true meaning and the benefits of service/servitude and demonstrates how much he has learned to care for the well-being of others. The realization that service to others is both a strategy for survival and an obligation is essential to his coming of age and to his moral development. Rutherford learns to "serve" through the example of the caretakers in the text: Isadora (Rutherford's girlfriend he has abandoned in New Orleans); the Allmuseri Africans, especially Baleka and her mother; and his brother Jackson, his alter ego.

Middle Passage suggests that a necessary part of transformation into a more humane and decent society would be the acquisition of what are traditionally considered characteristics of female culture, particularly where caretaking and service to others are concerned. This idealized version of womanhood, as the harmless and natural embodiment of servitude, is held in contrast to male culture. In fact, the text often reads like a critique of male culture. Situations without female influence are crude, barbaric, destructive. In a pub in New Orleans which appears to be a microcosm of the flotsam of American society—all seamen (a pun, perhaps) are equal because they are all armed:

> darkly lit, rum-smelling [. . .] stinking of whale oil [. . .] scowling and jabbering like pirates, squirting jets of brown tobacco juice everywhere except in the spittoons—a den of Chinese assassins, scowling Moors, English scoundrels, Yankee adventurers, and evil-looking Arabs. Naturally, I [Rutherford] felt pretty much right at home. (18)

The crew of the *Republic*, truly the nation at sea, is "flea-infested, foul-tongued" (22). They are united by their failure in life and are "refugees from responsibility [. . .] miscreants, dreamers, and fools" (40). Most revealing are the manhood tests and criteria to which the crew subject themselves as a way to prove gender purity and worthiness:

> The *Republic* was, above all else, a ship of *men*. Without the civilizing presence of women, everyone felt the pressure, the masculine imperative to prove himself equal to a vague standard of manliness in order to be judged "regular." To fail at this in the eyes of the other men could, I needn't tell you, make your life at sea quite miserable. It led to posturing among the crew, a tendency to turn themselves into caricatures of the concept of maleness: to strut, keep their chests stuck out and stomachs sucked in, and talk monosyllabically in surly mumbles or grunts because being good at language was womanly. [. . .] You had to *work* at being manly [. . .]. The crewmen had drinking contests nearly every day. They gambled on who could piss the farthest over the rail, or on

> whose uncircumcised schlong was the longest, and far into the night lie awake in their hammocks swapping jokes about nuns sitting on candles. (41)

Any man who dares to not participate in these manhood rituals, such as the first mate Cringle, is not respected and is ostracized.

In contrast to masculine culture, which includes the most virulent forms of opportunism and venality, is that of certain aspects of what is typically regarded as feminine culture, which are clearly intended as positive contrast, by comparison. Feminine characteristics, for the most part, are qualities to be aspired to, most prominently the presumed willingness to put the comfort and welfare of others before one's own. It is a form and a model of constructive servitude.[81]

Isadora Bailey, the schoolteacher who tries to blackmail Rutherford into marriage by paying off his debts to a gangster, has many of the requisite qualities of a caretaker. Isadora has "a religious respect for Work" (6), and she keeps her apartment as a refuge for disabled and abandoned animals—a "menagerie of crippled beasts" (7) on whom she showers attention, affection and complete devotion. For Isadora, Rutherford is simply in many ways another disabled creature, and her attempts to snag him come from an impulse to both take care of him and to remake him into a respectability he resists, equating it with a kind of enslavement: "she saw me as clay. Something she could knead beneath her tiny brown fingers into precisely the sort of creature I—after seeing my brother shackled to subservience—was determined not to become: 'a gentleman of color'" (9). Nevertheless, Rutherford eventually sees the value of Isadora's point of view and way of life. Whatever her motives for trying to entrap Rutherford, as the conditions on the *Republic* worsen during the voyage he reflects back on her character and the qualities that impress him most about her—her commitment to service to others.

On the *Republic* an Allmuseri mother also provides an example for Rutherford of how to be responsible for the welfare of others. Understanding how precarious life was on the slave ship, and not knowing what would happen when they reached their destination, this woman singles out Rutherford as the most likely candidate to look after her small daughter, Baleka, if anything should happen to her, because he "looked most African" (79) of all the members of the crew. She tests his potential for this task by throwing back into his lap a moldy biscuit he had so magnanimously given to the hungry child, making it clear to him that it wasn't good enough for her, even under the circumstances. Rutherford passes the test because he decides that the mother is right and subsequently shares, reluctantly at first, all his meals with the child, who becomes very attached to him. When the mother is swept overboard Rutherford becomes Baleka's guardian and protector, and during the storm at sea he clings with one hand to the foremast and with the other to Baleka. When it becomes clear to him that the crew and/or captain may be sexually molesting her, Rutherford becomes a father to her, declaring, "I could not let her die, a dark pawn, caught between Falcon and the ship's proletariat. I knew that now" (118). When Rutherford becomes extremely ill, this eight-year-old child takes care of him, which reinforces the idea of reciprocity and responsibility for this former self-serving reprobate.

Rutherford's older brother Jackson offers perhaps the most obvious example of constructive service and servitude, and this is particularly significant because it occurs within the context of enslavement. Jackson is a man who transcends the confines and abuses of slavery by making choices to behave in an honorable and responsible manner. His reward for his efforts is that his master, Reverend Peleg Chandler, eventually sets him free (as Chandler is approaching his own death). Jackson has *earned* his freedom through word and deed. Johnson somewhat complicates Jackson and his decision to stay after he is freed—many slaves, having nowhere else to go and no resources, stayed on their plantations after emancipation. But Jackson's decision to stay serves another purpose in this text. His decision underscores the notion that servitude, forced or otherwise, is a noble endeavor in that it offers opportunities that may contribute to the development of the moral character and evolution of those who serve. Self-effacement, humility, responsibility to self and others are what matter most, even in controlled, limited and oppressive or abusive circumstances.

Jackson is the perfect slave, servant and caretaker, possessing a constitution and sensibility that correspond perfectly with the feminine model, "laying out [Reverend Chandler's] clothes each morning, combing his dry, brittle hair, fetching his nightly footbaths" (113). His apparent submissiveness and servility serve many purposes. Ostensibly he is obsequious, perhaps even a coward with little or no sense of self. But ultimately, Johnson positions Jackson as a martyr, an altruist, a big brother, a family man—with *all* human beings as part of his family. While it is true that Jackson is the perfect servant to his master, he lives to serve humanity. Rutherford is forced to acknowledge, however grudgingly, Jackson's contribution and sacrifice:

> To his credit, he stayed, thereby assuring me of having *some* family. [. . .] Rightly or wrongly, he thought it possible to serve his people by humbly being there when they needed him—whites too, if they weren't too evil, and he was incapable of locking anything out of his heart. There can be, as I see it, no other way to unriddle why my brother, more than any other bondman, was generally faithful to Reverend Chandler [. . .]. [He was] just as regular in the performance of his appointed tasks for the other servants, standing there by

> everyone's side through family death and sickness; Jackson was a Sunday preacher in the slave quarters, the model of propriety, and had twice the patience of St. Francis.

The youthful Rutherford is a complete contrast, "*his* shadow-self, the social parasite, the black picklock and worldling—in whom he saw, or said he saw, our runaway father. He was ashamed of Riley Calhoun. And of me" (113). Eventually, Rutherford learns from Jackson's example. After he begins to change because of his experiences on the *Republic*, Rutherford sees his brother in a different light and relates to him for the first time:

> "God," I asked, "is this some kind of *test?*" My worldly wits gone, and I knew, there on my aching knees, the personal devastation that was my brother's daily bread: burning for things to work out well, knowing the lives of his loved ones depended on this [. . .]. I cried for all the sewage I carried in my spirit, my failures and crimes, foolish hopes and vanities, the very faults and structural flaws in the blueprint of my brain. (126–127)

As the conditions on the sinking *Republic* worsen, the social contract breaks down completely as a result of rapidly occurring and multiple crises, but the reformed Rutherford has what is for him a new response to difficulties. He becomes healer and peacemaker—a caretaker like his brother Jackson—puts others before himself and comes to understand his own metamorphosis. He has become useful, and within his newly emerging hunger to be useful fathoms a viable identity within any context, including that of enslavement and servitude. His need emerges to give back some of what he has stolen, to make amends for a wasted life, to derive some meaning out of a misguided existence, to give of himself to others; to calm, to heal, to lead, to serve as a role model and inspiration, to give hope. When he feels that he is dying his only wish is for his comrades: "I was dying, no doubt about that, and I did not care for myself anymore, only that my mates should survive" (181), and he is ready to sacrifice himself for others:

> the first thing I was forced to do was forget my personal cares, my pains, and my hopes before repairing to the deckhouse where the sufferers were sprawled. I placed a hand on each of their foreheads and listened. Though tired and sleepless, I clowned and smiled for the children; I told American jokes that failed miserably in translation. I prayed, like my brother, that all would be well, [. . .] the "useful fiction" of this lie got the injured through the night and gave the children reason not to hurl themselves overboard [. . .]. If you had known me in Makanda or New Orleans you would have known that I

> doubted whether I truly had anything of value to offer to others. [. . .] [But] I was but a conduit or window through which my pillage and booty of "experience" passed. And momentarily the injured were calmed, not by the lie [. . .] but by the urgent belief they heard in my voice, and soon enough I came to desperately believe in it myself, for them I believed we would reach home, and even I was more peaceful. (161–163)

As he practices his newfound skill of providing multiple services for others, Rutherford continues to learn from Cringle, who makes the ultimate sacrifice—giving the survivors of the storm, mutiny and slave uprising permission to use his decimated and diseased body for food. Squibb, the ship's cook, and all the other remaining survivors put aside their class-consciousness, job descriptions, racial, ethnic and philosophical differences to work for survival and the common good because, as he confides to Rutherford, "[a] ship's a society, if you get my drift. A commonwealth, Mr. Calhoun" (175). The result of his new outlook and a willingness to transform allows Rutherford to actually metamorphose psychologically and emotionally into a mother; his transformation is absolute, as he explains to Isadora after his rescue from the sea: "Whenever Baleka is out of my sight I am worried. If she bruises herself, *I* feel bruised. Night and day I pray all will go well for her, even after I am gone. [. . .] I cannot *eat* [. . .] until I am sure she has eaten first, nor sleep if she is restless and, to make matters worse, if she is quiet for too long, I worry about that as well . . ." (195). He has metamorphosed into a more evolved being who now has "no need to possess or dominate, only appreciate in the ever extended present" (187) through amalgamation and the willingness to sacrifice and serve. The sea, the storm and living with the knowledge that each moment could be his last taught him the value of cooperation and the skill of living in the moment.

Johnson also primes Rutherford for service to others and for transformation by exposure to the Allmuseri slaves on the *Republic.* On the ship there are rumors that "[t]hem niggers is weird. A tribe of witches and strangelings. They kin *do* things" (84); that they are magicians or sorcerers; and, that because they had no science, in the way it was typically understood, "[t]o Falcon that made them savages" (78). But the Allmuseri are largely misunderstood by the crew, and Johnson takes pains to contrast their culture to that of the *Republic* in a way that leaves no doubt as to which is truly savage. Although they attempt to save themselves by rising up in bloody insurrection—they clearly do not want to be enslaved—they have been specially targeted for transport because their reputation as perfect servants precedes them.

Rutherford calls them "popular servants," which sounds more like a job or a career choice than the compulsory subjugation that it is. They are destined for slavery. They are sought after for slaves because their religion dictates a respect for life, therefore they are less apt to harm themselves or others. They are vegetarians, and therefore "easy to feed. Disliking property, they were simple to clothe. Able to heal themselves, they required no medication. They seldom fought. They could not steal. They fell *sick*, it was said, if they wronged anyone. As I live, they so shamed me [Rutherford] I wanted their ageless culture to be my own." The Allmuseri belief in karma influences every aspect of their behavior. They sweep the ground before them to respect the insects and tiny creatures that have a right to their lives. This reverence for life makes the shedding of blood by them almost inconceivable. They also possess a language that is pictographic, metaphoric, lyrical, poetic, beautiful. They are a highly evolved people and culture. Although enormously attracted to their culture, but not having any part of it, Rutherford wishes not to "insult them" by insinuating himself into or appropriating it (78, 77–78).

The motives for slave insurrection require no explanation. Nevertheless, the Allmuseri in *Middle Passage* have a karmic debt to pay for their bloodletting: damnation and billions of rebirths to achieve human status once more, because, according to their beliefs, every thought and deed has consequences and is part of a cosmic equation that must be balanced. Accompanying this prospect is a great sense of remorse for having resorted to violence to solve their problem, "[a]nd so they placed their foreheads on the deck in shame and supplication, praying that the killing would not be carved forever into their nature" (140–141). The Allmuseri believe that they have failed because they violated their most cherished principles. But most important, and crucial to disclosing the point of view of the novel, is that they have been thoroughly contaminated and then destroyed by their *responses* to their enslavement and brutalization, not by the brutalization itself. Totally demoralized, they ask Rutherford to convince the "captain to plot a new course for us" (141). They have allowed their circumstances to disconnect them from their values and have literally lost their way. The lesson they learn is not lost on Rutherford, or the reader.

To Charles Johnson, and resounding through *Middle Passage*, is the idea that slavery need not be *the* defining moment for African Americans; that brutality need not be answered with brutishness. The message is clear: if one can entertain the possibility of transformation and transcendence in the worst of times and under the worst of conditions, then there is not only hope, but an obligation and necessity to embrace this possibility today. *Middle Passage* demonstrates this particularly through the evolution of Rutherford Calhoun, and through the constant example of constructive servitude and sacrifice provided by Isadora, the Allmuseri, Cringle, and most of all by Calhoun's brother Jackson, the faithful servant.

Johnson acknowledges in the introduction to *Proverbs* that in our age of "Relativism, or situational ethics, perhaps even of nihilism," this book in the Bible for some will

> seem right-wing and patriarchal, oppressive and harsh, dogmatic and illiberal. Many will regard its contents as obsolete for the conditions we face at the eleventh hour of the twentieth century because, above all else, we moderns value individual freedom. Unfortunately, our passion for liberty is often misunderstood as license or, more accurately, as licentiousness. [. . .] [But] *Proverbs* not only speaks powerfully to our morally adrift era, but describes rather well my own often benighted, rebellious-on-principle generation (the Baby Boomers) when it says, "There is a generation that curseth their father, and doth not bless their mother. There is a generation that are pure in their own eyes, and yet is not washed from their filthiness" (30:11–12). Chilling.[82]

Even so, moral relativism and situational ethics dominate *Middle Passage*. Rutherford cries "I'm not on *anybody's* side! I'm just trying to keep us *alive!* I don't know who's right or wrong on this ship anymore, and I don't much care! All I want is to go *home!*" (137). Must one choose sides? In his effort to write a philosophical novel and to present a more varied and comprehensive point of view in which the psyche of the white Other is inhabited, *Middle Passage* does not meet the expectations one might have of a black writer to in some way denounce those responsible for slavery, or to offer some sense of the long-term catastrophic effects of slavery and servitude. These are clearly not Johnson's intentions, but are consistent with his ideas about the nonmonolithic nature of experience.

Johnson eschews the notion that any artist can speak for any given group and does not see himself as a spokesperson for African Americans.[83] In fact, he asserts that "no one can speak for 33 million black Americans. Our continuum of voices ranges from Thomas Sowell to Al Sharpton, Walter Williams and Ken Hamblin to Louis Farrakhan. Would anyone ask John Updike to speak for white Americans? The idea is absurd."[84] A single representative or spokesperson for any group is a denial of individuality and an insult.

Aside from its purely literary value, *Middle Passage* is ultimately a call to examine assumptions about morality and responsibility—to self and others. Confronting the past without surrendering to its effects, acknowledging individuation within all contexts and accepting amalgamation and mongrelization as givens are all part of this responsibility. It is a call to acknowledge the need and criteria for transcendence; a transcendence that must be grounded, as Johnson himself says, in "a life that embodies humility, service, and a culture's loftiest ideals," through "wisdom and love; and love is realized through work and undefatigable [sic] service to the things loved." Because in "building, serving, creating [. . .] [one] mightily strives to be righteous."[85] Most significant, this text is ultimately a counterpoint to the idea of the perpetual and presumed degradation of black people because of slavery and servitude. Victimization is a state of mind that can and must be ameliorated by self-reliance and self-respect, by sacrifice and service to others. These are the essential constituents for decency, moral social evolution and survival in *Middle Passage*, and for Charles Johnson.

Chapter 5

Elegy for a Dream

Toni Morrison's Song of Solomon

We did our hours of constructive work, all of us, from eight to eleven-thirty: Sid in his study, Sally and Charity with their babies and house plans and shopping and village volunteerism, I in the moving shade of the treetops of the guest-house porch, the cook in her kitchen, the nurse girl in the nursery, and God, presumably, in His Heaven.

—Wallace Stegner

[T]hey protect themselves from their guilt in the Negro's condition and from their fear that their cooks might poison them, or that their nursemaids might strangle their infant charges, or that their field hands might do them violence, by attributing to them a superhuman capacity for love, kindliness and forgiveness.

—Ralph Ellison[1]

"My mode of writing is sublimely didactic"[2]

At first glance, Toni Morrison's *Song of Solomon* may seem an unlikely example of retrospective fiction in which African American servitude is a significant factor. Because there is so much else to consider in this exquisitely provocative coming-of-age tale, it is not a text that shouts out the relevance of black servitude. Heritage, family and individual dysfunction, class and color consciousness, retaliatory violence, redemption and transcendence contend for consideration and resolution for the characters, as well as for the reader. Even so, the presence of and references to black servitude, however oblique or subtle, effectively facilitate an engagement with these elements of the story and many more. Black servitude brings to the fore the complexities and impact of racism, achievement and identity, and elucidates the social and historical contexts that give rise to social consciousness.

African American servitude in *Song of Solomon* also makes visible the conditions essential to the acquisition of what is commonly called the American Dream—surely a misnomer. Liberty, happiness, financial security and a home, protection and stability for self and loved ones, freedom from intimidation and fear and many other criteria considered to be peculiarly the aspirations of Americans have been desired by many people over time, the world over. The ability to employ servants, and the expectation of who will serve or be served, distinguishes those who merely aspire to the Dream from those who may truly own it.

As the first epigraph to this chapter suggests, all is right with the world when one is in a position to live with ease, secure in the knowledge that basic maintenance and the menial demands of domestic life have been delegated. As the second epigraph suggests, such an assumption is delusional and potentially dangerous. America has been regarded, and rightly so, as a place amenable for achieving the Dream, for some people. In *Song of Solomon* black servitude draws attention to how the so-called American Dream is defined and sought after, and the frustration, futility and rage that result not only from inaccessibility to it for most African Americans, but the expectation that blacks play a serving and supporting role for those who do have access to it. Morrison complicates, deflates and finally detonates the "whole tradition of 'universal' yearnings collapsed into that well-fondled phrase, 'the American Dream.'"[3] Furthermore, *Song of Solomon* discloses how black affluence—even some approximation of or proximity to the American Dream—in and of itself, is not a cure-all for the problems that besiege black people in America. Acquisition of the Dream is subverted not only because of race, although this is a principal determinant, but because it is an inherently flawed value system that promises a sense of security and happiness it can never deliver—a system grounded in an excessive regard for possessions.

For the reader of *Song of Solomon*, black servitude is "sublimely didactic."[4] Morrison's fiction derives from her understanding of history and its effects and her own personal insights shaped by her experience as an African American woman. It all adds dimension to her work. She affirms: "I have claimed what I know. As a black and a woman, I have had access to a range of emotions and perceptions that were unavailable to people who were neither."[5] It is Morrison's mission to present a more comprehensive, multidimensional view of

African Americans in her writing than has heretofore been available. Misrepresentation has often been a product of ignorance, disinterest or a political agenda which deliberately misrepresents or perverts reality. For Morrison

> the reclamation of the history of black people in this country is paramount in its importance because while you can't really blame the conqueror for writing history his own way, you can certainly debate it. There's a great deal of obfuscation and distortion and erasure, so that the presence and the heartbeat of black people has been systematically annihilated in many, many ways and the job of recovery is ours.[6]

Morrison even asserts that the tie that binds African and African American writers is "the clear identification of what the enemy forces are, not this person or that person and so on, but the acknowledgment of a way of life dreamed up for us by some other people who are at the moment in power, and knowing the ways in which it can be subverted. That *is* a connection: we know who he is."[7] She is, as Patricia Storace points out, "relighting the angles from which we view American history, changing the very color of its shadows, showing whites what they look like in black mirrors."[8]

Morrison learned about what it meant to grow up as a slave from her great-grandparents. Her parents grew up in the sharecropping system.[9] Most important, she is uniquely qualified to understand servitude, as a writer who has experienced it firsthand. As a young girl Morrison knew that her family was "very poor,"[10] and she began domestic work at the age of thirteen: "That was the work that was available: to go to a woman's house after school and clean for three or four hours. The normal teen-age jobs were not available. Housework always was. You got to work these gadgets that I never had at home: vacuum cleaners. Some of the people were nice. Some were terrible. Years later, I used some of what I observed in my fiction."[11]

It is hard to see how Morrison's early exposure to the realities of enslavement along with her own experiences in servitude, would not, in some way, inform her work. Morrison often writes or talks about the ways in which socialization affects a writer's work. She believes that "writers transform aspects of their social grounding into aspects of language."[12] Her assessment of and attitude toward servitude ("when I was working in kitchens, I did good work"),[13] has enabled her to fashion characters, circumstances and situations regarding black servitude with depth and insight and a dimension rarely seen in literature.

In *Song of Solomon* there are the usual usages of black servants: the yardman, the washerwoman, the railroad porter, the maid, the former slave and servant, the all-purpose flunky. But there are also, fully realized in these representations, situations and characterizations that engender unique ways to consider black servitude; ways that amplify the enormous impact of history on the lives of individuals. A wealthy and educated black woman takes a job as a maid, the only one available to her because of her color, as a means to acquire emotional independence and wholeness; a former railroad porter obsessed with white violence against black people turns vigilante; a former slave and servant tries to live forever to witness the ruination of a murdering, thieving white family.

Briefly, *Song of Solomon* is about a journey toward spiritual sentience and transcendence. It is a quest, almost in the classical sense, in which the goal of the hero is treasure, "in this case, the self-knowledge gained through a journey into history."[14] Milkman Dead, the self-absorbed son of the wealthiest black people in a Michigan town, is corrupted by parental material overindulgence and emotional neglect. He is caught between his parents, Macon and Ruth Dead, who deeply dislike and disrespect each other. Milkman's attention and time are consumed with his preoccupation with material things, drinking, hanging out with his best friend Guitar Bains, an older youth from the wrong side of town, and having sexual relations with his own cousin, Hagar. Milkman is an uncomfortable, imperfect hero, "unimaginative and uncommitted, a reluctant confidant, a poor listener who does not pay attention to words, asks the wrong questions, and offers erroneous interpretations. He is ill equipped for the quest."[15]

Milkman mistakenly comes to believe that his aunt Pilate, an independent, self-fashioned bootlegger who is estranged from her brother Macon Dead, is hoarding gold. Prodded by his father, Milkman leaves his home on a mission to find the gold, some of which is ostensibly earmarked for operational purposes for Guitar's vengeful black organization, the Seven Days. The Seven Days is a group of black revolutionaries that targets whites at random for physical violence or execution as a response to an identical act perpetrated against a black person. Milkman's expedition turns into a spiritual quest. Away from his embittered family, his unhealthy relationships with both Hagar and Guitar and his usual meaningless pursuits, Milkman has the critical distance that allows him to begin to develop a value system apart from the gross materialism of his family and to quell his emotional turbulence. He comes to understand the importance of history, tradition and family and begins to acquire a new sense of who he is and his place in the world through discovery of his ancestral past. Slavery, racial oppression and injustice, and their effects, especially on his own family, become real to Milkman for the first time. Through Milkman's dawning sense of historical causality, and his subsequent embarkation toward enlightenment, "Morrison transforms the moment of coming to grips with slavery as an allegory of liberation."[16] Guitar, who has become obsessed with the phantom gold and believes he has been cheated, stalks Milkman and then kills Pilate. In the enigmatic ending, Milkman leaps toward Guitar, who has come to kill him.

As Valerie Smith argues, *Song of Solomon* "powerfully explores the nature of family, identity, and culture within a society still burdened by the legacy of slavery and its aftermath of racial violence."[17] The narrative begins with the suicide of Robert Smith (a member of the Seven Days) in 1931. His suicide works as the anchor for events that amble between Reconstruction and the mid-twentieth century, with references to slavery. Morrison's commitment to confronting the past is certain: "It is the past, not the future, which is infinite. Our past was appropriated. I am one of the people who has to reappropriate it,"[18] which explains why, "even though *Solomon* does come up to 1963, it's sort of back there somewhere."[19] *Song of Solomon* is not set in the remote past, but is retrospective in that it continually evokes and is entirely dependent on the past. Every action and consequence has antecedents, which not only make comprehensible the present in the text, but suggest a future. Writing about the past is a way to give life to history, and to work through unresolved or unanswered questions about the past. For Morrison, "what makes one write anyway is something in the past that is haunting, that is not explained or wasn't clear so that you are almost constantly rediscovering the past. I am geared toward the past, I think, because it is important to me; it is living history."[20]

Pullman Porter, Revolutionary

Cheryl Lester writes that, "[f]or the purpose of ethical action, Morrison believes that language users should aim to express the historical specificity of their knowledge and experience, should place truth before beauty, and should recognize their expressive activity as a moral imperative."[21] In fact, Morrison believes engagement with sociohistorical concerns is crucial not only to literature itself, but to contemporary literary dialogue. She submits: "I don't think it is possible to discuss a literature without taking into consideration what is sociologically or historically accurate, but most of the criticism in this country stops here."[22] Although she believes that writing "should not even attempt to solve social problems, [. . .] it should certainly try to clarify them."[23] Considering her convictions, it is almost inconceivable that Morrison would construct such a character as Railroad Tommy, a former railroad servant turned deadly revolutionary, without considering history and the context of experience within the historical moment.

African American Pullman porters, the labor force assembled by George Mortimer Pullman after the Civil War, were considered to be part of the black aristocracy, individuals who enjoyed the privilege (as it was seen to be) of working a clean job that provided steady income and therefore status within the community. What could motivate someone like Railroad Tommy, who has these advantages, to become a vigilante?

The reality was that job expectations for the Pullman porter echoed the expectations of slavery. As Beth Tompkins Bates explains in *Pullman Porters and the Rise of Protest Politics in Black America, 1925–1945*, the porter "was a servant whose job was to attend to all the needs of passengers as they traveled across the country on Pullman's luxurious hotels on wheels." The "porters were ever mindful of servile relations engendered in the antebellum South, for the work culture for porters, nurtured by the Pullman Company, was inherited from slavery." In the Pullman cars "a white person could be pampered and waited on in the manner once reserved for privileged gentry in the antebellum South. [. . .] [T]he company featured a smiling, submissive-looking black servant in its advertisements for Pullman sleepers." Apparently, "[w]hen discussing their work, Pullman porters sometimes noted that 'Lincoln freed the slaves, and the Pullman Company hired 'em.'" Asa Philips Randolph, principal organizer of the Brotherhood of Sleeping Car Porters and Maids labor union, was concerned that servility was a legacy of slavery that continued to impede full realization of citizenship and equality for African Americans, and that it perpetuated the negative social relations of slavery between blacks and whites.

The porters, exploited by low wages and long work hours, were an asset to the Pullman Company as mascots in publicity and advertising. There was no upward mobility, they often had to endure the insult of bowing and scraping for tips to compensate for low wages and avail themselves of leftovers and handouts as part of a strategy to survive. The individuality of thousands of black porters was erased, and they were further objectified and emasculated by the use of the common term "George," the name of the owner of the Pullman Company, and after the fashion of slave ownership.[24]

I agree with Cynthia Davis, who argues that

> oppression in Morrison's world is more often psychic violence. She rarely depicts white characters, for the brutality here is less a single act than the systematic denial of the reality of black lives. The theme of "invisibility" is, of course, a common one in black American literature, but Morrison avoids the picture of the black person "invisible" in white life (Ellison's Invisible Man trying to confront passersby). Instead, she immerses the reader in the black community; the white society's ignorance of that concrete, vivid, and diverse world is thus even more striking.[25]

The invisibility factor, in which blacks are invisible in a white world—a continuing aspect of the master-mistress/slave dynamic—extended in bizarre, peculiarly sexualized ways into the culture of railroad portering. "The *visibility* accorded white service workers makes it hard to imagine a white woman undressing in front of a white hotel bellboy." But "[v]eteran porters talked about white women who thought nothing of undressing in front of them, as if they were invisible"—a compulsory spectatorship for black men who were forced to do what was normally punishable by death—gaze upon the forbidden white woman. The pain of being invisible and disrespected was surely devastating:

> The Pullman porter rode his car, silent with all the chaff round him, always most agreeable when he was of the old school, accepting the generic designation of "George" as though it were a balm instead of an affront, a domestic apparently unaltered by the passage of time or the Emancipation Proclamation. . . . Any white man who spoke to him spoke consciously to a Negro, [. . .] life was a process of enforcing recognition of his personality from a world which treated him as possessed of color without feature. It was always mixing him up with the porter in the car ahead and asking him in simple bewilderment if he was its porter, because he was, after all, only a piece of furniture set out for the convenience of persons who saw no need to be connoisseurs of this sort of furniture.[26]

Railroad Tommy in *Song of Solomon* is such a George. Yes, he later serves as a barber in his community, but, like the service of maintaining the racial ratio through his activities in the Seven Days, it is an act of love. It is a way to take care of and look out for the interests of his people. The humiliating aspects of being a railroad porter, a part of the cheap but classy labor force, belie the clean crisp appearance, a veneer that masks an ugly truth about a society reluctant to change. Through Railroad Tommy, the reader is left to imagine the white world, which, though invisible in the text, hovers at the edges of the black world as an adversarial force or context that must be reckoned with.

From the mouth of Railroad Tommy we get an eloquent insider's point of view about what it means to be a servant—to have one's face pressed up against the window of the American Dream without the possibility of attaining it.[27] He recalls with pride the satisfied feeling of getting a dining car and galley kitchen in perfect order late at night; it was a "thrill" (59). Although Railroad Tommy is proud of his abilities as a porter, one of the best and most coveted jobs for a black man at that time, he has no illusions about the status of black people in America, and taunts teenage Guitar and thirteen-year-old Milkman about what they will never have in life. Prominent on the list of things they will never have are people waiting on them; there is no personal service in their futures because they are black:

> a valet and a cook and a secretary to travel with you and do everything you say. Everything: get the right temperature in your hot-water bottle and make sure the smoking tobacco in the silver humidor is fresh each and *every* day. That's something else you not going to have. [. . .] [Y]ou not going to have no breakfast tray brought to you early in the morning with a red rose on it and two warm croissants and a cup of hot chocolate. Nope. Never. (60)

Railroad Tommy's seemingly good-natured teasing of the two young men is laced with razor-sharp menace and barely suppressed rage. Undergirding his rage, which makes possible his participation in the Seven Days, is, undoubtedly, the weight of history, the continuing refusal of white America to accept blacks as full and equal citizens and the seemingly interminable iniquity of the American judicial system in racial matters, particularly in the South. As Wahneema Lubiano puts it:

> The language of political and economic reality that is prehistory for the boys forms the core of Railroad Tommy's lyrical warning to Guitar and Milkman and is also a site for the change of time. While Railroad Tommy "signifies" on the boys' present petty unfulfilled desires, he scrolls the pages of past history and the reader "reads" Guitar and Milkman's future. He makes visible certain aesthetic pleasures that are part of the workingman's life on the trains in order to make the boys feel the absences of those pleasures, present and future.[28]

In 1831 Nat Turner and his band of determined slave revolutionaries attempted to obtain freedom from slavery in a revolt considered to be the most serious slave insurrection in American history. They failed. After sixty white deaths, swiftly followed by their own, there was little doubt that slaves were both motivated and capable of organizing an uprising. It was also clear that the consequences for such actions were and would always be severe, for black and white. In 1931, one hundred years later, the fictive Robert Smith, who had continued the work of Turner, so to speak, relinquishes his position with the Seven Days through suicide. One must wonder: Was Smith driven to suicide by his own actions as a vigilante, or by the ineffectiveness and utter futility of those actions, or any others, to change the prospects for blacks in America? The Seven Days fight the same fight as Nat Turner. The need for equality and justice for African Americans is still at issue; however, the approach to acquiring it requires new methods—organized retaliatory violence in a secrecy and stealth necessitated by potential consequences.

May we simply write off Railroad Tommy as a sociopath, a psychotic thrill-seeker with too much time on his hands, or, simply, just another angry black man? These dismissive, reductive and very familiar explanations for black rage are evasions that trivialize the experience and the needs of an entire people. In *Song of Solomon* Morrison references the horrors visited upon black people, actual historical events stretching from slavery through the 1960s, which make clear the reasons the Seven Days feel not only justified in their actions, but obliged to act. As Genevieve Fabre so aptly describes it, "the craziness of the black world is only matched by the insanity of the white world's devices."[29] In their way of thinking, their guerilla and terrorist tactics, which do not target the actual perpetrators of violence against African Americans, are self-defense and will help ensure the continuation of their people; they strike against forces they believe are bent on genocide. To understand the Seven Days, and Railroad Tommy, one must understand black rage. Enslavement aside, the short list thereafter is still a litany of grievances that legitimizes their despair.

Jim Crow America carefully delineated the spatial boundaries between blacks and whites. Laws that regulated segregation focused on public and private institutions, recreation facilities and means of transportation, and prohibitive covenants denied blacks access to better neighborhoods. Parentless children were segregated in orphanages. The detritus and forgotten of society, black and white criminals and the insane, were isolated from each other by color. In the same land that claimed in its Pledge of Allegiance to be "One nation, under God, indivisible," black and white could not worship together in church under Jim Crow. Even the dead were made to observe the strictures that segregated black from white in morgues and cemeteries. The spirit of these laws and customs bolstered a climate of racial hatred and intimidation, and ensured the continuance of deeply ingrained beliefs of white superiority and black inferiority. Access to better schools was denied until the 1954 Supreme Court decision that outlawed racial segregation in public schools. The resulting resistance and violence toward blacks seeking to test this law are legendary. As Morrison remarks: "The faces of those white women hovering behind that black girl at the Little Rock school in 1957 do not soon leave the retina of the mind."[30]

Woodrow Wilson's administration unabashedly supported racial segregation and fomented discord. Some of the most horrific violence against African Americans, especially wholesale lynching without consequences for the perpetrators, occurred during his administration. But African Americans became increasingly determined to resist abuse. When blacks were assaulted in the urban riots of 1919 that combusted in twenty-six cities, they fought back.

In the context of such mindless violence and hostility toward blacks, Morrison introduces the Seven Days, founded "in 1920, when that private from Georgia was killed after his balls were cut off and after that veteran was blinded when he came home from France in World War I" (155). Black participation in World War I failed to secure for them a new place in American society. Black soldiers in an Armistice Day parade in Philadelphia were attacked by spectators and police (233). In *Song of Solomon* the insults and abuses visited upon black people, even in the face of their patriotism and sacrifice, are carefully interwoven in the reflections and conversations of those who have been subjected to them. Even if they join the black air force pilots of the 332nd Fighter Group and single-handedly defeat Hitler and win the war, they will not have that morning breakfast tray brought to them by a servant, Railroad Tommy assures his listeners. Not only did black soldiers not get the good life for their contribution to the war effort, after doing their patriotic duty, often with distinction, some were lynched in their uniforms with absolute impunity. Under Franklin Delano Roosevelt there were changes, many made possible by the New Deal, which gave African Americans unprecedented opportunities for employment, especially as federal employees. However, the hope of recognition as full and equal citizens was stymied in completely predictable ways. Roosevelt refused to integrate the armed services in a law "that prohibited the intermingling of 'colored and white' army personnel in the same regiments," an act denounced by A. Philip Randolph and the NAACP whose "*Crisis* carried the headline: 'WHITE HOUSE BLESSES JIM CROW.'"[31] As Eric Foner explains, "in the 1930s," there were no "moves to incorporate black workers within Social Security. Roosevelt gave no assistance to the antilynching initiative."[32] Truman "*called for* abolishing the poll tax, making lynching a federal crime, and *limiting* discrimination in employment," but as part of a political strategy to secure the Northern black vote (my emphasis).[33] In a society in which the struggle for acknowledgement of full equality for blacks under the law was not yet realized, the acknowledgement of equality by white America could only be an absurdity.

Unspoken, but understood by all who gather around to listen to Railroad Tommy, is that not having a servant is irrelevant to their reality, that even being hired as a servant is not guaranteed for a black person, no matter what they have accomplished or who they or their fathers are. In fact, of the 12,000 African American porters employed by the Pullman Company by World War I, "many [. . .] [were] the best-educated black men in the country."[34] They were grossly underemployed in respect to their skills and level of education—a fact that speaks volumes about the state of affairs for blacks in the United States. Ronald Takaki reports that black soldiers in World War II were subjected to degrading camp conditions, segregated training programs, "servile work assignments," regardless of their level of skill or education, and hostility and violence both on the military bases and in society in general. The appeals of black leaders and intellectuals to the American government and white society for definitive resolution—legal, economic and social equity, during and after both world wars—fell largely on deaf ears. The tenacious resistance to acknowledging black equality was increasingly defined, by many blacks, as an unremediable national evil, understandably so, given the circumstances.

Morrison believes that "Black people in general don't annihilate evil. We are not well known for erecting stoning centers or destroying people when they have disagreements. We believe that evil has a natural place in the universe. We try to avoid it or defend ourselves against it but we are not surprised at its existence or horrified or outraged."[35] Nevertheless, she makes comprehensible how, for the Seven Days, the evil of oppression and violence against blacks must be challenged with equal violence—a fire-to-fight-fire approach. They see no other solution. Clearly, as Ralph Story asserts, "[i]n the course of Morrison's meticulously revealing this society, she gives readers a glimpse of black rage, the certainty of which has, for a variety of reasons, tended to remain undisclosed. (The urban riots of the 1960s offered a dramatic piece of public testimony.)"[36]

The continuing horrors of racism in America are historical context and causality in *Song of Solomon.* Emmett Till, a teenage black boy from Chicago, is lynched in Mississippi in 1955 (80, 81). In 1963 a church in Birmingham, Alabama is bombed, and four little girls in a Sunday School class die (173).

During this period, civil rights leader Martin Luther King, modeling his nonviolent protest methods on Mahatma Gandhi's example, is repeatedly arrested. The heroic efforts of those committed to changing the status of blacks in America are met with reactions ranging from consternation and stern resistance, to disabling and often fatal violence. The scenes are now familiar. Throughout the 1950s and 1960s peaceful civil rights demonstrators and workers—who attempt sit-ins, boycotts, voter registration—have attack dogs turned loose on them, are beaten and hosed by police and other angry whites and are jailed. President Kennedy is finally forced to send out troops to quell the riots. Two hundred thousand nonviolent freedom marchers descend on Washington, D.C. The protest politics of blacks and other supporters of civil rights make serious efforts, and modest and significant inroads in legislation. Nevertheless, one hundred years after the Emancipation Proclamation, the Civil Rights Act of 1964 was needed to further attempts for equality for African Americans.

In the aftermath of the urban riots of the 1960s (Harlem, Watts, Detroit, Cleveland, Newark), and the assassinations of Malcolm X and Martin Luther King, with the nation reeling from these and other racially charged events and situations, it was certain that the race problem was as incendiary as it had been a century earlier. There was progress, victories even, in the effort to change the economic and social status of blacks, particularly during Lyndon Johnson's administration. His vision of a Great Society had no place for poverty and can claim "the legislative triumphs of the civil rights era—the Civil Rights Act of

1964, the Voting Rights Act of 1965, and the Fair Housing Act of 1968."[37] Yet, these legislations could not check the activities of the Ku Klux Klan, which was increasingly successful in recruitment and terrorism. The accelerating activities of the John Birch Society were so ominous that they became a concern for the U.S. Senate. It would take more than laws to stabilize, much less improve, the racial situation in America. Martin Luther King's "Dream" could not force white America to change long-cherished ideas and attitudes toward African Americans. There were other frustrations and disappointments, such as the refusal of the majority of unions to accept black members, and the failure of the Socialist and Communist parties—once so attractive to many black intellectuals, artists and workers—to address the particular concerns of blacks in America. John Hope Franklin argues that the 1960s began as a time of hope, but gradually

> the optimism gave way to pessimism and even cynicism. It was not merely the opposition to equality on the part of the white citizens councils or the Northern white mothers who railed against school desegregation or the white construction workers who bitterly opposed the employment of black journeymen and apprentices, but the feeling, bolstered by bitter experience, that justice and equality were not to be extended to blacks under any circumstances that created the gloomy atmosphere out of which the Black Revolution emerged.[38]

In the world of *Song of Solomon*, during the entire period from 1920 through the 1960s, invisible black civilian militants, the self-anointed soldiers in an undeclared war, go to work—Railroad Tommy among them. The Seven Days offers deadly retribution to an oppressive and unjust society in secret. They mete out their own brand of justice and attempt to keep the racial ratio between black and white the same—efforts to stay the tide of the genocide they fear.

The civil rights movement began to lose momentum in the late 1960s, particularly after the assassination of King. In his discussion of the failure of legislation to change the fundamental social status of blacks in America, Senator Fred Harris, a member of the National Advisory Commission on Civil Disorders, makes a blatant admission of what African Americans have understood for centuries:

> There should be no mistake about this, for the future of America is too important: the root cause of the black wrath that now threatens to destroy this nation is the unwillingness of white Americans to accept Negroes as fellow human beings. This is precisely what we meant by racism. [. . .] [D]espite the passage of five civil rights bills since 1957, despite the erosion of legal supports

> for segregated institutions, despite greater acceptance of Negroes into our major institutions, both public and private, it is still no easy thing to be a black person in America.[39]

Black people in America needed no National Advisory Commission to understand that their frustration and rage were justified. In their study of black rage in the immediate aftermath of the struggles of the 1960s, African American psychiatrists William Grier and Price Cobbs determined that

> [i]f racist hostility is to subside, and if we are to avoid open conflict on a nationwide scale, information is the most desperately needed commodity of our time. And of the things that need knowing, none is more important than that all blacks are angry. White Americans seem not to recognize it. They seem to think that all the trouble is caused by only a few "extremists." They ought to know better. We have talked to many Negroes under the most intimate of circumstances and we know better.[40]

This thumbnail sketch of the racial climate and its effects on black Americans during the tenure of the Seven Days is vital to making sense of Railroad Tommy's involvement with this group. Through this character, Morrison, whose "hope is simultaneously to reveal and to heal, to strip away the illusions to show why African-American life remains to many an embattled existence, and to minister to a beleaguered population,"[41] effectively demonstrates how an otherwise ordinary human being, someone who takes pride in his job as a servant on the railroads, can be conscripted for such lethal purposes. It is the poor, powerless and downtrodden who truly and desperately dream of equality and justice. In the midst of such travail to which black Americans were subjected, most black porters attempted to better their lot by organizing a union. Railroad Tommy finds another forum in which to channel his rage. The absence of a breakfast tray delivered by a servant was the least of worries for African Americans in Jim Crow America, or for Railroad Tommy. It is what the absence of the servant-delivered tray represents that matters most—the withholding of equal opportunity, the denial of equality.

In a society in which the prospects for full and equal citizenship for black people are uncertain, and in which history, its effects, and the realities of the present are denied, the prognosis for a secure and healthy American future is in question. Although he co-owns a barbershop, which is surely a step up the economic ladder, in his musings about the way things are, Railroad Tommy considers his former position as a servant, and his inability to truly rise above it. To be forever denied the simple pleasure of having a breakfast tray brought to him underscores his reality: expectation and hope must be rigidly curtailed because of his color—he can go no further. This denial seems to be the proverbial straw that breaks Railroad Tommy, and is also a catalyst for helping him to clarify his thinking about the overall history and plight of blacks in America. A sense of futility and despair rule his thinking.

There has been an observable decline in physical violence against blacks in comparison to the first half of the twentieth century. There is also a decline in aggressive political activity on behalf of black civil rights since the civil rights movement, marked by an almost deafening silence. It is a silence fractured, immeasurably, by those, black and white, who deny the consequences of history. The occasional but very vocal assertions of some African American intellectuals and politicians that there is now a level playing field in America bolsters the notion that racism is not a determining factor for success or for acquiring the American Dream; that Martin Luther King's Dream has become a reality. Yet, who would argue that, today, working class, un- or underemployed African Americans, subscribe to this belief? Railroad Tommy does not subscribe to such a belief.

An absence of violence or political activity does not mean there is an absence of rage. Partial though measurable success does not ensure an absence of rage. Unarticulated, the question still looms large in *Song of Solomon:* What if African Americans, hardworking and ordinary people like Railroad Tommy, succumbed to frustration and despair? The potential for retaliatory violence is a terrifying and sobering reality in this text.

Black Social Stratification and Servitude

Characteristics that define Americanness, and that are requisite for acquiring the American Dream, include level of education, profession, lineage, color, power and influence, recognition by those already established in the ranks and, of course, one's net worth or a demonstrated ability to amass money and goods. Ultimately, to have the means to delegate domestic labor—to have someone to wash clothes, cook, clean up the house or yard—ranks high in the criteria for American success. Repeatedly in her work, Toni Morrison engages with "what it means to be black and privileged."[42] Social stratification within the African American community, the defining characteristics of class and caste and the dynamics of upward mobility resound through *Song of Solomon.* For African Americans, particularly the middle class and elite, black servitude was particularly problematic from the late nineteenth through the first half of the twentieth century. This often tension-filled and irreconcilable arrangement between black servants and black employers was the result of a species of class and caste consciousness that was peculiar to African American society, a consciousness notable in *Song of Solomon.*

The discomfiture between black employers and domestics may be attributed, to some extent, to the usual complaints one hears about those with new money. A certain Ms. Evans, a maid in Judith Rollins's study of black women domestics, declared: "I won't work for somebody who just got their two cents together. They don't know what they're doing. They're insecure about their positions. And they don't know how to relate to their help."[43] Willard Gatewood argues in *Aristocrats of Color* that although elite African Americans in the late nineteenth and early twentieth centuries employed African American servants in the South, Scandinavian, German, Swedish and Polish immigrants, and some English women "were preferable as maids because they were more tractable than others. [. . .] A common complaint by aristocrats of color was that they could not secure black servants, and if they did, the blacks refused to show proper deference toward their employers." Furthermore, African American servants did not want to work for African Americans. "According to Archibald Grimké, the 'colored servant class' unfortunately had 'adopted the white race's contempt for colored people' and preferred to remain unemployed rather than work for a colored family."[44]

In early-twentieth-century black society in *Song of Solomon*, prosperous Negroes certainly spelled trouble for young Pilate Dead when she worked as a domestic servant. As a teenager on her own in the world, she "did not want a steady job [as a domestic] in a town where a lot of colored people lived. All her encounters with Negroes who had established themselves in businesses or trades in those small Midwestern towns had been unpleasant. [. . .] [T]hough the men saw many raggedy black children, Pilate was old enough to disgrace them" (144). Eventually, she avoided these situations.

Pilate's older brother, Macon Dead, a slumlord and the most financially successful black man in town, is the embodiment of this prosperous class of Negroes. His driving principle is: "Money is freedom [. . .]. [T]he only real freedom there is" (163). Determined to continue his ascent on the social ladder, Macon is ashamed and feels disgraced by Pilate, who he believes has degenerated into a filthy, immoral bootlegger. He fears that her very presence has the power to lower his status and confuse and damage his relations with white bankers in the town. He is, as Samuel Allen describes him, the "industrious, ambitious businessman, standard-bearer of bourgeois horrors." Macon's hearth and home are desolated by his greed, indifference to his family, hatred for his wife.

On the other hand, Pilate is a celebration of life and love, "deformed in the world's view and derelict, but whose gift is forbearance and love and a surrendering to life to possess it."[45] Her value system, and happy if unconventional home, offer an alternative to materialism. It is only the encroachment of the outside world that causes problems for Pilate, and for her daughter and granddaughter, Reba and Hagar, who make up the rest of her household. It is Pilate, with her openness and wisdom, who truly parents Milkman and starts him on a path of self-actualization and enlightenment. As Jan Furman argues, Pilate "has already defined her priorities: family and relationships are important, while money and manners are not. Over time, Milkman acquires a similar understanding, but ultimately his achievement is possible only because of Pilate's example."[46] Pilate is a good soul. She is willing to share all she has, what little there is of it. Through the contrasts of Macon and Pilate, Morrison draws attention to the direct relationship between unbridled pursuit of property and goods, and loss of self. She "uses the contrast between the artificial and natural to dramatize the two value systems represented by the Dead brother and sister."[47] In fact, as Susan Willis has pointed out, "[t]he utopian aspect of Pilate's household is not contained within it, but generated out of its abrupt juxtaposition to the bourgeois mode of her brother's household. In contrast to Macon's world, which is based on accumulation, Pilate's household is devoted in true 'potlatch' fashion to non-accumulation."[48]

The contrast is stunning. Macon is utterly desensitized and corrupted by his obsession with money and with the material trophies of his success, which have blunted his social consciousness and moral sensibilities. For Macon, "all human relationships have become fetishized by their being made equivalent to money. His wife is an acquisition; his son, an investment in the future; and his renters, dollar signs in the bank."[49] His determination is palpable: As a shrewd businessman Macon knew that there were some opportunities even then, although he also understood that "as a Negro he wasn't going to get a big slice of the pie. [. . .] There was quite a bit of pie filling oozing around the edge of the crust in 1945. Filling that could be his" (63). He meant to not share his filling with anyone else, even someone in great need. Destitute Mrs. Bains, Guitar's grandmother, who scrambles to keep a roof over her grandchildren's heads, identifies the social malady of indifference that presumably afflicts middle-class and elite blacks who are indifferent to the struggles of those who do not enjoy the same material comforts. With dignified resignation, Mrs. Bains simply acknowledges what to her is a fact of life when Macon Dead refuses to give her a break on paying the rent: "A nigger in business is a terrible thing to see. A terrible, terrible thing to see" (22). Macon's reasoning is thoroughly capitalist and strategic and could be that of any slaveholder describing his methods and actions. He imparts his wisdom to his son as though he has discovered the meaning of life: "Own things. And let the things you own own other things. Then you'll own yourself and other people too. Starting Monday, I'm going to teach you how" (55).

Relationships between black employers, many of whom come from this class of successful businessmen, and their black servants are complicated and freighted with struggles for dominance and power that are not, typically, part of the white employer/black servant dynamic. The caste/class differentials and the boundaries are clearly defined in a white employer/black servant configuration. There is no struggle for dominance because it is always clear who has the power.

Consider Freddie, more pathetic than malicious, who is a "born flunky, he loved gossip and the telling of it. He was the ear that heard every murmur of complaint, every name-calling; and his was the eye that saw everything: the secret loving glances, the fights, the new dresses" (24–25). He uses his information to show off and get attention. Servant, janitor, general factotum of the Dead family, Freddie takes liberties no one else would dare with his employers, because "he purchased [them] with the services he rendered" (15). As J. Brooks Bouson argues, Morrison "not only ridicules them [the Deads] for their class pretensions, but also actively humiliates them by insisting on their family pathology and by exposing the shameful family secrets that haunt them."[50] Freddie functions as the means to expose the class tensions and secrets not only of the Dead family, but of African American society.

Ruth Dead has many secrets, most having to do with her dead father, the wealthy Dr. Foster, and her son. Freddie peeks in the window and discovers Ruth in a dark room breastfeeding her son who, though still a child, is beyond the age when it is appropriate to do so. He laughs, "Have mercy, I be damn" (14). Emboldened because he has caught her in a compromising position, Freddie violates normal employer/servant spatial and behavioral boundaries by entering the house uninvited and in a proprietary fashion. He seeks them out with a false, jovial familiarity: "'Miss Rufie. Miss Rufie. Where you? Where you all at?' He opened the door to the green room as though it were his now. 'I be damn, Miss Rufie. When the last time I seen that?'" (14). Freddie feels a falling away of a social hierarchy that, in the presence of his social betters, would normally make him ingratiate himself or even grovel, behaviors with which he is accomplished, obsequious lackey that he is. A leveling with Ruth occurs because she is lowered in status by the discovery of her sexual perversion.

Phyllis Palmer writes that

> [h]istorians have often noted the cultural distinctions between "good" women and "bad" women based on standards of purity and licentiousness, and the issue of sexual propriety continues to simmer in feminist scholarship. The home has been reified as the setting for good women, virtuous wives and mothers. Its work has been haloes with maternal imagery. [. . .]

> Through creating a proper home and through contrast with a servant, the MCH [middle-class housewife] found her identity as a good woman.[51]

Ruth has sacrificed her standing as a good woman because of her daily breast-feeding ritual with her son. Both Freddie and Ruth are confirmed in her guilt by her reaction when she is discovered, and by the fact that she never again nurses her son after this incident. The image that Freddie sees through the window is not maternal, but inappropriately sexual. Presumptions of Ruth's purity are forfeit. Freddie seizes his opportunity to exercise his new power, and wastes no time spreading the nasty secret in the community. He also has the power to effectively rename Ruth's son "Milkman," "a name he was never able to shake" (15). Still, a white employer would never brook such meddling and sniveling obsequiousness, which is obvious disrespect, from someone who served them. The glaring question: Why do both Macon and Ruth Dead allow it?

Of course, Freddie is clearly useful for the services he provides, typically things the Deads would never themselves do, the most common function of servants in general. His job is mundane, which is to be expected, but also extreme in that it includes surrogacies which denote his expendability. To protect himself from potential danger, Macon uses the reluctant Freddie to fetch his rent payment from the drunken, shotgun-waving Porter: "Go get me my money" (26). Also, Macon finds Freddie useful for the information he freely provides about the goings-on in his community that Macon, as an antisocial and self-imposed outsider, is not privy to otherwise. "Macon knew Freddie as a fool and a liar, but a reliable liar. He was always right about his facts and always wrong about the motives that produced the facts" (25).

Aside from his usefulness as a multipurpose servant, insecurity could explain the Deads' tolerance of Freddie's improper conduct. But Macon is clearly not intimidated by the likes of Freddie, and although Ruth was caught in a compromising position and has her insecurities, she is accustomed to wealth and the prerogatives of privilege.

Freddie functions as a reminder of the fact that the Deads are not, themselves, that far removed from the possibility of being servants, if not slaves. The specter of slavery, and the economic need for continuing in service after slavery, was the reality for the majority of African Americans in the first decades of the twentieth century. A very few years earlier, and under different circumstances, Ruth and Macon would be serving, not served. This newly forming social class of African Americans has yet to work out a comfortable working relationship with their African American servants. History gets in the way. On one hand, they may overcompensate because of a misplaced and unacknowledged sense of guilt because of their own advantages. This may account for the Deads' tolerance of Freddie's transgressions. But black employers were also often noted for severe treatment of their black employees, another overcompensation and effort, perhaps, to distance themselves and enforce the distinctions of class and status.

African American society began the process of redefining and restructuring itself after emancipation. The caste system, which was based more on color coding (privileging light skin) than achievement and wealth, gradually deteriorated. Servants, regardless of color, lost social status in the black community as the hierarchy became more meritocratic and wealth-based. According to E. Franklin Frazier in *Black Bourgeoisie: The Rise of a New Middle Class in the United States*, for example, after World War I "Negroes who had constituted Negro 'society' because they were mulattoes and acted like 'gentlemen' were pushed aside because they were engaged in personal services. The Negro doctors, dentists, lawyers, and businessmen [. . .] were becoming the leaders of Negro 'society.'"[52] This growing trend explains Macon's conviction that he could secure an esteemed place in his community based on his achievements as a businessman, even though he is dark-skinned. It may also explain his disdain for Pilate, who has had three positions that rank very low on the merit scale—washerwoman, domestic, bootlegger.

Toni Morrison says, "I don't think the class problems among black people are as great as the class problems among white people. I mean, there's just no real problems with that in terms of language and how men relate to one another—black men relate to one another whatever class they come from."[53] Nevertheless, the same presumed equality, even fraternity, among African Americans because of race and a shared history may actually contribute to the awkwardness of the black employer/servant relationship. The Deads and Freddie travel in different social circles and have extremely different financial situations and prospects in life. They are—different. In *Song of Solomon*, servitude is one factor that divides classes in the black community. But servitude is also, ultimately, the great equalizer.

First Corinthians Dead, the lemony-yellow, middle-aged daughter of Ruth and Macon and older sister to Milkman, is a refined, educated, well-to-do woman whose life is narrowly defined and constricted by her father's belief that she and her sister Magdalene are too good to, as Corinthians puts it, "mix with . . . people" (195). Her family life is beleaguered with tension, bitterness, anger and hatred. The older she becomes, the more her options dwindle in life. It becomes clear that she will never marry and have children; she will be forever, herself, a child in her father's house. Morrison explains that "Corinthians is kept like a child [. . .] because her father and mother believed, at least to some degree, that the American Dream was worthwhile. And part of that dream is to remain infantized [sic] and to regard innocence as a virtue that's supposed to last forever."[54] Eventually her frustration and loneliness, and the fact that life is passing her by, motivate Corinthians to seek a life outside her dysfunctional, stultifying home. She becomes a maid.

Ruth Dead loves the idea of what she believes Corinthians is doing. "Amanuensis. [. . .] The rickety Latin word made the work her daughter did (she, after all, wasn't required to work) sound intricate, demanding, and totally in keeping with her education. [. . .] It was a lie, of course, even as the simpler word 'secretary' was a lie [. . .]. She did not know then, and never found out, that Corinthians was Miss Graham's maid" (187). Ironically, the position of amanuensis, a fancy-sounding word that suggests some noble or intellectual engagement, historically ranks low in the job hierarchy: "Historical context illuminates the irony of the passive, receptive role of the amanuensis, who, as a mere transcriber, was always held in low regard by teachers of classical rhetoric and who, later in the history of Western letters, was a person of low social and political status, similar to the historical status of women. We might recall the status of Milton's daughters in this regard."[55] An amanuensis is, arguably, a servant. Clearly, "being the granddaughter of the eminent Dr. Foster should have culminated in something more than the two uniforms that hung on Miss Graham's door" (188), or something more than being an amanuensis.

Corinthians belongs to a class of elite black people in a position to often avoid the full impact, "the insults, the substandard treatment, and the poor facilities that the Jim Crow laws had left for blacks" by virtue of their wealth and social isolation. Lawrence Otis Graham provides a context in *Our Kind of People: Inside America's Black Upper Class* for understanding this privileged black world in the 1960s during the civil rights movement, through the coping attempts of his great-grandmother:

> But like many blacks of her class, she was able to limit the interactions that she and her family had with such indignities. Rather than ride at the back of the bus and send her daughter to substandard segregated schools, she and her husband bought a car and paid for private schooling. For my great-grandmother, life had been generous enough that she could create an environment that buffered her family against the bigotry she knew was just outside her door.

Graham describes his own polite detachment as a youngster from the civil rights movement:

> What I now recall was lacking—at least in my own Jack and Jill experience—was any real sense of the anger and dissatisfaction that the rest of black Amer-

> ica was expressing in the late 1960s and early 1970s. Martin Luther King had been shot, cities had been burned, Nixon and Agnew were in the White House, and yet we were learning how to ride horses, make leather belts, or commandeer a small yacht. [. . .] In retrospect, it all seemed as if we were operating in a world that was separate from what we saw on TV news or in the local newspapers. [. . .] [T]o suburban kids like me and my brother, the "community," the "struggle," and the "cause" were just terms we nodded at before we turned to the Jack and Jill kid next to us and politely said, "It's my turn to drive the boat."[56]

There are, of course, diverse political ideologies within the African American community. Jacqueline Jones argues, for example, that the emerging black middle class actually "played a large part in the development of Afro-American political consciousness. This class owed its status to male household heads who managed—through luck, hard work, and determination—to maintain their tenuous positions as skilled craftsmen or entrepreneurs within an increasingly hostile Jim Crow environment."[57] But it is clear that Corinthians comes from such a situation in which social consciousness is not an issue. Although the battle for civil rights is waged outside her door, and played out graphically in the media, there is just enough material comfort to create an illusion of well-being and to foster indifference. Nevertheless, black is black, as Corinthians discovers when she begins to look for a job in 1961. The America outside her home and neighborhood remind her of who and what she is not.

Corinthians' situation is complicated. After college and travel abroad, she returns to a society in which there is "one and only one kind of work" available for "colored girls, regardless of their background" (189)—domestic service. Resigned to her fate, Corinthians accepts a job as a maid to get out of the house, to have something all her own that does not come from or have anything to do with her father and to stave off depression. There are other factors that may have contributed to Corinthians' limited options for employment. Her lack of work experience; a liberal and elite education that did not prepare her for other work in life, such as teaching; the length of time from the completion of her education and her job seeking (twenty-one years), for example. However, making a new life offers very particular challenges for Corinthians because she is a black woman. Race and the time period ultimately determine her portion.

Corinthians worries about and takes great pains to keep the nature of her job a secret, for obvious reasons. The charade: She carefully avoids any contact with the other maids on the city bus she takes to her job, dresses in beautiful street clothes and high-heeled shoes so as not to be associated with them, carries no bag with uniforms or comfortable shoes in them but leaves these at her employer's house. She carries a book written in French, which she strategically handles and displays as an indicator of her different and superior status from the other maids. "Once she was in Miss Graham's house she changed into her uniform (which was a discrete blue anyway, not white) and put on a pair of loafers before she dropped to her knees with a pail of soapy water" (190). As Mary Romero points out in *Maid in America*, "[w]hite uniforms are used to distinguish the maid from families and friends, particularly when employers fear that others might mistake the reason for her presence."[58] But for Corinthians, the blue uniform signifies another important distinction between herself and other maids who wear white—it is one more way, pitiful though it may be, for her to affirm her superiority over them.

It is this job, however, that gives Corinthians a new life and sense of herself; it gives her hope, an eagerness to confront the possibilities which are only available outside her own door. Morrison is able to construct such a character as Corinthians because she understands that domestic work—typically regarded as lowly and undignified—can, and has, empowered many black women who had no other occupational alternatives. She states:

> black women have had some enormous responsibilities, which in these days people call freedoms—in those days, they were called responsibilities—they lived, you know, working in other people's, white people's, houses and taking care of that and working in their own houses and so on and they have been on the labor market. And nobody paid them that much attention in terms of threats, and so on, so they had a certain amount of "freedom." But they did a very extraordinary job of just taking on that kind of responsibility.[59]

Morrison has enormous respect for black women who have had to work, and for what is often the unacknowledged resiliency, perseverance, and moral constitution demonstrated by black women under extreme pressure and responsibility. She explains:

> It seems to me historically true that Black women have a special place in this culture which is not always perceived as an enviable one. One of the characteristics of Black women's experience was that they did not have to choose between a career and a home. They did both. [. . .] Because of the dual responsibility that Black women had—when they were left, they didn't collapse. They didn't have crutches in the first place, so with nothing but themselves to rely on they just had to carry on. And that, I think, is absolutely extraordinary and marvelous.[60]

This job of servitude, from which blacks could not escape for hundreds of years as slaves, and subsequently as free people, is one that offers some benefits for Corinthians. Her self-respect increases as she thrives in her job. She takes pride in earning her own money and comes to understand that she has been a child in her parents' house, passively receiving an allowance doled out to her. She acquires freedom, independence and a sense of self. "We can only congratulate her for making this leap that for her must be into a kind of abyss."[61]

Her life begins to open up. Educated at Bryn Mawr and in France, a woman considered unsuitable for any black man because she was too elegant and unused to struggle, Corinthians finds her opportunity for love in a yardman. Henry Porter, the first and only man to ever show interest in Corinthians, is also in service. She finds Porter as a result of her willingness to go out into the world, and discovers that she can deal with situations she would have felt otherwise degrading because of her socialization, status, and lack of training and experience. Porter and Corinthians first become friends and then lovers, but she keeps the relationship a secret for the same reason that she keeps her employment as a maid a secret—she is ashamed of her involvement with a man who has such humble employment and who must live accordingly. In fact, at times "she hated him a lot for the shame she felt. Hated him sometimes right in the middle of his obvious adoration of her, his frequent compliments about her looks, her manners, her voice" (194). Although she now clearly understands the social circumstances that severely limit employment opportunities for blacks because of her own new experience, she is unable to face the judgments of her community, and especially her own family, for this act of defiance and class apostasy (193, 195).

Eventually, on the verge of breaking up with Corinthians because he is tired of the secrecy and sneaking around, Porter tells her he doesn't want a doll baby, he wants a real woman, a grown-up woman. Out of conditioning, habit and pride, she holds herself above and thinks herself better than the other maids on the bus and abuses them terribly to Porter. She tries to hurt him for preferring what she thinks they represent; over what she has to offer as a "lady" (197). The maids on the bus are, to Corinthians, illiterate, desperate, low class, fat, easy, loose and disproportionately grateful for anything they may get from a man (196–197). But, so much is at stake that Corinthians, probably for the first time in her life, tries to examine her own assumptions and values. She wonders: "Did he mean like the women who rode on the bus? The other maids, who were not hiding what they were? Or the black women who walked the streets at night?" (196).

Both examples of being "real" are women who may "serve" in very different ways, but who have in common the fact that they are open and honest, qualities that have nothing to do with the nature of their employment. Through the choice of being either a maid or a prostitute in order to qualify as "real," Corinthians discovers that she is, in fact, not real, but a made-up person with a sham of public and private personae, who lives a fantasy and a lie out of a misplaced sense of shame. With this realization, and with her growing ability to accept her new life and partner, her shame begins to lose its power over her. This "daughter of a wealthy property owner, and the elegant Ruth Foster, granddaughter of the magnificent and worshipped Dr. Foster [. . .] a woman who had turned heads on every deck of the *Queen Mary* and had Frenchmen salivating all over Paris [. . .] was now banging on the car-door window of a yardman" (197–198).

Being with such a man as Porter, choosing such a man, would have been inconceivable to Corinthians without her experience as a maid. They may be from polar ends of African American society, but servitude is ultimately the great equalizer and wipes out Corinthians' class consciousness and their class differences. She has expanded her horizons by taking a public bus into a wealthy white neighborhood to get down on her knees and scrub floors. Servitude may be the expectation in America for the likes of Porter and Corinthians; but it is their sole hope for employment, and the tie that binds them together.

Slave, Servant, Timeless Adjudicator

Circe, the live-in domestic of the Butler family, is the most enigmatic character in *Song of Solomon*. She is, as J. Brooks Bouson puts it, "a deliberate parody of the traditional white representation of the loyal white servant."[62] When I think of Circe, I recall the parabolic old woman in Morrison's Nobel Lecture in 1993,

> the daughter of slaves [. . .] [who] lives alone in a small house outside of town. Her reputation for wisdom is without peer and without question. Among her people she is both the law and its transgression. The honor she is paid and the awe in which she is held reach beyond her neighborhood to places far away, to the city where the intelligence of rural prophets is the source of much amusement.[63]

But Morrison constructs this tiny, toothless servant who is benign, by all appearances, as one who wields incredible power. She is a healer and caretaker, someone who would be a respected person in another society (246). Circe is midwife to people and dogs, bringing new life into the world, and stands attendance at their deaths by natural or unnatural means. It is she who ensures the continuation of the Dead family line by concealing Jake (Mason the elder) Dead's children, Pilate and Macon, in the home of their father's murderers. Like the Odyssean Circe, she is a dispenser of information, and tells Milkman what he needs to know to find his way home—a metaphor for finding his family history and roots. Most important, she is witness, sentinel, justice and patient chastener. Circe metes out retribution for Jake's murder, the confiscation of his property and the orphaning and dispossession of his children.

Jake Dead was born a slave, but he had extraordinary resolve to have a life, to make a good life despite all obstacles. He completely refused to let his beginnings as a slave define him or his future. Jake made no excuses, worked hard and had no interest in explanations or excuses for lack of effort. His farm and his life were a model and inspiration to his admiring friends and neighbors. With Horatio Alger determination, Jake believed fervently in the tenets of the American Dream and stirred the aspirations of his fearful, reluctant, downtrodden brethren. His beautiful, bountiful property

> spoke to them like a sermon. "You see?" the farm said to them. "See? See what you can do? Never mind you can't tell one letter from another, never mind you born a slave, never mind you lose your name, never mind your daddy dead, never mind nothing. Here, this here, is what a man can do if he puts his mind to it and his back in it. Stop sniveling," it said. "Stop picking around the edges of the world. Take advantage, and if you can't take advantage, take disadvantage. We live here. On this planet, in this nation, in this county right here. *No*where else! We got a home in this rock, don't you see!"

And, they did see. He "was the farmer they wanted to be. [. . .] He had come out of nowhere, as ignorant as a hammer and broke as a convict, with nothing but free papers, a Bible, and a pretty black-haired wife, and in one year he'd leased ten acres, the next ten more" (235).

But after the Butlers "shot the top of his head off and ate his fine Georgia peaches," the black community was devastated and disheartened; it "was the beginning of their own dying" (235). His murder left them without hope and focus, and with a lesson hard to unlearn. It left them with yet another example of how a black man can make every effort to have a certain kind of life and have it all taken away, with absolute impunity, by avaricious white people. Jake's killers were never caught because they never went anywhere. They didn't have to. They were never arrested. "Everybody knew who did it. Same people Circe worked for—the Butlers. [. . .] Wasn't nothing to do. White folks didn't care, colored folks didn't dare. [. . .] Folks just was thankful the children escaped" (232). Hard work, self-determination, decency are clearly not enough to succeed in a hostile environment where you have no rights or protection under the law. Circe set a different goal than Jake, one that was well within her power, one she could do in secret. She found a way to succeed, according to her own terms, in this hostile environment.

Circe worked for the Butlers "in a large house—a mansion—outside Danville, for a family of what was then called gentlemen farmers" (166). After their father is murdered for his property, Circe hides young Macon and Pilate in the Butler's storage rooms. If the Butlers had found Circe to be hiding the two orphans, she possibly would have been in danger of losing more than her job. Circe knew that her employers had killed Jake, but theirs was the safest place because no one would think to look for the orphans there (232). Subterfuge, stealth and cunning were her methods as she went quietly about her business of looking after the Dead children, and serving the Butlers. The only way the black people in the area even knew that the children were alive was that Circe brought the boxed earring that Pilate wore for repairs (231); the Butlers never found out what had happened to them.

Circe becomes a law unto herself. Eventually, the Butlers' money runs out, and their family dies off. Circe watches and waits and makes certain that nothing good comes from the Butler's actions. Clearly, "[w]here there is dirt there is not only revenge, but payoff or pleasure,"[64] and "[a]cting as an agent of black revenge, Circe [. . .] symbolically dirties—that is, shames—the once powerful and superior white family, representatives of the prejudiced white culture that has historically shamed blacks by treating them as dirty and dissmelling objects of contempt."[65] The last Miss Butler kills herself rather than live and work as her black servant had done all her life. The thought, not only of living without servants, but having to work like one, was more than she could bear. With each servant she has to let go, her will to live diminishes, and she finally chooses death over humiliation.

But Circe, their servant, remains in their mansion long after they are all gone. Along with the pack of Weimaraners who roam the filthy, dilapidated mansion, Circe watches the house disintegrate. Like her namesake in Greek mythology who turns men into animals, Circe is a sorceress. It is plain to see that the dogs are, in fact, the Butlers incarnate who are cursed to be spectators of and participants in the final ruination of all they had acquired by murder and theft. When Milkman visits Circe, these dogs assess him with their "intelligent child's eyes [. . .]. Calm, sane, appraising eyes" (240), which denote their awareness of their circumstances.

Filled with a pride and conviction unabated by time, Circe attempts to make Milkman understand her mission. The expectation for Circe, her purpose in the Butlers' world, as well as in the larger society, is to serve. But she decides her legacy will be to serve justice, not the Butlers: "They loved this place. Loved it. [. . .] Stole for it, lied for it, killed for it. But I'm the one left. Me and the dogs. And I will never clean it again. Never. Nothing. Not a speck of dust, not a grain of dirt, will I move. Everything in this world they lived for will crumble and rot" (247).

This impossibly old woman, "older than death" (219), who may in fact be dead, is larger than life. Milkman, who comes to know her in his search to learn about his family's past, knows only her first name, and it is possible that she does not have a last name (227). The lack of a surname is, of course, part of the legacy of slavery, but Circe is possibly older than this. She is, arguably, the continuing embodiment or the spiritual descendant of her mythological namesake, with the "strong, mellifluent voice of a twenty-year-old girl" (240), which signifies her timelessness.[66] Circe is likened to the witch in Hansel and Gretel, a woman whose house (her island, so to speak), is ostensibly a place of refuge with special treats as an inducement for those lost, curious, hungry or unwary. Those in search of protection or some other yearning will disregard any trepidation to go into this house, "[e]specially if the object of his craving is not gingerbread or chewy gumdrops, but gold" (219).

Although Circe is powerful, she has limitations. Milkman knows that Circe will not last, but the Weimeraners, her bewitched progeny, are reproducing. Hers is a revenge made less sweet by the realization that it is the dogs who will continue. Their power will diminish because of their transformation from human form, but they will survive, nonetheless. They will inherit what is left, and will take what they need to continue (257). This striking metaphor for the inexorable force and survivability of greed reminds us of the power of those who believe they are entitled to and will take what does not belong to them.

Voluntary Servitude

The issue of "voluntary" black slavery/servitude is pervasive in *Song of Solomon.* Voluntary slavery/servitude presumes a servile state of mind that manifests itself in the conduct of African Americans in the presence of or where white people are concerned. It is a deference disproportionate to the circumstances and people at hand, is accomplished without any apparent coercion, is most often perceived to be some form of Uncle Tomism and is demeaning and self-defeating. It is typical, or habitual, to regard this type of behavior simply as a manifestation of self-loathing or cowardice. But Morrison complicates each seeming instance of "voluntary" servitude by demonstrating how individual identity may be shaped and behavior influenced by the social context of the historical moment, and how "voluntary" slavery/servitude is often a crucial part of a strategy for survival for African Americans.

Corinthians is an unusual example of voluntary servitude in that she, even though from a wealthy family, self-conscripts into servitude. But her reasons for making this choice are similar to others in this text who may be identified as acquiescing to servitude. She does it to protect her interests, in her case, to save her sanity and maybe her life. Most of the indignities to which Corinthians willingly submits are not the menial aspects of the job, which is honest work. The social and historical context is significant. Corinthians' greatest indignity is having to pretend that she is something other than what she is because American society persists in viewing black women as domestics and as not fit for another kind of work; because her employer is both attracted to and conflicted by Corinthians' obvious refinement and education, which her employer must regard as marginal; and, because of the class pressures from her own society.

Corinthians has a complex utility and "serves" her employer, Michael-Mary Graham, in ways other than work. Corinthians is hired because her name appeals to Miss Graham's poetic sensibility; she is a trophy maid. Miss Graham is thrilled to have an educated, refined black servant with such good manners and literary tastes, but has no idea how educated Corinthians is, or who she really is. Corinthians conceals her true identity; she is "not a complete fool. She never let her mistress know she had ever been to college or Europe or could recognize one word of French that Miss Graham had not taught her (*entrez*, for example)" (190). She pretends that she is less educated than she is in order to assuage the ego of her white employer, and knowingly allows herself to be treated as a trophy or mascot for the benefit of her employer. Corinthians' genteel deference is gratifying to Miss Graham and makes her feel good about herself—liberal and magnanimous—and simultaneously reinforces her superiority to "have a maid who read and who seemed to be acquainted with some of the great masters of literature. So nice to give a maid a copy of *Walden* for Christmas rather than that dreary envelope, and to be able to say so to her friends. In the world Michael-Mary Graham inhabited, her mild liberalism, a residue of her Bohemian youth, and her posture of sensitive lady poet passed for anarchy" (190). Miss Graham tolerates Corinthians' lack of imagination and skill in cooking, and hires a Swedish cook and a white man to do the heavy work when she has large dinner parties, out of consideration for Corinthians. One might argue that this is an indication that times were beginning to change. But Corinthians' relationship with Miss Graham demonstrates the often fragile and fraudulent nature of aspiring liberalism.

Racial hierarchy is a requirement of Miss Graham's liberalism; a requirement unknown to herself. However subtle they may be, the indicators of social rank based on color and the need for hierarchy lurk beneath every action and motive. Miss Graham's behavior is a classic example of the "psychological exploitation" that Judith Rollins describes as one of the most insidious aspects of domestic service—the expectation, requirement even, of intimacy or friendship, or at least the appearance of it, between a white employer and black servant. Rollins writes that this type of exploitation "has two essential functions of affording employers the self-enhancing satisfactions that emanate from having the presence of an inferior and validating the employers' lifestyle, ideology, and social world, from their familial interrelations to the economically and racially stratified system in which they live." Corinthians provides that "window to exotica," Miss Graham craves, a form of "psychological exploitation [which] need not be overtly harsh," but is nonetheless "just as powerful when it is disguised in maternalism, in gift-giving, and in tolerance for irresponsibility."[67] When Corinthians self-conscripts into servitude, she finds that she must adapt in ways she could not have foreseen. She must shore up her employer's ego at the expense of her own honesty.

There is no evidence, however, that Corinthians is in any way traumatized by her playacting. In fact, in a calculated presentation or withholding of evidence of her education, as is strategically warranted, she protects her interests. Through careful management of her employer, she demonstrates an uncanny ability for "racial savvy"[68] and plays the game masterfully. She gets what she needs from the arrangement—money and independence. An acknowledgment of and resignation to the realities of the arrangement appear to be the extent to which she suffers. Corinthians suffers more from her association with servitude than from the servitude itself. Interestingly, Corinthians, for the first time, appears like an adult when she appeases the childish needs of Miss Graham. Miss Graham's need to feel superior is shown to be sad and pathetic, as is Corinthians' need to be distinguished from other maids.

Guitar Bains is the most outspoken character about voluntary slavery/servitude and finds this a convenient pejorative to apply to many of the people in his life. Macon Dead subscribes to "voluntary slavery," according to Guitar, because he "keep[s] his knees bent. Why does he love them so?" Guitar is appalled at Macon's extreme conciliatory behavior, especially considering that he had, as a child, seen his father shot dead by white people. He condemns Pilate as "worse. She saw it too and, first, goes back to get a cracker's bones for some kind of crazy self-punishment, and second, leaves the cracker's gold right where it was! Now, is that voluntary slavery or not?" (224). Pilate had left the gold in the cave where years ago Macon killed a white man. She had retrieved the man's bones to become lifelong curator of them, which sickens and infuriates Guitar.

In another event Pilate and Macon come to get Milkman and Guitar out of jail (after they have stolen from Pilate), and behave in an uncharacteristically self-abasing way. Guitar is incapable of feeling gratitude, or of understanding that their behavior is a ploy; it is merely performative, superficial theater. Increasingly reductive in his thinking, and as his gold fever and paranoia intensify, he sneers at this woman who has shown him only hospitality and friendliness, and never given any offense, because "[s]he slipped into those Jemima shoes cause they fit" (224). Milkman also feels shame at Pilate "as he watched and listened. [. . .] Not just her Aunt Jemima act, but the fact that she was both adept at it and willing to do it—for him" (209).

Macon's and Pilate's conduct are part of a successful strategy for disarming their jailors. Both Guitar and Milkman completely misapprehend Macon's and Pilate's motives because of their hypersensitivity to anything having to do with white people, and, for Guitar, because he has gold fever. They are unable to see this kind of deferential behavior as anything but degrading, and it *is* absolutely insulting for them to behave so. Yet, in the world in which they live, it is also clever manipulation for survival, a game, a charade, "racial savvy,"[69] the results of which benefit both Guitar and Milkman. Guitar and Milkman cannot see that Macon assumes an inferior position before the white policemen because, as Thomas March points out:

> While the necessity of this behavior clearly acknowledges the limits of African-American power as demarcated by white racism, Macon reveals in his behavior not that success is equated with whiteness, but that his success depends on the degree to which he can communicate a docility that allows him to maintain his position and his wealth, to divorce himself from the hint of threat, in either direction.[70]

Pilate is able to shape shift immediately when out of the presence of the jailors, and acts as though nothing has happened or is wrong. Indeed, there is nothing wrong with Pilate. The experience has not made her lose her stride or affected her core self. What is wrong is the society that requires such behavior. As Brenda Marshall so aptly affirms:

> The policeman to whom she misquotes the Bible and the nephew she subtly mocks in doing so are never the wiser as this seemingly old subservient black woman gives her bizarre explanation of why she carries around a bag of bones. We can almost hear the amused "these people" under the breath of the policeman, but we're chuckling under our breath with Pilate, because we know what she knows: that things aren't always what they seem with Pilate. [. . .] [I]t is her awareness of these metamorphoses, it is what she knows, that allows her to maintain her dignity in any guise.[71]

The idea of voluntary slavery/servitude extends even to Guitar's own mother, whom he judges harshly because she accepts a payoff of forty dollars instead of the life insurance to which she is entitled for the work-related death of her husband. Guitar

> remembered anew how his mother smiled when the white man handed her the four ten-dollar bills. More than gratitude was showing in her eyes. More than that. Not love, but a willingness to love. Her husband was sliced in half and boxed backward. He'd heard the mill men tell how the two halves, not even fitted together, were placed cut side down, skin side up, in the coffin. [. . .] Even so, his mother had smiled and shown that willingness to love the man who was responsible for dividing his father up throughout eternity. (224)

Guitar does not consider that his mother has limited alternatives for response. To Guitar, she is flawed and weak. He is incapable of considering that she is emotionally disabled by shock and grief; habituated to receiving less than she deserves, but with what grace and dignity she can muster; and, that she may be taking the high ground rather than abasing herself with tears, recriminations and belligerence that would yield nothing, perhaps not even the forty dollars. His easy assessment and hate-filled mindset will also not allow him to consider, with empathy and love, that she is conditioned to acquiesce out of fear—she is a product of the world in which she lives. She is not to be blamed, rather the society in which she lives that makes such behavior necessary. Like Pilate and Macon, Guitar's mother plays a role scripted for her hundreds of years ago, and she does not have the power to rewrite it.

Circe is, presumably, another case of voluntary servitude. Milkman misapprehends Circe's motives, which are unimpeachable, for staying on in the decaying ruins of the Butler mansion. Milkman—arrogant, judgmental and derisive in his attitude toward her—thought Circe stayed on in voluntary servitude because she "loved those white folks that much" (246). Circe defends herself, and explains:

> "You don't listen to people. Your ear is on your head, but it's not connected to your brain. I said she killed herself rather than do the work I'd been doing all my life!" Circe stood up, and the dogs too. "Do you hear me? She saw the work I did all her days and *died*, you hear me, *died* rather than live like me. Now, what do you suppose she thought I was? If the way I lived and the work I did was so hateful to her she killed herself to keep from having to do it, and you think I stayed on here because I loved her, then you have about as much sense as a fart!" (247)

Circe is determined to watch the Butler property disintegrate, wills herself to live (stay) long enough to see what the murdering Butlers loved and killed for go completely to ruin. This solitary mission, the sacrifice of her life, is volunteerism indeed, but in the service of honor and righteousness—a justice denied by law and society.

Black Servitude and Victimization

Some critics, such as Stanley Crouch, think that Morrison turns her considerable literary gifts to the portrayal of blacks as victims. He "concluded that Morrison was 'immensely talented. I just think she needs a new subject matter, the world she lives in, not this world of endless black victims.'"[72] Morrison herself has said that "we are all of us, in some measure, *victims* of *something*. Each one of us is in some way at some moment a victim and in no position to do a thing about it." But for Morrison, the critical question is that, considering the universal nature of victimization, "how does one remain whole—is it just impossible to do that?"[73] *Song of Solomon* offers possibilities to consider not only the certainty and reality of victimization, but how its subjects resist its effects in an effort to remain whole.

There are those characters, such as Jake, who are clearly victims, "and in no position to do a thing about it."[74] Jake is murdered, his story ends there. The consequences of his murder are far-reaching; most immediate is the impact on his young children, who are certainly victimized by the loss of their father. It is undeniable that Macon and Pilate Dead carry with them damage inflicted by the loss of their father. Neither, despite the burden of memory and the very real hardships they endure as orphaned youngsters, surrenders to victimization. They both become, in very different ways, successful in the lives they choose for themselves.

It comes down, I think, to one's definition of victim. A victim is, typically, someone who is harmed and made to suffer. Pilate and Macon qualify. However, when an individual who carries the pain of affliction transcends the circumstances of their suffering, it seems inappropriate to view them as victims, especially in the face of what is certainly a heroic effort to overcome. Victims do not triumph over their circumstances.

Macon is not a victim. In an interview, Morrison is told, "we don't admire Milkman's father." Morrison responds: "Why not? The people in these novels are complex. [. . .] It seems to me that one of the most fetching qualities of black people is the variety in which they come. It is a compelling thing for one because no single layer is 'it.' If I examine those layers, I don't come up with simple statements about fathers and husbands, such as some people want to see in books."[75] Macon is, in fact, the most prosperous black businessman in town, even if he does serve only his own interests. Although most of the characters in this text have been victimized, particularly because of their color, "victim" is not a fitting label with which to describe them. Prominent among them are those who are quite literally pressed into service, but who do not allow that experience to determine their identity. They are clearly individuals independent of the work they do, and the circumstances that force them to do it.

As a young teenager on her own, destitute, homeless, friendless, Pilate needed work and settled on a town with limited choices for employment for black women—laundry or prostitution:

> The next day Pilate was hired as a washerwoman at ten cents a day. She worked there, ate there, slept there, and saved her dimes. Her hands, well calloused from years of harvesting, were stripped of their toughness and became soft in the wash water. Before her hands could get the different but equally tough skin of a laundress, her knuckles split with the rubbing and wringing, and ran blood into the rinse tubs. She almost ruined an entire batch of sheets, but the other girls covered for her, giving the sheets a second rinse. (145)

The sisterhood of washerwomen gave the homeless young girl a place to sleep and covered for her on the job while her hands healed and became accustomed to the work because they understood, without having to know the details, that she was in great need. Keeping this difficult, backbreaking job as a washerwoman was the only thing standing between Pilate, and the other washerwomen, and the whorehouse. They are clearly victimized by their limited choices in life. However, they do not act like victims, but make the most of what's available to them under the circumstances.

Pilate is victimized in numerous ways: her mother dies giving birth to her; she suffers rejection by society because of her absence of a navel and rejection by her brother because she does not live according to his standards; and, she is illiterate. Pilate eventually rejects the life of a washerwoman for one that would give her autonomy. As an adult, Pilate is self-employed as a bootlegger, a profession that gives her independence and control, and places her in a position from which she can provide a community service, so to speak, for wealthy and poor alike. Any "adult, child, or beast" (24) was welcome at her wine house. Morrison herself says that Pilate is "a totally generous free woman. She's fearless. She's not afraid of anything. She has very few material things. [. . .] She doesn't run anybody's life. She's available for almost infinite love. If you need her—she'll deliver. And she has complete clarity about who she is"[76]—not a description of a victim. To see her as such undermines her efforts, resourcefulness and skill at survival. It is crucial to acknowledge the harm that Pilate and the other washerwomen may suffer. It is also necessary to acknowledge their strength and courage. This makes them victimized but not victims.

The wealthy Corinthians becomes a maid and rejects the life of an emotionally abused dependent for one that would give her autonomy. Circe does not wring her hands and slink away in defeat after the death of Jake, or after the deaths of her employers. Slavery and servitude have honed her clarity and power, and given her a mission to protect and ensure the final dissolution of the Butler home for the sake of justice. The servant Freddie is no victim; he makes the most of his limited talents and circumstances by making himself useful, even independent. As town crier, he receives the attention he craves to feel an important part of the community. Porter, the yardman, totters on the brink of succumbing to victimization. He is driven to drink and almost to madness by the plight of black people in America, and perhaps because of his own participation in the Seven Days. It is his steady work as a yardman that provides some stability and enables him to connect with Corinthians. Former railroad servant Railroad Tommy refuses to accept the constraints and debilitations of victimization. Yes, it can be argued that he is emotionally and spiritually disfigured by the failure of America to address the treatment of black people, but he fights back. He is co-owner of a barbershop, and he takes matters of justice and retribution into his own hands as one of the Seven Days.

I am in complete agreement with Valerie Smith, who writes:

> In each of her novels, Morrison boldly undermines the assumptions and hierarchies that historically have legitimated the oppression of people of color, women, and the poor in U.S. culture. Her prose simultaneously invokes the lyrical and historical, the supernatural and the ideological; she seeks to show the place of "enchantment" for people like the ones among whom she came of age, even as she explores the complex social circumstances within which they live out their lives.[77]

One may have unresolved issues, poor human relations skills, an unkempt home and appearance or a taste for vengeance and not be a victim. Many in *Song of Solomon* are wounded, some of them bone or soul deep. Yet, they acknowledge, on some level, the challenges they face, the odds against them and aggressively attempt to do something about it. Simply regarding these characters and their choices as products of victimization denies their full humanity as well as their complexity as subjects in the text itself. Although Morrison calls into question the definition of victim, she never sanitizes the lives of her characters, mitigates the pain and frustration they must surely feel or absolves the perpetrators of oppression or wrongdoing, racial or otherwise. The capacity these characters have not only for survival, but for, in some cases, transcendence, is a celebration of the human spirit. The injury they all suffer, and their efforts to transcend their suffering, make them splendidly human.

Eric Foner contends that for Morrison history "is both a burden *and* a form of self-knowledge."[78] I would like to suggest that for Morrison it is the denial of history that is a burden; it is the denial of history that disables self-knowledge, for individuals and for societies. Black servitude, its function and usages in American society as both ideal and expectation, is a preoccupation if not an obsession for many African American authors, understandably so. Toni Morrison is no exception.

In *Song of Solomon*, the significance of black servitude is underscored definitively through an experience Pilate Dead has as a young domestic. Pilate's male employer appears to be having a stroke or heart attack, and she holds him up from behind to keep him from "falling off a cliff" (41). The man's wife discovers them locked together in this way, and is at first disbelieving of Pilate's explanation. But, it becomes clear that Pilate has literally kept the man fastened to life. When she lets go, he falls down dead. In this scene, as metaphor, we can see that without the support and service of African Americans, the collapse of American society is inevitable. The inability of the sickened man's wife to see this simple truth, her willingness to jump to a negative and erroneous explanation without considering other possibilities, represents a society intent on misreading, or denying, the role that black people have played in shaping and sustaining America. As Betty Fussell argues, Morrison's "vision is strong, even heroic, and like James Joyce, she explodes institutionalized mythologies to invent her own. While she attacks racial and sexual stereotypes, she reserves her full anger for those who would deny they exist."[79]

History and black servitude enjoy a complex relationship in *Song of Solomon*. Morrison demonstrates the consequences of American history, but simultaneously elucidates the resiliency and determination of African Americans through the representation of black servitude. The effects of history are undeniable in the intricate relationship between affluent black employers and their black servants. It is impossible to imagine Railroad Tommy's involvement in the Seven Days without understanding his rage, which derives from historical truths about blacks in America, or without knowing something of the possible context of his former employment as a railroad servant. Although, even as the daughter of a wealthy man, Corinthians Dead is forced to accept domestic service as employment, she embraces servitude as the means to emotional and financial independence, and adulthood. She finds peace in performing her housekeeping tasks as a maid. Circe strategically positions herself as savior to orphaned children as a servant—in this way, it is a position of power. But, ultimately she repudiates her role as a servant when her last employer dies; her declaration of independence—a passionate cry that she refuses to ever clean someone else's dirt again. Pilate finds comfort and support from her fellow washerwomen, women who made a safe place for her during her confused destitution. Pilate's experience as a servant also taught her that there was, surely, something else that she could do other than domestic work.

One could argue that the ability to transcend victim status is an important component of the American Dream. Accordingly, many of the characters in *Song of Solomon* have, in some measurable way, made progress toward that end. But it is the burden of history, and the burden of a society resistant to change, that demands such an effort to begin with. Morrison calls into question the defining characteristics of the Dream. Is it a Dream that encourages unhealthy acquisitiveness, which desensitizes and corrupts? Does it create a craving for social hierarchy, which encourages abuse and oppression? Is it a system that is dependent, by design, on the historical designations of served and servant? In *Song of Solomon*, it is a Dream in need of review and revision.

Epilogue

We think and write about history because it has formed us, influences the choices we imagine available to us.

—Marge Piercy

Outside the whale is the unceasing storm, the continual quarrel, the dialectic of history. Outside the whale there is a genuine need for political fiction, for books that draw new and better maps of reality, and make new languages with which we can understand the world. Outside the whale we see that we are all irradiated by history, we are radioactive with history and politics; we see that it can be as false to create a politics-free fictional universe as to create one in which nobody needs to work or eat or hate or love or sleep.

—Salman Rushdie

Although we think the past is gone and the future is not yet here, if we look deeply, we see that reality is more than that. The past exists in the guise of the present, because the present is made from the past. In this teaching, if we establish ourselves firmly in the present and touch the present moment deeply, we also touch the past and have the power to repair it.

—Thich Nhat Hanh[1]

Black servitude in retrospective fiction has much to reveal about American history, culture and values. Robert Penn Warren, E. L. Doctorow, Charles Johnson and Toni Morrison confront political, social and economic situations of the past through the representation of black servitude in their tales that engage historical context. Mark Carnes writes in *Novel History: Historians and Novelists Confront America's Past (and Each Other)* that the "fossilized facts of the historical record are reanimated with imaginative meaning and aesthetic truth. Novel history, like alchemy, is an inaccessible science and elusive art, but to readers who seek understanding of themselves and the world, its riches are real."[2] Each of the authors in this book is such an alchemist, imbuing the past with imaginative meaning, which also reveals a distinctive world view. They do not *read* or *misread* history, they *imagine* history and the historical moment in particular ways for specific reasons.

Most significant, their ideas about race and race relations are embodied in the representation of African American servitude and the issues that surround it within the context of the historical moments in which the stories take place. These representations serve theoretical and philosophical as well as literary purposes. I have endeavored in this book to disclose "the ways in which the presence of Afro-Americans has shaped the choices, the language, the structure—the meaning" of these particular works, to help flush out "the ghost in the machine."[3]

Black servitude has enormous utility for these writers, and they strategically deploy African American servants and slaves and engage with the idea of black servitude in ways that encourage a rethinking of our conceptions of the historical past. *Band of Angels*, *Ragtime*, *Middle Passage* and *Song of Solomon* are vehicles through which social issues, particularly those that continue to remain problematic and unresolved, and that continue to resonate in American society, are vetted and expressed. In this interpretive process, they make or suggest connections between the past and the present. They offer possibilities for how we, as a nation, imagine ourselves and how we mythologize our society.

It is conceivable that for Robert Penn Warren black servitude in *Band of Angels* provides a context from which to draw a connection between the Civil War period, the period in which the story takes place, and the one in which *Band of Angels* was written, the early years of the civil rights movement. Apparent in the text is the emphasis on and affirmation of the perception of black inferiority—moral, cultural and aesthetic. Black people are presented as co-conspirators in their own oppression as a direct result of an inherent deficiency. Along with the suggestion of the "innocence" in the cultural and social principles and practices of the southern planter aristocracy, Warren elucidates the white racialist attitudes which made possible the enslavement and continued persecution of black people. These were clearly issues that Warren struggled with in his own journey toward enlightenment.

E. L. Doctorow uses the personal tribulations of a black washerwoman to create an explosive set of circumstances for an upper-middle-class white suburban family, the town in which they live, New York City and to some extent the nation in the early twentieth century in *Ragtime*. Through the denial or resolution of the circumstances surrounding this servant, Doctorow contends with issues of great personal concern for him: the nature of justice, equality and compassion.

In *Middle Passage* Charles Johnson utilizes the idea of black servitude, primarily through a representation of issues surrounding slavery and its effects, to challenge the idea of permanent disfigurement for African Americans because of oppression and injustice. While ratifying the deleterious effects of enslavement, the narrator of his tale advocates the idea of transcendence in spite of and perhaps because of any and all circumstances. Personal responsibility and the acknowledgement of choice determine fate. This point of view makes manifest Johnson's concerns about the state of African American society and cultural production today.

Finally, of great interest to Toni Morrison is the disparity between the professed values of American society and the reality, especially in matters of race. Morrison, subtly but deliberately, constructs a world in which black people are both serving and served. Through flashbacks and an involuted timeline in *Song of Solomon* we must consider how everything and nothing has changed where race in America is concerned. Although circumstances are such that by the mid-twentieth century a black man may own a barbershop or become a wealthy property owner, the effects of the violence and abuse of slavery remain. Black servitude is the locus for evincing the status and prospects of blacks in America, amid a climate of continuing oppression and violence toward African Americans and retaliatory violence by blacks. The tenacity of racism in America is unremitting subtext in *Song of Solomon.*

One of the things that attracted me to these very different retrospective texts, written by authors who have very different political and cultural sensibilities, is that they actually share some things in common. Issues of historical and personal significance are played out through the representation of black servitude. They all employ the past to elucidate the present and sometimes offer a prognosis based on the current state of affairs.

There are numerous connections, similar issues and concerns, all manifested in very different ways. Black servitude is a way in which to think about victimization. How do we define "victim"? Who is one? What makes one? Is it all a matter of perspective? One of the most compelling concerns is black rage. What are the causes of it? Is it justified? What would "cure" it? Does it matter? Racial amalgamation in American society is another. Each text considers, in some way, resistance to heterogeneity, as well as the inevitability of it. The well-intentioned white person who is in a position of power over African American slaves or servants is an interesting operative in each text—the individual who is able or attempts to act outside the influences of their society. The potential consequences for a society driven by material consumption resonates through the representation of black servitude. Survival strategies employed by black servants are a powerful commentary for what is required for blacks to survive in America. When black servants step out of their designated supporting roles, whatever that situation may be, things begin to quickly fall apart. The destabilization of hierarchy is often the result, and the effort to achieve some sense of normalcy thereafter says much about the challenges America faces around the race issue. Black servitude is the axis upon which these issues, and many more, turn. It raises crucial questions about social triage and the interference of race and hierarchy in human relations.

The labels are easy, for text or author: militant, liberal, racist, conservative. Must we choose? Labels shut down the possibility of engaging with the complexity of the texts themselves and reduce the author to a mere reporter for a particular point of view. They tell us little and are more often than not misleading. Toni Morrison has said that

> spaces [. . .] can conceivably be filled in with other significances. [. . .] The point is that into these spaces should fall the ruminations of the reader and his or her invented or recollected or misunderstood knowingness. The reader as narrator asks the questions the community asks, and both reader and "voice" stand among the crowd, within it, with privileged intimacy and contact, but without any more privileged information than the crowd has.[4]

It is the objective of this investigation to look beneath and beyond the label. Peel it away, and myriad spaces of exquisitely layered beauty and meaning appear.

As readers we must be alchemists and trust that this "inaccessible science and art" will render up "its riches [which] are real."[5] We may not learn the absolute "truth" of the past in the investigation of history or retrospective fiction, and it may be unknowable. But the representation of black servitude in retrospective fiction moves us along in this effort. Through engagement with the idea of black servitude, we may enlarge our understanding of the works, the authors and the history of the nation in which we live.

Notes

Preface

1. *The Holy Bible.* King James Version. 1 Corinthians 3:9 (Cleveland, OH: The World Publishing Company).
2. "Let Me Walk with Thee," W. G. Gladden, arr. by H. B. Britt, *Baptist Standard Hymnal with Responsive Readings*, ed. A. M. Townsend (Nashville: Sunday School Publishing Board, National Baptist Convention, 1924) 393.
3. William A. Henry III, *In Defense of Elitism* (New York: Doubleday, 1994) 15.
4. Harold Bloom, ed. and intro., *Bloom's BioCritiques: Toni Morrison* (Philadelphia: Chelsea House, 2002) ix.
5. Gerda Lerner, *Black Women in White America: A Documentary History* (1972; New York: Vintage-Random House, 1992) 226.
6. William Faulkner, "That Evening Sun," *The Norton Anthology, Shorter Sixth Edition*, ed. Nina Baym, et al. (New York: Norton, 2003) 2166.

Chapter 1

1. Georg Wilhelm Friedrich Hegel, *Philosophy of History* (1832), qtd. in George Bernard Shaw, "The Revolutionist's Handbook," *Man and Superman* (1903). Francis Parkman, introd., *Pioneers of France in the New World*, 11th ed. (1865; Boston: Little, Brown, 1874). Charles Chaplin, *My Autobiography* (1964; New York: Harmondsworth, 1966).
2. Rpt. in Howard Zinn, *A People's History of the United States, 1492-Present*, 20th Anniversary ed. (1980; New York: HarperCollins, 1999) 1. See Bartolomé de las Casas, *History of the Indies* (New York: Harper & Row, 1971).
3. Henry Wiencek, *An Imperfect God: George Washington, His Slaves, and the Creation of America* (New York: Farrar, Straus and Giroux, 2003) 41. Some sources cite 1501, or other dates, for the introduction of the idea of importing Africans as slaves.
4. Bernard Grun, ed., *The Timetables of History: A Horizontal Linkage of People and Events*, 3rd rev. ed. (New York: Touchstone-Simon & Schuster, 1991) 227.
5. Cotton Mather, "On the Conversion of the Negroes," *The Negro Christianized*, rpt. in *The Minority Presence in American Literature: 1600–1900*, ed. Philip Butcher, vol. 1 (1706; Washington, D.C.: Howard UP, 1977) 71.
6. Harriet Martineau, *Society in America* (1837; New Brunswick: Transaction, 1981) 220.
7. Frederick Douglass, *Narrative of the Life of Frederick Douglass, An American Slave, Written by Himself* (1845; New York: Signet, 1968) Appendix 121.

8. Thomas Jefferson, *Notes on the State of Virginia, 1784–85*, rpt. in *The Portable Thomas Jefferson*, ed. Merrill D. Peterson (New York: Penguin, 1975) 454–455.
9. Alexis de Tocqueville, *Democracy in America*, ed. J. P. Mayer, trans. George Lawrence (1835; New York: Perennial, 1988).
10. Wiencek 5.
11. Thomas L. Connelly, "Robert Penn Warren as Historian," *A Southern Renascence Man: Views of Robert Penn Warren*, ed. Walter B. Edgar (Baton Rouge: Louisiana State UP, 1984) 1.
12. Robert Penn Warren, "The Uses of History in Fiction," *Southern Literature Journal* 1.2 (1969): 70. Transcription of panel discussion with Ralph Ellison, William Styron and Robert Penn Warren, moderator C. Vann Woodward, thirty-fourth annual meeting, Southern Historical Association, Jung Hotel, New Orleans, Louisiana, Nov. 6, 1968.
13. Connelly 15.
14. Catherine Clinton, *Tara Revisited: Women, War & the Plantation Legend* (New York: Abbeville, 1995) 120.
15. E. L. Doctorow, "'Fiction is a System of Knowledge': An Interview with E. L. Doctorow," with Christopher D. Morris, *Michigan Quarterly Review* 30.3 (Summer 1991): 446.
16. E. L. Doctorow, "A Spirit of Transgression," interview with Larry McCaffery, *E. L. Doctorow: Essays & Conversations*, ed. Richard Trenner (Princeton, NJ: Ontario Review Press, 1983) 43.
17. See Derek Wright "*Ragtime* Revisited: History and Fiction in Doctorow's Novel," *International Fiction Review* 20.1 (1993): 14. Wright states in support of Doctorow's claim that historians do imagine and fabricate a specific view of the past, and that "history, insofar as it is always narrowly partial and selective, is one of the least trustworthy and potentially one of the most fictional of narrative forms. As the opening pages of *Ragtime* demonstrate, whole racial groups have been written out of American history simply by not being mentioned, and the task of the novelist, as conceived by Doctorow, is to write them back in."
18. Barbara Foley, "From *U.S.A.* to *Ragtime:* Notes on the Forms of Historical Consciousness in Modern Fiction," *American Literature: A Journal of Literature, History, Criticism and Bibliography* 50 (1978): 96.
19. E. L. Doctorow, "An Interview with E. L. Doctorow," with Michael Wutz, *Weber Studies: An Interdisciplinary Humanities Journal* 11.1 (Winter 1994): 15.
20. Charles Johnson, "An Interview with Charles Johnson," with Jonathan Little, *Contemporary Literature* 34.2 (Summer 1993): 166.
21. Molly Abel Travis, "*Beloved* and *Middle Passage:* Race, Narrative, and the Critic's Essentialism," *Reading Cultures: The Construction of Readers in the Twentieth Century* (Carbondale: Southern Illinois UP, 1998) 80.
22. Wolfgang Binder, "Uses of Memory: the Middle Passage in African American Literature," *Slavery in the Americas*, ed. Wolfgang Binder (Wurzburg: Konigshausen & Neumann, 1993) 555, 556.
23. Susan Willis, *Specifying: Black Women Writing the American Experience* (Madison: U of Wisconsin P, 1987) 3.
24. Toni Morrison, "'The Language Must Not Sweat': A Conversation with Toni Morrison," 1981, interview with Thomas LeClair, *Conversations with Toni Morrison*, ed. and introd. Danille Taylor-Guthrie (Jackson: UP of Mississippi, 1994) 122, rpt. from *New Republic* 18 (March 21, 1981): 25–30.
25. Marilyn Sanders Mobley, "Call and Response: Voice, Community, and Dialogic Structures in Toni Morrison's *Song of Solomon*," *New Essays on Song of Solomon*,

The American Novel Series, ed. and introd. Valerie Smith (New York: Cambridge UP, 1995) 42–43.

26. I find this term extremely useful in conceptualizing the representation of these figures in that it effectively describes the "mechanical" aspects of the African American literary slave and servant. In this capacity, the servant may be regarded as a device that manages vital cultural information. Servants are powerfully influential in this way in that they measure, shape, process and then transmit information. They are not simply passive implements that are utilized, they are devices that control.
27. Toni Morrison, *Playing in the Dark: Whiteness and the Literary Imagination* (New York: Vintage-Random House, 1993) 17.
28. Doctorow, "False Documents" 25.
29. Mark C. Carnes, *Novel History: Historians and Novelists Confront America's Past (and Each Other)* (New York: Simon & Schuster, 2001) 21.
30. C. Vann Woodward, panel moderator, "The Uses of History in Fiction," *Southern Literature Journal* 1.2 (1969): 58. See Woodward's explanation for the historical antecedents shared by the two disciplines, 58–60.
31. Warren I. Susman, *Culture as History: The Transformation of American Society in the Twentieth Century* (New York: Pantheon, 1984) 288, 21. See Susman's discussion on the historical novel in his chapter "History as Myth and Ideology" for the uses of history in the works of Ezra Pound, William Carlos Williams and Hart Crane, 21–23.
32. James R. Thompson, "'Categories of Human Form': Some Notes on E. L. Doctorow and Historical Consciousness," *Caliban* 28 (1991): 18.
33. Peter Freese, "Doctorow's 'Criminals of Perception', or, What Has Happened to the Historical Novel," ed. Gunter H. Lenz, *Reconstructing American Literary and Historical Studies* (Frankfurt: Campus, 1990): 346–347.
34. Doctorow, "False Documents" 26.
35. Doctorow, "The Writer as Independent Witness," interview with Paul Levine, Morris *Conversations* 50, my emphasis.
36. Joseph W. Turner, "The Kinds of Historical Fiction: An Essay in Definition and Methodology," *Genre* 12 (1979): 333. See Turner also for a discussion on problems of definition of the historical novel, voice and uses of the past, authenticity, reliable narrator and authority, and his critique of Avrom Fleisher's theoretical discussion of the historical novel in *The English Historical Novel: Walter Scott to Virginia Woolf* (Baltimore: The Johns Hopkins Press, 1971).
37. Doctorow, "False Documents" 24.
38. Susman xii. Ragtime music and historical narrative employ similar principles of structure.
39. Doctorow, "Fiction is a System" 440–441.
40. Turner 339. James qtd. from "Anthony Trollope," *Partial Portraits* (New York: Macmillan, 1888), rpt. in *The Art of Fiction and Other Essays*, ed. Morris Roberts (New York: Oxford UP, 1948) 59–60. See also Georg Lukács, *The Historical Novel*, trans. Hannah and Stanley Mitchell (1937; London: Merlin Press, 1962) 241–242.
41. Woodward 58.
42. Turner 345.
43. In a letter to John Adams in 1813, Jefferson decries the English social system in which "an artificial aristocracy founded on wealth and birth" determines an individual's place in and value to society. Similarly, he fulminates against such an arbitrary social equalizer as gunpowder which "armed the weak as well as the

strong." Jefferson repudiates any system that defers to brute strength, superior weaponry or accident of birth, because rank in such a system is based solely on circumstances outside the control of the individual. He proudly takes credit for his part in the development of the laws that "divid[e] the lands of intestates equally among all [the] children, or other representatives [. . .] [which] laid the axe to the foot of pseudo-aristocracy," which were written immediately after the Declaration of Independence. See Jefferson letter to John Adams, October 28, 1813, Monticello, in Peterson 534.

44. Jefferson, *Notes* 188, 193. See also letter to Benjamin Banneker, August 30, 1791, Philadelphia, rpt. in *The Portable Thomas Jefferson*, ed. Merrill D. Peterson (New York: Penguin, 1975) 454–455.
45. Tocqueville 576.
46. Paul Fussell, *Class: A Guide Through the American Status System* (New York: Touchstone, 1992) 17.
47. John Marshall Harlan, "Dissenting Opinion," *Plessy v. Ferguson*, 1896.
48. President George H. W. Bush qtd. in Benjamin DeMott, *The Imperial Middle: Why Americans Can't Think Straight About Class* (New Haven: Yale UP, 1990) 10, from an article by George Will in *The Washington Post* Nov. 3, 1988: A27. DeMott writes that "Will called it 'a national travesty that a presidential candidate denies class realities.'"
49. William A. Henry III, *In Defense of Elitism* (New York: Doubleday, 1994) 31.
50. P. Fussell 15.
51. According to plate tectonics theory the layers of the earth's crust move at infinitesimally slow rates, sometimes less than centimeters per year, which ultimately creates new plates, destroys old ones and totally reconfigures the surface of the planet as a result—all completely indiscernible to human perception. This movement eventually results in the very gradual formation of surface structures such as mountains and reconfigures bodies of water, but also causes catastrophic geological events such as earthquakes and volcanic activity. I use the term *relational tectonics* to elucidate the inconspicuous, often imperceptible shifting of behaviors, allegiances, etc., of servants and others under the influence of variable social pressures because of the striking similarities of this process with the subterranean shifting of tectonic plates in continental drift. The term *relational tectonics* is a useful and illustrative way to explain and visualize the dynamics of servants with their social superiors from which both gradual and catastrophic social events arise, often with far-reaching social and historical consequences.
52. DeMott 27.
53. Annette Kuhn, *The Power of the Image: Essays on Representation and Sexuality* (London; Boston: Routledge & Kegan Paul, 1985) 54.
54. C. W. Harper, "Black Aristocrats: Domestic Servants on the Antebellum Plantation," *Phylon* 46 (June 1985): 126.
55. Jefferson, *Notes* 190.
56. Barbara Christian, "Black Women in Afro-American Literature," *Black Feminist Criticism: Perspectives on Black Women Writers* (New York: Pergamon Press, 1985) 3, 2.
57. S. F. Bennett and J. P. Webster, "Sweet By and By," *Progressive Baptist Hymnal*, Bicentennial Edition, ed. D. E. King (1940; Washington, D.C.: Broadman Press, 1976) #344.
58. Douglass provides examples of how slaves were punished for telling the truth about their circumstances. In one instance, a slave is questioned by a stranger on the road about his treatment. He responds politely but truthfully about not being

treated well, having to work too hard and not being fed properly, not knowing that he was speaking to his own master who he has never seen on the large plantation where he lives. He is subsequently sold away from family and friends for his transgression. The lesson, then, according to Douglass is "the maxim, that a still tongue makes a wise head. They suppress the truth rather than take the consequences of telling it" (35–36), for the sake of survival.

59. Harper 132, 131.
60. The practice of feigned deference did not end with slavery. See Annie S. Barnes, "White Mistresses and African-American Domestic Workers: Ideals for Change," *Anthropological Quarterly* 66 (Jan. 1993): 24–25, for a discussion of how a female servant today "stays in her place" in order to get along with her employer and to protect her employment.
61. Cornel West, *Race Matters* (Boston: Beacon Press, 1993) 13.
62. David J. Cherrington, *The Work Ethic: Working Values and Values that Work* (New York: Amacom, 1980) 39.
63. Donald L. Kanter and Philip H. Mirvis, *The Cynical Americans: Living and Working in an Age of Discontent and Disillusion* (San Francisco: Jossey-Bass, 1989) 1.
64. Gillian Brown, *Domestic Individualism: Imagining Self in Nineteenth-Century America* (Berkeley: U of California P, 1990) 63.
65. Ernest Hardy, "Whoopi's Hollywood Shuffle: *Bogus* lives down to its name," *Los Angeles Weekly* Sept. 6–12, 1996: 33–34.
66. Henceforth, for this discussion I use *servant* as a general term to denote all categories of those who serve, except when referring specifically and only to slaves.
67. Sander L. Gilman, *Difference and Pathology: Stereotypes of Sexuality, Race, and Madness* (Ithaca: Cornell UP, 1985) 21, 15.
68. Catherine Clinton writes that "Black artists and critics rightfully deplore [. . .] the lack of diversity in depiction of the African American experience. Indeed, media commentators have noted that in the 1990s, more black women have been relegated to playing maids in films and television programs than ever before." *Tara* 22.
69. George Watson, "The Silence of the Servants," *The Sewanee Review* 103 (Summer 1995): 480. Watson uses as an example the representation of servants in *The Remains of the Day* by Kazuo Ishiguro, both novel and film adaptation, which he says are misguided and outrageous; perhaps the result of inexperience and ignorance.
70. Bonnie Thornton Dill, "'Making Your Job Good Yourself': Domestic Service and the Construction of Personal Dignity," *Women and the Politics of Empowerment*, eds. Ann Bookman and Sandra Morgen (Philadelphia: Temple UP, 1988) 36–37. In her study Dill describes the defensive disclaimers used by domestics to hide their shame about their occupations.
71. Frances Trollope, *Domestic Manners of the Americans* (1832; Oxford: Oxford UP, 1984) 44, 46. Trollope resided in the United States from 1827 to 1830.
72. Late-nineteenth-century observer Lucy Maynard Salmon reported the same difficulties in acquiring a servant. Even after securing help "it was difficult to keep white servants for any length of time in a country where land was cheap and the servant soon in turn became a master. It was undoubtedly this difficulty that led to the substitution for white servants of Indians and negro [sic] slaves." Lucy Maynard Salmon, *Domestic Service* (1897; New York: Arno, 1972) 49. See Salmon's note on the writing of Elkanah Watson, who discusses the notion of upward mobility, which apparently impairs the usefulness of American servants, but also "adds to his self-respect as a man." *Men and Times of the Revolution*

169–170. Of course, such a notion was not pertinent to black and Indian slaves, who had no hope of becoming master.

73. David R. Roediger, *The Wages of Whiteness: Race and the Making of the American Working Class* (New York: Verso, 1996) 47, 49. See especially Roediger's chapter 3, "'Neither a Servant Nor a Master Am I': Keywords in the Languages of White Labor Republicanism," for a discussion on the development of working-class terms that distinguished the free from the unfree, and subsequently white from black, and that provided dignity and a sense of upward mobility for white workers.
74. See T. H. Breen, "The 'Giddy Multitude': Race and Class in Early Virginia," from "A Changing Labor Force and Race Relations in Virginia, 1660–1710," rpt. in *From Different Shores: Perspectives on Race and Ethnicity in America* 2nd ed., ed. Ronald Takaki (New York: Oxford UP, 1994) 107–117; from *Journal of Social History* 7 (Fall 1973): 3–18.
75. Some of the significant changes in servitude are the demographics; the decrease in the number of live-in servants; changes in the nature of the work because of technology; to some extent, the social and working relationship between employer and employee; fringe benefits, i.e., health insurance, retirement, and paid sick leave and vacation time in some instances.
76. Judith Rollins, *Between Women: Domestics and Their Employers* (Philadelphia: Temple UP, 1985) 58–59.
77. Salmon 140, 163.
78. Mary Romero, *Maid in the U.S.A.* (New York: Routledge, 1992) 7, 12.
79. Barnes 25, 27.
80. Frazer Ward, "Foreign and Familiar Bodies," from *Dirt and Domesticity: Constructions of the Feminine*, exhibition at the Whitney Museum of American Art at Equitable Center, June 12-August 14, 1992, ed. Jesús Fuenmayor, Kate Haug, Frazer Ward (New York: Whitney Museum of American Art, 1992) 8. Ward discusses anthropologist Mary Douglas's idea that concepts of dirt and dirtiness are subjective social constructs and not absolute, and "that these ideas symbolize social relations." Mary Douglas, *Purity and Danger: An Analysis of the Concepts of Pollution and Taboo* (1966; London: Ark Paperbacks, 1984) 35.
81. Morrison, *Playing in the Dark* 47, 63, 5, 47.
82. Henry Louis Gates, Jr., ed., *"Race," Writing, and Difference* (Chicago: U of Chicago P, 1985) 4.
83. The preface also states that it is "the Executive Board of the American Anthropological Association, acting on a draft prepared by a committee of representative American anthropologists," and therefore does not reflect the views of all. See AAA "Statement on 'Race,'" May 17, 1988, at www.aaanet.org/stmts/racepp.htm.
84. Anthony Appiah, "The Uncompleted Argument: DuBois and the Illusion of Race," in Gates, *"Race"* 21.
85. For opposing positions on affirmative action and reparations see Randall Robinson, *The Debt: What America Owes to Blacks* (New York: Plume, 2001), and Stephen L. Carter, *Reflections of an Affirmative Action Baby* (New York: Basic-Harper Collins, 1991). For recent scholarship on race culture, race hierarchy and biological determinism see: Dinesh D'Souza, *The End of Racism: Principles for a Multiracial Society* (New York: Free Press, 1995); Philippe J. Rushton, *Race, Evolution, and Behavior: A Life History Perspective* (New Brunswick, NJ: Transactions Publishers, 1994); Richard J. Herrnstein and Charles Murray, *The Bell Curve: Intelligence and Class Structure in American Life* (New York: Free Press, 1994); Sey-

mour W. Itzkoff, *The Decline of Intelligence in America: A Strategy for National Renewal* (Westport, CT: Praeger, 1994).

86. See Werner Sollors' chapter 1, particularly the discussion on "The Limits of Ethnicity," *Beyond Ethnicity: Consent and Descent in American Culture* (New York: Oxford UP, 1986) 39.
87. Roger Sanjek, "The Enduring Inequalities of Race," *Race*, eds. Steven Gregory and Roger Sanjek (New Brunswick, NJ: Rutgers, UP, 1996) 8–9, 1.
88. DeMott 12.
89. Christopher Miller, "Theories of Africans: The Question of Literary Anthropology," in Gates, *"Race"* 288.
90. Barbara Johnson, "Threshold of Difference: Structures of Address in Zora Neale Hurston," in Gates, *"Race"* 323.
91. Bruce Robbins, *The Servant's Hand: English Fiction from Below* (Durham, NC: Duke UP, 1993) 9.
92. Robbins, *Servant's Hand* 15.
93. Bruce Robbins, "The Butler Did It: On Agency and the Novel," *Representations* 6 (Spring 1994): 90.
94. Morrison, *Playing in the Dark* xii.

Chapter 2

1. *The Holy Bible*, King James Version. Samuel Eliot Morison, *The Oxford History of the American People: Volume Three, 1869 Through the Death of John F. Kennedy, 1963* (1965; New York: Meridian-Penguin, 1994).
2. Dana D. Nelson, *The Word in Black and White: Reading "Race" in American Literature, 1638–1867* (New York: Oxford UP, 1993) xii. Nelson borrows the term "violence of representation" from Nancy Armstrong and Leonard Tennenhouse, *The Violence of Representation: Literature and the History of Violence* (New York: Routledge, 1989).
3. Joseph Blotner, *Robert Penn Warren: A Biography* (New York: Random House, 1997) 300. According to Blotner, critical reception of the novel at its first release was mixed but generally favorable (298). Critics have been eager to agree with this assessment, with notable exceptions such as John R. Strugnell, who writes that the novel "is very like the costume novels which Penn Warren says he hates" ("Robert Penn Warren and the Use of the Past," *Review of English Literature* 4.4 [1963]: 100).
4. Lucy Ferris, "Sleeping with the Boss: Female Subjectivity in Robert Penn Warren's Fiction," *Mississippi Quarterly* 48 (Winter 1994–95): 147.
5. Warren, "The Uses of History in Fiction" 60–61.
6. Clinton, *Tara* 198.
7. Warren was born April 24, 1905 in Guthrie, Kentucky.
8. Blotner 300.
9. Clinton, *Tara* 182.
10. Lillian Smith, *Killers of the Dream* (1961; New York: Norton, 1978) 90.
11. Grace Elizabeth Hale, *Making Whiteness: The Culture of Segregation in the South, 1890–1940* (New York: Vintage, 1999) 9, 8, 195, 196.
12. Morison, 109. See Morison for a discussion on the rise of racism during this period including Klan activity against Catholics and Jews, and how Henry Ford fomented racial hatred against Jews in particular. Some of the worse race riots in American history occurred in East St. Louis in 1947, with forty-seven people dead, hundreds wounded; in 1919 in Washington D.C., six people were killed

when police and thousands of troops attempted to restore order; and, also in 1919, in Chicago with thirty-six killed. Other "major racial disorders" occurred in "New York and Omaha, and at least seven in the South" (218–219). Also see 109, 338–339. Morison also points out that Roosevelt, however, "did not attempt the colossal task of forcing it [integration] on Southern states and committees, or of putting blacks on their electoral rolls" (339); see also 419. Many of Truman's policies were part of a political strategy. Hale writes that "[u]nder the assumption that congress would pass none of his proposals, Truman called for abolishing the poll tax, making lynching a federal crime, and limiting discrimination in employment. This strategy [. . .] gained Truman the grateful swing votes of northern blacks without losing the traditional white southern Democratic vote" (287).

13. Hale 289.
14. See Lerner, "The Ordeal of the Children" 414–424.
15. For a discussion about the "two white societies in the South" (78), see James A. Perkins, "Racism and the Personal Past in Robert Penn Warren," *Mississippi Quarterly* 48 (Winter 1994–95): 73–82.
16. See *The American Dream: The 50s*, Time-Life Books, ed. and for. Hugh Downs (Alexandria, VA: Time-Life, 1998) 108, for a photographic overview of the 1950s.
17. The Southern Agrarians were a group of twelve intellectual southern men (known in their earliest association as The Fugitives) in Nashville in the 1920s, many of whom were affiliated with Vanderbilt University. This group of poets, critics and social commentators published in *The Fugitive*, their literary magazine, and in other periodicals as well.
18. Louis D. Rubin, Jr., ed. and introd., *I'll Take My Stand: The South and the Agrarian Tradition, By Twelve Southerners* (1930; Baton Rouge: Louisiana UP, 1977) xiii. Concerned that they would be largely misunderstood by modern academics and intellectuals, for good reason, Rubin argues that the Agrarians were humanists, "thoughtful men" united by "deeply felt historical loyalties and sectional self-defense" (xiv), whose main interest was "the erosion of the quality of individual life by the forces of industrialization and the uncritical worship of material progress as an end in itself" (xv), and who were working in the "pastorale" tradition which celebrated "the humane virtues of a simpler, more elemental, nonacquisitive existence" (xv).
19. Robert Penn Warren, *Selected Letters of Robert Penn Warren, Volume One: The Apprentice Years, 1924–1934*, ed. and introd. William Bedford Clark (Baton Rouge: Louisiana State UP, 2000) 179. Blotner calls Warren's part of the project "the most difficult task: locating the position of the Negro in this [the Agrarian] economic and social order" (106).
20. Warren, *Selected Letters* 185.
21. Robert Penn Warren, "The Briar Patch" (250), in Rubin, *I'll Take My Stand.* See Booker T. Washington, "The Atlanta Exposition Address," *Up From Slavery* (1901; New York: Penguin, 1986). A significant part of Washington's strategy to diffuse white hostility (especially violence and lynching) was to convince white people that blacks were not a threat to them, and that black people were willing to "learn to dignify and glorify common labour and put brains and skill into the common occupations of life" (220). Most important, he assuaged their fears of integration and miscegenation with the assurance that "[i]n all things that are purely social we can be as separate as the fingers, yet one as the hand in all things essential to mutual progress" (221–222). See response and counterargument of W. E. B. DuBois, *The Souls of Black Folk* (1903; New York: Signet NAL, 1982),

especially "Of Our Spiritual Strivings," in which Du Bois discusses the resulting burden and psychological damage black people suffer from being considered a "problem." See also, "The Talented Tenth." See David Levering Lewis, *W. E. B. Du Bois: Biography of a Race, 1868–1919* (New York: Macrae-Henry Holt, 1993); and, Thurgood Marshall's "The Brown Decision," in *Let Nobody Turn Us Around: Voices of Resistance, Reform, and Renewal, An African American Anthology*, eds. Manning Marable and Leith Mullings (Lanham, MD: Rowman & Littlefield, 2000) 357–364.

22. Hale 145.
23. Warren, "Briar Patch" 251, 259, 251, 257, 252, 253, 264. "Briar Patch" is not the only indication of Warren's earlier racial attitudes. See poetry, such as "Pondy Woods," and also Henry Louis Gates, Jr.'s commentary, *The Signifying Monkey: A Theory of African American Literary Criticism* (New York: Oxford, 1988) 122.
24. Robert Penn Warren, "Warren on the Art of Fiction," interview with Ralph Ellison and Eugene Walter, *Talking with Robert Penn Warren*, eds. Floyd C. Watkins, John T. Hiers and Mary Louise Weaks (Athens: U of Georgia P, 1990) 33; from original uncut manuscript, held in Ellison's apartment, 1956, American Academy of Rome.
25. Robert Penn Warren, "Of Bookish Men and the Fugitives," interview with Thomas L. Connelly, Feb. 10, 1982, in Watkins, *Talking* 384. See also Blotner, who explains that Donald Davidson thought "Briar Patch" was too progressive and wanted to reject it (112). Warren could not foresee how the piece "would haunt him, or how he would be judged a racist by people ignorant of his later repudiation of the 'separate but equal' doctrine" (113). Although he later supported Dr. Martin Luther King and spoke out against the brutality with which students were treated when trying to sit-in at an all-white lunch counter, Warren was continuously called upon to defend his stance in "Briar Patch."
26. Warren, *Selected Letters* 186–187.
27. Robert Penn Warren, *The Legacy of the Civil War: Meditations on the Centennial* (1961; Cambridge: Harvard UP, 1983).
28. Blotner 301. Ralph Ellison and Warren became close personal friends and companions. The Ellisons often stayed as weekend guests with the Warrens and attended many of their parties. Ellison wrote: "We [he and his wife] were introduced to an array of people—writers, artists, curators, publishers, academics—whom otherwise we might not have encountered, [and] as far as we were aware no other writers gave parties that encompassed such a diversity of backgrounds and talent" (qtd. in Blotner 302–303). It is clear that as his opinions altered, Warren increasingly made an effort to know and associate with people of different backgrounds and races.
29. Robert Penn Warren, "Robert Penn Warren: An Interview" with Marshall Walker, Sept. 11, 1969, in Watkins, *Talking* 158, 159.
30. Clark, *Selected Letters* 2.
31. Qtd. in Blotner 344. Warren even stated in an interview: "By the way, my sympathies are with Black Power—as I would interpret it. The psychological need I'm deeply sympathetic with, and I think Black Power, in terms of its long-range meaning, is essential." Walker, "Interview" 165.
32. Apparently Warren was not the only participant in the Southern Agrarians who made adjustments in his thinking about the race question during the period from 1930 to the early sixties. In fact, in his introduction to the 1962 edition of *I'll Take My Stand*, Louis Rubin said little about the position on segregation in the book in spite of its prominence in the ideologies of the group and in the text. His

explanation is that "[s]o much had happened in the three decades since *I'll Take My Stand* first appeared that many of the racial assumptions in it no longer represented the views of Tate, Ransom, Warren, and certain other contributors to the symposium" (xvii).

33. After graduation from Vanderbilt, Warren received an M.A. from the University of California; attended Yale on a graduate fellowship; and, was a Rhodes scholar at Oxford. He taught at, among others, the University of Iowa and the University of Minnesota, traveled to many places including Europe and North Africa, and lived in many other places including New York, San Francisco, Connecticut, Vermont, Italy, France and England.
34. Hale 285. Hale attributes the publicity to work done by the NAACP, particularly on the 1934 lynching of Claude Neal which was an extraordinarily gruesome spectacle and sensationalized in the press. Neal was tortured for over ten hours, his mutilated body photographed for postcards, his body parts sold for souvenirs—common practices in lynching.
35. Hale 291. For a detailed personal account of growing up black in the rural South of the 1940s and 1950s see Anne Moody, *Coming of Age in Mississippi* (New York: Laurel-Dell, 1968).
36. Walker, "Interview" 159.
37. Warren, *Legacy*.
38. Robert Penn Warren, *Band of Angels* (1955; Baton Rouge: Louisiana State UP, 1994) 2. All subsequent references cited parenthetically in the text. Quote by A. E. Housman. *Band of Angels* is based on a true incident in antebellum Kentucky. A wealthy white man who was the father of two little black girls died without having told them of their lineage. They were sold on the auction block as part of the estate. See Blotner for particulars of incident, 291. See Werner Sollors, *Neither Black Nor White Yet Both: Thematic Explorations of Interracial Literature* (Cambridge, MA: Harvard UP, 1997) 483n32, who writes: "The white father who dies intestate, bringing his children—most especially daughters—in danger of being sold may be considered a topos of interracial literature, including writers from Ignaz Franz Castelli to Robert Penn Warren. As Brown, *The Negro in American Fiction*, 46, pointed out: 'Too often the kindly disposed master dies suddenly, without having chance to fulfill his promises of freedom." Sollors refers to Sterling Brown's *The Negro in American Fiction* (1937; New York: Atheneum, 1969).
39. Henry Louis Gates, Jr., *Figures in Black: Words, Signs, and the "Racial Self"* (New York: Oxford UP, 1987) xviii.
40. Blotner 299.
41. Warren, *Legacy*.
42. Robert Penn Warren, "Why Do We Read Fiction?," *New and Selected Essays* (New York: Random House, 1989) 64, 65.
43. Blotner does concede, however, that even "the generally sympathetic Leslie Fiedler" commented on the "indulgence of melodrama and romance" (300) in the text.
44. The absence of irony may be attributed to a stylistic or technical challenge Warren faced in his writing. Warren does admit very early in his career that he has difficulty in creating irony. In a letter to Andrew Lytle in 1925 he writes: "I have never achieved a real irony which is the true alloy. [. . .] [A] true irony alloys the softer ore of romanticism and makes it usable. [. . .] I have felt the trouble vaguely but have not been able to phrase it for lack of self honesty" (*Selected Letters* 71).
45. Morrison, *Playing in the Dark* 17.

46. Gates, *Figures in Black* 104, 105. See also chapter 1, "Literary Theory and the Black Tradition" on the "self-evidence" of black inferiority, based particularly on "the absence of published writing among blacks."
47. L. Smith 27–28.
48. Forrest G. Robinson, "A Combat with the Past: Robert Penn Warren on Race and Slavery," *American Literature* 67 (Sept. 1995): 527, 513.
49. James Justus, "The Slavery of Freedom in *Band of Angels*," *The Achievement of Robert Penn Warren* (Baton Rouge: Louisiana State UP, 1981) 236.
50. Robinson quotes from *American Literature: The Makers and the Making*, eds. Cleanth Brooks, R. W. B. Lewis and Robert Penn Warren, 2 vols. 1.1048 (New York: St. Martin's Press, 1973) 528.
51. Hale 282.
52. Carnes 16.
53. Hale 284. See also the film version of *Band of Angels* (1957), dir. Raoul Walsh with Clark Gable, Yvonne de Carlo and Sidney Poitier—a sappy, watered-down adaptation; a completely unambiguous love story about Bond and Amantha.
54. Douglass 24.
55. Winthrop D. Jordan, *White over Black: American Attitudes Toward the Negro, 1550–1812* (Chapel Hill: U of North Carolina P, 1968) 18.
56. Hale quotes Mildred L. Rutherford, "the best known amateur historian in the early twentieth century" (61, 62). Also see Hale 312n35.
57. Eugene D. Genovese, *Roll, Jordan, Roll: The World the Slaves Made* (New York: Vintage-Random House, 1972) 91.
58. Genovese 144, 145.
59. See Clinton, *Tara* 109–124. Clinton quotes from Myrta Lockett Avary, *Dixie After the War* (New York: D. Appleton & Co., 1903) 263, and from Jane Pickett in a letter to her mother, July 25, 1863, Montevallo, Boddie Family Papers MSA. See also Clinton, *Tara* 171–177. For more discussion about slave desertion see Daniel E. Sutherland, "A Special Kind of Problem: The Response of Household Slaves to Their Masters and Freedom," *Southern Studies* 20.2 (1981): 151–166. Also, Annalucia Accardo, "A Spy in the Enemy Country: Domestic Slaves as Internal Foes," *The Black Columbiad: Defining Moments in African American Literature and Culture*, ed. Werner Sollors (Cambridge: Harvard UP, 1994) 77–87.
60. See Jefferson *Notes* as an example of early American discourse on the evils of "admixture," one of the most provocative of the earliest American writings on color coding and human essence. He states: "Are not the fine mixtures of red and white, the expressions of every passion by greater or less suffusions of color in the one, preferable to that eternal monotony, which reigns in the countenances, that immovable veil of black which covers the emotions of the other race? Add to these, flowing hair, a more elegant symmetry of form, their own judgment in favor of the whites, declared by their preference of them" (186–187). See Jefferson's discussion on beauty, which is a factor in animal husbandry, "thought worthy [of] attention in the propagation of our horses, dogs, and other domestic animals; why not in that of man?" (*Notes* 187). See 186–191. See also "The Calculus of Color" in Sollors, *Neither Black* 112–141.
61. Sollors, *Neither Black* 76.
62. In a letter dated Sept. 20, 1786, Thomas Jefferson cautioned his daughter Maria about keeping herself protected from the sun so that she would not become tanned: "Remember too as a constant charge not to go out without your bonnet because it will make you very ugly and then we should not love you so much." The beauty of southern women was based "on a standard of facial pallor." *Family*

Letters, ed. Betts and Bear (30). Qtd. in Catherine Clinton, *The Plantation Mistress: Woman's World in the Old South* (New York: Pantheon Books, 1982) 100. Jefferson was subscribing to the common belief, the "self-flattering assumption in Western culture that mankind's initial color must have been white—and the problem thus became how to explain, not the diversity of human pigmentation as such, but most especially the appearance of *blackness*" (Sollors, *Neither Black* 76). If a highly educated intellectual such as Jefferson thinks this way about color, it's not surprising that an entire society is similarly afflicted, slaveholding or otherwise, as well as an identity-challenged mixed-race teenager during slavery.

63. L. Smith 90.
64. Another of many examples is that Amantha takes a rather imperious, haughty pose in her introduction to Rau-Ru by Bond. She may be nervous but has the presence of mind, nevertheless, to contrast Rau-Ru's appearance with her own—ever conscious of her white skin and physiognomy: "aware of the whiteness of my own small hands laid decorously together at my waist." She takes great pleasure as she tells of her awareness of his blackness and his "nigger finery" (119).
65. See Jefferson on black inferiority and the association with body odor. *Notes* 187.
66. Lillian Smith writes: "I knew that my old nurse who had cared for me through long months of illness, who had given me refuge [. . .] was not worthy of the passionate love I felt for her but must be given instead a half-smiled-at affection similar to that which one feels for a dog. [. . .] I learned to cheapen [. . .] one of the profound relationships of my life" (28–29). See also 131–133.
67. Clinton, *Plantation Mistress* 202.
68. Clinton, *Plantation Mistress* 202.
69. Clinton, *Tara* 212, 205, 204.
70. Elizabeth Fox-Genovese, *Within the Plantation Household: Black and White Women of the Old South* (Chapel Hill: U of North Carolina P, 1988) 109, 196, 202, 203.
71. Fox-Genovese 292. See also Clinton, *Plantation Mistress* 199–204.
72. See Deborah Gray White, *Ar'n't I a Woman: Female Slaves in the Plantation South* (New York: Norton, 1985), especially chapter 1, "Jezebel and Mammy: The Mythology of the Female Slave," about the mythologies surrounding black women, particularly in the extreme polarization of stereotypes in the wanton Jezebel and the maternal mammy. The characterization of black women in *Band of Angels* relies heavily upon both types. White argues that "[t]he uniqueness of the African American female's situation is that she stands at the crossroads of two of the most well-developed ideologies in America, that regarding women and that regarding the Negro" (27).
73. See Noliwe M. Rooks on the politics of hair in *Hair Raising: Beauty, Culture, and African American Women* (New Brunswick, NJ: Rutgers UP, 1996).
74. L. Smith 103.
75. See Clinton for a discussion about the "sexual hypocrisy" of the planter aristocracy, and the outrage of black leaders after slavery who denounced the increasing and inflammatory rhetoric that made the black man the sexual aggressor after white women. The reality being, of course, that it was white men who had the power to act against black women with impunity, and who would not, in the words of Reverend Henry McNeal Turner, "*let our ladies alone*" (*Tara* 178). See also 178–182.
76. See Harriet Jacobs, *Incidents in the Life of a Slave Girl* (1861; New York: Oxford UP, 1988); especially the chapters "The Trials of Girlhood," "The Jealous Mistress" and "A Perilous Passage in the Slave Girl's Life."

77. Justus 237. See also Allen Shepherd, "Toward an Analysis of the Prose Style of Robert Penn Warren," *Studies in American Fiction* 1 (1973): 196–197.
78. Clinton, *Plantation Mistress* 204.
79. So named because of an incident in 1973 in Stockholm in which a bank robbery hostage became involved with one of her captors. It has come to represent the psychological state of submission, empathy and identification with one's kidnapper or abuser.
80. Alma A. Ilacqua, "Amanda [sic] Starr: Victim of Her Own False Assumptions," *University of Hartford Studies in Literature: A Journal of Interdisciplinary Criticism* 8 (1976): 179, 181, 182.
81. Justus 246.
82. See Frances E. W. Harper's *Iola Leroy* (1892), and Jacobs's *Incidents in the Life of a Slave Girl.*
83. Lucy Ferris, "Sleeping" 165. For a discussion on interracial love relationships during slavery see Patricia Hill Collins, *Black Feminist Thought: Knowledge, Consciousness, and the Politics of Empowerment*, rev. Tenth Anniversary ed. (New York: Routledge, 2000). Collins argues that "even under slavery, to characterize interracial sex purely in terms of the victimization of Black women would be a distortion, because such depictions strip Black women of agency. [. . .] More difficult to deal with, however, is the fact that even within these power differentials, genuine affection characterized some sexual relationships between Black women and White men" (d'Emilio and Freedman 1988, 100–104) 162–163. Clearly, within the enormous realm and potential for human interaction love was a possibility in some of these circumstances. But Clinton's assessment reflects the dynamics of power and forced submission that typically dominated these situations; an apt point well taken.
84. Clinton, *Plantation Mistress* 213.
85. Lucy Ferris, "From Manty to Cassie: The Evolution of Warren's Female Persona," in *"To Love So Well the World": A Festschrift in Honor of Robert Penn Warren*, ed. Dennis Weeks (New York: Peter Lang, 1992) 269.
86. Justus 240.
87. Lucy Ferris, "Female Persona" 260.
88. Fox-Genovese 374.
89. W. Jordan 151.
90. White 29.
91. W. Jordan 35. Quotes are from William Smith, *New Voyage to Guinea*, 146; Barbot, *Description of the Coasts*, Churchill, comps., *Voyages*, V, 34; and, Smith, *New Voyage to Guinea*, 221–222, "clearly based on Bosman," *New and Accurate Description*, 206–207.
92. See Clinton, *Plantation Mistress* 202.
93. Fox-Genovese 101.
94. Fox-Genovese 292.
95. White 35, 38.
96. See Douglass 23, on the untenable domestic situation when masters have children with their slaves.
97. Jefferson, *Notes* 193.
98. Genovese 4, 5.
99. Fox-Genovese 200, 201, 64.
100. See chapter 1 of Wiencek's splendid discussion about Washington's provisions in his will for freeing his slaves. Also Jefferson, *Notes* 215.
101. Justus 240.

102. Fox-Genovese 35. See her discussion about slaveholding women in the South who supported, benefited and derived their identities from holding slaves, in her chapter "And Women Who Did Not," 334–371.
103. Justus 246.
104. Genovese 146.
105. Genovese 91.
106. Warren, *Legacy.*
107. Warren, "Why Do We Read Fiction?" 56, 61, 64. Warren makes it clear that he is not suggesting that fiction is a "combination of opium addiction, religious conversion without tears, a home course in philosophy, and the poor man's psychoanalysis. [. . .] But it is not; it is fiction" (64).
108. Blotner 299, 291, 298. Warren qtd. in Blotner, 291.
109. W. Jordan 177–178.
110. Robert Penn Warren, *Jefferson Davis Gets His Citizenship Back* (Lexington: U of Kentucky P, 1980) 112, qtd. in Robinson 528–529.
111. Robert Penn Warren, *Segregation: The Inner Conflict in the South,* for. William Bedford Clark (1956; Athens: U of Georgia P, 1994) 63, my emphasis.
112. Warren, "Divided South Searches for Its Soul," *Life* (July 9, 1956): 111, qtd. in Blotner (303).
113. Lewis P. Simpson, "Robert Penn Warren and the South," *Southern Review* 26 (Winter 1990): 8.
114. Hugh Ruppersberg, "Robert Penn Warren and the 'Burden of Our Time': Segregation and Who Speaks for the Negro?" *Mississippi Quarterly* 42 (Spring 1989): 117, 116. Blotner writes that the material that made the book was "too inflammatory for *Life:* the epithets and expletives, and sheer hatred and the vitriolic anti-NAACP and anti-Negro fulminations" (304).
115. Christopher Metress, "Fighting Battles One by One: Robert Penn Warren's *Segregation,*" *Southern Review* 32 (Winter 1996): 167. Metress goes on to argue that "Briar Patch" actually reflects the beginnings of profound changes in Warren's ideas about race. He states: "Changed attitudes about race make it difficult for us today to see anything but an unreconstructed Warren in 'The Briar Patch,' but bitter though his defense of segregation may seem to modern sensibilities, it contained the seeds of uncertainty and self-criticism, seeds that would yield a more pleasing fruit when Warren returned to the race question in the 1950s" (167).
116. Warren, "Why Do We Read Fiction?" 65, 64.
117. Warren, Walker "Interview" 162.
118. See Warren, Walker "Interview," 188–202.
119. Ferris, "Sleeping" 165.
120. Jefferson, *Notes* 215.
121. Warren, *Legacy.*
122. Warren, "Why Do We Read Fiction?" 57.
123. Warren, "Why Do We Read Fiction?" 61, 57, 63.

Chapter 3

1. E. L. Doctorow, "E . L. Doctorow: Novelist," interview with Bill Moyers, in Bill Moyers, *Bill Moyers: A World of Ideas*, Public Affairs Television, Inc., rpt. in Morris, *Conversations* 147. Bessie Smith, "Washwoman Blues," recorded August 24, 1928. John Kenneth Galbraith, *The Culture of Contentment* (Boston: Houghton Mifflin, 1992) 6. Galbraith borrows the quote from Arthur Schlesinger, Jr., *The*

Coming of the New Deal, vol. 2 of *The Age of Roosevelt* (Boston: Houghton Mifflin, 1958) 479. Emma Goldman, *New York Tribune* Oct. 7, 1893.

2. Wright 15–16.
3. David Emblidge, "Marching Backwards Into the Future: Progress as Illusion in Doctorow's Novels," *Southwest Review* 62 (1977): 405.
4. E. L. Doctorow, "The Belief of Writers," *Michigan Quarterly Review* 24.4 (Fall 1985): 614. Rpt. lecture delivered at The University of Michigan, April 1985, Hopwood Awards, rev. by the author for publication.
5. E. L. Doctorow, "The Myth Maker: The Creative Mind of Novelist E. L. Doctorow," interview with Bruce Weber, rpt. in Morris, *Conversations* 95; from *The New York Times Magazine* Oct. 20, 1985: 24+. Weber writes that *Big As Life* is Doctorow's only book that does not have "a storyteller within the story" (95).
6. E. L. Doctorow, "An Interview with E. L. Doctorow," with Winnifred Farrant Bevilacqua, Sept. 3, 1988, Budapest, Hungary, rpt. in Morris, *Conversations* 138.
7. Morris, *Conversations* xvii. Morris points out that Liesl Schillinger's interview, "A Talk with E. L. Doctorow," was the first to note the historical progression. See Morris, *Conversations* xviii and 109. See also Cobbett Steinberg, "History of the Novel: Doctorow's *Ragtime*," *University of Denver Quarterly* 10.4 (1976): 125–130.
8. Douglas Fowler, *Understanding E. L. Doctorow* (Columbia: U of South Carolina P, 1992) 1. Fowler quotes Trenner, *Essays* 1–2, 3.
9. Doctorow, Wutz "Interview" 13.
10. Doctorow, "Myth Maker" 95.
11. E. L. Doctorow, "A Spirit of Transgression," interview with Larry McCaffery, in Trenner, *Essays* 43.
12. Doctorow, "Myth Maker" 95.
13. Doctorow, "Doctorow, Novelist" 153–154.
14. Doctorow, "Myth Maker" 93. Also see Cobbett Steinberg, who suggests that in *Ragtime* "history becomes the novel's main protagonist (or is it antagonist?)" (126).
15. See Vincente Minnelli's *Meet Me in Saint Louis* (1944) about the experiences of an upper-middle-class family during the 1904 World's Fair, and George Marshall's *Papa's Delicate Condition* (1963).
16. E. L. Doctorow, "History and the Forms of Fiction: An Interview with E. L. Doctorow," with Jared Lubarsky. *Eigo Seinen* 124 (1978): 150–52, rpt. in Morris, *Conversations* 37.
17. Doctorow, "Forms of Fiction" 36.
18. E. L. Doctorow, *Ragtime* (New York: Bantam, 1975) 3–4, 4. All subsequent references cited parenthetically in the text.
19. Lawrence W. Levine, *Highbrow / Lowbrow: The Emergence of Cultural Hierarchy in America* (Cambridge, MA: Harvard UP, 1988) 175–176.
20. Doctorow acknowledges his debt to early-nineteenth-century German writer Heinrich von Kleist's character Michael Kohlhass, after whom Coalhouse Walker is modeled and named. For Kohlhass, the possessions of contention were horses. Also on the source of the story see Patricia O. McGhee, "*Ragtime's* Coalhouse Walker, Jr.: Deja Vu," *Literature and Film Quarterly* 16.4 (1988). See various interviews in Morris, *Conversations*.
21. Arthur Saltzman, "The Stylistic Energy of E. L. Doctorow," in Trenner, *Essays* 90.
22. Richard Hofstadter, *The Age of Reform: From Bryan to F.D.R.* (New York: Vintage, 1955) 175.

23. For an illustrative account of how the laborer was "protected" see "The Process of Adjustment: 1880–1930s" in Leonard Dinnerstein, Roger L. Nichols and David M. Reimers, *Natives and Strangers: A Multicultural History of Americans* (New York: Oxford UP, 1996). "In 1910, for example, approximately 3,000 railroad workers were killed and over 95,000 injured. [. . .] There were tales of Polish children earning $2.68 for a sixty-hour week in the Shenandoah coal mines and of a fifteen-year-old girl in Chicago taking home $27 for 245 days of labor. Slavic women and boys earned 75 [cents] to $1 a day in Pittsburgh's spike, nut and bolt, and steel wire factories. Women also sweated for ten hours daily, at wages of 10 [cents] an hour, in the city's steam laundries. They stood continuously in pools of water with their shirts soaking from the steam" (147), and "[m]ost unbelievable is that Italian women continued working fifteen- and sixteen-hour days in which all they received for their efforts was 50 [cents] or 60 [cents]" (148). But "Blacks fared worse than immigrants, earning the lowest wages for the most menial and degrading work" (147).
24. Theodore Roosevelt, a speech given before The Knights of Columbus, New York City, Oct. 12, 1915.
25. Dinnerstein et al. 222.
26. Henry Claridge, "Writing on the Margin: E. L. Doctorow and American History," *The New American Writing: Essays on American Literature Since 1970*, ed. Clark Graham (New York: St. Martin's Press, 1990) 12.
27. Claridge 17.
28. John Seelye, "Doctorow's Dissertation," *New Republic* CLXXIV (April 10, 1976): 22.
29. Freese, "Doctorow's 'Criminals'" 358–359.
30. Phyllis Palmer, *Domesticity and Dirt: Housewives and Domestic Servants in the United States, 1920–1945* (Philadelphia: Temple UP, 1989) 65.
31. Jacqueline Jones, *Labor of Love, Labor of Sorrow: Black Women, Work, and the Family from Slavery to the Present* (New York: Vintage, 1985) 113.
32. Faye E. Dudden, *Serving Women: Household Service in Nineteenth-Century America* (Middletown, CT: Wesleyan UP, 1983) 143.
33. J. Jones 165. "The 108,342 servants and 46,914 laundresses not in commercial laundries totaled almost two-thirds of all gainfully employed black women in the North" (164). See also 165–166.
34. Dudden 90. See also Anthony Trollope, *North America* 5th ed. (London: Chapman and Hall, 1866) 151, and the Rosine Association of Philadelphia, *The Sketch-book of a Manager*, 333.
35. Jones reports that in 1866 "the 'colored washerwomen' of Jackson, Mississippi, organized themselves and established a price code for their services. Though the strike in June of that year was unsuccessful, according to Philip Foner it marked the 'first known collective action of free black workingwomen in American history, as well as the first labor organization of black workers in Mississippi'" (56–57). See Philip S. Foner, *Women and the American Labor Movement: From Colonial Times to the Eve of World War I* (New York: Free Press, 1979) 124–125. In 1881 the washerwomen of Atlanta organized through their churches and went on strike. Their demand: $1 per twelve pounds of laundry. "The white establishment in Atlanta wasted little time in marshaling the full weight of both the private and public sectors in an effort to destroy the association. Landlords threatened to raise the strikers' rents to exorbitant levels, and the city council debated a resolution that would require every laundress to pay $25 for a business license," which they could not afford (J. Jones 148). The leaders were arrested and

fined. See Dudden for discussion of attempts of washerwomen to organize in Galveston in 1877. Their demand: $1.50 per day (232–233). All of these efforts were defeated. See also Palmer on the history of domestics and labor unions, particularly with the help of the YWCA, and the resistance to contracting for domestic help by employers who seemed to regard it as a family matter in her chapter "Negotiating the Law of Service" (111–135).

36. Dudden 206, 205–219.
37. Rollins 82.
38. Dudden 225. See also Ellen Dwyer, "Categories of Female Insanity: A Case Study of Nineteenth-Century Black Women," unpublished paper, Department of Forensic Studies, University of Indiana, 11–13.
39. Recorded by Bessie Smith, August 24, 1928.
40. Robbins, *Servant's Hand* 12.
41. Doctorow, "Doctorow, Novelist" 155.
42. Doctorow, "Forms of Fiction" 37–38.
43. Doctorow, "Transgression" 44.
44. E. L. Doctorow, "Mr. Ragtime," interview with Jonathan Yardley, *The Miami Herald*, Dec. 21, 1975, rpt. in Morris, *Conversations* 11.
45. Robbins, *Servant's Hand* 3.
46. Christopher D. Morris, *Models of Misrepresentation: On the Fiction of E. L. Doctorow* (Jackson: UP of Mississippi, 1991) 102–103.
47. Rollins 209, 210. See Rollins' discussion on the devaluation and erasure of nonwhites in colonialism, and the explanations of Albert Memmi and Frantz Fanon on the socialization that perpetuates this thinking, which "takes on an exaggerated form when the person of color also holds a low-status occupational and gender position—an unfortunate convergence of statuses for the black female domestic servant" (212).
48. David Katzman, *Seven Days a Week: Women and Domestic Service in Industrializing America* (New York: Oxford UP, 1978) 188.
49. bell hooks, *Black Looks: Race and Representation* (Boston: South End Press, 1992) 168.
50. Katzman 188.
51. Prominent among those who sought to raise the social consciousness of the public were, of course, John Dewey, philosopher and educational reformer who advocated participatory learning over rote; Upton Sinclair, novelist, social reformer, politician, and writer of political treatises whose book about the Chicago meatpacking industry, *The Jungle*, was directly responsible for the passage of the Pure Food and Drug Act in 1906; Lincoln Steffens, who as a journalist exposed governmental corruption in newspaper articles, and many others. See Hofstadter's chapter V, "The Progressive Impulse," for a detailed discussion about muckrakers who, he points out, "were working at a time of widespread prosperity, and their chief appeal was not to desperate social needs but to mass sentiments of responsibility, indignation, and guilt. Hardly anyone intended that these sentiments should result in action drastic enough to transform American society. In truth, that society was getting along reasonably well, and the muckrakers themselves were quite aware of it" (196–197).
52. Doctorow, "Doctorow, Novelist" 155.
53. J. Jones 131.
54. Katzman 159.
55. Romero 124–125, 76, 77.
56. Rollins 179, 180.

57. David Wellman, "Red and Black in White America: Discovering Cross-Border Identities and Other Subversive Activities," *Names We Call Home: Autobiography on Racial Identity*, eds. Becky Thompson and Sangeeta Tyagi (New York: Routledge, 1996) 37.
58. Gloria Anzaldúa, *Borderlands/La Frontera: The New Mestiza* (San Francisco: Spinsters/Aunt Lute, 1987) 77.
59. Deborah Fairman Browning, "Toilers within the Home: Servants' Quarters in Nineteenth-Century New England," *Journal of American Culture* 15 (Spring 1992): 97, 93, 96. See Browning's detailed discussion about the construction, quality, and location of servants' living spaces, and how those spaces compare to and accommodate the family space and enforce the division of middle class from lower class.
60. Rollins 180.
61. Romero 108.
62. In an interview with Michael Wutz, Doctorow himself expresses some uncertainty about the identity of the narrator: "The hidden narrator of *Ragtime* is probably the little boy in later times," he states. Wutz interrupts and asks: "Why do you say 'probably'?" and Doctorow responds: "Because he was hidden to me for so much of that book. At a certain point quite near the end he betrays a personal relationship to everything he has narrated and appears to be the son of Mother and Father, namely the little boy. I'm pretty sure that's who it is, but I'm not sure that that is essential for reading the book to know that. [. . .] There's a tremendous advantage writing from a child's point of view. [. . .] Childhood is full sentient being and powerlessness combined" (10–11).
63. Dudden 150. For an overview of the history of discourse on the child/servant relationship, and on prevailing fears of moral contamination of children by servants, especially of a sexual nature, see Ann Laura Stoler's *Race and the Education of Desire: Foucault's History of Sexuality, and the Colonial Order of Things* (Durham, NC: Duke UP, 1995), chapter 5, particularly the section "On Whiteness and Native Nursemaids" 149–164.
64. Robert Coles qtd. from *Privileged Ones: The Well-off and the Rich in America* (Boston: Little, Brown & Co., 1977) in Dudden 151; see also Dudden 147.
65. Peter Stallybrass and Allon White, *The Politics and Poetics of Transgression* (Ithaca, NY: Cornell UP, 1986) 153. See also for an interesting discussion of Freud's ideas about sexual coming of age and attachment and obsession with maids, and how "servants bear a symbolic part mainly as displacements of the biological parents. [. . .] Hence, the physical debasement of the maid is displaced by the exceptional scene of bourgeois 'animality'" (149–169).
66. J. Jones 125–126. Jones uses as her sources the United States Department of Commerce, Bureau of the Census, Bureau of the Census, *Statistics of Women at Work* (Washington, D.C.: Government Printing Office, 1916) 166; Ransom and Sutch, *One Kind of Freedom*, 37–38; Fleming, "Servant Problem," 4–5; Rabinowitz, *Race Relations*, 74; Janiewski, "From Field to Factory," 38, 174; Woofter, "Negroes of Athens," 42, 44–45; William Pickens, *Bursting Bonds* (Boston: Jordan and More, 1923) 41.
67. J. Jones 127.
68. Dudden 64. She goes on to say that "[s]ince service lay at the bottom of the occupational scale, there was nowhere else for blacks to go" (65).
69. Bridget, Brigit and Biddy were generic and demeaning terms for Irish women servants. See Rollins for discussions on the considerable stereotyping to which Irish servants were subjected, on how "the Irish were particularly despised as

'vulgar,' 'childlike,' 'barbaric,' 'ignorant,' 'unclean,' and worst of all, not Christian," and how this affected their servant status" (51–52); see Palmer on how Irish servants "were stigmatized in racial terms as slovenly, licentious, and dark" (146); and, Dudden on the characterization of immigrant Irish women servants as "most faithless [. . .] most strange, not just personally but culturally" (65–71).

70. See Dinnerstein et al. for a discussion of the problem of Irish and immigrant fear of African Americans as a threat to their own job security because they were often used as strikebreakers and would also work for lower wages. Much of the conflict is the result of the perception of unfair competition for limited resources. In fact, African Americans also faced competition for different reasons; "most employers preferred to use whites, at least until World War I" (122), and "[i]n nearly all of these jobs, however, black workers faced considerable discrimination. They usually were common laborers in the industries where they were employed and were paid less than whites. Immigrant workers competed with them for some of the better jobs, forcing many blacks to seek employment as menials or as domestic servants in the homes of white folks" (152). See also 122. See Gerda Lerner's discussion "Doing Domestic Work," in which she states: "At various periods in history when white immigrant labor was available, black women were crowded out of domestic work or, at the least, displaced from the better-paying servants' jobs" (226).
71. Little Boy admires Houdini, who, according to his profession as an escape artist, manages to escape from all manner of traps, imprisonments, obstacles. Houdini is a metaphor for Jewish immigrants who circumvent (escape) the confines of prejudice and social restriction; his welcome through the front door of the family's home along with his popular and commercial success are evidence of this. See Doctorow's *Ragtime* 7–8.
72. L. Levine 177.
73. See Wright 16.
74. Barbara Cooper, "The Artist as Historian in the Novels of E. L. Doctorow," *Emporia State Research Studies* 29.2 (1980): 35–36.
75. Emblidge 407.
76. Josie Campbell, "Coalhouse Walker and the Model T Ford: Legerdemain in *Ragtime*," *Journal of Popular Culture* 13 (1979): 303.
77. Saltzman 95.
78. Mark Busby, "E. L. Doctorow's *Ragtime* and the Dialectics of Change," *Ball State University Forum* 26.3 (1985): 42.
79. Doctorow, "Independent Witness" 51.
80. Doctorow, "Independent Witness" 51.
81. Emily Miller Budick, *Fiction and Historical Consciousness: The American Romance Tradition* (New Haven, CT: Yale UP, 1989) 186.
82. Doctorow, "Independent Witness" 49.
83. Doctorow, "Doctorow, Novelist" 147.
84. Cooper 36.
85. Maureen Howard, "New Books in Review," *Yale Review* 65 (1975–76): 404. In any case, *Ragtime* received the National Book Critic's Circle Award. For a discussion of publication history, and critical and popular reception of *Ragtime*, see Kathy Piehl's "E. L. Doctorow and Random House: The Ragtime Rhythm of Cash," *Journal of Popular Culture* 13 (1980): 404–411. Also, for popular reception of *Ragtime* see Bernard Rodgers, "Ragtime," *Chicago Review* 27.3 (1976): 138–144.
86. Doctorow, "False Documents" 24.

87. Fredric Jameson, *Postmodernism, or, The Cultural Logic of Late Capitalism* (1991; Durham, NC: Duke UP, 1999) 24–25.
88. Emblidge 405.
89. Doctorow, "Transgression" 43.
90. Doctorow, "Belief" 617.

Chapter 4

1. Rudolph D. Byrd, ed., *I Call Myself an Artist: Writings by and about Charles Johnson* (Bloomington: Indiana UP, 1999) xiii. Johnson, *Middle Passage* 179. All subsequent references cited parenthetically in the text. Mohandas K. Gandhi, *Non-Violence in Peace and War*, see chapter 142, vol. 1 (1942; New York: Schocken Books, 1951). James Baldwin, "Notes from a Hypothetical Novel," *Nobody Knows My Name: More Notes of a Native Son* (1961; New York: Dell, 1967). George Bernard Shaw, "Maxims for Revolutionists: Liberty and Equality," *Man and Superman* (1903).
2. Charles Johnson, "The Second Front: A Reflection on Milk Bottles, Male Elders, the Enemy Within, Bar Mitzvahs, and Martin Luther King Jr.," *Black Men Speaking*, eds. Charles Johnson and John McCluskey (Bloomington: Indiana UP, 1997) 178.
3. In fact, Johnson asserts that anything is possible with the right attitude and effort. He states: "If I wanted to be a cartoonist, a philosopher, a fiction writer, a college professor, an essayist, a screenwriter, a martial artist, all I needed to achieve any or all of these things was my own talent, disciplined labor, and the blessing of God. In other words, the self was a verb, not a noun—a process, not a product. You defined your life through action, deeds." Michael Boccia, "Interview with Charles Johnson," *African American Review* 30:3 (1996 Winter): 617.
4. Charles Johnson, Northwestern University Commencement Address, 1994, rpt. in Byrd, *Artist* 142.
5. Johnson, Little "Interview" 177, 178.
6. Charles Johnson, "I Call Myself an Artist," in Byrd, *Artist* 6.
7. Byrd, *Artist* xiii.
8. Controversy is familiar territory for Johnson, who, as S. X. Goudie puts it, "has been both a marksman and a marked man" primarily because of his own criticism of black fiction, which he sees largely as shallow, limited, derogatory, and uninteresting. "'Leavin' a Mark on the Wor(l)d': Marksmen and Marked Men in *Middle Passage*," *African American Review* 29:1 (Spring 1995): 109. Johnson acknowledges that his work is off the beaten track for African American writers. In the introduction to *Oxherding Tale* he writes about the bewilderment and concern of those who do not understand: "If he is a creator of color, they will wonder why he is doggedly pursuing a project so unusual it bears no resemblance whatsoever to other Negro books—'protest novels' in particular—presently being ballyhooed and blessed with awards and attention. And their confusion will be all the greater if his dream-novel, this project that (for him) is more about breaking new ground than fitting into ephemeral literary fashions, also challenges most of the racial and sociological presuppositions in the air during the time of the book's composition" (1982; New York: Plume, 1995) ix-x.
9. The Allmuseri are a fictional tribe, an imaginative composite of many cultures, African and otherwise. See Charles Rowell, "An Interview with Charles Johnson," *Callaloo: A Journal of African-American and African Arts and Letters* 20.3 (Summer 1997): 545; William Nash, "A Conversation with Charles Johnson,"

New England Review 19.2 (Spring 1998): 6; Rob Trucks, "A Conversation with Charles Johnson," *TriQuarterly* 107/108 (Winter/Spring/Summer 2000): 10.

10. See Vincent O'Keefe, who argues that *Middle Passage* is Rutherford's "narrative of perceptual transformation from Captain Falcon's imperial psychology of presupposition, product, and dualism to the African Allmuseri tribe's holistic ideals of humility, process, and reciprocity." "Reading Rigor Mortis: Offstage Violence and Excluded Middles 'in' Johnson's *Middle Passage* and Morrison's *Beloved*," *African American Review* 30.4 (Winter 1996): 635.
11. John Haynes, review qtd. in Goudie 110. See also Virginia Whatley Smith, who writes: "The query portends Johnson's revisioning of the black experience after anxiety-filled years when his early novels met with failure," suggesting perhaps that Johnson's frustration had a bearing on his decision to structure his novel in such a way. "Sorcery, Double-Consciousness, and Warring Souls: An Intertextual Reading of *Middle Passage* and *Captain Blackman*," *African American Review* 30.4 (Winter 1996): 659.
12. Richard Hardack, "Black Skin, White Tissues: Local Color and Universal Solvents in the Novels of Charles Johnson," *Callaloo: A Journal of African-American and African Arts and Letters* 22.4 (Fall 1999): 1030, 1038. Hardack also writes that "[w]hat is disturbing is not that Johnson writes purely ontological fictions—the prerogative of all artists and the ideal of many postmodern science fiction writers—but that he systematically denies a post-racial history in pursuing a preracial aesthetics" (1032), and that for Johnson slavery is a "metaphysical condition, and 'Negroness' a performative one" (1037).
13. Johnson, Little "Interview"164.
14. Daniel M. Scott, "Interrogating Identity: Appropriation and Transformation in *Middle Passage*," *African American Review* 29.4 (Winter 1995): 653.
15. Travis, "*Middle Passage:* Transcending Race Through Narrative," in *Reading Cultures* 77.
16. Binder 557.
17. Johnson reports that he "accumulated research on the slave trade for *Middle Passage*" for seventeen years, and spent six years reading about the "tradition of the sea," which included Melville, London, Sinbad stories and Homer. Rowell "Interview" 540–541. For a discussion of the literary antecedents of *Middle Passage* see Deborah Wyrick, "Charles Johnson's Battle of the Books," *Postcript* 11 (1994): 1–9.
18. See Ashraf H. A. Rushdy, "The Properties of Desire: Forms of Slave Identity in Charles Johnson's *Middle Passage*," *Arizona Quarterly: A Journal of American Literature* 50.2 (Summer 1994). Rushdy gives historical accounts of slave theft and the rationalizations for it, most of which argue that a slave is merely transferring the master's property, and cannot himself own it or steal it because *he* himself is property, and he is only making use of it for the benefit of the owner. Rutherford is a "phenomenological thief" (79).
19. See O'Keefe, who argues that "[a]fter his [Rutherford's] transformation on the *Republic*, he no longer thinks in dualist terms of thievery and violation" (639).
20. Johnson, "Black Images and Their Global Impact," in *Artist* 139.
21. Hardack argues that Johnson's ideas about self-reliance disregard the dynamics of victimization and the real reasons for failure. He writes: "In Johnson's fiction, African Americans fail in the hermeneutic, not social, arena: their actual suffering and even deaths come from lacking an ontology. (In Wai Chee Dimock's terms, this would be called blaming the victim: in Johnson's terms it would be institutionalized whining.)" (1044).

22. Johnson, "Black Images and Their Global Impact," in *Artist* 139.
23. Although Johnson uses many of the rhetorical strategies of the African American slave narrative genre, there are significant differences, prominent among them are Rutherford's attitude toward and easy intimacy with his reader. Molly Abel Travis writes: "Narrators such as Frederick Douglass and Harriet Jacobs were uncomfortably aware of the distance between their experiences and those of their readers. One reason why the slave remained the other/object was because the genre of the slave narrative diverted the reader's attention from the individual slave's experiences and shifted the focus to slavery as an institution." Rutherford "manifests none of the anxiety that the traditional slave narrator expressed in writing for a white audience. From the first sentences of his shiplog, Calhoun sounds not only comfortable but droll," Travis, *Reading Cultures* 72, 77–78.
24. Johnson, "I Call Myself an Artist" 23, 22.
25. Johnson, "Philosophy" 81.
26. Johnson, Little "Interview" 181.
27. Johnson, Nash "Conversation" 8.
28. Johnson, Little "Interview" 166. Johnson acknowledges the influence of Maurice Merleau-Ponty for the view "that philosophy, and fiction—both disciplines of language—are about, at bottom, the same business." Charles Johnson, *Being and Race: Black Writing since 1970* (Bloomington: Indiana UP, 1988) 32. See Maurice Merleau-Ponty, *Sense and Non-Sense*, trans. Herbert L. Dreyfus and Patricia A. Drefus (Evanston, IL: Northwestern UP, 1964) 26.
29. Johnson, "Philosophy" 80.
30. Johnson, *Being and Race* 17, 8.
31. Johnson, "Philosophy" 84.
32. Travis, *Reading Cultures* 84.
33. Johnson, *Being and Race* 11.
34. Johnson, "Philosophy" 82.
35. Johnson, "Philosophy" 80, 81.
36. Johnson, Little "Interview" 172.
37. Jonathan Little, *Charles Johnson's Spiritual Imagination* (Columbia: U of Missouri P, 1977) 3.
38. Johnson, *Being and Race* 45.
39. For a firsthand account of the Middle Passage experience, see Olaudah Equiano, *The Interesting Narrative of the Life of Olaudah Equiano, or Gustavus Vassa, The African, Written by Himself*, ed. Werner Sollors (1789; New York: W. W. Norton, 2001), particularly chapters 1–4, vol. 1, 19–70. See also Nathan Irvin Huggins, *Black Odyssey: The Afro-American Ordeal in Slavery* (New York: Pantheon, 1977).
40. Fritz Gysin, "The Enigma of Return," in *Black Imagination and the Middle Passage*, eds. Maria Diedrich, Henry Louis Gates, Jr., and Carl Pederson (New York: Oxford UP, 1999) 186. For a discussion about Rutherford's precarious status between the Allmuseri and the white crew, and his "confinement to the middleness of [. . .] [a] colonial moment, and the transcendence of coloniality via enunciation from the point of confinement" (625), see Brian Fagel's "Passages from the Middle: Coloniality and Postcoloniality in Charles Johnson's *Middle Passage*," *African American Review* 30.4 (Winter 1996). Fagel argues that Rutherford "is incapable of experiencing togetherness with the Allmuseri [. . .] [he] finds himself too far removed from any sense of African roots" (627).
41. See O'Keefe, 643. Also, see Trucks, who argues that Johnson identifies "[o]ther kinds of slavery, such as psychological, sexual, metaphysical" (3).
42. Johnson, Little "Interview" 160–161.

43. Johnson, *Speaking* 178. Johnson quotes Dr. Joseph Scott from "his memoir of a Depression-era Detroit childhood."
44. Johnson, *Oxherding Tale* xix.
45. Scott 653.
46. Johnson, *Being and Race* 30, 31.
47. See, for example, J. P. Kennedy's *Swallow Barn; or, A Sojourn in the Old Dominion*, the Uncle Remus stories of Joel Chandler Harris, and Margaret Mitchell's *Gone with the Wind.*
48. Johnson, Rowell "Interview" 544.
49. Johnson, "Second Front" 178.
50. Johnson, *Being and Race* 43.
51. Johnson, Rowell "Interview" 542–543.
52. Johnson states in an interview: "You've got black people who own slaves—blacks owned other black people and in some cases didn't free them. It's so complex" (Rowell "Interview" 544).
53. Charles Johnson, "Accepting the Invitation," *Tricycle: The Buddhist Review* 10.1 (Fall 2000): 64. Johnson is a practicing Buddhist.
54. Johnson, *Speaking* 178. Johnson quotes Dr. Joseph Scott.
55. Johnson, Rowell "Interview" 544.
56. Byrd xiii.
57. Aside from the obvious philosophical similarities, see Goudie, who points out the parallels between the lives of Johnson and Rutherford. Goudie writes: "Certainly the novel speaks to Johnson. Like his protagonist, Johnson was trained in philosophy; Calhoun on the plantation of the Reverend Chandler in Southern Illinois, and Johnson at Southern Illinois University. Calhoun, as a result of his contact with the Allmuseri, becomes a disciplined martial artist; Johnson has practiced as a martial artist for many years. Calhoun ultimately marries the schoolteacher who was partly responsible for his remarkable journey; Johnson is married to a schoolteacher who has enabled his own" (121n29).
58. Among other things, Reagan attempted to reinstate tax exemptions for private schools that discriminated against African Americans and repeatedly supported efforts to circumvent affirmative action in hiring, promotion and admissions; supported the reversal of *Roe v. Wade;* reduced Medicare supplementation and unemployment; attempted to eliminate the Department of Education; sought deregulation in environmental matters such as land use and pollution. Zinn, chapter 21, "Carter-Reagan-Bush: The Bipartisan Consensus," particularly 577–582.
59. See V. P. Franklin's *Black Self-Determination: A Cultural History of African American Resistance*, for. Mary Frances Berry (1984; New York: Lawrence Hill Books, 1992), for a historical perspective of African American ideologies, objectives and strategies for self-reliance and self-determination.
60. Ebenezer Falcon is not alone in his concern for the alleged deleterious consequences of affirmative action, clearly subtext in this dialogue. For discussions by African Americans who question or oppose affirmative action policies see Carter's *Reflections;* Thomas Sowell's *A Conflict of Visions: Ideological Origins of Political Thought* (New York: Basic Books, 2002), especially his thoughts on compensatory policy; Shelby Steele's *The Content of Our Character: A New Vision of Race in America* (New York: St. Martin's Press, 1990); and, Ward Connerly's *Creating Equal: My Fight Against Race Preferences* (San Francisco: Encounter Books, 2000).
61. Johnson, "Second Front" 182–183, 184, 187. See also Whatley Smith, who argues that Johnson "offers a different, civilian-based premise regarding warfare in

1990. [. . .] [H]e stresses that African Americans may aspire to a Romantic sense of oneness with their African heritage, but in reality they should maintain their American roots and redress the critical issues of black-on-black crime recurring from their slave past" (673).

62. Johnson, "Black Images and Their Global Impact" 137–138, 138.
63. Charles Johnson, introduction to *Proverbs*, authorized *King James Version*, Pocket Canon Series (New York: Grove Press, 1998) viii.
64. Johnson, "Second Front" 182.
65. Gates, *Signifying* 4.
66. Johnson, Little "Interview" 164.
67. Johnson, *Being and Race* 43.
68. Travis, *Reading Cultures* 82–83.
69. See Ashraf H. A. Rushdy, "The Phenomenology of the Allmuseri: Charles Johnson and the Subject of the Narrative of Slavery," *African American Review* 26.3 (Fall 1992): 373–394.
70. See Ivan Van Sertima, *They Came before Columbus: The African Presence in Ancient America* (New York: Random House, 1976), particularly chapter 2, "The Visible Witnesses," and center text photographic evidence.
71. Johnson's views on racial identity are much criticized. In an interview he explains that "as a Buddhist, I see 'race' as an illusion, a product of the mind. [. . .] I certainly did not start writing in order to address only racial issues. That would, I'm afraid, bore me to death because this mysterious, wondrous universe we inhabit has so much more in it than the illusion of race. [. . .] But no, it's not central to my aesthetic position as a phenomenological Buddhist" (Johnson, Nash "Conversation" 4). Johnson's study of Buddhism, and the concept that "Gautama's phenomenological insight that desire was the origin of suffering, his beautiful description of impermanence, the rightness of a life devoted to *ahimsa* ('harmlessness toward all sentient beings'), and the very zen truth that ontological dualism was one of the profoundest tricks of the mind," lead Johnson to question: "Was race an illusion, a manifestation of *Maya?*" (introduction to *Oxherding Tale*) xi.
72. Timothy Parrish, "Imagining Slavery: Toni Morrison and Charles Johnson," *Studies in American Fiction* 25.1 (Spring 1997): 82.
73. Hardack 1037.
74. Johnson, Boccia "Interview" 618, 612.
75. Johnson, *Being and Race* 43.
76. Fagel 627
77. See Du Bois for a discussion of this phenomenon. Du Bois argues that the Negro American necessarily possesses a duality of mind and spirit because he is always forced to view himself as both a Negro and an American. He writes: "It is a peculiar sensation, this double-consciousness, this sense of always looking at one's self through the eyes of others, of measuring one's soul by the tape of a world that looks on in amused contempt and pity. One ever feels his twoness,—an American, a Negro; two souls, two thoughts, two unreconciled strivings; two warring ideals in one dark body, whose dogged strength alone keeps it from being torn asunder" (45).
78. Fagel 628.
79. Fagel 631.
80. Johnson, *Being and Race* 44.
81. I do agree, however, with Elizabeth Muther's ideas about the representation of Isadora Bailey. Muther writes: "Johnson creates her under a consistent mask of

misogyny, though it is arguably Calhoun's and not his own. And Isadora appears in the action only in the frame story of the novel—the first and ninth chapters—and even here is treated with contemptuous humor. [. . .] [S]he is a composite of misogynistic stereotypes" (649). But this "predatory female" may also be a "signal of male inadequacy, a rote performance, doubling other ritualized male acts of evasion of responsibility" (650); a "moral compass of sorts" (651). "Isadora at Sea: Misogyny as Comic Capital in Charles Johnson's *Middle Passage*," *African American Review* 30.4 (Winter 1996): 649–658.

82. Johnson, *Proverbs* ix.
83. See Marjorie Williams, "The Author's Solo Passage: Charles Johnson on Race and Writing," *Washington Post*, Dec. 4, 1990: D1+.
84. Johnson, Nash "Conversation" 3.
85. Johnson, *Proverbs* xiv, xv, xvi.

Chapter 5

1. Wallace Stegner, *Crossing to Safety*, 2002 edition (New York: The Modern Library, 1997) 153. Ralph Ellison, *Shadow and Act* (New York: Random House, 1964) 92.
2. Toni Morrison, "The One Out of Sequence," interview with Ann Koenen, Lenz, *History and Tradition;* rpt. in Taylor-Guthrie, *Conversations* 74.
3. Morrison, *Playing in the Dark* 33.
4. Morrison, "Sequence" 74.
5. Toni Morrison, "Author Toni Morrison Discusses Her Latest Novel *Beloved*," an interview with Gail Caldwell, rpt. in Taylor-Guthrie *Conversations* 243; from the *Boston Globe* Oct. 6, 1987: 67–68.
6. Toni Morrison, "An Interview with Toni Morrison," with Christina Davis, 1986, rpt. in Taylor-Guthrie *Conversations* 224–225; from *Presence Africaine: Revue Culturelle Du Monde / Cultural Review of the Negro World*, 1145 (1988): 141–150.
7. Morrison, Davis "Interview" 229.
8. Patricia Storace, qtd. in "Ghosts in the House: How Toni Morrison Fostered a Generation of Black Writers," Hilton Als, *The New Yorker*, Oct. 27, 2003: 66.
9. Bloom, *BioCritiques* 7. An interesting contrast in adult life for Morrison was her experience of hiring a white housekeeper to look after her small children when she was a single mother: "the role reversal pleased her" (12). Later, Morrison taught at Princeton, which "had once been an all-white university, a school for rich boys who arrived on campus with their black servants" in tow (30).
10. Toni Morrison, "Chloe Wofford Talks about Toni Morrison," interview with Claudia Dreifus, *The New York Times Magazine*, Sept. 11, 1994, 73.
11. Morrison, "Chloe Wofford" 73.
12. Morrison, *Playing in the Dark* 4.
13. Morrison, "Chloe Wofford" 73.
14. Jacqueline de Weever, *Mythmaking and Metaphor in Black Women's Fiction* (New York: St. Martin's Press, 1991) 28.
15. Genevieve Fabre, "Genealogical Archaeology or the Quest for Legacy in Toni Morrison's *Song of Solomon*," in *Critical Essays on Toni Morrison*, ed. Nellie Y. McKay (Boston: G.K. Hall, 1988) 108.
16. Willis, *Specifying* 96.
17. V. Smith, *New Essays* 11.
18. Morrison, Taylor-Guthrie *Conversations* xiii–xiv.

19. Morrison, "Toni Morrison," interview with Charles Ruas, 1981, rpt. in Taylor-Guthrie, *Conversations* 110; from Charles Ruas, *Conversations with American Writers* (New York: McGraw Hill, 1984) 215–243.
20. Toni Morrison, "An Interview with Toni Morrison," Bessie W. Jones and Audrey Vinson, 1985, rpt. in Taylor-Guthrie *Conversations* 171; from *The World of Toni Morrison: Explorations in Literary Criticism*, Bessie W. Jones and Audrey Vinson (Dubuque, IA: Kendall Hunt, 1985) 127–151.
21. Cheryl Lester, "Meditations on a Bird in the Hand: Ethics and Aesthetics in a Parable by Toni Morrison," in *The Aesthetics of Toni Morrison: Speaking the Unspeakable*, ed. and introd. Marc C. Conner (Jackson: UP of Mississippi, 2000) 125.
22. Morrison, "Sequence" 67.
23. Toni Morrison, "Memory, Creation, Writing," *Thought* 59 (1984): 389.
24. For my understanding of the history, culture and politics of black railroad porters I am indebted to Beth Tompkins Bates' excellent *Pullman Porters and the Rise of Protest Politics in Black America, 1925–1945* (Chapel Hill: U of North Carolina P, 2001) 17, 5, 18, 20. Randolph was not alone in thinking that the lot of African Americans could only be improved when "this race long stigmatized by servitude" was granted economic rights. Historian Carter Woodson, qtd. in Bates, 6. See David Levering Lewis, *When Harlem Was in Vogue* (New York: Oxford UP, 1979) 23 (quotation), 17–24.
25. Cynthia A Davis, "Self, Society and Myth in Toni Morrison's Fiction," in *Toni Morrison: New Casebooks*, ed. and introd. Linden Peach (New York: St. Martin's Press, 1998) 27.
26. As qtd. in Bates 18; Murray Kempton, *Part of Our Time: Some Ruins and Monuments of the Thirties* (New York: Simon and Schuster, 1955) 259, 240–242. Many black men opted for "[w]ork in the stockyards [which] may have been dirty, smelly, and dangerous, but porters usually worked for fifteen years before they received a token 5 percent increase in pay"; they typically earned about $60 for 400 hours of work per month. Bates 22, 26.
27. The culture of black barbershops has always been central to the social life of black communities. Ralph Story writes that "[a]s Ralph Ellison said some thirty years ago, 'There is no place like a Negro barbershop for hearing what Negroes really think.' The barbershop is the one place in both Morrison's novel and actual black communities where black males speak openly and candidly. In the late 1960s, black barbershops were also noteworthy for the political discussions which frequently took place within them. Morrison's Railroad Tommy and Hospital Tommy, two more members of the Seven Days, are therefore very realistic and believable. [. . .] [I]n her use of the barbershop as the group's informal meeting place, Morrison delineates a class and race history of Afro-American political thought so accurate that her genius in this particular area has yet to be fully appreciated." Ralph Story, "An Excursion into the Black World: 'The Seven Days' in Toni Morrison's *Song of Solomon*," in *Modern Critical Interpretations: Toni Morrison's Song of Solomon*, ed. and introd. Harold Bloom (Philadelphia: Chelsea House, 1999) 88.
28. Wahneema Lubiano, "The Postmodernist Rag: Political Identity and the Vernacular in *Song of Solomon*," in V. Smith *New Essays* 105.
29. Fabre 111.
30. Toni Morrison, "What the Black Woman Thinks About Women's Lib," *The New York Times Magazine*, 22 (August 1971): 15.

31. Ronald Takaki, *Double Victory: A Multicultural History of America in World War II* (Boston: Little, Brown and Company, 2000) 23, 8–57.
32. Eric Foner, *The Story of American Freedom* (New York: W. W. Norton, 1998) 209.
33. See Hale 287.
34. Bates 23.
35. Toni Morrison, "Complexity: Toni Morrison's Women," interview with Betty Jean Parker, 1979, rpt. in Taylor-Guthrie *Conversations* (62); from *Sturdy black Bridges*, ed. Roseann Bell et al. (Garden City, NJ: Doubleday, 1979) 251–257.
36. Story 87.
37. E. Foner, *American Freedom* 284.
38. John Hope Franklin, *From Slavery to Freedom: A History of Negro Americans*, 5th ed., (1947; New York: Alfred. A. Knopf, 1980) 484.
39. Senator Fred R. Harris, for., *Black Rage*, William H. Grier, M.D. and Price M. Cobbs, M.D. (1968; New York: Basic Books, 1980) vi.
40. Grier and Cobbs, *Black Rage* 4. More than two decades later, Ellis Cose describes a society in which black professionals, those one might assume to have "made it," who have, ostensibly, obtained the American Dream, as one that requires embarrassing and rage-producing strategies to be treated with a modicum of respect, such as dressing up to hopefully signal to store employees that they can afford their purchases and are not there to steal. A white grocery store cashier or salesman has the power to remind African Americans that they are not only not truly welcome, but that they are suspect. The injury to pride and dignity because of excessive and obvious surveillance is immeasurable. African Americans, professional and otherwise, are wounded and enraged by the assumption that they are dishonest. Stereotypes die hard, or not at all. See Ellis Cose, *The Rage of a Privileged Class: Why are middle-class blacks angry? Why should America care?* (New York: Harper Collins, 1993). See also the introduction to Cornel West's *Race Matters.*
41. Conner xxiv.
42. Valerie Smith, "Black Feminist Theory and the Representation of the 'Other,'" in *Changing Our Own Words: Essays on Criticism, Theory and Writing by Black Women*, ed. Cheryl A. Wall (New Brunswick:NJ: Rutgers UP, 1989) 52.
43. However, Rollins, whose interviews with domestics were conducted in the early 1980s, discloses, for the most part, a more comfortable and congenial relationship between most black employers and their servants, which was clearly evidence of changing times. Rollins reports that maids were not only satisfied but preferred to work for black employers, that they were treated with respect, their female employers often worked along with them, they developed real friendships, and were invited to social functions with family and friends. She attributes this to a sense of kinship and empathy on the part of "[b]lack employers, [who] lacking racism and with a class prejudice modified by the heterogeneity of most black families and a history that has bred a sensitivity to the less fortunate, appear to establish a very different kind of relationship with their black domestics than white employers do perhaps even with their white domestics" 148, 149.
44. Willard B. Gatewood, *Aristocrats of Color: The Black Elite, 1880–1920* (Bloomington: Indiana UP, 1993) 196.
45. Samuel Allen, "Review of *Song of Solomon*," in McKay *Essays* 30.
46. Jan Furman, ed. and introd., *Toni Morrison's Song of Solomon: A Casebook* (New York: Oxford UP, 2003) 6.
47. Barbara Christian, "Community and Nature: The Novels of Toni Morrison," Bloom's *BioCritiques* (88).

48. Susan Willis, "Eruptions of Funk: Historicizing Toni Morrison," *Black American Literature Forum*, 16.1 (Spring 1982): 38.
49. Willis, "Historicizing" 38.
50. J. Brooks Bouson, *Quiet As Its Kept: Shame, Trauma, and Race in the Novels of Toni Morrison* (Albany: State U of New York P, 2000) 80.
51. Palmer 138.
52. E. Franklin Frazier, *Black Bourgeoisie: The Rise of a New Middle Class in the United States* (1957; New York: Collier Macmillan, 1962) 165.
53. Toni Morrison, "Intimate Things in Place: A Conversation with Toni Morrison," Robert Stepto, 1976, rpt. in Taylor-Guthrie *Conversations* 21; from *The Massachusetts Review* 18 (1997): 473–489.
54. Morrison, "Sequence" 69.
55. Joyce Irene Middleton, "From Orality to Literacy: Oral Memory in Toni Morrison's *Song of Solomon*," V. Smith *New Essays* 30.
56. Lawrence Otis Graham, *Our Kind of People: Inside America's Black Upper Class* (New York: Harper Collins, 1999) 2. Jack and Jill is an almost eighty-year-old exclusive "national invitation-only social group for black kids from well-to-do families" xi.
57. J. Jones 142–143.
58. Romero 113.
59. Morrison, "Intimate Things" 17.
60. Morrison, "Sequence" 72–73.
61. Stephanie A. Demetrakopoulos, "The Interdependence of Men's and Women's Individuation," Bloom, *Modern Critical Interpretations* 53.
62. Bouson 95.
63. Toni Morrison, "Nobel Lecture," 1993 in *Toni Morrison: Critical and Theoretical Approaches*, ed. Nancy J. Peterson (Baltimore: The Johns Hopkins UP, 1997) 267.
64. Patricia Yaeger, *Dirt and Desire: Reconstructing Southern Women's Writing, 1930–1990* (Chicago: U of Chicago P, 2000) 268.
65. Bouson 96.
66. For an in-depth analysis of Morrison's usages of Homer's Odyssey in *Song of Solomon* see Trudier Harris, *Fiction and Folklore: The Novels of Toni Morrison* (Knoxville: U of Tennessee P, 1991).
67. Rollins 156, 157.
68. Johnson, *Middle Passage* 28.
69. Johnson, *Middle Passage* 28.
70. Thomas March, "Filling in the Gaps: The Fictional World of Toni Morrison," in Bloom, *BioCritiques* 48.
71. Brenda Marshall, "The Gospel According to Pilate," *American Literature* 57:3 (Oct. 1985): 486.
72. Stanley Crouch qtd. by Ellyn Sanna, "Biography of Toni Morrison," in Bloom, *BioCritiques* 32.
73. Toni Morrison in "The Seams Can't Show: An Interview with Toni Morrison," with Jane Bakerman, 1977. *Black American Literature Forum* 12:2 (Summer 1978): 60.
74. Morrison, "Seams" 60.
75. Toni Morrison, "An Interview with Toni Morrison," interview with Nellie McKay, 1983, rpt. in Taylor-Guthrie *Conversations* 145; from *Contemporary Literature* 24.4 (1983): 413–429.
76. Toni Morrison in "A Conversation with Toni Morrison," with Bill Moyers, 1989, rpt. in Taylor-Guthrie *Conversations* 269; from *A World of Ideas II*, ed. Andie Tucher (Garden City, NJ: Doubleday, 1990).

77. V. Smith *New Essays* 10.
78. Eric Foner, "The Canon and American History," *Michigan Quarterly Review*, The University of Michigan, vol. xxviii.1 (Winter 1989): 49.
79. Toni Morrison, "All That Jazz," interview with Betty Fussell, Taylor-Guthrie *Conversations* 283. From *Lear's* 5.8 (Oct. 1, 1992): 68.

Epilogue

1. Marge Piercy, *City of Darkness, City of Light* (New York: Fawcett Columbine, 1996) ix. Salman Rushdie, *Imaginary Homelands: Essays and Criticism, 1981–1991* (New York: Penguin, 1992) 100. Thich Nhat Hanh, *The Path of Emancipation: Talks from a 21-Day Mindfulness Retreat* (Berkeley: Parallax Press, 2000) 103.
2. Carnes 25.
3. Toni Morrison, "Unspeakable Things Unspoken: The Afro-American Presence in American Literature," the Tanner Lecture on Human Values, University of Michigan, Oct. 7, 1988, *Michigan Quarterly Review* xxviii.1 (Winter 1989): 11.
4. Morrison, "UnspeakableThings" 29.
5. Carnes 25.

Works Cited

Accardo, Annalucia. "A Spy in the Enemy Country: Domestic Slaves as Internal Foes." *The Black Columbiad: Defining Moments in African American Literature and Culture.* Ed. Werner Sollors. Cambridge, MA: Harvard UP, 1994. 77–87.

Allen, Samuel. "Review of *Song of Solomon.*" *Boston University Journal* 26:1 (1978): 67–69. Rpt. in McKay *Essays* 30–32.

Als, Hilton. "Ghosts in the House: How Toni Morrison Fostered a Generation of Black Writers." *The New Yorker* Oct. 27, 2003: 62–75.

American Anthropological Association. "Statement on 'Race'" May 17, 1998. www.aaanet.org/stmts/racepp.htm

Anzaldúa, Gloria. *Borderlands/La Frontera: The New Mestiza.* San Francisco: Spinsters/Aunt Lute, 1987.

Appiah, Anthony. "The Uncompleted Argument: DuBois and the Illusion of Race." Gates *"Race"* 21–37.

Armstrong, Nancy and Leonard Tennenhouse. *The Violence of Representation: Literature and the History of Violence.* New York: Routledge, 1989.

Bakerman, Jane. "The Seams Can't Show: An Interview with Toni Morrison." 1977. *Black American Literature Forum* 12.2 (Summer 1978): 56–60.

Baldwin, James. "Notes from a Hypothetical Novel." *Nobody Knows My Name: More Notes of a Native Son.* 1961. New York: Dell, 1967.

Barnes, Annie S. "White Mistresses and African-American Domestic Workers: Ideals for Change." *Anthropology Quarterly* 66 (Jan. 1993): 22–36.

Bates, Beth Tompkins. *Pullman Porters and the Rise of Protest Politics in Black America, 1925–1945.* Chapel Hill: U of North Carolina P, 2001.

Bennett, S. F. and J. P. Webster. "Sweet By and By." *Progressive Baptist Hymnal,* Bicentennial Edition. Ed. D. E. King. 1940. Washington, D.C.: Broadman Press, 1976. #344.

Bevilacqua, Winnifred Farrant. "An Interview with E. L. Doctorow." Budapest, Hungary. Sept. 3, 1988. Morris *Conversations* 129–143.

Binder, Wolfgang. "Uses of Memory: the Middle Passage in African American Literature." *Slavery in the Americas.* Ed. Wolfgang Binder. Wurzburg: Konigshausen and Neumann, 1993. 539–564.

Bloom, Harold. Ed. and Introd. *Bloom's BioCritiques: Toni Morrison.* Philadelphia: Chelsea House, 2002.

———.ed. and introd. *Modern Critical Interpretations: Toni Morrison's Song of Solomon.* Philadelphia: Chelsea House, 1999.

Blotner, Joseph. *Robert Penn Warren: A Biography.* New York: Random House, 1997.

Boccia, Michael. "An Interview with Charles Johnson." *African American Review* 30.3 (Winter 1996): 611–618.

Bouson. J. Brooks. *Quiet As Its Kept: Shame, Trauma, and Race in the Novels of Toni Morrison.* Albany: State U of New York P, 2000.

Breen, T. H. "The 'Giddy Multitude': Race and Class in Early Virginia." "A Changing Labor Force and Race Relations in Virginia, 1660–1710." *Journal of Social History* 7 (Fall 1973): 3–18. Rpt. in *From Different Shores: Perspectives on Race and Ethnicity in America.* Ed. Ronald Takaki. 2nd ed. New York: Oxford UP, 1994. 107–117.

Brooks, Cleanth, R. W. B. Lewis, and Robert Penn Warren, eds. *American Literature: The Makers and the Making.* 1:1048. New York: St. Martin's Press, 1973.

Brown, Gillian. *Domestic Individualism: Imagining Self in Nineteenth-Century America.* Berkeley: U of California P, 1990.

Brown, Sterling. *The Negro in American Fiction.* 1937. New York: Atheneum, 1969.

Browning, Deborah Fairman. "Toilers within the Home: Servants' Quarters in Nineteenth-Century New England." *Journal of American Culture* 15 (Spring 1992): 93–98.

Budick, Emily Miller. *Fiction and Historical Consciousness: The American Romance Tradition.* New Haven: Yale UP, 1989.

Busby, Mark. "E. L. Doctorow's *Ragtime* and the Dialectics of Change." *Ball State University Forum* 26.3 (Summer 1985): 39–44.

Bush, President George H. W. Qtd. by George Will. *The Washington Post* Nov. 3, 1988: Sec. A27. Qtd. by DeMott Benjamin. *The Imperial Middle: Why Americans Can't Think Straight About Class.* New Haven, CT: Yale UP, 1990.

Butler, Octavia. *Parable of the Sower.* New York: Aspect-Warner, 1993.

Byrd, Rudolph D. Ed. and Preface. *I Call Myself an Artist: Writings by and about Charles Johnson.* Bloomington: Indiana UP, 1999.

Caldwell, Gail. "Author Toni Morrison Discusses Her Latest Novel *Beloved.*" *Boston Globe* Oct. 6, 1987: 67–68. Rpt. in Taylor-Guthrie *Conversations* 239–245.

Campbell, Josie. "Coalhouse Walker and the Model T Ford: Legerdemain in *Ragtime.*" *Journal of Popular Culture* 13 (1979): 302–309.

Carnes, Mark C. *Novel History: Historians and Novelists Confront America's Past (and Each Other).* New York: Simon & Schuster, 2001.

Carter, Stephen L. *Reflections of an Affirmative Action Baby.* New York: Basic-HarperCollins, 1991.

Chaplin, Charles. *My Autobiography.* 1964. New York: Harmondsworth, 1966.

Cherrington, David J. *The Work Ethic: Working Values and Values that Work.* New York: Amacom, 1980.

Chopin, Kate. *The Awakening.* 1899. New York: Norton, 1976.

Christian, Barbara. *Black Feminist Criticism: Perspectives on Black Women Writers.* New York: Pergamon Press, 1985.

———."Community and Nature: The Novels of Toni Morrison." Bloom *BioCritiques* 75–91.

Claridge, Henry. "Writing on the Margin: E. L. Doctorow and American History." *The New American Writing: Essays on American Literature Since 1970.* Ed. Clark Graham. New York: St. Martin's Press, 1990. 9–28.

Clark, William Bedford. Ed. and Introd. *Selected Letters of Robert Penn Warren, Volume One: The Apprentice Years, 1924–1934.* Baton Rouge: Louisiana State UP, 2000.

Clinton, Catherine. *The Plantation Mistress: Woman's World in the Old South.* New York: Pantheon Books, 1982.

———.*Tara Revisited: Women, War & the Plantation Legend.* New York: Abbeville, 1995.

Cobbs, Price M., M.D. and William H. Grier, M.D. *Black Rage.* 1968. New York: Basic Books, 1980.

Coles, Robert. *Privileged Ones: The Well-off and the Rich in America.* Boston: Little, Brown & Co., 1977.

Collins, Patricia Hill. *Black Feminist Thought: Knowledge, Consciousness, and the Politics of Empowerment.* Rev. Tenth Anniversary ed. New York: Routledge, 2000.

Connelly, Thomas L. "Of Bookish Men and Fugitives." Interview with Robert Penn Warren. Feb. 10, 1982. Watkins et al. *Talking with Robert Penn Warren* 374–389.

———."Robert Penn Warren as Historian." *A Southern Renascence Man: Views of Robert Penn Warren.* Ed. Walter B. Edgar. Baton Rouge: Louisiana State UP, 1984. 1–17.

Conner, Marc C. Ed. and Introd. *The Aesthetics of Toni Morrison: Speaking the Unspeakable.* Jackson: UP of Mississippi, 2000.

Connerly, Ward. *Creating Equal: My Fight Against Race Preferences.* San Francisco: Encounter Books, 2000.

Cooper, Barbara. "The Artist as Historian in the Novels of E. L. Doctorow." *Emporia State Research Studies* 29.2 (1980): 5–44.

Cooper, James Fenimore. *Satanstoe, or The Littlepage Manuscripts, A Tale of the Colony.* 1845. Albany: State U of New York P, 1990.

Cose, Ellis. *The Rage of a Privileged Class: Why are middle-class blacks angry? Why should America care?* New York: HarperCollins, 1993.

Crouch, Stanley. Qtd. in Ellyn Sanna. "Biography of Toni Morrison." Bloom, *Bloom's BioCritiques* 3–37.

Davis, Christina. "An Interview with Toni Morrison." 1986. *Presence Africaine: Revue Culturelle Du Monde / Cultural Review of the Negro World* 1145 (1988): 141–150. Rpt. in Taylor-Guthrie *Conversations* 223–233.

Davis, Cynthia A. "Self, Society and Myth in Toni Morrison's Fiction." Peach *New Casebooks* 27–42.

de las Casas, Bartolomé. *History of the Indies.* New York: Harper & Row. 1971.

Demetrakopoulos, Stephanie A. "The Interdependence of Men's and Women's Individuation." Bloom *Modern Critical Interpretations* 41–56.

d'Emilio, John and Estelle Freedman. "Race and Sexuality." *Intimate Matters: A History of Sexuality in America.* New York: Harper and Row, 1988.

DeMott, Benjamin. *The Imperial Middle: Why Americans Can't Think Straight About Class.* New Haven, CT: Yale UP, 1990.

de Weever, Jacqueline. *Mythmaking and Metaphor in Black Women's Fiction.* New York: St. Martin's Press. 1991.

Diedrich, Maria, Henry Louis Gates, Jr. and Carl Pederson. Eds. *Black Imagination and the Middle Passage.* New York: Oxford UP, 1999.

Dill, Bonnie Thornton. "'Making Your Job Good Yourself': Domestic Service and the Construction of Personal Dignity." *Women and the Politics of Empowerment.* Eds. Ann Bookman and Sandra Morgen. Philadelphia: Temple UP, 1988. 33–52.

Dimock, Wai Chee. *Empire for Liberty: Melville and the Poetics of Individualism.* Princeton, NJ: Princeton UP, 1989.

Dinnerstein, Leonard, Roger L. Nichols and David M. Reimers. *Natives and Strangers: A Multicultural History of Americans.* New York: Oxford UP, 1996.

Doctorow, E. L. "The Belief of Writers." *Michigan Quarterly Review* 24.4 (Fall 1985): 609–619. Lecture. Hopwood Awards. The University of Michigan. April 1985. Rev. by the author for publication.

———,"E. L. Doctorow, Novelist." Interview with Bill Moyers. 1990. Bill Moyers, *Bill Moyers: A World of Ideas.* Public Affairs Television. Doubleday. Rpt. in Morris *Conversations* 147–164.

———."False Documents." Trenner *Essays & Conversations* 16–27.

———,"'Fiction is a System of Knowledge': An Interview with E. L. Doctorow." Christopher D. Morris. *Michigan Quarterly Review* 30.3 (Summer 1991): 439–456.

———,"History and the Forms of Fiction: An Interview with E. L. Doctorow." Interview with Jared Lubarsky. 1978. *Eigo Seinen.* Rpt. in Morris *Conversations* 35–40.

———,"An Interview with E. L. Doctorow." Interview with Winnifred Farrant Bevilacqua. Sept. 3, 1988. Budapest, Hungary. Morris *Conversations* 129–143.

———,"An Interview with E. L. Doctorow." Interview with Michael Wutz. *Weber Studies: An Interdisciplinary Humanities Journal* 11.1 (Winter 1994): 6–15.

———,"Mr. Ragtime." Interview with Jonathan Yardley. *The Miami Herald* Dec. 21, 1975. Rpt. in Morris *Conversations* 7–13.

———,"The Myth Maker: The Creative Mind of Novelist E. L. Doctorow." Interview with Bruce Weber. *The New York Times Magazine* Oct. 20, 1985. 24+. Rpt. in Morris *Conversations* 92–101.

———.*Ragtime.* 1975. New York: Bantam, 1981.

———,"A Spirit of Transgression." Interview with Larry McCaffery. Trenner *Essays and Conversations* 31–47.

———,"The Writer as Independent Witness." Interview with Paul Levine. Rpt. in Morris *Conversations* 41–52.

Douglas, Mary. *Purity and Danger: An Analysis of the Concepts of Pollution and Taboo.* 1966. London: Ark Paperbacks, 1984.

Douglass, Frederick. *Narrative of the Life of Frederick Douglass, An American Slave, Written by Himself.* 1845. New York: Signet, 1968.

Downs, Hugh. *The American Dream: The 50s.* For. Hugh Downs. Eds. of *Time-Life Books.* Alexandria, VA: Time-Life, 1998.

Dreifus, Claudia. "Chloe Wofford Talks about Toni Morrison." *The New York Times Magazine* Sept. 11, 1994. 72–75.

D'Souza, Dinesh. *The End of Racism: Principles for a Multiracial Society.* New York: Free Press, 1995.

DuBois, W. E. B. *The Souls of Black Folk.* 1903. New York: Signet NAL, 1982.

Dudden, Faye E. *Serving Women: Household Service in Nineteenth-Century America.* Middletown, CT: Wesleyan UP, 1983.

Dwyer, Ellen. "Categories of Female Insanity: A Case Study of Nineteenth-Century Black Women." Unpublished paper. Department of Forensic Studies, University of Indiana. 11–13.

Edgar, Walter B. *A Southern Renascence Man.* Baton Rouge: Louisiana State UP, 1984.

Ellison, Ralph. "The Uses of History in Fiction." Transcription of panel discussion with Ralph Ellison, William Styron and Robert Penn Warren. Moderator C. Vann Woodward. Thirty-fourth annual meeting of the Southern Historical Association. Jung Hotel. New Orleans, Louisiana. Nov. 6, 1968. *Southern Literature Journal* 1.2 (1969): 57–90.

———,"Warren on the Art of Fiction." 1956. Interview with Robert Penn Warren and Eugene Walter held in Ellison's apartment. American Academy of Rome. Watkins et al. *Talking with Robert Penn Warren* 25–51.

Emblidge, David. "Marching Backwards Into the Future: Progress as Illusion in Doctorow's Novels." *Southwest Review* 62 (1977): 397–409.

Equiano, Olaudah. *The Interesting Narrative of the Life of Olaudah Equiano, or Gustavus Vassa, The African, Written by Himself.* Ed. Werner Sollors. 1789. New York: Norton, 2001.

Fabre, Genevieve. "Genealogical Archaeology or the Quest for Legacy in Toni Morrison's *Song of Solomon.*" McKay *Essays* 105–114.

Fagel, Brian. "Passages from the Middle: Coloniality and Postcoloniality in Charles Johnson's *Middle Passage.*" *African American Review* 30.4 (Winter 1996): 625–633.

Faulkner, William. "That Evening Sun." *The Norton Anthology of American Literature. Shorter Sixth Edition.* Ed. Nina Baym et al. New York: Norton, 2003. 2166–2177.

Ferris, Lucy. "From Manty to Cassie: The Evolution of Warren's Female Persona." *"To Love So Well the World": A Festschrift in Honor of Robert Penn Warren.* Ed. Dennis Weeks. New York: Peter Lang, 1992. 259–272.

———."Sleeping with the Boss: Female Subjectivity in Robert Penn Warren's Fiction." *Mississippi Quarterly* 48 (Winter 1994–95): 147–167.

Fiedler, Leslie. *New Republic* Sept. 26, 1955. 30.

Fleisher, Avrom. *The English Historical Novel: Walter Scott to Virginia Woolf.* Baltimore: The Johns Hopkins UP, 1971.

Foley, Barbara. "From *U.S.A.* to *Ragtime:* Notes on the Forms of Historical Consciousness in Modern Fiction." *American Literature: A Journal of Literature, History, Criticism and Bibliography* 50 (1978): 85–105.

Foner, Eric. "The Canon and American History." *Michigan Quarterly Review.* The University of Michigan. xxviii.1 (Winter 1989): 44–49.

———.*The Story of American Freedom.* New York: Norton, 1998.

Foner, Philip S. *Women and the American Labor Movement: From Colonial Times to the Eve of World War I.* New York: Free Press, 1979.

Fowler, Douglas. *Understanding E. L. Doctorow.* Columbia: U of South Carolina P, 1992.

Fox-Genovese, Elizabeth. *Within the Plantation Household: Black and White Women of the Old South.* Chapel Hill: U of North Carolina P, 1988.

Franklin, John Hope. *From Slavery to Freedom: A History of Negro Americans.* Fifth ed. 1947. New York: Alfred A. Knopf, 1980.

Franklin, V. P. *Black Self-Determination: A Cultural History of African American Resistance.* For. Mary Frances Berry. 1984. New York: Lawrence Hill Books, 1992.

Frazier, E. Franklin. *Black Bourgeoisie: The Rise of a New Middle Class in the United States.* 1957. New York: Collier Macmillan, 1962.

Freese, Peter. "Doctorow's 'Criminals of Perception', or, What Has Happened to the Historical Novel." Lenz *Reconstructing* 345–371.

Furman, Jan., Ed. and Introd. *Toni Morrison's Song of Solomon: A Casebook.* New York: Oxford UP, 2003.

Fussell, Betty. "All That Jazz." Interview with Toni Morrison. *Lear's* 5.8 (Oct. 1, 1992): 68. Rpt. in Taylor-Guthrie *Conversations* 280–287.

Fussell, Paul. *Class: A Guide Through the American Status System.* 1983. New York: Touchstone, 1992.

Galbraith, John Kenneth. *The Culture of Contentment.* Boston: Houghton Mifflin, 1992.

Gandhi, Mohandas K. *Non-Violence in Peace and War.* Vol. 1. 1942. New York: Schocken Books, 1951.

Gates, Henry Louis, Jr., Maria Diedrich and Carl Pederson. Eds. *Black Imagination and the Middle Passage.* New York: Oxford UP, 1999.

———.*Figures in Black: Words, Signs, and the "Racial" Self.* New York: Oxford UP, 1987.

———, ed. *"Race," Writing, and Difference.* Chicago: U of Chicago P, 1985.

———.*The Signifying Monkey: A Theory of African American Literary Criticism.* New York: Oxford UP, 1988.

Gatewood, Willard B. *Aristocrats of Color: The Black Elite, 1880–1920.* Bloomington: Indiana UP, 1993.

Geismer, Maxwell. *Nation* Oct. 1, 1955. 287.

Genovese, Eugene D. *Roll, Jordan, Roll: The World the Slaves Made.* New York: Vintage-Random House, 1972.

Gilman, Sander L. *Difference and Pathology: Stereotypes of Sexuality, Race, and Madness.* Ithaca, NY: Cornell UP, 1985.

Gladden, W. G. "Let Me Walk with Thee." Arr. H. B. Britt. *Baptist Standard Hymnal with Responsive Readings.* Ed. A. M. Townsend. Nashville: Sunday School Publishing Board. National Baptist Convention, 1924.

Goldman, Emma. *New York Tribune* Oct. 7, 1893.

Goudie, S. X. "'Leavin' a Mark on the Wor(l)d': Marksmen and Marked Men in *Middle Passage.*" *African American Review* 29.1 (Spring 1995): 109–122.

Graham, Clark. Ed. *The New American Writing: Essays on American Literature Since 1970.* New York: St. Martin's Press, 1990.

Graham, Lawrence Otis. *Our Kind of People: Inside America's Black Upper Class.* New York: Harper Collins, 1999.

Gregory, Steven and Roger Sanjek. Eds. *Race.* New Brunswick, NJ: Rutgers UP, 1996.

Grier, William H., M.D. and Price M. Cobbs, M.D. *Black Rage.* For. Senator Fred R. Harris. 1968. New York: Basic Books, 1980.

Grun, Bernard. Ed. *The Timetables of History: A Horizontal Linkage of People and Events.* 3rd rev. ed. New York: Touchstone-Simon & Schuster, 1991.

Gysin, Fritz. "The Enigma of Return." Diedrich 183–190.

Hahn, Thich Nhat. *The Path of Emancipation: Talks from a 21-Day Mindfulness Retreat.* Berkeley: Parallax Press, 2000.

Hale, Grace Elizabeth. *Making Whiteness: The Culture of Segregation in the South, 1890–1940.* New York: Vintage-Random House, 1999.

Hardack, Richard. "Black Skin, White Tissues: Local Color and Universal Solvents in the Novels of Charles Johnson." *Callaloo: A Journal of African-American and African Arts and Letters* 22.4 (Fall 1999): 1028–1053.

Hardy, Ernest. "Whoopi's Hollywood Shuffle: *Bogus* lives down to its name." Rev. of *Corinna, Corinna.* Dir. Jessie Nelson. *Los Angeles Weekly* Sept. 6–12, 1996: 33–34.

Harlan, John Marshall. "Dissenting Opinion." *Plessy v. Ferguson.* 1896.

Harper, C. W. "Black Aristocrats: Domestic Servants on the Antebellum Plantation." *Phylon* 46 (June 1985): 123–135.

Harper, Frances E. W. *Iola Leroy.* 1892. Boston: Beacon Press, 1987.

Harris, Senator Fred R. Forward. Grier and Cobbs. *Black Rage.* vi-vii.

Harris, Trudier. *Fiction and Folklore: The Novels of Toni Morrison.* Knoxville: U of Tennessee P, 1991.

Haynes, John. Qtd in Goudie. "'Leavin' a Mark on the Wor(l)d'" 109–22.

Hegel, Georg Wilhelm Friedrich. *Philosophy of History.* 1832. In Shaw's "The Revolutionist's Handbook." *Man and Superman.*

Henry, William A. III. *In Defense of Elitism.* New York: Doubleday, 1994.

Herrnstein, Richard J., and Charles Murray. *The Bell Curve: Intelligence and Class Structure in American Life.* New York: Free Press, 1994.

Hofstadter, Richard. *The Age of Reform: From Bryan to F.D.R.* New York: Vintage-Random House, 1955.

The Holy Bible. King James Version. Cleveland, OH: The World Publishing Company. Jeremiah 31:29. 1 Corinthians 3:9.

hooks, bell. *Black Looks: Race and Representation.* Boston: South End Press, 1992.

Housman, A. E. Epigraph. *Band of Angels.* Robert Penn Warren. 1955. Baton Rouge: Louisiana State UP, 1994.

Howard, Maureen. "New Books in Review." *Yale Review* 65 (1975–76): 404.

Huggins, Nathan Irvin. *Black Odyssey: The Afro-American Ordeal in Slavery.* 1977. New York: Pantheon, 1990.

Ilacqua, Alma A. "Amanda [sic] Starr: Victim of Her Own False Assumptions." *University of Hartford Studies in Literature: A Journal of Interdisciplinary Criticism* 8 (1976): 178–189.

Itzkoff, Seymour W. *The Decline of Intelligence in America: A Strategy for National Renewal.* Westport, CT: Praeger, 1994.

Jacobs, Harriet. *Incidents in the Life of Slave Girl.* 1861. New York: Oxford UP, 1988.

Jameson, Fredric. *Postmodernism, or, The Cultural Logic of Late Capitalism.* 1991. Durham, NC: Duke UP, 1999.

Jefferson, Thomas. *Notes on the State of Virginia, 1784–85.* Ed. Merrill D. Peterson. *The Portable Thomas Jefferson.* New York: Penguin, 1975.

———."To Maria Jefferson." Letter from Thomas Jefferson. Sept. 20, 1786. *Family Letters*. Ed. Betts and Bear. Qtd. in Clinton *Tara*.

Johnson, Barbara. "Threshold of Difference: Structures of Address in Zora Neale Hurston." Gates *"Race"* 317–328.

Johnson, Charles. "Accepting the Invitation." *Tricycle: The Buddhist Review* 10.1 (Fall 2000): 63–64.

———.*Being and Race: Black Writing since 1970*. Bloomington: Indiana UP, 1988.

———."Black Images and Their Global Impact." 1993. Byrd *Artist* 137–139.

———,ed. with John McCluskey. *Black Men Speaking*. Bloomington: Indiana UP, 1997.

———,"A Conversation with Charles Johnson." William R. Nash. *New England Review* 19.2 (Spring 1998): 49–61. <newfirstsearch.oclc.org/WebZ/FSP> 1–9.

———,"A Conversation with Charles Johnson." Rob Trucks. *TriQuarterly* 107/108 (Winter/Spring/Summer 2000): 537–560. <newfirstsearch.oclc.org/WebZ/FSP> 1–12.

———."I Call Myself an Artist." Byrd *Artist* 3–30.

———,"An Interview with Charles Johnson." Michael Boccia. *African American Review* 30.3 (Winter 1996): 611–618.

———,"An Interview with Charles Johnson." Jonathan Little. *Contemporary Literature* 34.2 (Summer 1993): 159–181.

———,"An Interview with Charles Johnson." Charles Rowell. *Callaloo: A Journal of African American and African Arts and Letters* 20.3 (Summer 1997): 531–547.

———.*Middle Passage*. New York: Plume, 1990.

———.Northwestern University Commencement Address. 1994. Byrd *Artist* 141–144.

———.*Oxherding Tale*. 1982. New York: Plume, 1995.

———."Philosophy and Black Fiction." Byrd *Artist* 79–84.

———."The Second Front: A Reflection on Milk Bottles, Male Elders, the Enemy Within, Bar Mitzvahs, and Martin Luther King Jr." Johnson and McCluskey *Black Men Speaking* 177–188.

Jones, Jacqueline. *Labor of Love, Labor of Sorrow: Black Women, Work and the Family, From Slavery to the Present*. 1985. New York: Basic Books. Vintage-Random House, 1995.

Jordan, Winthrop D. *White over Black: American Attitudes Toward the Negro, 1550–1812*. Chapel Hill: U of North Carolina P, 1968.

Justus, James. "The Slavery of Freedom in *Band of Angels*." *The Achievement of Robert Penn Warren*. Baton Rouge: Louisiana State UP, 1981. 236–248.

Kanter, Donald L. and Philip H. Mirvis. *The Cynical Americans: Living and Working in an Age of Discontent and Disillusion*. San Francisco: Jossey-Bass, 1989.

Katzman, David. *Seven Days a Week: Women and Domestic Service in Industrializing America*. New York: Oxford UP, 1978.

Kennedy, John Pendelton. *Swallow Barn; or, A Sojourn in the Old Dominion*. Intro. Lucinda H. MacKethan. The Library of Southern Civilization. Ed. Lewis Simpson. 1832. Baton Rouge: Louisiana State UP, 1986.

Kincaid, Jamaica. *Lucy*. New York: Plume, 1991.

Koenen, Anne. "The One Out of Sequence." Interview with Toni Morrison, 1980. Lenz *History and Tradition* 207–221. Rpt. in Taylor-Guthrie *Conversations* 67–83.

Kuhn, Annette. *The Power of the Image: Essays on Representation and Sexuality*. London; Boston: Routledge and Kegan Paul, 1985.

Le Clair, Thomas. "'The Language Must Not Sweat': An Interview with Toni Morrison." 1981. *New Republic* 184 (March 21, 1981): 25–29. Rpt. in Taylor-Guthrie *Conversations* 119–128.

Lenz, Gunter H. Ed. *History and Tradition in Afro-American Culture*. Frankfurt: Campus, 1984.

———,ed. *Reconstructing American Literary and Historical Studies*. Frankfurt: Campus, 1990.

Lerner, Gerda. *Black Women in White America: A Documentary History.* 1972. New York: Vintage-Random House, 1992.

Lester, Cheryl. "Meditations on a Bird in the Hand: Ethics and Aesthetics in a Parable by Toni Morrison." Conner *Toni Morrison* 125–138.

Levine, Lawrence W. *Highbrow/Lowbrow: The Emergence of Cultural Hierarchy in America.* Cambridge, MA: Harvard UP, 1988.

Levine, Paul. "The Writer as Independent Witness." Interview with E. L. Doctorow. Morris *Conversations* 41–52.

Lewis, David Levering. *W. E. B. Du Bois: Biography of a Race, 1868–1919.* New York: Macrae-Henry Holt, 1993.

———.*When Harlem Was in Vogue.* New York: Oxford UP, 1979.

Little, Jonathan. *Charles Johnson's Spiritual Imagination.* Columbia: U of Missouri P, 1997.

———."An Interview with Charles Johnson." *Contemporary Literature* 34.2 (Summer 1993): 159–181.

Lubarsky, Jared. "History and the Forms of Fiction: An Interview with E. L. Doctorow." *Eigo Seinen.* 1978. Rpt. in Morris *Conversations* 35–40.

Lubiano, Wahneema. "The Postmodernist Rag: Political Identity and the Vernacular in *Song of Solomon.*" V. Smith *New Essays* 93–116.

Lukács, Georg. *The Historical Novel.* Trans. Hannah Mitchell and Stanley Mitchell. 1937. London: Merlin P, 1962.

March, Thomas. "Filling in the Gaps: The Fictional World of Toni Morrison." Bloom *BioCritiques* 39–60.

Marshall, Brenda. "The Gospel According to Pilate." *American Literature* 57:3 (Oct. 1985): 486–489.

Marshall, Thurgood. "The Brown Decision." *Let Nobody Turn Us Around: Voices of Resistance, Reform, and Renewal, An African American Anthology.* Eds. Manning Marable and Leith Mullings. Lanham, MD: Rowman & Littlefield, 2000. 357–364.

Martineau, Harriet. *Society in America.* 1837. New Brunswick, NJ: Transaction, 1981.

Mather, Cotton. "On the Conversion of the Negroes." 1706. *The Negro Christianized.* Rpt. in *The Minority Presence in American Literature: 1600–1900.* Ed. Philip Butcher. Washington, D.C.: Howard UP, 1977. 71–76.

McCaffery, Larry. "A Spirit of Transgression." Interview with E. L. Doctorow. Trenner *Essays and Conversations* 31–47.

McCluskey, John and Charles Johnson. Eds. *Black Men Speaking.* Bloomington: Indiana UP, 1997.

McGhee, Patricia O. "*Ragtime's* Coalhouse Walker, Jr.: Deja Vu." *Literature and Film Quarterly* 16.4 (1988): 272–275.

McKay, Nellie Y. Ed. *Critical Essays on Toni Morrison.* Boston: G. K. Hall, 1998.

———."An Interview with Toni Morrison." 1983. *Contemporary Literature.* 24.4 (1983): 413–429. Rpt. in Taylor-Guthrie *Conversations* 138–55.

Merleau-Ponty, Maurice. *Sense and Non-Sense.* Trans. Herbert L. Dreyfus and Patricia A Dreyfus. Evanston: Northwestern UP, 1964.

Metress, Christopher. "Fighting Battles One by One: Robert Penn Warren's *Segregation.*" *Southern Review* 32 (Winter 1996): 166–171.

Middleton, Joyce Irene. "From Orality to Literacy: Oral Memory in Toni Morrison's *Song of Solomon.*" V. Smith *New Essays* 19–39.

Miller, Christopher. "Theories of Africans: The Question of Literary Anthropology." Gates "*Race*" 281–300.

Mitchell, Margaret. *Gone with the Wind.* 1936. New York: Pocket Book-Macmillan. 1968.

Mobley, Marilyn Sanders. "Call and Response: Voice, Community, and Dialogic Structures in Toni Morrison's *Song of Solomon.*" V. Smith *New Essays* 41–68.

Moody, Anne. *Coming of Age in Mississippi.* New York: Laurel-Dell, 1968.

Morison, Samuel Eliot. *The Oxford History of the American People: Volume Three, 1869 Through the Death of John F. Kennedy, 1963.* 1965. New York: Meridian-Penguin, 1994.

Morris, Christopher D. Ed. and Introd. *Conversations with E. L. Doctorow.* Jackson: UP of Mississippi, 1999.

———."'Fiction is a System of Knowledge': An Interview with E. L. Doctorow." *Michigan Quarterly Review* 30.3 (Summer 1991): 439–456.

———. *Models of Misrepresentation: On the Fiction of E. L. Doctorow.* Jackson: UP of Mississippi, 1991.

Morrison, Toni. "All That Jazz." Interview with Betty Fussell. *Lear's* 5.8 (Oct. 1, 1992): 68. Rpt. in Taylor-Guthrie *Conversations* 280–287.

———,"Author Toni Morrison Discusses Her Latest Novel *Beloved.*" Interview with Gail Caldwell. 1987. *Boston Globe* Oct. 6, 1987: 67–68. Rpt. in Taylor-Guthrie *Conversations* 239–45.

———,"Chloe Wofford Talks about Toni Morrison." An interview with Claudia Dreifus. *The New York Times Magazine* Sept. 11, 1994. 72–75.

———,"Complexity: Toni Morrison's Women." Interview with Betty Jean Parker. *Sturdy Black Bridges.* Ed. Roseann Bell, et al. Garden City, NJ: Doubleday, 1979. 251–257. Rpt. in Taylor-Guthrie *Conversations* 60–66.

———,"A Conversation with Toni Morrison." Interview with Bill Moyers. 1989. *A World of Ideas II.* Ed. Andie Tucher. Garden City, NJ: Doubleday, 1990. Rpt. in Taylor-Guthrie *Conversations* 262–274.

———.*The Dancing Mind.* Speech upon Acceptance of the National Book Foundation Medal for Distinguished Contribution to American Letters on the Sixth of November, Nineteen Hundred and Ninety-Six. New York: Borzoi-Knopf, 1996.

———,"An Interview with Toni Morrison." Interview with Christina Davis. *Presence Africaine: Revue Culturelle Du Mond / Cultural Review of the Negro World* 1145 (1988): 141–150. Rpt. in Taylor-Guthrie *Conversations* 223–233.

———,"An Interview with Toni Morrison." Interview with Bessie W. Jones and Audrey Vinson. 1985. Bessie W. Jones and Audrey Vinson. *The World of Toni Morrison.* 127–151. Rpt. in Taylor-Guthrie *Conversations* 171–187.

———,"An Interview with Toni Morrison." Nellie Y. McKay. 1983. *Contemporary Literature* 24.4 (1983): 413–429. Rpt. in Taylor-Guthrie *Conversations* 138–155.

———,"Intimate Things in Place: A Conversation with Toni Morrison." Interview with Robert Stepto, 1976. *The Massachusetts Review* 18. 1997. 473–489. Rpt. in Taylor-Guthrie *Conversations* 10–29.

———,"'The Language Must Not Sweat': An Interview with Toni Morrison." Interview with Thomas Le Clair. 1981. *New Republic* 184 (March 21, 1981): 25–29. Rpt. in Taylor-Guthrie *Conversations* 119–128.

———."Memory, Creation, Writing." *Thought* 59 (1984): 385–390.

———."Nobel Lecture." 1993. Ed. Nancy J. Peterson. *Toni Morrison: Critical and Theoretical Approaches.* Baltimore: The Johns Hopkins UP, 1997. 267–273.

———,"The One Out of Sequence." Interview with Anne Koenen. 1980. Lenz, *History and Tradition.* 201–221. Rpt. in Taylor-Guthrie *Conversations* 67–83.

———.*Playing in the Dark: Whiteness and the Literary Imagination.* New York: Vintage-Random House, 1993.

———,"The Seams Can't Show: An Interview with Toni Morrison." Interview with Jane Bakerman. 1977. *Black American Literature Forum* 12.2 (Summer 1978): 56–60.

———.*Song of Solomon.* New York: Alfred A. Knopf, 1977.

———,"Toni Morrison." Interview with Charles Ruas, 1981. Charles Ruas. *Conversations with American Writers.* New York: McGraw Hill, 1984. 215–243. Rpt. in Taylor-Guthrie *Conversations* 93–118.

———."Unspeakable Things Unspoken: The Afro-American Presence in American Literature." The Tanner Lecture on Human Values. University of Michigan. Oct. 7, 1988. *Michigan Quarterly Review* xxviii.1 (Winter 1989): 1–34.

———."What the Black Woman Thinks About Women's Lib." *The New York Times Magazine* Aug. 22, 1971. 15.

Moyers, Bill. "A Conversation with Toni Morrison." 1989. Bill Moyers. *A World of Ideas II*. Ed. Andie Tucher. Garden City. NJ: Doubleday, 1990. Rpt. in Taylor-Guthrie *Conversations* 262–274.

———,"E. L. Doctorow, Novelist." Interview with E. L. Doctorow. Moyers *A World of Ideas*. Public Affairs Television. Doubleday. Rpt. in Morris *Conversations* 147–164.

Muther, Elizabeth. "Isadora at Sea: Misogyny as Comic Capital in Charles Johnson's *Middle Passage*." *African American Review* 30.4 (Winter 1996): 649–658.

Nash, William R. "A Conversation with Charles Johnson." *New England Review* 19.2 (Spring 1988): 49–61. <newfirstsearch.oclc.org/WebZ/FSP> 1–9.

Nelson, Dana D. *The Word in Black and White: Reading "Race" in American Literature, 1638–1867*. New York: Oxford UP, 1993.

O'Keefe, Vincent A. "Reading Rigor Mortis: Offstage Violence and Excluded Middles 'in' Johnson's *Middle Passage* and Morrison's *Beloved*." *African American Review* 30.4 (Winter 1996): 635–647.

Palmer, Phyllis. *Domesticity and Dirt: Housewives and Domestic Servants in the United States, 1920–1945*. Philadelphia: Temple UP, 1989.

Parker, Betty Jean. "Complexity: Toni Morrison's Women." Interview with Toni Morrison. *Sturdy Black Bridges*. Ed. Roseann Bell, et al. Garden City, NJ: Doubleday, 1979. 251–257. Rpt. in Taylor-Guthrie *Conversations* 60–66.

Parkman, Francis. Intro. *Pioneers of France in the New World*. 11th ed. 1865. Boston: Little, Brown, 1874.

Parrish, Timothy L. "Imagining Slavery: Toni Morrison and Charles Johnson." *Studies in American Fiction* 25.1 (Spring 1997): 81–100.

Peach, Linden. Ed. and Introd. *Toni Morrison: New Casebooks*. New York: St. Martin's Press, 1998.

Pederson, Carl, Henry Louis Gates, Jr. and Maria Diedrich. Eds. *Black Imagination and the Middle Passage*. New York: Oxford UP, 1999.

Perkins, James A. "Racism and the Personal Past in Robert Penn Warren." *Mississippi Quarterly* 48 (Winter 1994–95): 73–82.

Peterson, Merrill D. Ed. and Introd. *The Portable Thomas Jefferson*. New York: Penguin, 1975.

Peterson, Nancy J. *Toni Morrison: Critical and Theoretical Approaches*. Baltimore: Johns Hopkins UP, 1997.

Piehl, Kathy. "E. L. Doctorow and Random House: The Ragtime Rhythm of Cash." *Journal of Popular Culture* 13 (1980): 404–411.

Piercy, Marge. *City of Darkness, City of Light*. New York: Fawcett Columbine, 1996.

Robbins, Bruce. "The Butler Did It: On Agency and the Novel." *Representations* 6 (Spring 1994): 85–97.

———.*The Servant's Hand: English Fiction from Below*. Durham, NC: Duke UP, 1993.

Robinson, Forrest G. "A Combat with the Past: Robert Penn Warren on Race and Slavery." *American Literature* 67 (Sept. 1995): 511–530.

Robinson, Randall. *The Debt: What America Owes to Blacks*. New York: Plume, 2001.

Rodgers, Bernard. "Ragtime." *Chicago Review* 27.3 (1976): 138–144.

Roediger, David R. *The Wages of Whiteness: Race and the Making of the American Working Class*. 1991. New York: Verso, 1996.

Rollins, Judith. *Between Women: Domestics and Their Employers*. Philadelphia: Temple UP, 1985.

Romero, Mary. *Maid in the U.S.A.* New York: Routledge, 1992.
Rooks, Noliwe M. *Hair Raising: Beauty, Culture, and African American Women.* New Brunswick, NJ: Rutgers UP, 1996.
Roosevelt, Theodore. Speech. The Knights of Columbus. New York City. Oct. 12, 1915.
Rowell, Charles. "An Interview with Charles Johnson." *Callaloo: A Journal of African American and African Arts and Letters* 20.3 (Summer 1997): 531–547.
Ruas, Charles. "Toni Morrison." Interview with Toni Morrison. 1981. Charles Ruas. *Conversations with American Writers.* New York: McGraw Hill, 1984. 215–243. Rpt. in Taylor-Guthrie *Conversations* 93–118.
Rubin, Jr., Louis D. Ed. and Introd. *I'll Take My Stand: The South and the Agrarian Tradition, By Twelve Southerners.* 1930. Baton Rouge: Louisiana UP, 1977. xi-xxxv.
Ruppersberg, Hugh. "Robert Penn Warren and the 'Burden of Our Time': Segregation and Who Speaks for the Negro?" *Mississippi Quarterly* 42 (Spring 1989): 115–128.
Rushdie, Salman. *Imaginary Homelands: Essays and Criticism, 1981–1991.* New York: Penguin, 1992.
Rushdy, Ashraf. H. A. "The Phenomenology of the Allmuseri: Charles Johnson and the Subject of the Narrative of Slavery." *African American Review* 26.3 (Fall 1992): 373–394.
———."The Properties of Desire: Forms of Slave Identity in Charles Johnson's *Middle Passage.*" *Arizona Quarterly: A Journal of American Literature* 50.2 (Summer 1994): 73–108.
Rushton, Philippe J. *Race, Evolution, and Behavior: A Life History Perspective.* New Brunswick, NJ: Transactions Publishers, 1994.
Rutherford, Mildred L. Speeches. 1912 and 1914. Qtd. by Grace Elizabeth Hale. *Making Whiteness: The Culture of Segregation in the South, 1890–1940.* New York: Vintage, 1999. 43–84.
Salmon, Lucy Maynard. *Domestic Service.* 1897. New York: Arno, 1972.
Saltzman, Arthur. "The Stylistic Energy of E. L. Doctorow." Trenner *Essays & Conversations* 73–108.
Sanjek, Roger. "The Enduring Inequalities of Race." *Race.* Ed. Steven Gregory and Roger Sanjek. New Brunswick, NJ: Rutgers UP, 1996. 1–17.
Sanna, Ellyn. "Biography of Toni Morrison." Bloom *BioCritiques* 3–37.
Schlesinger, Jr., Arthur. *The Coming of the New Deal. The Age of Roosevelt.* Vol. 2. Boston: Houghton Mifflin, 1958.
Scott, Daniel M. "Interrogating Identity: Appropriation and Transformation in *Middle Passage.*" *African American Review* 29.4 (Winter 1995): 645–655.
Seelye, John. "Doctorow's Dissertation." *New Republic* CLXXIV (Apr. 10, 1976): 22–23.
Shaw, George Bernard. "Maxims for Revolutionists: Liberty and Equality." *Man and Superman.* 1903.
Shepherd, Allen. "Toward an Analysis of the Prose Style of Robert Penn Warren." *Studies in American Fiction* 1 (1973): 188–202.
Simpson, Lewis P. "Robert Penn Warren and the South." *Southern Review* 26 (Winter 1990): 7–12.
Smith, Bessie. "Washwoman Blues." Williams and Grainger. Recorded August 24, 1928.
Smith, Lillian. *Killers of the Dream.* 1949. New York: Norton, 1994.
Smith, Valerie. "Black Feminist Theory and the Representation of the 'Other." Wall *Changing Our Own Words* 38–57.
———.ed. and introd. *New Essays on Song of Solomon.* The American Novel Series. New York: Cambridge UP, 1995.
Smith, Virginia Whatley. "Sorcery, Double-Consciousness, and Warring Souls: An Intertextual Reading of *Middle Passage* and *Captain Blackman.*" *African American Review* 30.4 (Winter 1996): 659–674.

Sollors, Werner. *Beyond Ethnicity: Consent and Descent in American Culture*. New York: Oxford UP, 1986.

———,ed. *The Black Columbiad: Defining Moments in African American Literature and Culture*. Cambridge, MA: Harvard UP, 1994.

———.*Neither Black Nor White Yet Both: Thematic Explorations of Interracial Literature*. Cambridge, MA: Harvard UP, 1997.

Sowell, Thomas. *A Conflict of Visions: Ideological Origins of Political Thought*. New York: Basic Books, 2002.

Stallybrass, Peter and Allon White. *The Politics and Poetics of Transgression* Ithaca, NY: Cornell, 1986.

Steele, Shelby. *The Content of Our Character: A New Vision of Race in America*. New York: St. Martin Press, 1990.

Stegner, Wallace. *Crossing to Safety*. 1986. New York: The Modern Library, 2002.

Steinberg, Cobbett. "History of the Novel: Doctorow's *Ragtime*." *University of Denver Quarterly* 10.4 (1976): 125–130.

Stepto, Robert. "Intimate Things in Place: A Conversation with Toni Morrison." Interview. *The Massachusetts Review* 18 (1997): 473–489. Rpt. in Taylor-Guthrie *Conversations* 10–29.

Stoler, Ann Laura. *Race and the Education of Desire: Foucault's History of Sexuality, and the Colonial Order of Things*. Durham, NC: Duke UP, 1995.

Storace, Patricia. Qtd. in "Ghosts in the House: How Toni Morrison Fostered a Generation of Black Writers." Hilton Als. *The New Yorker* Oct. 27, 2003. 62–75.

Story, Ralph. "An Excursion into the Black World: The 'Seven Days' in Toni Morrison's *Song of Solomon*." Bloom *Modern Critical Interpretations* 85–93.

Strugnell, John R. "Robert Penn Warren and the Uses of the Past." *Review of English Literature* 4.4 (1963): 93–102.

Susman, Warren I. *Culture as History: The Transformation of American Society in the Twentieth Century*. New York: Pantheon, 1984.

Sutherland, Daniel E. "A Special Kind of Problem: The Response of Household Slaves to Their Masters and Freedom." *Southern Studies* 20.2 (1981): 151–166.

Takaki, Ronald. *Double Victory: A Multicultural History of America in World War II*. Boston: Little, Brown and Company, 2000.

———,ed. *From Different Shores: Perspectives on Race and Ethnicity in America*. 2nd ed. New York: Oxford UP, 1994.

Taylor-Guthrie, Danille. *Conversations with Toni Morrison*. Jackson: UP of Mississippi, 1994.

Thompson, Becky and Sangeeta Tyagi. Eds. *Names We Call Home: Autobiography on Racial Identity*. New York: Routledge, 1996.

Thompson, James R. "'Categories of Human Form': Some Notes on E. L. Doctorow and Historical Consciousness." *Caliban* 28 (1991): 17–24.

Tocqueville, Alexis de. *Democracy in America*. Ed. J. P. Mayer. Trans. George Lawrence. 1835. New York: Perennial, 1988.

Travis, Molly Abel. *Reading Cultures: The Construction of Readers in the Twentieth Century*. Carbondale: Southern Illinois UP, 1998.

Trenner, Richard. *E. L. Doctorow: Essays and Conversations*. Princeton, NJ: Ontario Review Press, 1983.

Trollope, Anthony. *North America*. 5th ed. London: Chapman and Hall, 1866.

Trollope, Frances. *Domestic Manners of the Americans*. 1832; Oxford: Oxford UP, 1984.

Trucks, Rob. "A Conversation with Charles Johnson." *TriQuarterly* 107/108 (Winter/Spring/Summer 2000): 537–560. <http://newfirstsearch.oclc.org/WebZ/FSP> 1–12.

Turner, Henry McNeal. "'*let our ladies alone*'" 1866. Qtd. in Clinton *Tara* 178.

Turner, Joseph W. "The Kinds of Historical Fiction: An Essay in Definition and Methodology." *Genre* 12 (1979): 333–355.

Van Sertima, Ivan. *They Came before Columbus: The African Presence in Ancient America.* New York: Random House, 1976.

Vinson, Audrey and Bessie W. Jones. "An Interview with Toni Morrison." 1985. Bessie W. Jones and Audrey Vinson. *The World of Toni Morrison: Explorations in Literary Criticism.* Dubuque, IA: Kendall Hunt, 1985. 127–151. Rpt. in Taylor-Guthrie *Conversations* 171–187.

Walker, Marshall. "An Interview." With Robert Penn Warren. Sept. 11, 1969. *Robert Penn Warren: A Vision Earned.* Ed. Marshall Walker. New York: Harper and Row, 1979. 188–202. Rpt. in Watkins et al. *Talking with Robert Penn Warren* 147–169.

———,ed. *Robert Penn Warren: a Vision Earned.* New York: Harper and Row, 1979.

Wall, Cheryl A. Ed. *Changing Our Own Words: Essays on Criticism, Theory and Writing by Black Women.* New Brunswick, NJ: Rutgers UP, 1989.

Walter, Eugene. "Warren on the Art of Fiction." 1956. Interview with Robert Penn Warren and Ralph Ellison. Sept. 11, 1969 in Ellison's apartment. American Academy of Rome. Watkins et al. *Talking with Robert Penn Warren* 25–51.

Ward, Frazer. "Foreign and Familiar Bodies." *Dirt and Domesticity: Constructions of the Feminine.* Exhibition at the Whitney Museum of American Art. Equitable Center. June12-August 14, 1992. Ed. Jesús Fuenmayor, Kate Haug and Frazer Ward. New York: Whitney Museum of American Art, 1992.

Warren, Robert Penn. *Band of Angels.* 1955. Baton Rouge: Louisiana State UP, 1994.

———."The Briar Patch." Rubin 246–264.

———."Divided South Searches for Its Soul." *Life.* July 9, 1956.

———,*Jefferson Davis Gets His Citizenship Back.* Lexington: U of Kentucky P, 1980. Warren qtd. in Forrest G. Robinson. "A Combat with the Past: Robert Penn Warren on Race and Slavery." *American Literature* 67 (Sept. 1995): 511–530.

———.*The Legacy of the Civil War: Meditations on the Centennial.* 1961. Cambridge, MA: Harvard UP, 1983.

———,"Of Bookish Men and the Fugitives." Interview with Thomas L. Connelly. Feb. 10, 1982. Edgar *A Southern Renascence Man.* Rpt. in Watkins et al. *Talking with Robert Penn Warren* 374–389.

———,"Robert Penn Warren: An Interview." Marshall Walker. Sept. 11, 1969. Walker *A Vision Earned.* Rpt. in Watkins et al. *Talking with Robert Penn Warren* 147–169.

———.*Segregation: The Inner Conflict in the South.* 1956. For. William Bedford Clark. Athens: U of Georgia P, 1994.

———.*Selected Letters of Robert Penn Warren, Volume One: the Apprentice Years, 1924–1934.* Ed. and introd. William Bedford Clark. Baton Rouge: Louisiana State UP, 2000.

———."The Uses of History in Fiction." Transcription of panel discussion with Ralph Ellison, William Styron and Robert Penn Warren. Moderator C. Vann Woodward. Thirty-fourth annual meeting of the Southern Historical Association. Jung Hotel. New Orleans, LA. Nov. 6, 1968. *Southern Literature Journal* 1.2 (1969): 57–90.

———,"Warren on the Art of Fiction." 1956. Interview with Robert Penn Warren and Ralph Ellison. In Ellison's apartment. American Academy of Rome. *Paris Review.* 1957. Rpt. in Watkins et al. *Talking with Robert Penn Warren* 25–51.

———."Why Do We Read Fiction?" *New and Selected Essays.* New York: Random House, 1989. 55–66.

Washington, Booker T. "The Atlanta Exposition Address." *Up From Slavery.* 1901. New York: Penguin, 1986.

Watkins, Floyd C., John T. Hiers and Mary Louise Weaks. Eds. *Talking with Robert Penn Warren.* Athens: U of Georgia P, 1990.

Watson, George. "The Silence of the Servants." *The Sewanee Review* 103 (Summer 1995): 480–486.

Weber, Bruce. "The Myth Maker: The Creative Mind of Novelist E. L. Doctorow." Interview with E. L. Doctorow. *The New York Times Magazine* Oct. 20, 1985. 24+. Rpt. in Morris *Conversations* 92–101.

Webster, J. P. and S. F. Bennett. "Sweet By and By," *Progressive Baptist Hymnal*, Bicentennial Edition. Ed. D. E. King. 1940. Washington, D.C.: Broadman Press, 1976. #344.

Weeks, Dennis L. Ed. *'To Love So Well the World': A Festschrift in Honor of Robert Penn Warren*. New York: Peter Lang, 1992.

Wellman, David. "Red and Black in White America: Discovering Cross-Border Identities and Other Subversive Activities." Eds. Becky Thompson and Sangeeta Tyagi. *Names We Call Home: Autobiography on Racial Identity*. New York: Routledge, 1996. 28–41.

West, Cornel. *Race Matters*. Boston: Beacon Press, 1993.

White, Deborah Gray. *Ar'n't I a Woman: Female Slaves in the Plantation South*. New York: Norton, 1985.

Wiencek, Henry. *An Imperfect God: George Washington, His Slaves, and the Creation of America*. New York: Farrar, Straus and Giroux, 2003.

Williams, Marjorie. "The Author's Solo Passage: Charles Johnson on Race and Writing." *Washington Post*. Dec. 4, 1990. D1+.

Willis, Susan. "Eruptions of Funk: Historicizing Toni Morrison." *Black American Literature Forum* 16:1 (Spring 1982): 34–42.

———.*Specifying: Black Women Writing the American Experience*. Madison: U of Wisconsin P, 1987.

Woodward, C. Vann. Panel moderator. "The Uses of History in Fiction." Transcription of panel discussion with Ralph Ellison, William Styron and Robert Penn Warren. Thirty-fourth annual meeting of the Southern Historical Association. Jung Hotel. New Orleans, LA. Nov. 6, 1968. *Southern Literature Journal* 1.2 (1969): 57–90.

Wright, Derek. "*Ragtime* Revisited: History and Fiction in Doctorow's Novel." *International Fiction Review* 20.1 (1993): 14–16.

Wutz, Michael. "An Interview with E. L. Doctorow." *Weber Studies: An Interdisciplinary Humanities Journal* 11.1 (Winter 1994): 6–15.

Wyrick, Deborah. "Charles Johnson's Battle of the Books." *Postcript* 11 (1994): 1–9.

Yaeger, Patricia. *Dirt and Domesticity: Reconstructing Southern Women's Writing, 1930–1990*. Chicago: U of Chicago P, 2000.

Yardley, Jonathan. "Mr. Ragtime." Interview with E. L. Doctorow. *The Miami Herald* Dec. 21, 1975. Morris *Conversations* 7–13.

Zinn, Howard. *A People's History of the United States, 1492-Present*. Twentieth Anniversary Edition. 1980. New York: HarperCollins, 1999.

INDEX